Collaboration in the Pharmaceutical Industry

Routledge Studies in the History of Science, Technology and Medicine

EDITED BY JOHN KRIGE, *Georgia Institute of Technology, Atlanta, U.S.A.*

Collaboration in the Pharmaceutical Industry

Changing Relationships in Britain and France, 1935–1965

Viviane Quirke

Routledge
Taylor & Francis Group
New York   London

Routledge
Taylor & Francis Group
270 Madison Avenue
New York, NY 10016

Routledge
Taylor & Francis Group
2 Park Square
Milton Park, Abingdon
Oxon OX14 4RN

© 2008 by Taylor & Francis Group, LLC
Routledge is an imprint of Taylor & Francis Group, an Informa business

Printed in the United States of America on acid-free paper
10 9 8 7 6 5 4 3 2 1

International Standard Book Number-13: 978-0-415-30982-0 (Hardcover)

Library of Congress Cataloging-in-Publication Data

Quirke, Viviane.
    Collaboration in the pharmaceutical industry : changing relationships in Britain and France, 1935-1965 / Viviane Quirke.
        p. ; cm. -- (Routledge studies in the history of science, technology, and medicine ; 18)
    Includes bibliographical references and index.
    ISBN 978-0-415-30982-0 (hardback : alk. paper)
    1. Pharmacy--Research--France--History--20th century. 2. Drugs--Research--France--History--20th century. 3. Pharmaceutical industry--France--History--20th century. 4. Pharmacy--Research--Great Britain--History--20th century. 5. Drugs--Research--Great Britain--History--20th century. 6. Pharmaceutical industry--Great Britain--History--20th century. 7. Pharmacy--Research--International cooperation. 8. Drugs--Research--Interrnational cooperation. 9. Pharmaceutical industry--International cooperation. I. Title. II. Series.
    [DNLM: 1. Drug Industry--history--France. 2. Drug Industry--history--Great Britain. 3. History, 20th Century--France. 4. History, 20th Century--Great Britain. 5. International Cooperation--history--France. 6. International Cooperation--history--Great Britain. 7. Technology, Pharmaceutical--history--France. 8. Technology, Pharmaceutical--history--Great Britain. QV 711 FA1 Q8c 2007]

RS122.Q57 2007
615'.1--dc22
        2007011046

Visit the Taylor & Francis Web site at
http://www.taylorandfrancis.com

and the Routledge Web site at
http://www.routledge.com

Contents

Acknowledgments

This book is based on my doctoral thesis, carried out at Oxford University, and completed in 2000. I am grateful for the guidance and opportunities, which my two supervisors Robert Fox and Paul Weindling gave me then, and continue to give me today. I have since then worked in collaboration with Frank James, Judy Slinn, and Roy Church. I thank all three for associating me with their stimulating projects. I am indebted to the Wellcome Trust, which funded my post-doctoral fellowship as well as my D.Phil., enabling me to continue working on pharmaceutical archives in France as well as in Britain. Working on these archives has been a rare privilege, for which I thank especially AstraZeneca and Sanofi-Aventis, and all those responsible for keeping their records and making them accessible to me, in particular Olivier de Boisboissel, Audrey Cooper, Dr Jean Gaillard, Carolyn Naylor, Dr David McNeillie, and Gérard Nichele.

Over the years the staff of the Pasteur Institute have given me invaluable assistance: Denise Ogilvie, Stéphane Kraxner, and Daniel Demellier in the archive centre, and Annick Perrot in the photographic library. Similarly, Hélène Chambefort has kindly guided me through the archives of INSERM, as has Eric Sidebottom, through the photographic collection of the Sir William Dunn School of Pathology in Oxford. The staffs of the Public Record Office (now the National Archives Centre), the Contemporary Medical Archives Centre, and the Bodleian Library, also deserve my acknowledgements for their hard work and dedication.

I am particularly grateful to scientists for granting me interviews, and allowing me a glimpse of their lives, especially the late Norman Heatley, whose kindness and encouragement gave me confidence as I embarked on what was for me then an unfamiliar subject, the history of penicillin. This book is therefore the result of a long, personal journey, which has taken me from the French school of social history, to the British school of history of science, technology and medicine. Along the way I have been lucky enough to receive help from numerous colleagues, many of whom I would now count as my friends. The meeting I had with Jonathan Liebenau and Mike Robson at the London School of Economics many years ago helped to launch me on my project to compare the French and British pharmaceutical industries. Since then, it has been enriched by published and unpublished material kindly made available to me by Pnina-Abir Am, Jon Agar, Carol Beadle, Jaye Chin-Dusting, Roger Cooter, Tony Corley, Diane Dosso, Desmond Fitzgerald, James Foreman-Peck, Jean-Paul Gaudillère, François Guinot, Sally Horrochs, Jean-Claude Jaignault, Christopher Lawrence, Muriel Le Roux, Ilana Löwy, Séverine Massat-Bourrah, Kim Pelis, Dominique Pestre, Judy Slinn, Jeff Sturchio, Steve Sturdy, Charles Suckling, and Keith Williams.

It has also benefited from discussions with colleagues who have read various chapters, especially Sophie Chauveau, Frank Bennetts, Jean-Paul Gaudillère, Muriel Le Roux, Jean-François Picard, Eric Sidebottom, and Judy Slinn. I am particularly grateful to John Krige, for his faith in the book, and for his constructive comments on an earlier draft. Needless to say any mistakes or shortcomings are entirely my own.

Finally I would like to thank Nick, whose career in industry and academia inspired this project, for his feedback and support. I dedicate the book to Thomas and Amélie, for whom it has been an almost constant companion over the years. May it encourage them to learn about and enjoy their two cultures, as I have done.

Introduction
A History of Collaborative Relationships

[Let us attempt] a small experiment in collaboration. One of your factory chemists, for example, could contact me in order to pursue Mr Firmenich's research, even if it means sending Firmernich the results of the work later for a publication.[1]

I agree with you that the scheme in the form which it has now reached is of little interest. I think however that it may still have a token value and may be useful in the future [...] This is truly an experiment in collaboration if nothing else![2]

The importance of co-operation in the conduct of everyday life, and in the organization of economic and political affairs has long been recognized.[3] In the last decades of the twentieth century, it has generally become accepted that innovation in high-tech industries is underpinned by collaboration between companies and scientists, especially academic scientists.[4] Although academic-industrial connections have sometimes led to concerns about academic freedom and conflicts of interest, it has also been observed that scientific advances often depend on these connections.[5] Reflecting the developments taking place in science and industry, the role of co-operation in generating scientific, technological and medical change has therefore received keen interest from historians and sociologists.[6] Network theory in particular has proved a rich vein for them to follow.[7] More recently, scholars studying the development of academic-government-industrial linkages in the second half of the twentieth century have written about the appearance of a 'triple helix',[8] and, by analogy with the scientific-military-industry complex of the Cold War, about the development of a 'biomedical complex'.[9] However, there have been relatively few histories of collaboration, and the exceptions have tended to focus on the United States of America.[10]

This book is on the history of collaborative relationships between scientists and drug companies, and the contribution these have made to the growth of the biomedical complexes of two countries usually left out of the literature on academic-industrial relations, Britain and France. It identifies the two countries' principal pharmaceutical research networks, and follows their development from the 1890s, when they emerged, until the 1980s, when faced with the rise of the new biotechnology and with global competition in the pharmaceutical industry, they underwent their most recent wave of change. The purpose of the book is therefore threefold: 1) to describe the growth of collaborative networks between scientists and drug companies in Britain and in France; 2) to analyse the changes that affected them; 3) to propose an explanation for these changes.

A. SOURCES AND ARGUMENT

While medical researchers are often less likely to confess their links with industry, chemists or pharmacists are generally less reluctant to admit to them. Nevertheless, because in the standard biographical material their importance is often played down, the best way to study such links is to look at primary, unpublished sources.[11] Using new evidence, based on private as well as public archives, and adopting a comparative approach in order to emphasize the similarities as well as the differences between Britain and France, I argue that, contrary to the common perception that scientists and companies in Britain and France learnt to co-operate as a result of World War Two[12] collaborations were already well established before the conflict broke out. Fruitful academic-industrial relations had developed between a small number of scientists and companies in response to growing scientific and industrial competition at the turn of the century.[13] They were strengthened by World War One, and expanded throughout the inter-war period. Although World War Two constituted an important turning point in the history of academic-industrial interactions, the relationship between scientists and pharmaceutical firms did not grow closer as a result of the conflict. The one-to-one relations that had been predominant until then were replaced by a looser, triangular relationship with the state, which thereafter became more actively involved in the 'experiments in collaboration' that were drugs. The period at the heart of this study (1935–65), which is often referred to as the 'golden age of drug discovery' or the Therapeutic Revolution,[14] was therefore one of transition, from one social order or model of behaviour to another. These changes, common to Britain and France, mirror the evolution of co-operative research in America, which has been described by John Swann.[15] This shared evolution begs an explanation.

It was the product of a common geopolitical context, but it was also driven by the science and technology that were embodied in drugs and, with them, crossed institutional and national boundaries. Thus, like the conflict out of which it emerged, penicillin was a turning point in the history of academic-industrial relations. The science and technology that produced penicillin also transformed the institutions, the companies and, beyond them, wider society.[16] The scientists quoted above were well aware that society, as well as science and technology, was being fashioned in their laboratories.[17] The evidence provided by this book fully supports their view. However, before summarizing it, I describe a basic problem which has long pervaded the literature on the interaction between science and industry. It is the problem of 'backwardness' and 'decline'.[18]

B. SCIENCE AND INDUSTRY IN BRITAIN AND FRANCE, OR THE PROBLEM OF BACKWARDNESS AND DECLINE

The alliance between science and industry has often been seen as the key to economic success.[19] Two countries whose economies underwent a considerable expansion in the late nineteenth and early twentieth centuries, Germany and the United States, have had their success attributed in large measure to the growth of industrial research laboratories, and to the close contacts established between these laboratories and academic institutions.[20] Conversely, when economic failure or industrial backwardness have been diagnosed, they have often been attributed to a poorly developed relationship between science and industry, as in the case of Britain and France for the same period.[21] These historical analyses echo the concerns of contemporaries, worrying about the state of decline of their two great nations.[22]

Such analyses, originally made about the sectors that led the Second Industrial Revolution (the chemical and electrical industries), have also been applied to the pharmaceutical sector, which came to greater prominence in the twentieth century. The literature on Germany and the United States suggests that, before World War Two, the co-operative relationship forged between academic scientists and drug companies was an important feature of the development of a modern pharmaceutical industry, that is to say an industry that is innovative, and characterized by high levels of concentration and investment in research.[23] In his book *Medical Science and Medical Industry*, Jonathan Liebenau has linked the growth of Philadelphia-based companies to the strong connections they developed with local medical practitioners.[24] Similarly, in the co-operative relationship established between academic scientists and firms such as Eli Lilly, Swann has seen the key to the expansion of the American pharmaceutical industry in the 1920s and 1930s.

On the other hand, the pharmaceutical industries of Britain and France, like their economies as a whole, have traditionally been considered as relatively backward until after World War Two.[25] It has also been assumed that their recent success has been due to the changes that occurred when, finally, they learnt from the example of their rivals, invested in research and development (R&D), and developed better links with academic institutions.[26] Such a body of literature prompts three questions. These provide the framework for the book, which is in three parts.

C. THE UNITED STATES: A MODEL?

The first question is therefore whether the American example, which is often held up as the epitome of modern entrepreneurship,[27] could be used as a model for the study of other countries. Could the argument be reversed, and could it be that where the pharmaceutical industry had not developed modern characteristics to the same degree as in the United States, for instance in Britain and France, there was little co-operation between companies and scientists outside the industry? In his thesis comparing the French and British pharmaceutical industries in the 1920s and 1930s, Mike Robson has suggested that this was indeed the case.

1. Comparing Britain and France with the United States

Robson has written that the co-operation between academic scientists and drug companies was less well developed in France than in Britain, and, in turn, was less well developed in Britain than in the United States.[28] He has reached his conclusions after applying the typology established by Swann for the same period.

Swann has distinguished between three types of collaboration at the time of expansion in university-industry interactions: there were collaborations with scientists as general consultants, as specialist-consultants, and as project researchers. Swann's typology is derived from the company Eli Lilly's own 'very elaborate system of contacts with the community of academic biomedical scientists'.[29] It is therefore based on the various functions scientists fulfilled for the benefit of a particular pharmaceutical firm. It is meant as a heuristic device, inviting comparisons with other sectors of the economy and with other countries. However, it also rooted in the institutional and organisational culture of the United States, and historians carrying out comparative investigations might wish to question its value as a tool for assessing other national contexts.[30]

Nevertheless, in his thesis Robson has attempted to apply Swann's typology to Britain and France. Although he has found that Swann's typology held quite well in the case of Britain, in the case of France, apart from Ernest Fourneau, he has seen no other example of general consultancy. Rhône-Poulenc's interaction with the Pasteur Institute seemed to have been mainly on the basis of particular research projects. The closest one came to specialist consultants in France was with the contacts established between companies and medical faculties for the clinical testing of new drugs. Robson has concluded that co-operation between scientists and the pharmaceutical industry was less well developed in France than it was in Britain.[31] However, he has admitted that the information was lacking in order to assess the French situation properly, especially with respect to small and medium companies.

Yet, Robson has found that the British and French situations represented a departure from the American model in two significant respects: the greater importance of institutional links, and the greater mobility of scientists between academic and industrial positions on this side of the Atlantic. In Britain, he has identified the Medical Research Council (MRC)'s Chemotherapy Committee, the National Institute of Medical Research (NIMR), which at times acted as 'a broker for technical information', and the Lister Institute-Allen & Hanburys connection.[32] To his British examples I would also add the enduring link between the Pasteur Institute and Rhône-Poulenc in France.

In Britain and France scientific institutions therefore played a similar role to that played by companies in the United States, in helping to shape the co-operative behaviour of scientists and pharmaceutical firms. However, individual researchers and their networks were also important. Thus, there was greater mobility between academic and industrial circles in Britain and France than there appeared to be in the United States. In Britain, there were many examples of career switches by senior scientists. In France, the practice of *cumul*, the accumulation of academic and/or industrial positions, at a senior level at least, created permeable boundaries between the academic and industrial realms. Before World War Two, the scientific professions may therefore not have been 'fixed' as either academic or industrial to the same extent in Britain and France as they were in the United States, or as they became later.[33]

As well as these two major differences between the model proposed by Swann and the French and British cases, there is another important aspect of the American example that is not necessarily applicable to either Britain or France. It is the extent to which interactions were regulated. As Leigh Hancher has pointed out in her book on government and the pharmaceutical industry, much of the literature on economic regulation is of American origin. As a result, it has 'been influenced by the historical, legal, and political development of regulation in the USA' and 'reflects certain implicit assumptions about the proper place of regulation in modern democratic systems'.[34]

This may also be true of the study of academic-industrial co-operation. The tendency to regard the United States, or Germany, as a model that other countries had to emulate in order to progress has long permeated the historiography on the interaction between science and industry, and has carried with it two assumptions: the first, that there is basically one road to progress, and that countries that deviate from it have in some way 'failed;[35] the second, that there is a scale of development, from 'backward', to less backward, to more advanced, which makes it possible to measure this progress.[36] A more fruitful approach may be to study academic-industrial relations on their own merits, without any preconceived ideas about whether they are the cause, or result, of economic success or failure.

2. Different kinds of co-operation?

There are a number of different typologies of co-operation, which suggests that the form and content of academic-industrial relations may not only vary according to the context in which they develop, but that they may also change over time. One such typology is Chin-Dusting et al.'s 'common types of academic-industrial relationships':

1. Consultations and fee for service including contract research outsourcing;
2. Competitive grants sponsored by industry;
3. Industrial sponsorship of investigator-led research;
4. institute-institute liaisons;
5. academia, industry and the government;
6. academic spin out companies.[37]

Although their typology fits particularly well the end of the twentieth/beginning of the twenty-first centuries in modern, Westernized nations, the authors have noted that the term 'relationship' implies a special connectivity, which goes far beyond the joint effort detailed under each heading.[38] The term 'collaborative relationships' is therefore broadly applicable to different times and different contexts. Hence it is used throughout this book, which spans both sides of the Channel, as well as a relatively long time period.

The collaborative relationship forged between Ernest Fourneau and Poulenc Frères (from 1928 a part of Rhône-Poulenc), which set the tone for other relationships in France,[39] was not based on a formal contract. As to Henry Dale, who influenced the development of a collaborative relationship in Britain,[40] he did not consult for industry after he left the Wellcome Physiological Research Laboratories (WPRL) for the NIMR. Nevertheless, before World War Two, co-operation with scientists occurred in Britain and France. However, it was often informally organized, in an *ad hoc* fashion, and was based on strong personal connections.

Consequently, it may be more difficult in Britain and France to reduce the interaction to the service rendered by scientists to drug companies, unlike in the United States where industry was the 'prime mover' in co-operative research. Until World War Two, British and French scientists and their institutions were prime movers, after which pharmaceutical firms took over the 'experiments in collaboration' that were drugs. Moreover, these scientists could not be exclusively described as 'academic', although I have often used the term as a matter of convenience, meaning 'non-industrial scientists'. Many of the men whose collaborative activities shaped the relationship between science and industry worked in government laboratories, or in medical research institutes whose research programmes reflected the public health policies of the State, such as the Pasteur Institute and the NIMR.

Although financial gain, personal advancement, and scientific interest in the research problems posed by industry were not absent from their motivations, they also pursued strong professional goals. They had a reforming agenda to bring science to medicine and develop research in industry, and by their cooperative behaviour they helped to make it a reality.

D. WERE THE FRENCH LESS CO-OPERATIVE THAN THE BRITISH?

Taking the comparison one level further, could it be that the French were less co-operative than the British?

1. Comparing Britain and France

Although their pharmaceutical sectors were similar with regard to structures and markets, the evidence from studies by economic historians, such as Mike Robson, but also by political scientists, for instance Maurice Wright, suggests that the relationship between drug companies and either government or academic institutions was very different on both sides of the Channel.[41] They have concluded that on the French side, co-operation was less well developed than on the British side. Their conclusion echoes complaints, often uttered by the French themselves, that there has always been a lack of co-operative spirit in France, especially when compared with Anglo-Saxon countries, not only in industry and government, but in science as well.[42]

Why this fascination with comparing Britain and France, and with differentiating them in terms of their cultures? The two countries fulfill the criteria for Marc Bloch's second, favourite type of comparison: close geographically, they have nonetheless evolved different political structures, and the outcome of events in their shared histories has often been very dissimilar.[43] The examples of Britain and France, therefore, have traditionally provided historians with a useful testing ground for their hypotheses concerning the relationship between agency and structure. Depending on whether they wished to lay their main emphasis on structure or agency, authors have often either stressed the differences, or else the similarities between Britain and France. For instance, in order to underline the structural causes of the differences she observed between the two countries, Leigh Hancher has contrasted their respective industries rather sharply. Similarly, Lacy Thomas has opposed Britain's success to France's failure in global pharmaceuticals, and explained this opposition in terms of the two countries' different economic and political systems.[44] On the other hand, Maurice Wright, whose main purpose is to emphasize the impact of World War Two on the French and British pharmaceutical sectors, has insisted on the similarities between them.[45]

My work, like Wright's, shows that historical events, and individual actors, played a more important role than structures in the evolution of academic-industrial relations in Britain and in France. It has been written that much of British industrial research before World War Two was carried out co-operatively.[46] I argue that this was also true of research in the pharmaceutical field, and in France. Although important organisational differences existed between the two countries, pharmaceutical research was carried out co-operatively even before the war in both Britain and France.

Thus, once the United States is abandoned as the yardstick by which to measure development in other countries, it becomes more difficult to say that co-operation there was better developed than in Britain, or that co-operation in Britain was better developed than in France. The literature surveyed above suggests that studies of co-operation benefit from being examined, not in terms of a 'model' that is being imitated, but in terms of local situations. These include the individuals, their networks, and the institutions or firms in which they work.

2. Comparing the co-operative cultures of Britain and France

Before comparing Britain and France, it is therefore useful to provide a definition of collaboration that is applicable to different contexts. Co-operation implies a reciprocal relationship, based on, or leading to, mutual trust.[47] It is perhaps the most important attribute of certain societies, compared with others that could be described as competitive.[48] In Britain and France, academic-industrial relations evolved in an institutional context in which medical research institutes often competed against private companies in the field of vaccines. Gradually, the co-operative culture of the small group of scientists (mainly chemists or biochemists in Britain, and chemists or pharmacists in France), who collaborated with pharmaceutical firms, and whose relationship was based on personal acquaintance, sometimes even long-lasting friendship, was disseminated along with the drugs, especially chemotherapeutic drugs, which they invented together. After spreading within their research institutions and the industry, it extended to government agencies as well.[49]

How does one identify the dominant culture of a sector of the economy, or of a professional group, and compare it with their counterparts in another country? There are three possible approaches, the first quantitative, the second qualitative, and the third a mixture of the two.[50] In the absence of comparable nation-wide databases, I have adopted a qualitative approach to study the most influential networks that defined academic-industrial relations in Britain and France. This makes it possible to describe and analyse the changes that affected them in the relatively long time-frame of the twentieth century.

3. Comparing networks

In France, the most important collaborative relationship was the one between the Pasteur Institute and Rhône-Poulenc; in Britain between the MRC and the group of 'reputable companies' (the expression was used by the Council), which co-operated for the development of insulin, and later penicillin. Through them, it is possible to gain a sense of the two countries' co-operative cultures. Indeed, whilst focusing on these two principal networks, I came across several other collaborative relationships.

The extent of these collaborations was a surprise, for co-operation in science had, until recently, been somewhat neglected by historians. On the one hand, in the traditional, heroic view of scientific endeavour, the scientist had been presented alone with his instruments, in his laboratory, isolated from the world outside; on the other hand, when historians of science began to rebel against this view, much of their attention was directed towards controversies in order to show that science is embedded in a social context.[51] By contrast, historians of technology, had begun focusing their studies on transfer mechanisms and on diffusion processes, and turned their attention towards the co-operative networks that shape technological change.[52]

As a result of the coming together of social studies of science and technology, science is increasingly being studied as a collaborative enterprise,[53] involving many unseen, because often unsung, helpers and participants in breakthrough discoveries as well as normal research.[54] This movement in the history of science parallels developments in economics, where the emphasis has started to shift away from competition, towards co-operation as an important aspect of economic life.[55] Thus, an important contribution of the relatively new discipline of economic sociology has been to explore the relationship between co-operation and competition, and in doing so to put culture back into economics.[56]

These approaches, which since the 1980s have gathered momentum, enable us to re-examine some of the assumptions that are implicit in much of the literature on the relationship between science and industry, and offer a more balanced picture of the academic-industrial interface, where co-operation and competition are both often present. As Sir Howard Florey, who played a key role in developing therapeutic penicillin, put it in 1962:

> It is not too difficult to get individual scientists to co-operate inside individual laboratories or in wider national and international spheres. Nevertheless, there is always underlying competition between individuals and between laboratories for prestige which to a large extent depends on making discoveries.[57]

A verbal symbol of this new focus on social interactions, the term 'network' has become commonplace in the history of science and technology since the work of Bruno Latour and Michel Callon and their British collaborators Steve Woolgar and John Law. It has also become widespread in several other branches of the social sciences, in particular in political theory and in studies of industrial organisation.[58] With the recent explosion in information technology, it has become almost too popular (says Latour), a convenient 'buzz word' to describe any kind of social interaction.[59]

In the volume entitled *Actor Network Theory and After*, both Latour and Law have distinguished between the earlier usage of the term, as an approach full of tensions and complexities, and its later transformation into a hardened 'theory'.[60] Even though Latour was happy to see the network approach change into something else, he believed that one of the original features of networks ought to remain: their non-human components (such as technological artifacts). These played a special role in preserving what he saw as one of the qualities of networks compared with other approaches: their flexibility, enabling them to overcome the central dilemma of the social sciences, that of structure *versus* agency. In addition, networks are well suited to the study of the interactions between science, technology and medicine.[61]

E. HOW AND WHY DID COLLABORATIVE RELATIONSHIPS CHANGE?

If, as I have argued, collaborative relationships between scientists and pharmaceutical firms were already well developed in Britain and France before World War Two, how and why did they change between 1935 and 1965?

1. The changing relationship between scientists and the pharmaceutical industry in Britain and in France

In his description of the American experience, Swann has shown that, although contacts between academic scientists and the pharmaceutical industry flourished between 1918 and 1945, in the 1950s and 1960s the number of collaborative projects declined, reaching their lowest point in the 1970s.[62] This was partly due to increased support for academic research by federal government agencies in areas of defense and aerospace, which had the effect of turning graduate students away from industrial careers. Swann, therefore, has identified World War Two as a turning point in the history of American academic-industrial relations.

Did World War Two have a similar effect on French and British cooperative behaviour in the pharmaceutical field? The answer is yes, but to varying degrees. In Britain, although academic-industrial interactions increased along with the number of drugs being developed, the experience of developing penicillin introduced formality and hierarchy into existing networks. By contrast, partly in reaction to the Vichy regime, and partly as a result of the sharp increase in fundamental research carried out in government laboratories,[63] French academic-industrial relations were driven underground. However, although at the institutional level they loosened or even became invisible, at the grass-roots research collaborations continued nonetheless. Pharmaceutical innovations such as chlorpromazine were the product of old as well as new alliances, in this case with clinicians, with whom Rhône-Poulenc developed relations under difficult wartime conditions, and which would blossom after the war.

Then, how and why could such different conditions, different economic and political structures and institutional organisation, produce an overall similar effect? Could it be that structures were, in fact, less important than agency (individuals and groups responding to historical events, such as war)? The role of war in producing change in science, technology, and medicine, but also in people's perceptions and behaviour, has become an important topic for historians.[64] In biological and medical science and industry, wartime is a moment when the battle against disease becomes closely identified with the battle against the enemy.[65] Such a collusion of interests is a powerful mobilising force.[66] Because the experience of war was so different in Britain and France, comparing Britain with France in the period before, during and after the conflict offers a qualitative way of measuring the impact of war on the two countries' co-operative cultures, and on their national systems of innovation in biomedicine.[67] Thus, as well as making a Franco-British comparison more practicable, the qualitative approach allows for a greater attention to be paid to the discourse used by the actors, to get as close to a history of 'mentalités' as sources permit, and identify a change-producing event in culture.

2. Penicillin and the victory of chemotherapy

Major chemotherapeutic advances were made in the period before, during, and after World War Two.[68] This period, which was one of social and political upheaval, has often been thought of a 'the golden age of drug discovery'.[69] Before the war, the first broad spectrum anti-bacterial drug sulphanilamide was developed, and that was quickly followed by penicillin. Antibiotics and other new groups of drugs, such as synthetic anti-histamines, psycho-depressant drugs, halogenated anaesthetics, were also developed then, and many of them were discovered in Britain and in France. One way to explain the changing relationship between scientists and the pharmaceutical firms in the two countries therefore is to place innovation at the center of the explanation.

One discovery stands out in this respect: penicillin. It functioned as 'crucial moment', as 'legacy' and as 'constitutive event', contributing to the passage of one pattern of behaviour to another, within the longer time-frame of the history of social interactions.[70] It emerged out of the war, and its impact on the post-war reconstruction of both countries was considerable. It became the symbol of American success, for the biomedical sciences as well as for the pharmaceutical industry.[71] It embodied the successful inter-action between science, government and industry, and its development in Britain and France was not only a goal in itself, but also an 'experiment in collaboration' to be reproduced and adapted in other contexts.

However, its impact on Britain and France was very different. This book therefore concludes that their divergent paths after the war had more to do with the two countries' different experiences of war, than with an inherent weakness of the co-operative spirit in France.[72]

F. BOOK OUTLINE

The book is written in three parts, each one including a comparison of the French and British contexts in chronological order. Throughout the text, the differences between Britain and France are weighed against the similarities. Part 1 describes the situation before World War Two. Chapter 1 lays out the common ground for the comparison between the two coun-tries, surveying the institutions, academic disciplines and industrial firms involved in collaborative research on pharmaceuticals. Chapter 2 describes the two countries' principal collaborative networks, through the history of two key innovations: insulin and sulphanilamide.

Part 2 focuses on the war period. Here, Britain and France are treated separately. The experience of developing penicillin helped to transform the relationship between scientists and pharmaceutical firms, therefore it provides the focal point for studying the impact of war on British and on France, and the divergence between them created by the conflict.

In Part 3, the separation between Britain and France is maintained. The changes brought by the experience of penicillin and by the period of post-war reconstruction are described through a series of short case-studies, including chlorpromazine, cortisone, anaesthetic halothane, and cepha-losporin. Whereas in Part 1 the academic side of the collaborations was emphasized, in Part 3, the industrial players come to the fore, as pharma-ceutical research shifts from a predominantly academic to a predominantly industrial environment, and pharmaceutical firms become prime movers in the 'experiments in collaboration' that are drugs.

Part I

Blurred Boundaries

Drug Research and Production in Britain and France before World War Two

INTRODUCTION

Historians have argued that the form and content of science have shaped the institutions and professional standards of modern medicine.[1] They have also shown the reverse to be true: the institutions and professional standards of modern medicine have shaped the form and content of science.[2] What have bound science and medicine together have been the reforming medical élites and their networks.

However, what exactly science has meant to medicine, when and where it has been embraced by the medical profession, has become the centre of historical debate. In the United States, the rise of the medical profession has been traced to the transformation of medicine in the nineteenth century, from a theory based on the specificity of disease, to knowledge generated and validated by experimental science. This new, experimental approach to medicine helped to place therapeutics at the centre of American physicians' professional identity.[3] However, therapeutics did not play an important part in the rise of the medical profession in all countries, for instance Austria, where the Vienna Medical School was characterized by 'brilliant clinical diagnosis', often accompanied by a skepticism of drugs and other interventive treatments.[4] Moreover, an anti-science movement persisted in German medicine until World War Two, under the influence of practitioners such as Erwin Liek.[5] In Britain, clinicians began adopting experimental methods during the inter-war period, although a certain amount of resistance persisted until World War Two.[6] In France, the shift from a more purely clinical to a predominantly scientific approach to medicine took place later still, in the 1960s, with the creation of Institut National de la Santé et de la Recherche Médicale (INSERM).[7]

This book can only lightly touch upon the resistance to science and therapeutics experienced in countries like Britain and France, whilst focusing on change, which the co-operative relations between scientists and pharmaceutical companies helped to bring about. Nevertheless, in the chapters that follow, it will become clear that resistance and change are interconnected. As Lord Robert Platt, a clinician associated with the MRC, put it:

[...] the phenomenal success of modern medical treatment seems to have depended almost wholly on non-clinical, often non-medical scientists, frequently working in, or in close collaboration with, the pharmaceutical industry.[8]

Platt suggested that the blame for resisting modern medical treatment might rest, at least in part, with clinicians. At the same time, he argued that the co-operation between scientists and pharmaceutical firms had contributed to the rise of modern medicine, i.e. one dominated by experimental medicine, centered on therapeutics. These scientists were often based in university or government laboratories, and were usually sought for their knowledge and expertise in chemistry, and the firms with which they collaborated had started developing their research facilities in search for novel treatments in the emerging fields of chemotherapy and replacement therapy. Their contribution is the subject of this book.

There are two angles from which to approach such a topic: the scientists, and the companies. Both are examined in Chapter 1, beginning with a description of the institutes of medical research, and ending with a history of the pharmaceutical industry in the two countries. However, I question the distinction between them, at least for the period between the wars.[9] Hence, I refer to it as a period of 'blurred boundaries', that is to say one in which research and production, and science and industry closely intermingled.[10] The French and British pharmaceutical industries showed strong similarities. Both shared an interest, if not a 'passion' for science, reflected in the growth of research laboratories between the wars.[11] Nevertheless, some differences between Britain and France are identified. In France, there was greater centralisation at institutional and national levels. In contrast, Britain was characterized by an extensive institutional network, loosely co-ordinated by the MRC through a system of committees.

Chapter 2 describes the expansion of co-operative research. In both countries, the most important collaborative relationships developed around the development of chemotherapeutic remedies, because of the perceived need to 'catch up' with Germany where chemotherapy had been 'invented'. This need was made all the more real by World War One, which interrupted supplies of German synthetic drugs. The shock of war reinforced notions of French 'backwardness' and British 'decline', and stimulated the development of co-operative networks in order to bring the two countries' pharmaceutical industry up to a par with its German counterpart. In France, it gave impetus to the close relationship between Ernest Fourneau's team at the Pasteur Institute and Poulenc Frères (part of Rhône-Poulenc after the 1928 merger). In Britain, it led to a network of university departments, pharmaceutical firms and government research institutions, under the aegis of the Royal Society and the Medical Research Committee (later Council) and Department of Scientific and Industrial Research (DSIR). Subsequently, whereas in the field of vaccines and sera there tended to be competition rather than co-operation between medical research institutions and pharmaceutical firms, in the field of the new biological remedies — hormones, vitamins and glandular extracts — co-operation blossomed, particularly in Britain, where it gave rise to a network of 'reputable companies'. These collaborated with the MRC for the production of insulin, and were to form the core of the Therapeutic Research Corporation, which became instrumental in developing penicillin in World War Two, and will be the subject of Chapter 3, in Part 2 of the book.

1   Research Institutions and Pharmaceutical Laboratories before World War Two

A. INTRODUCTION

This chapter describes the scientific and industrial context for the collaborations that burgeoned before World War Two. It begins with the institutes of medical research, which embodied a particular approach to the prevention and cure of disease, immunotherapy, associated with the sciences of bacteriology and immunology, and with the manufacture of vaccines and sera.[1] However, around the time of World War One, an alternative approach appeared within these institutes. It was chemotherapy, that is to say the prevention and treatment of illnesses using chemical substances.[2] Developed as a theory and a set of laboratory practices by Paul Ehrlich at the Institute for Experimental Therapy in Frankfurt-am-Main, chemotherapy was exported along with Salvarsan and the other synthetic drugs that came out of the Institute and German industrial laboratories, such as Bayer's, whose research programme was inspired by Ehrlich's.[3] Chemotherapy required the collaboration between organic chemists, physiologists, and bacteriologists.[4] Therefore, it became a privileged site for the development of co-operative networks of scientists and pharmaceutical firms. Thus, the history of the parallel, and at times conflicting, development of immunotherapy and chemotherapy constitutes the common ground for a comparison between Britain and France. It was common, because it was shared by an expanding international scientific community.[5]

In France, the Pasteur Institute dominated medical research until World War Two; hence it is studied in greater detail. In Britain, by contrast, an extensive network of institutions grew under the aegis of the MRC. Special attention is paid to the Lister Institute, which was modelled on the Pasteur, and allows a comparison to be made between the institutional structures and scientific cultures of the two countries. Thus, significant differences between Britain and France are identified. In France, there was greater centralisation at institutional and national levels,[6] and the style of leadership was more autocratic. In contrast, Britain's institutional network was loosely co-ordinated by the MRC through an ever-widening system of committees, which included the Salvarsan, Chemotherapy, Insulin and Therapeutic Trials Committees, and the style of leadership could be described as consensual.

Another difference that has been much discussed in the historiography is the relative stagnation of the biological and medical sciences in France compared with other countries, including Britain, where the inter-war period is widely recognized as the heyday of the British school of physiology.[7] The backwardness of French science has perhaps been over-stated by historians, keen to draw a contrast between the inter-war years and the spectacular take-off of the post-war period.[8] They may also have been influenced by contemporary accounts of decline that were a rhetorical device at the hands of reforming élites.[9] Although the evidence suggests that French science may indeed have suffered from relative stagnation, a number of inter-war research projects laid the foundations for innovative post-war developments, and deserve a mention.[10] For instance, the research on bacterial growth factors in the 1920s and 1930s by the microbiologist André Lwoff later led to ground-breaking work in genetics, for which he was awarded the Nobel Prize for Physiology or Medicine jointly with Jacques Monod and François Jacob in 1965.[11] In the pharmaceutical field, Ernest Fourneau and his team, which included a future director of the Pasteur Institute (Jacques Tréfouël) and a future Nobel Prize winner (Daniel Bovet), carried out innovative research on drugs of the sympathetic nervous system, sulphonamide drugs and synthetic anti-histamines.[12] The latter led Rhône-Poulenc to the neuroleptic drug chlorpromazine (Largactil), a discovery that transformed psychiatric care and stimulated the growth of psychopharmacology after World War Two.[13]

Despite the differences outlined above, the chapter, which ends with a study of the French and British pharmaceutical industries, also highlights strong similarities between the two countries. Both shared an interest, if not a 'passion' for science, reflected in the growth of research laboratories between the wars.[14] Furthermore, in both countries, the new biological remedies, including vitamins, hormones and organ extracts, opened up a third therapeutic way, which provided opportunities for collaborative research and underpinned the development of many small and medium firms.[15] A number of these, taking on the manufacture of vitamins and insulin, expanded greatly after World War Two with the production of antibiotics and corticosteroid drugs, and became major players in the international pharmaceutical industry, for instance Glaxo in Britain, and Roussel-Uclaf in France.[16]

B. FRANCE: AN INSTITUTIONAL MOSAIC

Some research was carried out in a number of Medical Schools, Science Faculties, in the Provinces as well as in Paris, and from 1927 also in the

Table 1.1 Chronology of Institutional Developments in Britain and France

Date	Institutional Developments
1881	Creation of Poulenc Frères in Paris
1888	Creation of the Pasteur Institute in Paris
1891	Creation of the Lister Institute in London
1896	Creation of the Wellcome Chemical Research Laboratories (WCRL) in London
1897	Creation of the Mérieux Institute in Lyon
1899	Creation of the Wellcome Physiological Research Laboratories (WPRL) in London
1900	Creation of the Biological Chemistry Department, which includes the Organic Chemistry Laboratory, within the Pasteur Institute Building of the first section of the Hôpital Pasteur
1909	Appointment of Major Greenwood to the first post of medical statistician, created for him at the Lister Institute
1910	Ernest Fourneau is appointed director of the Organic Chemistry Laboratory (renamed Therapeutic Chemistry Laboratory, TCL)
1911	Departure of Fourneau from Poulenc Frères for the Pasteur Institute Passing of the National Insurance Act
1913	Creation of the Medical Research Committee (reconstituted in 1920 as the Medical Research Council, MRC)
1914	Creation in Hampstead of the central laboratory of the MRC, later named National Institute for Medical Research (NIMR) Departure of Henry Dale from the WPRL for the NIMR, where he is appointed director of the Biochemistry and Pharmacological Laboratory Formation of the Chemical Sub-Committee (later renamed Drugs-Sub-Committee) of the Royal Society
1920-4	Oxygen Research Committee of the Department of Scientific and Industrial Research (DSIR) and the MRC
1921	Dunn Institute of Biochemistry created at Cambridge University
1926	Sir William Dunn School of Pathology created at Oxford University. Biochemistry Laboratory, also at Oxford Formation of Imperial Chemical Industries (ICI)
1927	Physicochemical Biology Institute (Institut de Biologie physicochimique) in Paris Creation of the Chemotherapy Committee of the MRC. Rhône-Poulenc takes over the British firm May & Baker
1928	Merger of Poulenc-Frères and the Société des Usines du Rhône (SCUR) to form Rhône-Poulenc Henry Dale is appointed director of the NIMR
1931	Therapeutic Trials Committee of the MRC
1938	Creation within the TLC of a Pharmacological Laboratory for Daniel Bovet

(Continued)

Table 1.1 Continued

Date	Institutional Developments
1940	Therapeutic Research Corporation (TRC)
1949	Death of Ernest Fourneau
1965	The Pasteur Institute acquires its semi-public status
1968	Death of Sir Henry Dale
1970	The TLC is dismantled
1975	Closure of the laboratories of the Lister Institute

Institut de Biologie physicochimique.[17] However, in the inter-war period the Pasteur Institute dominated French medical research. It requires to be studied in detail, not only because it was the principal institute of medical research, but also because it served as a model for many other institutes, in France and abroad.[18] As such, it provides a useful testing ground for hypotheses about the relative stagnation of French science between the wars and, more pertinently here, about the link between institutional structure and co-operative behaviour.

1. The Pasteur Institute: an institutional mosaic

Ilana Löwy has used the word 'mosaic' to describe the Pasteur Institute, that is to say a grouping of departments and laboratories loosely connected with each other, the main cement being the micro-organisms and micro-biological techniques developed for their study.[19] The term 'mosaic' implies that it is difficult to make generalisations about the institution as a whole and, therefore, any attempt to describe it must necessarily struggle with contradictions. It also suggests that there was relatively little co-operation between the various departments. If this was symptomatic of the culture of the Pasteur Institute, then the relations within the Institute may be expected to have coloured its interaction with the outside world, including industry.

Jacques Tréfouël certainly saw a link between internal and external co-operation. When, as Director of the Institute, he attempted to make it benefit from the lessons of penicillin after the war, he hoped to encourage better co-operation between all departments, indicating that he perceived it to be imperfect at the time.[20] Although his perception may have been derived from recent experience, the evidence suggests that the problem had begun long beforehand, in the inter-war period, when the Institute suffered from internal divisions. There were notorious personal rifts, such as between Charles Nicolle and Emile Roux,[21] or between Gaston Ramon and his colleagues.[22] Other disputes are less well known; for example, the 'serious disagreement' that opposed the physicist Pierre Lecomte du Nouy to

Louis Martin, Roux's successor, and led to Lecomte du Nouy's resignation in 1936.[23] He subsequently joined the pharmaceutical company Debat.[24] Inter-departmental rivalries have also been described by two historians of the Therapeutic Chemistry Laboratory, Jean Igolen and Daniel Bovet.[25]

What was the cause of these rifts and rivalries, which are suggestive of an individualistic, if not competitive culture?[26] In her study of the co-operative cultures of primitive peoples, the anthropologist Margaret Mead had postulated that material conditions influenced co-operation. Although she found no evidence that they did, it is nevertheless a useful hypothesis, for it might provide an explanation of behaviour in a society more technologically advanced than that of primitive peoples.[27] The rifts and rivalries within the Institute may therefore have been caused by the material difficulties it experienced between the wars.

The poverty of Besredka's immunology department was commented upon by a visitor from the Rockefeller Foundation in 1926, Harry Plotz. In one of his reports, he stated that the library lacked the most recent books, the laboratories lacked modern equipment, the old instruments were inadequate and falling into disrepair, and the staff managed without the barest of necessities.[28] Exacerbated by the crisis that affected the discipline all over the world,[29] the poor state of the immunology department appeared to have deleterious effects on the contribution of the Pasteur Institute to immunological research.[30]

However, Kim Pelis has shown that such material poverty was the result of a concept of science as a vocation involving personal sacrifice, and as an essentially non-profit activity, rather than a true lack of funds.[31] Moreover, a study of the Institute's budgets shows that it was the product of deliberate financial choices. During the inter-war period, the Institute was wealthy enough to commit funds to an extensive building programme. New laboratories for tuberculosis research and for the production of the BCG were built. They cost eight million francs, including a four million franc state subsidy, and still the reserve went up from three to four billion francs between 1929 and 1935. In the same period, the Institute was also capable of providing free medical care at the Hôpital Pasteur.[32]

Such intricacies highlight the danger of reducing explanations of backwardness or decline to a single factor, such as a lack of funding for research, or to culture.[33] In a complex institution like the Pasteur Institute, it is more likely that a number of inter-related factors were involved. A lack of inter-departmental collaboration, aggravated by the poverty of certain laboratories, the persistence of intellectual traditions that encouraged conservatism in the sciences,[34] a lack of 'enthusiasm' related to the crisis in immunology,[35] the isolation from clinical medicine,[36] all may have contributed to a gradual shift away from the centre to the periphery of medical research.[37] These factors are analyzed briefly in the following description of the Institute from its creation to 1939.

2. An Institute for Science and Industry

The Pasteur Institute was founded in 1888, after Louis Pasteur had gathered funds from an international subscription on the strength of his success with the rabies vaccine. The state also contributed funds, but the contributions by subscription were sufficient to guarantee the Institute's autonomous administration, which it guarded jealously until it finally became half-owned by the state in 1965. Income from the sale of vaccines was to return to the Institute, and help to support all research, which at the time meant research into vaccines. The purpose of the Institute was four-fold: it produced the rabies vaccine, which it distributed in a dispensary, carried out research into infectious diseases, and taught the Pasteurian discipline of microbiology.[38] Separate buildings were erected to serve the different purposes of the Institute, but there was considerable overlap, in particular between research and teaching. The boundaries between research, clinical medicine and the production of therapeutic remedies were also fluid. A certain amount of clinical research was carried out at the hospital, and research often accompanied the production of vaccines.

3. Research and teaching

Until World War Two, two main buildings were dedicated to teaching and research. They faced each other, on either side of the rue du Docteur Roux, then the rue Dutot (see Figure 1.1).

The first building housed the microbiology department, or 'service' to use the Pasteurian terminology. Teaching occupied a whole floor of the building, which included two large rooms used for almost a century for practical instruction, and several laboratories (see Figure 1.2). Emile Roux was in charge of the 'Grand Cours' (lecture course) until World War One, when the production of vaccines took precedence over the other functions of the Institute. In 1922, the course was re-established under René Legroux, a former pupil of Roux, and remained unchanged throughout the whole of the inter-war period. It provided the only instruction in microbiology in France until World War Two, and its particular value came from the way in which theory and practice were balanced. Its reputation was strong, not only in France, but also abroad. It attracted many scientists and doctors from other countries, and these foreigners were sometimes more numerous than the French students themselves.[39] The Institute's function as a training centre for scientists and doctors alike was essential for the inclusion of the Pasteur Institute in an international network of science, and of industry as well, which I describe in the next chapter. It was also crucial to the spread of Pastorianism as a scientific ideology.[40]

However, between the wars a lack of innovation in teaching became apparent, reflecting the conservatism of the Institute as a whole. The accusation of 'conservatism' was aimed more particularly at Roux, who

Figure 1.1 The Pasteur Institute ca 1900, Biological Chemistry building (courtesy of the Pasteur Institute).

remained in place as Director of the Institute until 1933. Although Legroux had incorporated some of the new developments in microbiology, the course remained unchanged, keeping the same structure and the same programme since 1914.[41] Nevertheless, after World War Two, it was slowly modernized, mainly under pressure from the microbiologist André Lwoff.[42] The new course included microbial physiology, biochemistry and genetics, and its renewal contributed to the Institute returning from the periphery back to the centre once again.

The second building housed the Biological Chemistry Department, and was erected in 1900, about eight years after microbiology. It was designed for the study of biological chemistry under Emile Duclaux, Professor at the Sorbonne. Teaching and research were combined in this building also. A course for the training of biochemists ran until 1939, when it moved back to the Sorbonne. Another course on fermentation began in 1900 under Fernbach, but was discontinued in 1939 and did not resume after the war. There were two main laboratories, the Biological Chemistry Laboratory, headed by Gabriel Bertrand from 1900 to 1937 (in 1942, he was replaced by Michel Macheboeuf), and the Organic Chemistry Laboratory, run by A. Etard.

Biochemistry illustrates well the lack of French development in the biological disciplines, by comparison with Germany and Anglo-Saxon

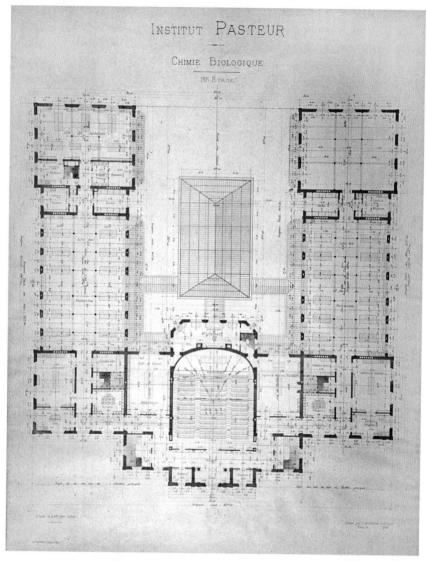

Figure 1.2 Plan of the Pasteur Institute, 1ˢᵗ floor of the Biological Chemistry building (courtesy of the Pasteur Institute).

countries. Until the 1960s, French biochemists remained essentially 'medical auxiliaries'.[43] Institutional restraints, intellectual traditions stemming from a national scientific culture, and individual personalities, all contributed to the relative backwardness of French biochemistry between the wars. The work of Gabriel Bertrand highlights this point. While directing the biological chemistry laboratory at the Pasteur Institute, he also held the chair of biochemistry at the Sorbonne, the only chair of biological chemistry in the country. His approach to biochemistry resembled, and, at the same time, reinforced that of other French biochemists, who worked in Faculties of Medicine or Pharmacy. Their brand of biochemistry was structural and analytical, reflecting an under-development of organic chemistry in France, and leading them to abandon work on cellular oxidation and respiration in the 1920s. Yet in the same period these were fertile areas of study in Germany (at the Kaiser Wilhelm Gesellschaft Biological Institute, under Otto Warburg), and in Britain (at Cambridge, under F.G. Hopkins), where they contributed to the development of general biochemistry. This did not happen in France until the 1960s, when biochemistry was, in fact, about to merge with the new discipline of molecular biology, in which a new generation of Pastorians would play a major role.[44]

The functions of research and teaching were closely associated with each other, and the evidence above suggests that the balance achieved at the Pasteur Institute preserved a central place for research. But what of the balance between research and production?

4. Research and production

Between the wars, the main vocation of the Institute became the applications of science, and more particularly the problems of production.[45] This was a cause of discomfort for the Institute, which disguised the reality behind a rhetoric of pure science.[46] Furthermore, a lack of clear separation between research and production became a cause for concern among a group of Pastorians, who perceived it not only as a threat to the financial security, but also as a hindrance to the scientific productivity of the Institute.[47] Their attempts to separate research from production in the period before World War Two are described below.

Although there were two separate production sites — the annex in Garches (a Paris suburb), for the production of diphtheria antitoxin, and the BCG building, for the production of the BCG vaccine against tuberculosis — throughout the Institute many smaller production units existed within the research laboratories. In the 1930s these units manufactured and sold a wide range of products, over which the Director and the Administrative Council had little control.[48] Similarly, they were unable to prevent the arrangements of a private nature between scientists and industry, which were felt to be detrimental to the quality of Pasteurian research.[49] These arrangements included contracts for the sale of products, or services.[50] Although it was not unusual for small pharmaceutical laboratories to rely on part-time workers to carry out essential research, the Institute perceived these arrangements as a threat to its scientific authority and to its existence as a collective body, with a single identity.

In 1933, the death of René Vallery-Radot, son-in-law of Louis Pasteur and President of the Administrative Council, and a few months later the deaths of Albert Calmette and Emile Roux, the last of Pasteur's old collaborators, created a void and provided opportunities for change.[51] A new President was elected: Alfred Lacroix, and Louis Pasteur Vallery-Radot replaced his father on the Council. The deputy Director, Louis Martin, became interim Director. Together, they prepared a reform of the Institute. Roux's power had been 'absolute', Lacroix announced in front of the Council, and his death had left the Institute 'decapitated', but ready for change.[52] As President of the Council, he was responsible for setting up a Commission to study the present situation.

In 1934, Pasteur Vallery-Radot presented a report on behalf of the Commission. It described a disparate grouping of laboratories, with no effective control either by the Director or by the Council.[53] Although the lack of a strong central (the term he used was 'rational') administration had not, as yet, had any serious consequences, he expressed fears for the future:

> It is true that the present organisation of the IP, which no longer fulfils its needs, has not caused any serious problems, thanks to the high caliber of its staff. However, it is to be feared that, some time in the future, the IP will suffer from administrative shortcomings. A more rational management is therefore required, as much for the scientific productivity of the Institute, as for its financial wellbeing.[54]

Among the recommendations, it was proposed to create a physical separation between the functions of research and production, by grouping all the production units together with the activities associated with production, such as sales and marketing, under a single roof. In a separate report, of which Charles Nicolle, whose clashes with Roux had been notorious, was the driving force, it was also proposed to create a Scientific Council. Its purpose would be to advise the Director on scientific matters and to give scientists a greater say in the running of the Institute. Only a few of the recommendations were implemented, and most of them did not attain their objective. Although a building was erected for the sale and marketing of pasteurian products, within the academic laboratories the confusion between research and production remained; although the Conseil Scientifique was put in place, the fact that it was nominated by the Conseil d'Administration restricted its power.[55] It contributed to the creation of an 'oligarchy',[56] and the community of Pastorians as a whole remained without a voice until the Institute acquired more democratic structures in the 1950s (these later developments are covered in Chapter 5). Otherwise, the situation remained unaltered, an indication of the Council's overall resistance to change.[57]

Nevertheless, an important idea had been sown in the minds of many Pastorians. This was the idea that the confusion between research and production was a principal cause of the Institute's decline. There is no evidence that this was the case, but the logical association that was established between its duality of purpose and decline in the 1930s created a precedent for future reform. However, in the short term, and with war looming on the horizon, the Institute comforted itself with the thought that practical applications of Pasteurian research, i.e. vaccines and sera, remained a treasured part of Pasteur's heritage and the 'natural extension of laboratory experiments'.[58]

Whatever caused the stagnation of the Institute between the wars, whether it was the poverty of certain of its laboratories, the persistence of intellectual traditions that encouraged conservatism in the sciences, or a lack of 'enthusiasm' related to the crisis in immunology, it did not affect the Therapeutic Chemistry Laboratory, which in this period reached its heyday. Rather than being hindered by its close contacts with industry, this laboratory greatly benefited from them. It was able to remain relatively independent from the rest of the Institute, both financially and intellectually, and this was beneficial to research. However, its existence as a source of tension within the institute needs to be explained here.

5. The Therapeutic Chemistry Laboratory: The academic arm of the pharmaceutical industry, and a thorn in the side of the Pasteur Institute?

In 1910, Ehrlich's success with Salvarsan was becoming known, for in 1909 Salvarsan had been introduced onto the market, and in that year he published his article on the experimental chemotherapy of spirochaetes.[59] When Etard died in the same year, Ernest Fourneau, who had been working in the Poulenc Frères research laboratories in Ivry, was chosen to replace him. The Organic Chemistry Laboratory was renamed 'Laboratoire de chimie thérapeutique', with the purpose of 'searching for new substances to be used in the treatment of infectious diseases'.[60] Not only would the new laboratory enable the Pasteur Institute to keep abreast of German developments, but it would also fit Roux's intentions to provide the Institute with a mixed source of funding, derived from synthetic remedies as well as vaccines.[61]

Roux hoped that a certain amount of collaboration would exist between the Therapeutic Chemistry Laboratory and other laboratories, and that the Institute as a whole would benefit from the experience acquired in dealing with this new category of therapeutic substances. Thus, products discovered in the laboratory would undergo physiological and therapeutic tests elsewhere in the Institute. For example, the research carried out on the anti-syphilitic drug Stovarsol in 1922 involved the collaboration of Constantin Levaditi.[62] Federico Nitti, who had been working in the Vaccine Department under A. Salembeni, began his long and fruitful collaboration with Fourneau's team in 1935 as a result of the sulphonamide investigation.[63] On another occasion, Noël Rist paid his cousin Daniel Bovet a visit, and returned from the Therapeutic Chemistry Laboratory with some samples of sulphone with a view to using them in the treatment of leprosy and tuberculosis.[64]

Although to some extent Roux's wish to foster internal collaborations was fulfilled, both Igolen and Bovet have stressed the inter-departmental rivalries, and even jealousies, of which the Therapeutic Chemistry Laboratory became the object.[65] These may have been caused by the competition between biological and chemical approaches to medicine. After Pasteur and his successor Duclaux, who had both given pride of place to chemistry, a biological approach had gained ground at the expense of chemistry, or so it seemed to Fourneau.[66] However, the divisions may also have been caused by envy. Chemotherapy soon became the largest department. It included up to thirty-five laboratories, and commanded one twelfth of the Institute's total budget.[67] Fourneau's collaboration with Rhône-Poulenc provided materials and equipment, and it boosted the numbers and salaries of its employees.

This created a climate beneficial to research. The Therapeutic Chemistry Laboratory produced scientific papers as well as drugs, some with fundamental implications such as the work on the pharmacology of the nervous system, which would lead to the first synthetic anti-histamines and a better understanding of allergic reactions. In 1935, when sulphanilamide threatened the field of sera, half of which eventually became obsolete, what had been suspicion from colleagues, soon became sharp division.[68] The discovery was greeted by silence within the Institute. This persisted until 1938, three years after the discovery of sulphanilamide, when the Director finally agreed to support the building of a pharmacological laboratory for Bovet.

Such tension and silence could have resulted from an incompatibility between the support given by industry, and the support, albeit reluctant, by the Institute, which based its image on the concept of science as a non-profit activity. On the other hand, the success of the laboratory may have encouraged the Institute to turn a blind eye to its links with industry. Nevertheless, when the conflict of interests was too great, for it threatened the very cement that held this complex mosaic together, the atmosphere became hostile.

The relationship between the Institute and the Hôpital Pasteur is probably the only one that could be described as a harmonious collaboration. There is a debate as to whether this close relationship inhibited the growth of a scientific approach to medicine in France. This debate is described briefly in what follows.

6. Which model for co-operation: science and the clinic, or science and industry?

The function of dispensary was added to the other functions of the Institute when a hospital, conceived for the isolation of patients treated with diphtheria antitoxin, was constructed in two sections: the first built in 1900, the second in 1903, and was run by Louis and then René Martin. The Hôpital Pasteur was the theatre of application of Pasteurian discoveries, from diphtheria antitoxin to sulphanilamide. It is where the first French-made penicillin was administered to a patient, and where, after the Liberation, a clinical laboratory for antibiotherapy was created. The Hôpital Pasteur helped to make the products of research accessible to the public, in the shape of diagnostic tests and treatments. It also provided publicity for the Institute, for instance when René Martin and Albert Delaunay described the cure of a child ill with streptococcal meningitis at a meeting of the Paediatric Society, and attracted an enthusiastic response from the audience.[69] Furthermore, the hospital produced knowledge of its own. Through treatment with the sulphonamides, which were active *in vitro* as well as *in vivo*, it was discovered that the drugs and dosages could be adapted to each individual case, and according to Claude Lapresle these findings revolutionized the treatment of infectious diseases.[70]

Roux's fruitful collaboration with Louis Martin at the Hôpital des Enfants Malades,[71] which served as a model for the co-operation between the Institute and the Hôpital Pasteur (once it had been built and Louis Martin placed at its head in 1900), has led some historians to suggest that the relationship between the Pasteur Institute and clinical medicine was fundamentally good. In his history of the Pasteur Institute, in 1962 Delaunay mentioned the 'union of the laboratory and the clinic' that was realized when Gaston Ramon and his friend Robert Debré, who was to reform the French clinic after World War Two, worked together on diphtheria.[72] On the other hand, the absence of a research tradition in many hospitals has led other historians to conclude that the ambiguous relationship between the Pasteur Institute and clinical medicine as a whole was so nefarious as to be one of the causes of the under-development of French biology between the wars.[73] This debate cannot be resolved here, but it should nevertheless be mentioned, for the collaboration between scientists and clinicians was believed by contemporaries (for instance, Heinrich Hörlein, director of IG Farben)[74] and is thought by many historians (such as Miles Weatherall)[75] to be a prerequisite for drug development.

There was a similarly complex relationship between the Institute and the pharmaceutical industry. Although co-operation between the Therapeutic Chemistry Laboratory and Rhône-Poulenc was excellent, the relationship between the Institute and the pharmaceutical industry as a whole was ambiguous.[76] This ambiguity was largely attributable to the founding paradox of the Institute: 'a private institution, dedicated to public health'.[77] The paradox was resolved in many ways, for instance by applying different criteria to vaccines and sera, which the Institute was determined to keep away from commercial concerns, and to other types of products. These were allowed to break away from the *maison-mère* (i.e. the parent company, as the Institute was sometimes referred to), and become independent companies, for instance d'Hérelle's 'Laboratoire du Bactériophage'.[78]

The 'elastic ideology' of the Paris Institute enabled it to resolve these ambiguities and project a powerful, coherent image of itself to the outside world.[79] However, the reality behind the façade remained complex. Paul Weindling has described the Pasteur Institute as 'pluralistic', in contrast with the more rigidly hierarchical Koch Institute in Berlin.[80] Centralized around Paris, and around personalities like Roux,[81] but fragmented, like the French system as a whole,[82] its structure provided order, at the same time allowing the expression of individual talents and ambitions.

Referring to the relations between the main Institute and its subsidiaries ('filiales'), Anne-Marie Moulin has used the term 'patriarchal network'.[83] This term also fits the relationship between the various departments and laboratories of the Pasteur Institute. It was hierarchical, as the term 'patriarch' suggests, but its control was loose enough for numerous collaborations to emerge, both inside and outside the Institute. This grouping of disparate laboratories and institutions was, historically and geographically, central to French medical research. Its influence was considerable, both within and outside France where it served as a model. Yet, as the case of the Lister Institute helps to show, it was not necessarily directly transferable to the British context.

C. BRITAIN: AN INSTITUTIONAL NETWORK

Compared with France, the British situation was very diverse, or 'multifaceted', as one historian has put it.[84] Unlike in France, or for that matter Germany, where the bacteriological laboratory reigned supreme as the symbol of scientific medicine, in Britain bacteriology co-existed and at times conflicted with other approaches, for instance medical statistics.[85] This diversity was reflected in the multiple sites for the production of medical knowledge, described below as an expanding network of research institutions.

1. Different approaches to medical science, and an expanding network of research institutions

The diversity of approaches to medical science is illustrated by the debate over the margin of error in the estimation of the famous 'opsonic index' (the ratio of a substance in blood — opsonin — to leukocytes in patients with a bacterial infection). This debate raged in 1910 between the bacteriologist Sir Almroth Wright, who ran the inoculation department at St Mary's Hospital in London, and Dr Major Greenwood, who occupied the first post of medical statistician in Britain,[86] a post created for him in 1909 by C.J. Martin, director of the Lister Institute, and a firm believer in the relevance of statistics to medical science.[87] Whereas Wright claimed that changes in the 'opsonic index' in patients' serum demonstrated the ability of therapeutic vaccines to promote the body's defences, Greenwood argued that such changes were statistically insignificant, and showed that therapeutic vaccines were inefficient. In 1919, when Greenwood left the Lister to become the newly created Ministry of Health's first senior Statistical Medical Officer based at the NIMR, the department at the Lister Institute closed down. However, by then, a 'triangular' dispute had developed between clinicians, bacteriologists, and statisticians over 'who should be the final arbiter of medical knowledge'.[88]

This dispute reflects the diversity of centres for medical research in Britain. Although the NIMR, which as well as Medical Statistics included departments of Applied Physiology and Endocrinology, Biochemistry and Pharmacology, and Biological Standards, was to play in Britain a role that was similar to the Pasteur Institute in France, it did not dominate medical research to the same extent. When it was set up in 1914, it shared the function of national research facility with the Lister, the first institute of medical research in Britain, which had been constructed on the model of the Pasteur in 1891.[89] In the 1920s and 1930s, they were joined by several other institutions that were connected with one another via the MRC.

Both the NIMR and the Lister Institute were built and developed at a time of expansion of medical research, begun inside the hospital system before World War One. In Britain, as in France, the clinical discipline of physiology had played an important role in bringing science to the bedside. However, unlike the French school of physiology, which suffered relative stagnation between the wars, the British school reached its heyday in the same period.[90] From its base in clinical laboratories, it gradually gave rise to fully-fledged departments within medical schools.[91] In almost all instances, these physiology departments provided a stimulus for the development of specialized subfields, such as biochemistry, which eventually acquired the status of independent disciplines.[92] Although the London teaching hospitals and universities of Oxford and Cambridge made a major contribution to these developments, regional centres with medical schools also played an important part. In some industrial cities, such as Sheffield, Manchester and Liverpool, medical research grew in response to local circumstances.[93] In addition, the Scottish university system, with two centres for medical research, Edinburgh and Glasgow, helped to counter-balance the weight of the London teaching hospitals and medical schools in the South.

However, several historians have argued that, paradoxically, the 'scientisation' of medicine could not be complete until the sciences related to medicine had acquired institutionally separate identities.[94] This occurred in the 1920s and 1930s in a number of British universities, under the influence of a reforming élite. Cambridge led the way, with F.G. Hopkins's Dunn Institute of Biochemistry, which was an off-shoot of Physiology (1921). The Sir William Dunn School of Pathology, and then the Biochemistry department were built next, in Oxford (in 1926).[95] Such a movement did not happen in France until after World War Two.[96]

The strength of Britain's physiological tradition made it possible for a distinctive approach to health and disease to develop in British medical schools and research institutions, although some reluctance to adopt scientific methods and practices subsisted among clinicians.[97] The use of drugs as investigative tools, in particular drugs for affections of the nervous system, contributed to the acquisition of knowledge about the normal functions of the body, in what has been called 'the physiological basis of medicine'.[98] The counterpart to a better understanding of physiology was an understanding of pathology (a point that appears to have been more controversial in France than in Britain),[99] and new concepts of disease emerged that were radically different from germ theory, for instance the concept of deficiency. According to Miles Weatherall, the impact of germ theory on medicine had been such that resistance to new approaches lingered on until World War Two. Hence a Medical Research Committee report in 1919 stated:

> Disease is so generally associated with positive agents — the parasite, the toxin, the *materies morbi* — that the thought of the pathologist turns naturally to such positive associations and seems to believe with difficulty in causation prefixed by a *minus* sign.[100]

Despite such resistance, the concept of deficiency gradually became established, as major discoveries in the fields of hormones and vitamins were being made.[101]

With such historical and geographical diversity, Britain was unlikely to develop a dominant ideology to the same extent as France, where medical research was largely concentrated in the Pasteur Institute in Paris. Although Almroth Wright greatly influenced British medical research between the wars, and this influence would have profound consequences on the early development of penicillin (see Chapter 3), his laboratory was only one amongst many.[102] The next section follows the development of medical research institutions chronologically, focussing on the Lister Institute and the NIMR. Other institutions that became pertinent to the history of penicillin are described in Part Two of this volume.

2. Similar, yet different: the Lister Institute

The Lister Institute (see Figure 1.3) was modelled on the Pasteur Institute and presented a British adaptation of the French example. Although there were important differences in their respective sizes, styles of leadership, and administration, the similarities between the two institutions were considerable. However, unlike the Pasteur Institute, the Lister's contribution is best considered not in isolation, but within the network of interconnected institutions that evolved under the aegis of the MRC. Much of the Lister's archive was destroyed during the war, therefore the following account is based on the history of the Lister by Harriet Chick et al., and on the remaining Lister papers, held in the Contemporary Medical Archives Centre.

Figure 1.3 The Lister Institute (with permission from the Wellcome Trust)

A few years after the foundation of the Pasteur Institute, a similar institution was created in London, called the British Institute for Preventive Medicine. Its early purpose was to produce the rabies vaccine, and a large private donation by the first Earl of Iveagh (of the Guinness family) made its construction possible. Renaming the Institute after a British scientist was a condition of the donation, and the name of Jenner was suggested. However, a small commercial enterprise called the Jenner Institute already existed in Battersea, so the new institute was christened after Joseph Lister.[103] Lister had been one of Pasteur's main defenders in the controversy surrounding the germ theory of disease. He is best known for putting it into practice, when he introduced anti-sepsis into surgery. There can be little doubt that the Pasteur Institute provided inspiration for the Lister Institute in London (see Figure 1.4). Several visits were made in order to study the organisation of the Parisian institution.[104] Thus, until World War One at least, the Lister Institute defined itself in relation to its French model. However, it contained the seeds of what made the British context 'unique', and a 'harbinger of things to come' in matters of medical science.[105]

Like the Pasteur Institute, the Lister fulfilled several functions: the first were to study infectious diseases, and to treat them with the help of vaccines and sera. Teaching and hospital care were later added to these two basic functions.[106] The Lister, like the Pasteur, experienced tension between its

Figure 1.4 Scientific staff of the Lister Institute ca 1925 (with permission from the Wellcome Trust)

'pure' (research) and 'applied' (production of vaccines) vocations. However, in the long run this tension was resolved differently in the two institutions. The differences between them, which were present from their creation, therefore suggest that different cultures were at work. This was reflected in their organisation and style of leadership, and in the science that was practised within their walls.[107]

Whereas the Pasteur Institute was the creation of one man, Pasteur, who surrounded himself with collaborators or 'disciples', the British Institute for Preventive Medicine was a spontaneous association of scientific men, similar to many others in Britain at the time. It was without a figurehead until the name of Jenner, and later Lister, was given to it, in order to offer a British equivalent to Pasteur.[108] Like the Pasteur Institute, the Lister relied on endowments (in this case, the Iveagh donation), on the sales of vaccines, and on a certain amount of state support. However, the Lister seemed to have a greater accountability to its benefactors. Lord Iveagh had specific wishes concerning the research to be carried out at the Lister, and as he and his successors were on the Governing Body, these wishes had to be respected. The Governing Body of the Lister was led by non-scientists as well as scientists like the Conseil d'Administration, but there was no equivalent of the Pasteurian Assemblée.

Some members of the Lister saw this structure as a drawback, and called for a 'senate' of professors to be created, along the lines of the Assemblée and the Kaiserliches Gesundheitsamt.[109] They envied the 'esprit de corps' that made the Pasteur appear, from the outside, as a coherent institution; whereas they perceived the Lister to be a disparate group of laboratories, in which individuals, with apparently little concern for seniority or authority, carried out their research. These members may have had an ulterior motive in drawing such a sharp contrast between the two institutions, or may simply have been unaware of the reality behind the façade of the Pasteur. However, the following quote from the authors of *War on Disease* suggests that the Lister was governed in a more democratic manner than the Pasteur, where power could be concentrated in the hands of the Director (as in the case of Emile Roux) and where reforms to counterbalance this power led to the creation of an 'oligarchy':[110]

> The government of the Institute is [...] not a self-perpetuating oligarchy, but a hierarchy in which the lowest tier, the members of the Institute, has some control over the actions and policy of the Governing Body. Until 1949, when the constitution of the Governing Body was amended, the Director was not *ex officio* a member of the Governing Body, but its servant.[111]

Two episodes in the early history of the Lister illustrate the extent to which its style of leadership and administration distinguished it from its French model. Shortly after being appointed Director (in 1903), C.J. Martin was sent to India to conduct the Plague Enquiry. Upon his return, he found an Institute where scientists had evolved personal research programmes, and were uncomfortable about discussing them with their Director.[112] The feeling that this lack of direction might be the cause of much mediocre research — perceived as 'too academic', i.e. cut off from medical applications and from teaching —[113] prompted a reorganisation of the Lister, which allowed a greater involvement of the Director in his colleagues' research. Nevertheless, in the almost thirty years that Martin remained as Director, from 1903 to 1930, he was remarkable for his non-interference in the activities of the researchers working under him.[114] In this he may have followed his personal preference, but perhaps also institutional policy, as the co-authors of the history of the Lister seem to suggest when they write:

> The practice of the Institute in making appointments *ad hominem*, rather than to a predetermined scheme, is nowhere more apparent than in the [biochemistry] department, for over the years a succession of likely young chemists were appointed to the staff, some to stay, others to depart to senior posts elsewhere, but all free to develop their own ideas.[115]

The Lister was governed by custom and practice, as well as by statutes, and was organized along the lines of the parliamentary system. An important event in its history illustrates this. This event also represents a watershed in the history of medicine in Britain, and is described below.

3. For and against amalgamation: shaping the future of British medical research on the eve of World War One

In 1911, the National Insurance Act, a precursor of the National Health Service, set up a scheme for basic health cover and made the funding of medical research possible. As a result, the Medical Research Committee, which became the MRC after the war, was created. Plans for a National Institute for Medical Research were made, and it was debated whether it might not be in the Lister's interest to amalgamate with the new government research institution.[116] With war approaching, co-operation between scientific institutions and government was deemed to be in the national interest. But how this co-operation should be implemented remained a matter for debate. Between 1912 and 1914, campaigns for and against amalgamation were conducted, and the arguments put forward by both camps allow us a glimpse of what was at stake.

In the first camp were those who saw in amalgamation an opportunity to benefit from government funding and carry out a certain amount of directed research, which this camp viewed as beneficial, whilst avoiding the dangers of competition from commercial houses.[117] In the second, were those who rejected the idea that scientific ideas could be manufactured to order, and thought that the best form of co-operation was an informal one. The latter considered government (the word used was: 'lay') interference to be a threat to scientific freedom and independence. The model of Johns Hopkins, described as 'the dictatorship of a national institute', was brandished as one to be avoided at all cost.[118] In the end, the argument between the two camps came down to a vote by the Governing Body, and the anti-amalgamation camp, although a minority, won the day because of its use of proxy votes.[119]

This decision was to have important consequences for the history of the medical sciences in Britain. It led to a division of labour between the two Institutes, and to the creation of an embryonic network of medical research institutions. While the NIMR studied pharmacology, chemotherapy, and chemistry, the Lister focussed on bacteriology and biochemistry, thus becoming the second oldest biochemistry department in the country after Liverpool. Martin's own interest in problems of nutrition made this a special area of biochemical study at the Lister. The cause of beri-beri was soon identified as a lack of a nutrient (called 'vitamine' by Casimir Funk, a guest worker from Warsaw) present in rice, bran and yeast, and eventually known as vitamin B_1.[120] After World War One, a joint research team from the Medical Research Committee and the Lister was sent to Vienna to study rickets, and established the value of cod liver oil in treating the disease.

After Martin's departure, Robert Robison took over the biochemistry department. His work on alcoholic fermentation, and on the process of ossification, broke new ground in the area of general biochemistry, which Jean-Paul Gaudillière has described as absent from the French scene.[121] Other research carried out in the department reflected the 'permeation of chemistry into the elucidation of mysterious vital processes', and the authors of *War on Disease* believed that this was made possible by the very nature of their Institute.[122]

Between the wars, valuable contributions were also made by the bacteriology department, for instance Joseph Arkwright's discovery of biological variations in the typhoid and dysentery group of vaccines.[123] The Lister's important place in British bacteriology justified the establishment of the National Collection of Type Cultures in 1922, under joint control of the MRC and the Lister.[124] What had begun as a domestic concern soon became a collection of international importance, comparable to that of the Pasteur.

Much of the work at the Lister was done in collaboration with the MRC, which helped it not only to receive government grants, but also to remain at the centre of medical research. Harriet Chick et al. has written of the extensive national and international network to which the Lister belonged between the wars. It was organized so as to provide visitors from Britain and abroad with training, in bacteriology especially; after 1933, it received Jewish scientists escaping from Nazi Germany.[125] It also became the centre of a formally organized network of female academics, the British Federation of University Women, which owed much to the Institute's special relationship with F.G. Hopkins's biochemistry institute at Cambridge.[126]

Such multi-disciplinary research was perhaps more likely to occur in a small, loosely directed institution such as the Lister,[127] which was at the heart of an expanding institutional network, than in a larger, hierarchical institution like the Pasteur, which dominated medical research in France and beyond, and where microbiology was the dominant discipline.[128]

However, in the field of vaccines and sera the Lister gradually drifted away from the centre towards the periphery. As the proponents of amalgamation had feared, a consequence of the 1914 decision was that it was compelled to remain in competition with commercial houses for the sale of vaccines. Although it had a formal agreement with Allen & Hanburys to commercialize vaccines and sera manufactured at their Elstree plant and, in exchange, to standardize commercial preparations of diphtheria antitoxin, its relationship with the pharmaceutical industry as a whole was weak. It also competed with other research institutions, most notably the inoculation department at St Mary's Hospital. Moreover, like the Pasteur, it suffered from a scattered production site. Its chief product, smallpox vaccine, was manufactured in laboratories in Cornwall from 1915 to 1935, while antisera (diptheria antitoxin, tetanus antitoxin and anti-gas gangrene) remained at the production site in Elstree.[129] The Lister was also marred by a lack of research associated with the production of biological remedies, at least until the latter part of the period, when a biochemical laboratory was added to the main production site in 1933, and new research topics were introduced, such as the study of viruses.

Although a thorough analysis of their financial accounts would have to be carried out for firm conclusions to be reached with respect to their relative financial situations, the evidence from secondary sources suggests that the Pasteur was much larger, with around 30 research departments and a budget reaching seven million francs in 1935, and by 1948 about a thousand researchers and a budget of one billion francs.[130] By contrast, between 1909 and 1950, the Lister was able to double its scientific staff from only about 24 to 49.[131] The Pasteur benefited from a constant stream of legacies, whereas in Britain reliance on endowments was a problem. The British public were not so keen to support medical research, partly because of the vigour of the anti-vivisection movement.[132] Furthermore, Pasteur's image may have been more effective at selling vaccines, and his Institute's strong national and international reputation helped to shield it from financial difficulties between the wars.[133]

The contribution of rhetoric to economic as well as scientific success is highlighted by the following paradox: whereas the Pasteur was relatively prosperous in the 1920s and 1930s, it defined itself increasingly in terms of pure science. By contrast, the Lister, which welcomed medical and other practical applications openly, suffered in the same period from serious financial difficulties. When demand for bacterial anti-sera dwindled with the advent of the sulphonamides, it received a blow from which, according to Miles Weatherall, it was never to recover.[134] It was unable to resolve the conflict between economics and innovation, and this eventually led to the closure of the laboratories in 1975.[135] Thanks to its elastic ideology, the Pasteur was able to manage the conflict between research and production until it was compelled in 1965 to make the decision, like the Lister fifty years earlier, either to remain private, or to become a state-owned laboratory. It chose the opposite course of action, reaching a compromise that gave it semi-public status, and it survived as a research institution.

The two institutes responded differently to different historical contexts. Before World War One, when the Lister Institute chose between amalgamation into a national research facility or continuation as a private institution, state funding for research was viewed with some suspicion. On the contrary, after World War Two, when the Pasteur Institute had to make a similar choice, state funding for research was encouraged (see Part 3 of this volume).

Different historical contexts, rather than different institutional cultures, may therefore explain these different outcomes. Nevertheless, one question arises: does the contrast which a comparison between the Pasteur and

Lister Institutes brings out indicate a weakness of the Lister, or British research institutions in general? In this chapter, I show that the British case is best considered, not in terms of individual institutions, but in terms of a network of inter-related laboratories, whose research was co-ordinated, rather than directed, by the MRC.

From 1914 onwards, this network included a central research laboratory, the future NIMR. Like the Pasteur, its goals were linked to the government's health policies through the MRC. However, unlike the Pasteur, its funding came entirely from the public purse. Nevertheless, the semi-autonomous status of the MRC allowed it to define its research objectives independently of government.[136] These objectives, and the role played by the NIMR in realising them, are studied next.

4. The scientific instrument of the MRC's strategy: the NIMR

Although in response to public health requirements a strong emphasis was placed on therapeutic research, when it was formed the MRC was given the right to define its own objectives. It kept these suitably wide, so as to modify them according to advances in medical knowledge.[137]

As the historian of the MRC, A.L. Thomson, explained in his opening chapter to Volume Two of *Half a Century of Medical Research*:

> If any narrow interpretation [that medical research must necessarily be directed to diseases as such] were ever in mind, it was effectively ruled out by the MRC's *own definition*, contained in the general scheme of research that was submitted formally to the Minister in November 1913 [my italics].[138]

The Minister endorsed the wide definition of medical research presented by the MRC to include 'all researches bearing on health and disease, whether or not such researches have any direct or immediate bearing on any particular disease or class of disease', on condition that these were 'judged to be useful' in relation to its main goal, described as 'the preservation of health by preventing or combating disease'.[139] The MRC was, therefore, left free to select the topics for funding, as well as the approaches to adopt for their study. Under its first Secretary, Walter (later Sir Walter) Morley Fletcher, a member of the Cambridge School of Physiology, it privileged the pre-clinical sciences.[140]

In the original programme, top priority was given to infectious diseases, and among these, tuberculosis headed the list. It had been the main impetus for the government's decision to support medical research, and represented a large fraction of the grants awarded as the result of the National Insurance scheme: 44 grants out of 104, totalling £8,875.[141] Second only to tuberculosis in terms of funding, the problem of rickets — as I mentioned earlier — was solved early in the programme. Its identification as a deficiency disease placed it in the field of nutrition research, soon to become the most important within the Council's general programme.

The MRC's initial approach was empirical. It distinguished between three broad divisions in medical research, corresponding to the alternative strategies available at the time: curative medicine, preventive medicine, and basic science. However, during the inter-war period the Council's approach was refined as a greater understanding of the causes of disease was achieved. These were defined as either 'intrinsic' (in the case of chronic illnesses and cancer) or 'extrinsic' (in the case of infectious and deficiency diseases). Although after World War Two the MRC's emphasis would shift towards research on the intrinsic causes, and the principal strategy to 'prevent and combat disease' would become that of the fundamental sciences, in the inter-war period its focus was on the extrinsic causes, more especially on infectious diseases, and its strategy was at once preventive and curative. Recognizing Britain's relative weakness in chemotherapy, in early programmes the Council concentrated its efforts on this area of research, more particularly on the treatment of tropical diseases.[142] The NIMR was to be an important instrument for implementing this strategy.

Until World War Two, one third of the MRC's budget was destined to the NIMR, while the rest was used to finance research projects throughout the country.[143] The institute began in Hampstead in 1914, on the site of the North London Hospital for Consumption. It was named the NIMR in 1920, after the Medical Research Committee had been reconstituted into the Medical Research Council, and later moved to new premises in Mill Hill. Originally, it was thought that Almroth Wright would be made overall Director. However, his style of leadership was deemed too autocratic, and different directors were assigned to each department until Henry Dale, then Head of Biochemistry and Pharmacology, became Director of the NIMR in 1928.[144] Dale, like Fourneau, had started his scientific career in one of the first pharmaceutical laboratories in the country, the Wellcome Physiological Research Laboratories (WPRL).[145] His appointment to the post of Director of the NIMR formalized a situation that had existed before, for he was clearly a dominant personality within the Institute, and his scientific expertise as well as his experience of industry placed him in a privileged position in relation to the MRC's research objectives.

One of these objectives, the development of chemotherapy, required the collaboration of chemists and biologists. Although the potential for multidisciplinary research was good inside the NIMR, at the national level such collaborations were more difficult to realize, partly because of the dearth of practically trained chemists and chemical engineers.[146] Following the precedent created by the Salvarsan Committees in World War One, with the help of the Department of Scientific and Industrial Research (DSIR), the MRC was able to encourage collaborations between chemists and biologists.[147] This was done at first by a Joint Committee (1926), and then by a Chemotherapy Committee (1927), on which chemists, who were paid by the Department to synthesize compounds for study, and biologists, who were funded by the Council to carry out experimental trials, could share information and ideas.[148] This committee was inspired by the screening operations organized by the German pharmaceutical industry, but seemed rather small without the 'effective co-operation' of the British pharmaceutical industry, which, according to Thomson, at the time showed little interest in chemotherapy.[149]

Nevertheless, as a result of these early collaborations, studies were made at the NIMR, particularly in its Biochemistry and Pharmacology Department, which had both applied and fundamental aspects. They included Dale and Dudley's work on the purification and standardization of insulin, Dale's research on acetylcholine and the chemical transmission of nerve impulses, the development of curare-like drugs for use in anaesthesia, and work on the chemotherapy of tropical diseases, for example the synthesis by Harold King of diamidine compounds, which proved useful in the treatment of kala-azar (a form of sleeping sickness). Last but not least, there was P. Fildes's and D.D. Woods's seminal work on the mechanism of action of sulphanilamide, which would have far-reaching implications for the study of structure-activity relations, and for drug discovery more generally after World War Two.[150]

Co-operation between the NIMR and clinical departments, although difficult at first, was later ensured through the Therapeutic Trials Committee. This Committee was created in 1931, partly under pressure from pharmaceutical companies, which by then had developed an interest in chemotherapy (according to Thomson, thanks to the Council's early efforts)[151] and were keen to have their remedies tested by clinicians.[152]

In order to ensure a more direct and fundamental contribution to chemotherapy after the discovery of sulphanilamide in 1936, plans were made to build a chemotherapy laboratory inside the Institute. This would follow the 'general line of action of a great commercial organisation', that is to say carry out an empirical study of chemically related compounds. However, unlike a pharmaceutical firm, the public laboratory would not suppress 'the scientifically valuable information incidentally obtained', especially concerning the relationship between the chemical structure and the biological activity of drugs.[153] World War Two interrupted the implementation of these plans, and, when they were reconsidered after the conflict, the advent of penicillin meant that a new design had to be drawn for the laboratory, so that it could take up the study of antibiotics, and investigate not only the chemical, but also the biological aspects of chemotherapy.[154]

To sum up, before World War Two, in both countries the boundaries between research and production were very fluid, despite attempts to keep the former separate from the latter. The development of institutes of medical research in Britain and in France at the turn of the century responded to a need created by public health measures, as well as by advances in science and medicine. These institutes produced remedies and carried out research which the pharmaceutical industry was, at least at first, either unwilling, or unable to do. They could, therefore, be considered as a branch of the pharmaceutical industry.

At the same time, academic-style institutes financed by pharmaceutical firms appeared, most notably the WPRL in Britain (1899), created by Henry Wellcome of Burroughs Wellcome, and — albeit on a smaller scale — the Institut Mérieux in France (1897), founded by Marcel Mérieux, a colleague of Emile Roux.[155] They were the industrial counterparts of the Lister and Pasteur Institutes, and produced vaccines and sera in competition with them. As such, it could therefore be said that they represented a branch of medical research. However, on the whole, the expansion of research facilities within British and French industry between the wars was attributable to new chemotherapeutic and biological remedies, rather than vaccines and sera, and this expansion is described in the next section.

C. THE PHARMACEUTICAL INDUSTRY IN BRITAIN AND IN FRANCE

Although the differences between Britain and France were significant, a comparison of their drug sectors highlights the similarities between them. In both countries, the pharmaceutical industry was transformed in the 1920s and 1930s by the appearance of new, purpose-built laboratories. These co-existed alongside more traditional forms of industrial science, for example analytical laboratories associated with factories, and collaborative research with academic scientists and medical practitioners. This section begins with a summary of the history of the drug industry in the two countries, before moving on to the growth of pharmaceutical research.

1. The British and French pharmaceutical industries before World War Two: demand-pull or discovery-push?

The pharmaceutical industry has long been a rather neglected area of history, especially in comparison with the chemical industry.[156] This may be because it is a sector that is difficult to define, due to its complexity, and to its variety of origins. However, in the last two decades, its importance to national economies and public health policies has attracted increasing numbers of scholars. It has therefore become easier to build up a picture of it, not only from the numerous company histories that have been published, but also from the historiography of national pharmaceutical industries that has begun to develop.[157] Overall these suggest that, between the wars, the British and French pharmaceutical sectors were market-pulled, rather than technology-pushed.[158] Nevertheless, the imitation of foreign — mainly German — competitors, and the discovery of new synthetic and biological remedies, stimulated their transformation into science-based and innovative sectors of the economy, a transformation that began around World War One.[159]

The British and French markets for drugs were more or less identical, with similar rates of the same diseases affecting the populations of the Metropole and Empire.[160] These were markets in which 'humble items using low technology' were sought after more than 'technologically advanced pharmaceuticals', and many such humble items have since then become household names, an indication of their lasting commercial success.[161] Nevertheless, some differences existed between the French and British tastes for medicines. While the French favoured mixed remedies — leading the Swiss pharmaceutical company Sandoz, for example, to manufacture special combinations of pharmaceutical preparations for their local customers — the British public appeared particularly fond of tonic wines.[162] However, these differences did not greatly affect the nature of the market, which continued to dominate pharmaceutical business in Britain and France until World War Two.

The British and French drug industries emerged out of a similar context, marked by the slow development of the fine chemical industry and the absence of a strong dyestuffs industry, and as such they differed from their German counterpart.[163] This helps to explain why the producers of galenical remedies (preparations of animal or plant origin), Allen & Hanburys

> [...] did not see themselves as competing in the same field as some foreign manufacturers. Synthetic drug manufacture did not play a significant part in its output and the firm did not seem to feel it should. [... It regarded] German synthetic drugs as a 'passing phase'.[164]

The company's reactive, rather than innovative, strategy was well suited to the niches in the market it occupied, to which it adapted its existing product line rather than developing novel drugs. Moreover, in an intellectual climate that regarded chemotherapy with some scepticism, Allen & Hanburys considered it more prudent to leave research in this field to the MRC.

The origin and structure of the French and British pharmaceutical industries were similar. Both grew out of the pharmacy or drug wholesaler and manufacturer, and remained predominantly small, family-owned concerns. However, British industry largely owed its structure to drug importers and wholesalers (as in the case of Allen & Hanburys), while French industry owed it more to pharmacy. This helps to explain why, although most firms were small to medium-sized in both countries, they tended to be smaller in France.[165]

In their responses to changes in science, technology and medicine, individual companies were not only affected by the origin and structure of the industry, and by the nature of the market in which they operated but they were also influenced by legislation. Before World War Two, patent law played a more prominent role than drug safety legislation in governing their activities within the market. Whereas the German pharmaceutical sector benefited from a patent law that stimulated innovation, in Britain and France legislation did not allow the patenting of drugs, judged unethical. Although other ways were found to protect discoveries, through brand names, and by patenting processes instead of finished products,[166] the lack of patent protection for drugs handicapped larger firms, which would have been able to invest in research.[167]

A distinctive feature of the French pharmaceutical sector compared with its British counterpart was the extent to which it was subjected to restrictive practices, for the preparation and sale of pharmaceutical products was, since the loi de Germinal passed in 1803, reserved to professional pharmacists.[168] Nevertheless, by the end of the nineteenth century, a number of pharmaceutical firms had succeeded in building an industrial base, thus becoming 'atypical' in the French context: Clin-Comar, Midy, Adrian, Fumouze, Coirre, and Byla.[169]

The economic, historical, and legal context described above was therefore favourable to small and medium companies, and these remained a predominant feature of Britain and France until World War Two. The internal organisation of companies was very varied, but on the whole they did not incorporate research departments of the kind found in German dyestuffs firms, such as BASF, where laboratories were part of an integrated corporate structure.[170] However, despite the relatively small size of many of French and British firms, research facilities did develop in the inter-war period, and the causes of change were almost as varied as the industry itself. They included the expansion of the chemical industry, which had a knock-on effect on the pharmaceutical sector; growing competition between firms because of economic recession, and developments in science, technology and medicine. In the next section, special attention is given to the latter, for these usually depended on collaborative research.

2. The growth of pharmaceutical research between the wars

Between the wars, pharmaceuticals became part of the core business of a number of chemical groups. For example, in 1928 Poulenc Frères amalgamated with the Société des Usines du Rhône (SCUR) to form Rhône-Poulenc, and in 1936 ICI created a Medicinal Section within their Dyestuffs Division.[171] These firms became trend setters in the pharmaceutical field, the former in the inter-war period, the latter during World War Two, and their efforts at bringing their business up to a par with their competitors abroad (the German firm IG Farben before, and American companies after the conflict) would in time benefit their two countries' drug sectors as a whole.[172]

However, French and British pharmaceutical firms also displayed a dynamism of their own, independently of the chemical industry. Robson has said of these often relatively small and disparate companies that:

> [...] they were each beginning in their different ways to exert influence over both medical and public opinion during the inter-war years. They did this by skilful use of advertising and salesmanship, by carrying out research on their own account, and by building relationships with key members of the medical profession.[173]

New developments in science, technology and medicine played an important part in this fundamental change, and are outlined below.

Several authors have pointed to diphtheria antitoxin, which was developed in the 1890s, as the single most important catalyst in the creation of a modern, science-based drug industry.[174] However, this may describe the American and German pharmaceutical sectors better than their British or French counterparts, which were slower to take on the production of biologicals. Important exceptions in Britain include Burroughs Wellcome,[175] and Evans Sons, Lescher & Webb. These two companies were among the first to refer to themselves as 'laboratories', and incorporated research facilities, developed in the case of Evans in connection with Liverpool University Medical School.[176] In France, as well as the Institut Mérieux mentioned earlier, several small companies produced vaccines and sera, and lent their bacteriological testing facilities to local hospitals. Many of these were dotted around the Paris area, and called themselves 'laboratoires de biochimie' or 'de biologie médicale'.[177]

The interruption of supplies of German synthetic drugs in World War One led a number of firms to acquire knowledge and expertise in organic chemistry. In Britain, it resulted in a collaborative project, which aimed to replace drugs such as the anti-syphilitic Salvarsan, and the local anaesthetic Novocaine, and in which the Royal Society acted as a forum for contacts between universities and industry.[178] Several pharmaceutical companies were involved, including Boots Pure Drugs Co. and Burroughs Wellcome. In France, the SCUR's position as chief producers of synthetic dyes was strengthened as a result of the war, when they began expanding their product line from dyes to pharmaceuticals by employing consultant-chemists picked from amongst the scientific élite.[179] On the other hand, thanks to the research carried out by the pharmacists Ernest Fourneau and Francis Billon in their laboratories in Ivry, Poulenc Frères had been imitating German synthetic drugs even before 1914. The sale of these drugs had not been a profitable activity, and the rationale behind the firm's commitment to research had initially been commercial, rather than industrial. Nevertheless, rendered more confident by the rise in sales experienced during the conflict, as well as by the prospect of diminished competition from

Germany afterwards, Poulenc decided to expand their production capacity in order to make it more profitable, and this, in turn, benefited research.[180]

The British company, May & Baker, was to profit greatly from Poulenc's growing scientific and technical expertise. The association between the two firms began in 1909 with the signature of an agreement, by which Poulenc's patents were to be transferred to May & Baker. This was achieved in 1916, and brought the British company in contact with chemotherapeutic research, resulting in the appointment of A.J. Ewins (formerly of Burroughs Wellcome) at the head of a new research laboratory constructed in Wandsworth.[181] In 1927, Poulenc took over May & Baker, and British laboratory staff subsequently began receiving technical training from the parent company. By 1927, the research department comprised four qualified chemists, two pharmacists and six laboratory assistants, which according to Judy Slinn represented quite a large research establishment for a company the size of May & Baker.[182]

Inter-company agreements, of the kind that existed between Poulenc and May & Baker, mergers, and international cartels were an important feature of the inter-war period. They limited competition, and allowed the transfer of technical know-how between firms.[183] They accelerated the spread of scientific discoveries, especially in the field of new biological remedies, which was to play an important part in the growth of the French and British pharmaceutical industries between the wars.

In the 1920s and 1930s, the discovery of insulin, sex hormones and vitamins stimulated companies in Britain and France into developing new product lines. The development of these novel remedies was often well suited to the type of research facility that was already in place, and coincided with the physiological and pharmacological approaches to therapy being developed at the time within medical research institutions.[184] Robson has noted that:

> Although the continuing German model of empirical research was envied out of a sense of awe, few tried to copy it directly. Instead, companies such as Burroughs Wellcome and Spécia [Rhône-Poulenc's pharmaceutical selling company] profited from a different research strategy beginning from a physiological or pharmacological perspective.[185]

These biological remedies also brought newcomers to the pharmaceutical industry. For instance Glaxo, baby food manufacturers, who diversified into pharmaceuticals as a result of a strong research programme in vitamins under their first research director Harry Jephcott.[186] French pharmaceutical companies were also quick to develop their own expertise in the field of hormones and vitamins. The largest company specializing in the new biologicals was Roussel (after 1928 Roussel-Uclaf).[187] Following Whipple's discovery in 1925 that raw liver extracts could be used to cure pernicious anaemia, a new range of products was born, called organotherapeutic or opotherapeutic remedies, and these were developed by several small and medium-sized companies in France. They included Byla and Choay.[188]

The impact of sulphanilamide on the pharmaceutical industry is recounted in many company histories. As a result of the co-operative research carried out between Fourneau, after he had moved to the Pasteur Institute in 1911, and Poulenc (later Rhône-Poulenc), a number of sulphon-amide drugs were developed in Britain and in France in the 1930s and 1940s. Rhône-Poulenc's product Septoplix reached the market in 1936.[189] May & Baker soon followed, by launching M&B 693, or Sulphapyridine, in 1938, and then Sulphathiazole (M&B 760).[190] The commercial success of these two drugs strengthened the British firm in relation to the parent company. The first sulphonamide drug to be marketed in France, Rubiazol, was manufactured by Roussel-Uclaf at the beginning of 1936, beating its rival Septoplix by a few weeks. It heralded Roussel-Uclaf's entry into the field of chemotherapy, and coincided with the company adopting the title of 'Laboratoire', as other French companies did in this period, for example Debat, Emile Bouchara, and Astier.[191]

Thus, throughout the inter-war period, French and British pharma-ceutical companies developed their research facilities, and many of them adopted what would become a 'modern' form of research, that is to say research carried out in separate, purpose-built laboratories. Even the more traditional Allen & Hanburys eventually developed a chemotherapeutic laboratory, in the 1950s. However, in their case, this did not happen as a direct result of the sulphonamides, but of penicillin.[192]

To conclude, the similarities between the British and French experiences in pharmaceuticals were overwhelming. However, according to Robson, the pharmaceutical French industry was not as quick to take up research as a central activity as its British counterpart at the time. For several Brit-ish companies, the knowledge and expertise acquired in producing new drugs, often in collaborative projects with academic research institutions and under the co-ordination of an official body (the Royal Society in World War One, and the MRC in the inter-war period), led them to transform their commitment to research from a cosmetic to a genuine concern. A group of five 'reputable' companies emerged, which in 1940 was to form the Therapeutic Research Corporation (TRC), composed of Burroughs Wellcome, British Drug Houses (BDH), Boots, May & Baker, and Glaxo. Of France, on the other hand, Robson has suggested that there was little evidence of research being carried out in French companies, apart from Rhône-Poulenc in collaboration with the Pasteur Institute.[193] His conclu-sions corroborate Terry Shinn's for French industry as a whole. According to Shinn, companies consistently chose to buy in technology by acquiring foreign licences rather than to develop their own research laboratories. He has cited three major exceptions: the Société des Produits Chimiques de Saint-Denis, Air Liquide, and the Société Française Radio-Electrique, in a context where industrial research was otherwise given low priority.[194] He has written that, on the whole, French entrepreneurs preferred organisational to scientific solutions to the problem of growing national and international competition.

Robson and Shinn have both made generalisations, and played down the role of the 'exceptions' they have cited. However, exceptions often set the trend for entire sectors of the economy, as Homburg has shown in describing the impact of BASF on the German dyestuffs industry in the late nineteenth century.[195] Moreover, Robson and Shinn have not questioned the assumption that industrial science must necessarily be carried out in purpose-built laboratories. Historians have begun to acknowledge that research could be done co-operatively, outside the boundaries of the company, and that research and production could be two closely inter-connected activities (and therefore often be hard to distinguish from each other).[196]

The next section shows that, although the research carried out by many small and medium pharmaceutical firms in Britain and France on the whole did not follow the model of the German BASF, or the American Du Pont, it was significant nonetheless. Without them, post-war developments cannot properly be understood. Rather than being 'opportunistic', as Liebenau has depicted British industry with regards to its research commitment,[197] it was the result of genuine scientific and technological enthusiasm, a characteristic shared by both countries between wars.[198]

3. What kind of industrial research?

Robert Fox has urged historians to define what they mean by industrial research:

> The modern conception of in-house chemical research as a fount of sophisticated new products or processes devised in a well-founded laboratory and destined, at least in principle, for commercial exploitation, is a late-comer in the history of industrial science. But that is not to say that industrial science itself is a late-comer.[199]

In the case of French and British pharmaceuticals, where the German model did not apply, the terms 'science', 'research', and 'laboratory' may cover realities that were different, but should not be dismissed merely as backward. After all, out of this different model a successful, innovative industry emerged that at various times has ranked amongst the world's leaders in pharmaceuticals.[200] This other model of pharmaceutical research, therefore, merits greater attention.

The preparation of traditional herbal and metallic remedies had involved certain chemical processes, for instance the extraction of alkaloids of vegetable origin, which in the nineteenth century were increasingly described in scientific terms, that is to say mainly by reference to chemistry.[201] In the official catalogue of the Great Exhibition of 1851, the beautiful crystalline forms obtained from vegetable alkaloids and mineral compounds were hailed as the result of the 'application of philosophic chemistry to the production of pharmaceutical preparations'.[202] The place where these were performed was often referred to as the 'laboratory', which became synonymous with the factory and the firm. The description of the laboratory facilities given in Tweedale's *At the Sign of the Plough* is very evocative, for there were:

> [...] furnaces, stills, steam apparatus, refrigerators and presses [...] a capacious sink, with water laid on, and perforated shelves fixed over it, for draining bottles, a fixed side table, for performing the smaller operations upon and, above this, a set of tests, test glasses, funnels, glass measures, and a perforated shelf, for supporting funnels [...]; a strong moveable table, which may be placed in any part of the laboratory; a druggist's root cutting or slicing knife; a large marble mortar, and an iron or bell mortar. There should also be a desk, on which to keep the journal of the operations of the laboratory, and above it a glass-case, containing the Pharmacopoeias and a few other books.[203]

In the first half of the twentieth century, herbal preparations and plant extracts were being superseded by the new biological and chemical remedies, although they were not totally displaced by them. In both Britain and France, there are examples of pharmaceutical companies that maintained their traditional specialties, while at the same time developing new chemical ones. Allen & Hanburys, who had pioneered the production of insulin in Britain, continued to make galenicals until 1958; the Laboratoires Houdé in France sold Stovaïne, antimony preparations and antipyretic drugs alongside their traditional herbal remedies.[204] Other galenical companies, for instance Dausse, did not change their product lines, but added experimental facilities (in this case an 'experimental farm') to those already in existence.[205]

In both countries, there appeared to be continuity, rather than discontinuity in the evolution of research facilities within the pharmaceutical industry, and this evolution was to some extent management-led.[206] Two examples of creation of research laboratories that were entirely management-led and of the type observed by Homburg in Germany were the WPRL in Britain, and the Poulenc laboratories in France. However, until World War Two, they were in the minority.

The modern pharmaceutical research laboratory in Britain and France evolved from the analytical laboratory established inside the factory, and grew with the perceived need to test and standardize preparations, sometimes even before legislation enforced these tests. In Britain, important laws included the Dangerous Drugs Act of 1922, and the Pharmacy and Poisons Act of 1933, which required the presence of trained pharmacists on production sites. In France, the 'loi de Germinal' was softened after World War

One (in 1918), and this led to a distinction between various pharmaceutical products, establishing a hierarchy between the producers of 'préparations magistrales' and the 'spécialités scientifiques', which were subject to special registration procedures.[207] Allen & Hanburys developed a separate analytical research division under Norman Evers, with seven chemists and a number of assistants, after 1922. It was the expertise of this embryonic research laboratory that made it a good choice for the production of insulin under the aegis of the MRC, and justified its partnership with BDH, which had been endowed with a large-scale production unit under Francis Carr (formerly of Burroughs Wellcome).[208] The experience acquired by Allen & Hanburys in producing insulin had a great impact on its research and production capabilities. This was described in a letter to the MRC:

> The unique experience which we gained in converting the laboratory production of Insulin into a large-scale process has combined with our resources for chemical and physiological research. The preparation and continued improvement of Insulin A&B (Allen & Hanburys and BDH) are the result of this combination.[209]

However, in the 1920s and 1930s, a new kind of laboratory began to take shape. Growing competition meant that science and research became part and parcel of firms' business strategies, and the 'one common, rather symbolic change, was to move away from traditional production facilities, often situated in a factory environment, into new facilities based on a laboratory environment'.[210] British companies chose to distance themselves from their origins as fine chemical producers and wholesalers by developing green field sites (for example May & Baker, Allen & Hanburys, BDH). A similar trend can be observed in France. Debat moved to a new site, in Garches, which was described by a journalist as the 'Trianon des usines'.[211] Rhône-Poulenc opened new pharmaceutical laboratories at Vitry-sur-Seine in 1930. Initially, they numbered eight laboratories, employing sixteen chemists, but they expanded again after 1935.[212]

These new laboratory facilities (see Figure 1.5) were an important element in a commercial strategy, in which 'scientific' was synonymous with 'quality', and which aimed to impress the medical profession. Nevertheless, the interest in disciplinary research that became apparent in the French and British pharmaceutical industries between the wars was genuine. A survey of pharmaceutical and other industrial laboratories carried out by the Centre National de la Recherche Scientifique (CNRS) in 1938 suggests that scientific research may have been taken more seriously than has hitherto been suggested in France.[213] On the British side, information about the employment of Ph.Ds, the production of patents and scientific publications indicates that the 'reputable' firms, at least, belonged to a network of research-oriented institutions in universities as well as industry.[214]

Figure 1.5 Inside a pharmaceutical research laboratory: one of Rhône-Poulenc's chemical labs in the 1930s (courtesy of Sanofi-Aventis).

Another important element in this strategy were the external contacts established with scientists and medical practitioners. For the smaller companies, these contacts compensated for a lack of extensive in-house research facilities, and the evidence suggests that co-operation between science and industry was more important than it is commonly believed.[215]

D. CONCLUSION

This chapter has highlighted some important national differences in the organisation of science in Britain and France. In France, there was greater centralisation at both institutional and national levels,[216] and the style of leadership was more autocratic. The term 'patriarchal network' is best suited to the French situation, for it combines the idea of hierarchical structure with that of relaxed control. In Britain, organisational structures were looser, the style of leadership consensual, and networks more extensive.

Contemporary observers believed these differences to be the cause of the stagnation of medical research in France, compared with other countries. Although it is not my purpose here to settle such a debate, my evidence suggests that accusations of decline are laden with ideological and political meaning.[217] At the Pasteur Institute, the spectre of decline was brandished in an effort to mobilize the Conseil d'Administration into reforming the

Institute after Emile Roux's death. A connection was established between what was described as its scientific decline under Roux's autocratic directorship, and the confusion between the functions of research and production. This created a precedent for reform in the post-war period. Paradoxically, the Lister Institute, which in the same period accepted more readily the applications of its research, was less successful as a producer of vaccines and sera, but made significant contributions in science as part of a growing network of British medical research institutions.

Otherwise, the similarities between the two countries are striking. The relationship between the Pasteur Institute as a whole and the pharmaceutical industry was both one of co-operation and competition.[218] In Britain, the Lister Institute had a similarly complex relationship with industry. Although it had an agreement with Allen & Hanburys for the sale of vaccines, it was often forced to compete with industry. The histories of the Pasteur and Lister Institutes illustrate the blurred boundaries that existed between the academic and industrial sectors in both countries before World War Two. Drug research (especially in the field of chemotherapy) remained largely academic. On the other hand, in the 1920s and 1930s, many pharmaceutical companies developed laboratories that were symptomatic of a new commitment to science.

In this chapter, I have shown that in both countries the conditions for the creation of collaborative relationships between scientists and pharmaceutical companies were favourable. But did the structural differences I have identified create different cultures with respect to co-operation, or were the similarities strong enough to produce a similar effect, that is to say well developed collaborative networks? This question is examined in the next chapter.

2   Scientific Communities and Networks before World War Two

A. INTRODUCTION

Having compared the organisation of science and industry in Britain and in France, I now turn to the development of collaborative networks in the period before World War Two. Whereas a lack of co-operation is often considered to be detrimental to academic as well as industrial research (an idea put forward to explain French 'backwardness' between World War One and World War Two),[1] too much co-operation, especially if it is government-sponsored, has also been described as unfavourable to industrial R&D (and identified as one of the roots of British industrial decline by David Mowery).[2] If opposite causes, that is to say either too little, or too much co-operation, can be shown to produce a similar effect, i.e. a lack of research, leading to backwardness or decline, then comparing Britain and France in terms of their collaborative cultures is a senseless task, unless studies of co-operation can first be separated from the issues of backwardness and decline. Separating alleged causes from their purported effects has become easier, since historians have begun to question the very idea of French backwardness and of British decline before World War Two.[3] Another fruitful approach has been to study the causes, including the slow development of industrial research.

Sally Horrocks and David Edgerton have shown that, contrary to the opinion expressed by Mowery, industrial R&D was not deficient in Britain before 1945, and therefore could not be the cause of the decline of British industry between the wars.[4] Recent research in French archives has also shown that, even in physics, which epitomized the French 'savant' in relation to business and the pursuit of money, academic-industrial co-operation was better developed in France than previously believed.[5] The concepts of backwardness and decline are, after all, relative to an external, perhaps even an ideal model that may not have existed in reality, but may have been used by French and British scientific élites to bring about institutional reform (see Chapter 1).[6]

Therefore, a fresh approach to comparing the French experience with the British may be best achieved by abandoning all preconceptions about

French 'backwardness' and British 'decline',[7] and by examining both countries on their own merits, as self-contained systems, before comparing
them with each other.[8] The first section of this chapter deals with France,
and shows that multi-disciplinary research teams and academic-industrial
collaborations were not absent in the inter-war period. The co-operation between Ernest Fourneau (see Figure 2.1) at the Pasteur Institute and
Rhône-Poulenc provided a model for the French pharmaceutical industry
as a whole, hence I examine it first. I then assess the French situation in
broader terms. Using a survey of industrial laboratories carried out by the
CNRS in 1938–40, I describe the existence of pharmaceutical networks,
and show that collaboration between firms and scientists in Paris and in the
provinces was not unusual on the eve of World War Two.

These networks began at the turn of the century within a close-knit
community of chemists and pharmacists for whom the boundaries between
science and industry were fluid. They expanded between the wars, as did
the research activities of scientific institutions and pharmaceutical companies. Despite important differences, in particular the greater involvement
of British government in academic-industrial collaborations through the
MRC and DSIR, and the greater public representation achieved by British
industry through the ABCM (Association of British Chemical Manufac-

Figure 2.1 Ernest Fourneau
in Biarritz (courtesy of the
Pasteur Institute).

turers) and FBI (Federation of British Industries), this chapter shows that a grass-roots co-operative culture existed in both countries, independently of government intervention, and that this culture produced similar, long-lasting collaborative relationships.

B. THE FRENCH EXPERIENCE

The French are seen, by themselves perhaps more than by others, as belonging to a non-co-operative culture.[9] A lack of co-operation within institutes or laboratories ('un laboratoire sans équipe'), and the absence of collaboration between scientific institutions and industry are often considered to be one of the causes of an alleged backwardness in French science in the 1920s and 1930s. Furthermore, the association between Ernest Fourneau's chemotherapeutic laboratory at the Pasteur Institute and Rhône-Poulenc has been dismissed as being 'the only example' of co-operation, and Poulenc (later Rhône-Poulenc)'s laboratory in Ivry (later Vitry) as the only pharmaceutical research laboratory in inter-war France.[10] Such interpretations play down the influence exerted both by Fourneau and by Rhône-Poulenc on French pharmaceutical research.

Marika Blondel-Mégrelis has argued, on the contrary, that the relationship between Fourneau and Rhône-Poulenc served as a model for, and transformed the industry.[11] I take her analysis one step further, by suggesting that the context in which their relationship developed was on the whole favourable to academic-industrial collaboration. This was a context of increasing international competition, and of growing research activity in scientific institutions and industry. Furthermore, between the wars, the relationship between Fourneau and Rhône-Poulenc was becoming the norm, rather than the exception.

1. Ernest Fourneau and Rhône-Poulenc

The link between Ernest Fourneau's Therapeutic Chemistry Laboratory and the Direction Scientifique at Rhône-Poulenc was based on a strong personal relationship, forged at the close of the nineteenth century as part of an emerging network of academic and industrial chemists and pharmacists, and developed during the first half of the twentieth century to become one of the most important academic-industrial connections in France. This section traces the relationship as it evolved from its beginnings.

Two brothers, Félix and Charles Moureu, played an important role in the earlier part of Fourneau's career. Félix was mayor of the Basque city of Biarritz, where Fourneau was born in 1872, and where his parents ran a hotel. Félix was also a pharmacist by profession, and Fourneau trained with him for three years, between 1890 and 1893. Charles was a chemist who taught Fourneau research methods in organic chemistry. Charles later became professor of chemistry at the Collège de France, where his laboratory was subsidized by Poulenc Frères,[12] and according to Marcel Delépine, Fourneau's obituarist, it was he who introduced Fourneau to the Poulenc brothers, Gaston, Emile and Camille.[13]

Having arrived in Paris to take his pharmacy exams, Fourneau met the pharmaceutical chemist Marc Tiffeneau, with whom he collaborated on a number of papers.[14] They formed a lasting friendship, strengthened by Tiffeneau's marriage to Fourneau's youngest sister Marguerite.[15] Together, Fourneau and Tiffeneau created the group known as 'La Molécule' in 1903. It welcomed both academic and industrial chemists, future pillars of the French pharmaceutical industry, such as Edmond Blaise, Albert Buisson, Marcel Delépine, Louis Givaudan, Nicolas Grillet.[16] It breathed new life into the Société Chimique de France, which had become somewhat moribund towards the end of nineteenth-century, and of which Fourneau was General Secretary from 1919 to 1932.[17]

In 1893, having moved to Paris to pursue his studies at the Faculté de Pharmacie, Fourneau took Auguste Béhal's course in organic chemistry. It was in his class that he became acquainted with Edmond Blaise, whom he later invited to join La Molécule, and would become his principal contact at the Research Laboratories of Rhône-Poulenc in the period between the wars.[18] In 1894, after successfully completing his diploma, Fourneau joined Charles Friedel's laboratory at the Sorbonne. There, he met Maurice Meslans, professor of pharmacy at Nancy, who became scientific and technical director of Poulenc-Frères in 1896, and began gathering a team of research chemists to work in the firm's first laboratory.[19]

Fourneau recalled that Meslans came looking for chemists in Friedel's laboratory, and that he offered a position to Fourneau, suggesting that he first spent some time in Germany in order to perfect his training in organic chemistry.[20] However, in *Une Chimie qui guérit*, Daniel Bovet has told a different story, describing how the German organic chemist Emil Fisher, on holiday in Fourneau's parents' hotel, had urged him to go and study organic chemistry in Germany.[21] Whatever prompted Fourneau's decision, over a period of three years, between 1898 and 1901, he visited the laboratories of Theodor Curtius, Ludwig Gattermann, Richard Willstätter, as well as Fisher.[22] Upon his return, he was appointed head of Poulenc's organic chemistry laboratory in Ivry, which according to Bovet he was instrumental in creating, having conceived the idea of a 'new kind of [industrial] research laboratory' during his stay in Germany.[23] It was in Ivry that he developed Stovaïne (a pun on his name, which in English means 'stove'), one of the first synthetic local anesthetics to be launched onto the French market, in 1904. Like another close collaborator of Poulenc, Francis Billon, who developed the anti-syphilitic drugs Arsenobenzol and Novarsenobenzol, manufactured and sold under licence from Poulenc by May & Baker in Britain under the names 'Arsenobenzol-' and 'Novarsenobenzol-Billon',[24] Fourneau owned a pharmacy. However, in 1905, having declared it unsuccessful as a business, he obtained from Poulenc that they award him a minimum of 6,000 FF per annum as his share of the profits from his inventions. As to Billon, he sold his pharmacy in 1907, so that he would be free to become company administrator, and receive a fixed fee for his services.[25]

Stovaïne, which was almost certainly the fruit of Fourneau's three-year-long experience in German laboratories, enhanced his reputation, and placed him in an advantageous position when Etard's post as head of the Organic Chemistry Laboratory became vacant at the Pasteur Institute in 1910. The purpose of the 'Laboratoire de chimie thérapeutique', as it was renamed, was to develop chemotherapeutic remedies. Although he had to compete against several other candidates, Fourneau was offered the post. The decision to award grants to two of the unsuccessful candidates, Simon and Paris, to work on such remedies in their own laboratories, is indicative of the Institute's commitment, under Roux, to this new approach to therapy.[26] However, a few years later, when antibacterial chemotherapy appeared to have reached a 'dead-end', and compared unfavourably with serumtherapy, which had produced sera against streptococcus, meningococcus, dysentery, plague and penumococcus, the Institute lost much of its interest in the approach.[27] This disinterest was combined with envy, and even resentment, when the magnitude of the industrial support received by Fourneau's laboratory became known.

When Roux had appointed Fourneau, he had announced to the Council of the Pasteur Institute that Fourneau would not retain any industrial connection. Later, in front of the Assembly, he described him as the inventor of Stovaïne, 'free from any attachment and ready to devote himself entirely to disinterested scientific research'.[28] By this, Roux meant that Fourneau's salary was to be paid by the Institute. At this point, the extent to which the laboratory would be supported by industry could not be guessed, although Bovet has written that an agreement had been signed between Fourneau and Roux, in which Fourneau insisted that he should maintain his connection with Poulenc, in order to obtain research materials and subsidies for additional staff.[29] However, according to Fourneau himself, Poulenc did not begin funding his laboratory until 1913, when he was asked to serve as an administrator and the company offered to pay for part of his research expenses 'without any objection or control', the industrial subsidy covering about half the running costs of the laboratory.[30] Fourneau's account of these events is corroborated by the historian of Rhône-Poulenc, Pierre Cayez, who has described how, out of a sense of remorse after his departure, the company appointed him as technical advisor and began paying him a fixed fee of 12,000 FF per annum, plus a share of the profits from his inventions.[31] Contrary to what has been written elsewhere, it is therefore unlikely that Poulenc 'sent Fourneau to the Pasteur Institute in order to ensure a link between the chemical and biological industries',[32] or that they 'made an unwritten gentleman's agreement with Roux'.[33] The indications are, rather, that Fourneau left Poulenc for financial reasons or as a matter of personal prestige, and not as a result of a strategic move by the company (see Figure 2.2).

While Mike Robson and Jonathan Liebenau have found no evidence of any contract linking the Institute and Poulenc,[34] my sources show that a formal contract was eventually exchanged in 1932, after the merger between Poulenc and the SCUR in 1928. Before then, the collaboration between Fourneau and the company had been informal, and based on what he described himself as 'mutual trust'. In a letter to Blaise, the new director of research of Rhône-Poulenc, he wrote that he had been happy with the absence of contract, and affirmed his loyalty to the company:

> [...] this state of affairs, which has proved itself, gives us total satisfaction, has all the flexibility one might wish for, and is based on a mutual confidence more powerful than any contract [...] I have been collaborating with Poulenc since 1900. I shall continue to do so until all my energies are spent.[35]

Nevertheless, Rhône-Poulenc's preference for a formal contract, which had the advantage of clarifying the situation for other collaborators as well as Fourneau ('car vous n'êtes pas seul en cause', wrote Blaise), prevailed, and in February 1932 the contract was exchanged, stating amongst other things the percentage of the sale of drugs to be attributed to Fourneau and his colleagues, and after Fourneau's death to his two sons.[36]

The collaboration, which evolved gradually, was initially based on a tacit understanding, and led to a reciprocal arrangement between the Pas-

Figure 2.2 Fourneau on a cruise on the Rhône with other members of the Conseil d'Administration of the SCUR in the 1920s (courtesy of Sanofi-Aventis).

teur Institute and Poulenc. While the Institute provided funds for buildings and equipment, the company paid the salaries or grants of some of the researchers and provided raw materials, which were often rare and expensive synthetic chemicals. Although it was not unusual for pharmaceutical companies to donate chemicals to external laboratories, it was uncommon for such companies to pay salaries and grants of researchers to the extent that Poulenc did at the Therapeutic Chemistry Laboratory. By the 1930s, as well as the laboratory workers, about one third of Fourneau's close collaborators were paid, some of them in part, others in total, by Rhône-Poulenc.[37]

During World War Two, the relationship between the Therapeutic Chemistry Laboratory and Rhône-Poulenc became more distant and complex. After Fourneau's death in 1949, it survived in the shape of a link that was institutional, rather than personal, until 1970, when the laboratory was finally dismantled. Few traces remain of Ernest Fourneau's laboratory in the Archives of the Pasteur Institute. After his death, his old collaborator Thérèse Tréfouël, by then also the wife of the Director of the Pasteur Institute, was able to salvage a part of his collection of published papers. However, after 1970, the collection of chemicals and other papers were dispersed. In the Rhône-Poulenc Santé Archive, the prolific correspondence that was exchanged between Fourneau and the research directors Edmond Blaise and, after 1942, Raymond Paul, survived for a time. The pages that follow are based on this archive, which I was able to consult before it was destroyed, when Rhône-Poulenc-Rorer merged with Hoechst to form Aventis (now part of Sanofi-Aventis). It makes it possible to build a picture of the laboratory, and the way in which co-operative research was carried out between the Therapeutic Chemistry Laboratory (see Figure 2.3) at the Pasteur Institute and Rhône-Poulenc from the date of the merger in 1928 until the death of Fourneau in 1949.[38] The next sections focus on the 1920s and 1930s, which was the most fruitful period of interaction between the industrial group and the research institution.

2. A multi-disciplinary research team in an academic laboratory

His collaboration with Rhône-Poulenc enabled Fourneau to gather around him a research team, although he never used the term himself. Indeed, he preferred to talk of them as his 'collaborators', by which he meant permanent members of staff rather than visiting researchers or students. Despite the problem of attracting, and especially keeping laboratory workers, by 1930, thanks to Rhône-Poulenc's support, Fourneau had the nucleus of a multi-disciplinary team. In Fourneau's opinion, the best approach to research was cross-disciplinary rather than purely theoretical, and he chose chemists, physiologists, bacteriologists, and later also physicists, to work with him.[39] The multi-disciplinary character of the group is reflected in Table 2.1.

Table 2.1 Fourneau's Collaborators at the Institute (in chronological order of joining the Therapeutic Chemistry Laboratory)[40]

Jacques Tréfouël	Docteur ès-sciences	1920
	Directeur de l'Institut Pasteur	
	Chef de Service	
Thérèse Tréfouël	Ingénieur Licence ès-sciences	1921
	Chef de Laboratoire Chim.	
Germaine Benoît	Ingénieur Docteur	1924
	Chef de Laboratoire -Chim.	
Vicomtesse Yvonne de Lestrange	(Chimiste bénévole)	1924
Joseph Sivadjian	Docteur ès-sciences- Bibliogr.	1926
Jean Matti	Ingénieur Docteur	1928
	Chef de laboratoire	
Daniel Bovet (Suisse)	Docteur ès-sciences	1929
	Chef de Laboratoire Physiologie	
Georges Montezin	Préparateur de physiologie	1930
Viviane Hamon	Licenc. Physique	1937
Federico Nitti	Docteur en Médecine	1938
	Chef de Service-Bactériol.	
Albert Funke	Ingénieur Docteur	1939
		(also in 1926–27)

This list, detailing the qualifications of members of Fourneau's laboratory, may seem unusual in a context which did not favour such research teams. Dominique Pestre has explained that the primary function of the French academic physics laboratory before World War Two was teaching, rather than research, and that multi-disciplinary teams were consequently very rare.[41] In Chapter 1, I have shown that teaching was also a very important function of the Pasteur Institute. The origins of Fourneau's team, which appears to have been exceptional, therefore needs to be explained.

John Beer has suggested that the multi-disciplinary research team had its roots in the research laboratory that appeared in the German dyestuffs Industry at the end of the nineteenth century.[42] By the inter-war period a number of such teams had appeared, in Britain as well as in France, in different scientific disciplines and industrial sectors, which suggests that they may have had multiple origins.[43] Nevertheless, because of Fourneau's experience in the laboratories of chemists such as Fischer and Willstätter at the turn of the century, it is very likely that the model for his research team

Figure 2.3 The Therapeutic Chemistry Laboratory of the Pasteur Institute in the 1930s (courtesy of the Pasteur Institute).

at the Pasteur Institute was German, and industrial in origin. However, the fact that his team worked in an academic rather than industrial environment may have lent it greater cohesion and stability.

The cohesion of the group has been described by Daniel Bovet in *Une Chimie qui guérit*.[44] Many of its members became friends, and as it included men and women in almost equal numbers, some were married. Jacques and Thérèse Tréfouël (see Figure 2.4) had joined the laboratory in 1920 and 1921 respectively. As a result of the work he carried out with Federico Nitti on sulphanilamide, Bovet met Nitti's sister Filomena, whom he married in 1938, and who joined the laboratory in 1940.[45] In addition to these friendships and marital collaborations, the loyalty that team members felt towards their 'patron' meant that many of his researchers remained until the end of the war, and a few of them were to stay with him until his death, in 1949.[46]

3. A 'stable' relationship[47]

Towards the end of his life and career, Fourneau commented to Raymond Paul that, contrary to popular belief, of all his collaborators, the women had been the most 'stable' (by which he meant loyal and reliable).[48] However, he and Rhône-Poulenc had always disagreed on hiring women

Figure 2.4 Jacques and Thérèse Tréfouël (courtesy of the Pasteur Institute).

researchers. Whereas the Direction Scientifique often refused to employ female scientists on the grounds that they would not fit well into an industrial laboratory, Fourneau found them to be not only loyal, but also very pleasant company. He commented on this in an interview with Radio Luxembourg on the occasion of the 50th anniversary of the Pasteur Institute, on 10 December 1938:

Speaking of Mme Tréfouël, I shall say a few words on what I think about women, about women working in laboratories of course... To say that I am pleased with female collaborators is not enough, for I cannot see how I would be able to manage without them. Moreover, all those who pay me the compliment of visiting my laboratory are struck by its friendly atmosphere, which is almost certainly due to the presence of young women. They come to realize that it is perfectly possible to combine hard work with beauty, and that gracefulness and science go perfectly well together.[49]

Many years later, Raymond Paul explained to a colleague why he thought that chemical engineering offered few possibilities for women: it involved physical effort; industrialists preferred to appoint men in charge of manufacturing; even in industrial research laboratories men were preferred, because when the time came to apply the research, the link with production was easier to achieve when a man was involved.[50] Therefore, the disagreement between the Direction Scientifique and Fourneau regarding the employment of women in the 1930s reflected two different cultures: the first, a factory-based engineering culture, and the second, an institution-based scientific culture. However, by the 1950s, the attitude of the company towards hiring women had changed. Indeed, in 1959 Raymond Paul promised a collaborator of Rhône-Poulenc, Claude Fromageot, that he would try to find a post for one of his female students.[51] In the same period, the industrial laboratory counted a number of women researchers, most notably the pharmacologist Simone Courvoisier, who was to play an important part in the development of chlorpromazine (see Chapter 5).

Nevertheless, in the 1920s and 1930s, these changes remained a long way off. In addition to disagreements about the appointment of women, frictions arose at times of uncertainty, for instance after the formation of Rhône-Poulenc, when the role of the Therapeutic Chemistry Laboratory needed to be redefined in relation to the firm's new pharmaceutical research facilities in Vitry, and Fourneau had to deal with Blaise at the Direction Scientifique of Rhône-Poulenc, rather than the Director of Pharmaceutical Research at Poulenc Frères as he had done previously. Although Blaise and Fourneau knew each other well, the nature and extent of their future collaboration was unclear. In order to protect Rhône-Poulenc's new laboratories against competition, Blaise insisted that external collaborators should be kept as a closed group. On the contrary, Fourneau believed that competition made it imperative for information to circulate as freely as possible. He threatened, if Blaise had his way, to withhold information concerning the work of his collaborators whose salaries were not paid by Rhône-Poulenc (an indication that, until then, he had perhaps helped to disseminate this kind of information).[52]

However, such an unpleasant exchange of letters was rare, and the friendly tone soon returned in their correspondence. When Fourneau wrote to Blaise in January 1937, he sent him his good wishes for the New Year, and expressed his hopes that their collaboration would continue, as their friendship, which would last for ever. This was more than a polite formula. Blaise and Fourneau had studied together at the Faculty of Pharmacy in Paris, and both were members of La Molécule. Like their compatriots in physics, who belonged to the close-knit community that has become known as the group of 'l'Arcouest' because of their shared holidays in Brittany, they were members of a community of professional scientists that was emerging at the turn of the century.[53]

Regular meetings and exchanges of letters between them ensured a close and stable relationship. Several years later, when Fourneau resigned from the Pasteur Institute after World War Two and began to make plans for his private laboratory in the company's headquarters in the rue Jean Goujon, there was uncertainty about what would be the focus of his new research.[54] Nevertheless, as had happened before, the relationship soon settled down, and Fourneau was given a free rein to choose his topics. He had always kept for himself certain subjects, especially if a student of his was carrying out a related piece of research. However, the new laboratory in the rue Jean Goujon was a personal gift, at the end of a long and fruitful collaboration, and he was left to do what he pleased (I will return to this in greater detail in Chapter 5).

Fourneau's collaboration with Rhône-Poulenc gave him access to important research facilities, without apparently harming his scientific reputation. In exchange, by monopolising his expertise, the company was able to corner the French market for synthetic drugs. In 1939, most French synthetic drugs were the product of their collaboration. They included the first chemotherapeutic remedy developed by Fourneau at the Pasteur Institute, the arsenical Stovarsol (against syphilis and trypanosomiasis); Moranyl (against sleeping sickness); and Rhodoquine (against malaria). Tropical medicine was therefore the main beneficiary of the work of the Therapeutic Chemistry Laboratory, until the advent of the first broad-spectrum antibacterial drug, sulphanilamide, in 1935. The collaborative research that led to these drugs seemed to follow a set procedure, based on a mutual understanding between Fourneau and Blaise, and consequently did not need to be enforced by rules or regulations. This allowed for greater flexibility and, on occasions, short-cuts could be taken when competition threatened the company's dominant market position, as happened with sulphanilamide.

4. The procedures of collaborative research

Projects usually began with Blaise sending an IG patent to Fourneau 'in search of new ideas', or of any information that could help them to put together their own version of a German drug. In fact, both Fourneau and Rhône-Poulenc watched closely developments taking place on the other side of the Rhine. France's patent legislation (neither medicines, nor even the processes leading to their manufacture — if these could be shown to be unique — were patentable),[55] meant that French firms could make medicines patented elsewhere, and then sell them in France and her colonies. Fourneau remarked that the Germans could, in principle, have been disadvantaged by this but, because of their head-start, having had the time to recoup their costs, they could meet the competition by dropping their prices.[56] On the other hand, French inventors were left unable to protect their own discoveries at home.

Copying foreign patents was not an unusual activity, and Rhône-Poulenc were not alone in adopting this R&D strategy.[57] With Rubiazol for instance, Roussel-Uclaf were suspected of having copied Bayer's Prontosil. Hence, Blaise asked Fourneau to analyze their rivals' product. After Fourneau had found that it was indeed very similar to the parent compound, Blaise remarked that, had they been more careful, the Faculty of Pharmacy might not have accepted Roussel-Uclaf's definition of *new* class of azo dye: 'Si la Faculté de Pharmacie faisait son métier, il est probable qu'elle n'accepterait pas cette définition de classe *nouvelle* de colorants aminoazoïques' (Blaise's own emphasis).[58] Eventually, Altwegg, Rhône-Poulenc's patent expert, found an article in the *Journal of the American Chemical Society* that pre-dated the IG patent and could have inspired Rubiazol, thereby reducing the scruples Roussel-Uclaf might have had in purely and simply copying the German group.[59]

Despite their limited ability to patent their drugs, patenting was nonetheless an important aspect of Rhône-Poulenc's, and other French firms's, business strategy. However, there were considerable differences in the manner in which Fourneau and the company viewed the use of patents. For Fourneau, they were a means of establishing his priority over discoveries that included not only new chemicals, processes, but even scientific hypotheses.[60] Thus, in 1940, he argued that a patent should be used to protect his hypothesis concerning the active principle of sulphone, which was based on his extensive experience with sulphanilamide.[61] In contrast, Blaise and his successor Raymond Paul often adopted a more cautious position, wishing to ascertain the market value of compounds and their specific pharmacological properties before applying for patents. According to Blaise, such a divergence of views reflected a relationship between the inventor and his inventions that was fundamentally different from that between the manufacturer and his products. Whereas the former wanted the best drug to be launched, the latter would only consider it, if it had the potential to replace other drugs already on the market.[62] However, their views about patents, like their attitudes towards the employment of women, never — as far as my sources show — led to full blown disagreement between Fourneau and Blaise, and later Paul.

The starting point for most projects was, therefore, a careful examination of German patents. This was followed by the selection for study of particular compounds and their derivatives, which were usually dyes that had been patented by IG Farben. These were then subjected to biological tests in Fourneau's laboratory, and by further tests in the firm's laboratories in Vitry, in order to reduce their numbers to a few promising candidates. The next stage consisted in organising small-scale, followed by large-scale clinical trials.

An early example of the kind of research that resulted from the study of German patents was the development of the anaesthetic properties of quinoline compounds, which had been patented by IG Farben in 1930.[63] Fourneau's scientific and technical expertise, in particular his extensive knowledge of chemical reactions, was relied upon by the company to select likely candidates among these compounds and their derivatives, according to criteria such as pharmacological activity, toxicity, cost and ease of preparation. Fourneau's team then carried out basic biological tests on the compounds. They were sent to Vitry for more extensive tests, which provided quantitative data upon which to base small-scale clinical trials (as few as seventeen cases could be involved in such trials). The Pasteur Institute's overseas subsidiaries were then mobilized for larger trials, which allowed comparative studies of two or more compounds to be made (in this case, Quiniostovarsol and Iso-plasmoquine, both tested by Sergent in Algiers). However, as a resource, Fourneau believed that these overseas subsidiaries were under-utilized by academic scientists and pharmaceutical companies alike. In a letter to Blaise, he cited the new Pasteur Institute in Brazzaville as an example of the much-needed middle ground between inventors and manufacturers, who he thought were all too easily discouraged by the difficulties and length of time required to carry out trials.[64]

Although the work on sulphanilamide also began with a careful examination of the German patent for Prontosil, by the mid-1930s, the research produced by the Fourneau-Rhône-Poulenc collaboration was becoming innovative in its own right. This progress, from imitation to innovation, is examined next.

5. From imitation to innovation

In what follows, the co-operative relationship between Fourneau and Rhône-Poulenc is shown to have created the potential for the French pharmaceutical industry to break free from the domination of IG Farben. By the mid-1930s, the combination of the various talents gathered around Fourneau, the physiologist Daniel Bovet, the chemists Jacques and Thérèse Tréfouël, and Yvonne de Lestrange, the chemical engineers Germaine Benoît and Jean Matti, gave the Therapeutic Chemistry Laboratory an innovative edge that it had not had before. The role of Bovet, in particular, was crucial. Fourneau wrote of him that he knew everything: 'c'est un homme très précieux; il sait tout: la chimie, la physique, la physiologie...'.[65] In 1929 he had moved to the Pasteur Institute from Spécia (Rhône-Poulenc's pharmaceutical selling company), and in the 1930s and 1940s was to play a key role in the research on the pharmacology of the nervous system, on sulphanilamide and the synthetic anti-histamines. After the war, in 1948, he left for the Istituto Superiore di Sanità in Rome, where for a time he and his wife Filomena remained consultants for Rhône-Poulenc. In recognition for his work, he was awarded the Nobel Prize for Physiology or Medicine in 1957.[66]

The discovery of sulphanilamide is described in detail in Bovet's book *Une Chimie qui guérit*.[67] In 1932, Gerhard Domagk, director of research in experimental pathology at Bayer, then part of the chemical group IG Farben, carried out experiments in mice infected with streptococci using a red dye, named *Prontosil rubrum*. He found that the animals treated with the dye survived, whereas the controls died. Later, Domagk succeeded in curing his own daughter, who had been suffering from a streptococcal infection, by treating her with Prontosil. By 1935, clinical trials were under way, and the results of Domagk's experiments and of the trials were published.[68] The study of Prontosil was then taken up by numerous centres in Germany and abroad, including the Therapeutic Chemistry Laboratory. Unlike their German colleagues, Fourneau's team was not steeped in a tradition of synthetic dye chemistry. Thus, they went on to show that Prontosil was broken down in the body and that, contrary to the belief that the bactericidal properties of dyes came from their ability to colour the vital elements of bacterial cells, its active principle was, in fact, the colourless compound *p*-aminobenzenesulphonamide ('sulfamide blanc' or sulphanilamide).[69] Their hypothesis about the action of Prontosil was confirmed when a similar activity was obtained with close derivatives of sulphanilamide prepared in Fourneau's laboratory. Because sulphanilamide had been known for a long time, it could not be patented, and this opened the way for companies in France and elsewhere to develop their novel drugs, all based on the sulphanilamide molecule. One of these, 1162 F (the 'F' standing for Fourneau), was launched in 1936 by Rhône-Poulenc as Septoplix, and was later followed by sulphapyridine, M&B 693, developed in 1937 by their British subsidiary, May & Baker.[70]

Following the discovery of the antibacterial action of sulphanilamide, the team's priority was speed of action, and this involved taking shortcuts, an aspect not conveyed by the publications. In particular, two routine scientific procedures were contravened: the sequence from small-scale to large-scale clinical trials, and the use of separate, but consistent biological tests. Small-scale clinical trials were carried out in Paris with 1162 F by Navarro-Martin, a Professor from the Faculty of Medicine in Valladolid, who had visited Fourneau's lab in the 1920s. His results were judged encouraging enough for a provisional patent to be applied for, even though they were felt to be less conclusive than if the trials had been extended to the colonies. Fourneau was told by Blaise that he could publish only once the patent was granted, but that in the meantime he could establish scientific priority by sending a sealed envelope to the Académie des Sciences, which would make it possible to preserve secrecy until the patent was obtained.[71] Once it had been granted, Fourneau and Blaise decided to publish their results in two separate articles of the *Comptes rendus de l'Académie des Sciences*. The reason for this was that the biological tests had been carried out under different conditions in the two laboratories, and that if their results had been published together in a single article, the discrepancies between them would have become obvious. Moreover, Fourneau was concerned that a joint publication might upset his colleagues at the Institute, many of whom regarded his collaboration with the industrial firm with a critical eye.[72]

Fourneau also hesitated about the idea of taking out a patent on 1162 F, which he feared would damage his friendship with Heinrich Hörlein, the director of IG Farben.[73] This hesitation helps to explain the delay in launching Septoplix, compared with Roussel-Uclaf's Rubiazol which reached the market a few weeks earlier.[74] The relationship between the Therapeutic Chemistry Laboratory and Rhône-Poulenc was therefore complicated by Fourneau's ambiguous relationship with Germany. He saw the large numbers of patents emerging from the German pharmaceutical industry as commercial propaganda that was rooted in international competition, and wished for France to improve its place on the international scene.[75] However, he also felt great admiration for German science and empathy towards German culture, developed close friendships with German scientists and officials, such as the German ambassador to France Otto Abetz,[76] and always acknowledged his debt to his former teachers.[77] But whatever his personal relationship with Germany, by the end of the 1930s, the Therapeutic Chemistry Laboratory and Rhône-Poulenc were breaking free from their German model. With their research on synthetic anti-histamines, in particular, they were becoming leaders, rather than followers.

6. Breaking free from IG

While studying the properties of anti-malarial drugs, in the early 1930s Bovet and Fourneau found that one of the compounds under study, 883 F (a derivative of 1,4-dioxane) was a sympatholytic (i.e. it blocked stimulation of the sympathetic nervous system, or SNS).[78] Because of the similarities between the chemical structures of adrenaline and acetylcholine, which both stimulated the SNS, and that of histamine, Bovet therefore began searching for substances capable of antagonizing histamine.[79] By 1936, he had a Ph.D. student, Anne-Marie Staub, working under his supervision on that very topic.

The implications of this research were at once scientific, and medical. Histamine, which had been isolated in 1910 by Henry Dale (then working at the WPRL), and subsequently shown by Dale and Laidlaw to cause contractions in smooth muscle, was suspected of being the principal agent in anaphylactic shock. This is an immediate hypersensitivity reaction, found in some extreme cases of allergy for instance, in which a sharp drop in blood pressure is one of the most dramatic symptoms, often with fatal consequences.[80]Anne-Marie Staub used the substantive 'anti-histamine' for the first time in 1939 to describe a small number of synthetic substances that antagonized histamine.[81] Among the compounds identified by Bovet and Staub, thymoxyethydiethylamine (929 F) showed clear anti-histaminic properties.[82] Although 929 F and its phenylethylenediamine derivative, 1571 F, which had even greater activity, were too toxic to be clinically useful, they helped to confirm the hypothesis about the link between histamine and allergic reactions, and led to the development of anti-histamine drugs, all of which to this day can be considered as derivatives of 929 F.[83]

After Staub left the Pasteur Institute, having completed her thesis, the anti-histamine research was pursued in Fourneau's laboratory by his son Jean-Pierre and his collaborator Yvonne de Lestrange, who prepared many more substances. Then, in 1940, it was taken over by Rhône-Poulenc, under the physiologist Bernard Halpern, who had been hired by the company in 1935, and who carried out further pharmacological tests with the series examined by Bovet and Staub. He found that the most active and least toxic compound was N-dimethylaminoethyl-N-benzylaniline, and this was commercialized by Spécia in 1942 under the name Antergan, the first of several successful synthetic anti-histamines made by the company (these developments will be examined more closely in Chapter 4).[84]

The anti-histamine work suggests that, after thirty years of collaboration with Fourneau's laboratory, Rhône-Poulenc had evolved into an organisation capable of carrying out innovative pharmaceutical research in its own right. It had matured through close co-operation with an academic laboratory and, through the introduction of basic research into the industrial laboratory,[85] would in time lead to ground-breaking work, with the psychotropic and anti-cancer drugs (studied in Chapter 5).

Thus, in response to problems set by industry, Fourneau's laboratory produced knowledge of a fundamental kind as well as drugs, helping not only to elucidate the relationship between chemical structure and biological action as in the case of sulphanilamide, but to unravel physiological mechanisms, such as those involved with histamine. The benefits of the collaboration were therefore clear, both for Fourneau and for Rhône-Poulenc. However, the benefits to the Pasteur Institute as a whole were less obvious. There is little doubt that it drew some advantages from the successes achieved in the field of chemotherapy, especially those which received wide scientific recognition like sulphanilamide. That the Institute was sensitive to this is demonstrated by the appointment of Jacques Tréfouël to be its director in 1940. On the other hand, how much money the Institute made from sources other than from private donations or the sale of vaccines is not known. Its accounts do not detail them, but it is unlikely that it gained great financial benefit from the Therapeutic Chemistry Laboratory's activities. Nevertheless, its link with Rhône-Poulenc was important enough to generate unease within the Institute. The strength of this relationship, which lasted six decades despite the unease it created, is therefore striking, and prompts the following question: was it possible, in fact, because, rather than an exception, such collaboration was becoming the norm in France?

The Therapeutic Chemistry Laboratory and Rhône-Poulenc collaborated most closely, although not exclusively, with each other. Rhône-Poulenc had connections with several academic scientists, many of whom had graduated from the Faculté de Pharmacie in Paris where they received their training in chemistry.[86] They were friends and colleagues of the first research director Blaise, and worked in Parisian and provincial academic institutions. Cayez has mentioned four laboratories which, in 1926, received financial assistance from Poulenc: Jean-Baptiste Senderens's at Barbachau, Béhal's at the Faculty of Pharmacy in Paris, Freyss's at Nancy, and Charles Moureu's at the Collège de France.[87] Moureu's successor, Marcel Delépine, gained a privileged place within Rhône-Poulenc for, like Fourneau, he cumulated his post as company administrator (more precisely of Spécia) with an academic position at the Collège de France.[88] As to Fourneau, he had connections with several small firms, and after the war was confident enough in his contacts to rely on them giving him staff 'free of charge' for his new laboratory in the rue Jean Goujon.[89]

These companies participated in a great variety of co-operative networks that included scientists like Fourneau, but also other pharmaceutical firms. These networks constitute the background against which the collaboration between Rhône-Poulenc and Fourneau should be considered. In the next section, they are brought to the foreground. The evidence suggests that, in pharmaceuticals, the French context as a whole was favourable to co-operation.

7. The CNRS, scientific mobilisation and pharmaceutical laboratories

Industrial laboratories remain a neglected topic,[90] even at a time of reappraisal of the importance of research in inter-war industry.[91] However, a document held in the Archives Nationales Contemporaines in Fontaine-bleau reveals that research in general, and collaborative research in particular, was a significant feature of the French pharmaceutical industry between the wars.[92]

This document is a survey of French laboratories, for which the physiologist André Mayer was responsible. It was launched after the Munich crisis in September 1938, and was carried out by the newly formed Centre National de la Recherche Scientifique, Section Appliquée (CNRSA), whose purpose was the co-ordination of laboratories in the context of economic recession and impending war, with a special emphasis on applied, rather than pure research.[93] The CNRSA, which modeled itself on the British DSIR, also sent researchers to study the organisation of science abroad.[94]

Between 1938 and 1941, about one hundred small and medium pharmaceutical companies responded to the survey, which represented an important step in the formulation of a science policy by the French state and its involvement in the funding of science. Such a development occurred later than in Britain, and is an important difference between the organisation of research in the two countries (see Chapter 1). However, the evidence suggests that a lack of government intervention did not cause co-operation to be less well developed on the French side.

8. Collaborative networks in the pharmaceutical industry

The overwhelming response to the survey revealed a scene described by Longchambon as 'anarchic'.[95] Nevertheless, it is a rich historical source, which makes it possible to capture the research activity of small companies ordinarily absent from descriptions of industrial laboratories of the Bell or Du Pont model.[96] The forms sent by the CNRSA contained questions about research equipment, scientific and technical personnel and, more importantly, about the co-operative nature of the research carried out by these firms. They reveal the existence of a variety of research networks within and around the French pharmaceutical industry on the eve of World War Two.

To the CNRS, there obviously was a link between research activity and co-operative behaviour, and this assumption formed the basis of its plans to mobilize French laboratories. As to pharmaceutical companies, the fact that they were prepared to answer the questionnaires reflects a realisation that research had an important role to play in building a relationship with government, and in ensuring their survival throughout the war and beyond.

Among the firms filling in the questionnaires, some admitted to doing no research whatsoever, and having no room set aside for the purpose of research. However, the majority perceived their activity as scientific research, whether it consisted of analytical work for the control of raw and finished products, or whether it involved experimentation, with or without animals. They employed between one and three scientists, at least one with a doctorate in pharmacy, and the others with a degree in chemistry or chemical engineering, and a few laboratory assistants and technicians. An exception were the Laboratoires Auguste Lumière, manufacturers of 'spécialités' in Lyon, where 34 scientists outnumbered 20 technicians.[97]

Several staff members had been trained at the Pasteur Institute, notably P. Séguin, a former assistant at the Pasteur, now employed at the Laboratoire de Biothérapie in the XVe arrondissement in Paris; J. Lepeut, former student at the Pasteur, and director of the Laboratoire Biologique manufacturing vaccines (XXe); the staff of the Laboratoire Laigle, who came from the Institut Pasteur in Tunis; and Thiroux, who had been head of department at the Pasteur, and consulted for the company Lizol.[98]

From the information contained in the survey, it is difficult to judge the level of sophistication of the research carried out by these small laboratories. However, it would be fair to say that they were as innovative as might be expected according to the standards of the time, that is to say before the therapeutic revolution (beginning in 1935 with sulphanilamide).[99] This would give pride of place to synthetic chemicals, have the effect of standardising research practices and the organisation of research in the pharmaceutical industry, and of raising public expectations of the efficacy of its products.

Moreover, these small and medium companies often considered their research to be innovative. Even in areas where research might have been more limited, as in galenicals and 'spécialités', innovation occurred, involving the search for new combinations of basic remedies, which could be described as 'variations upon a theme',[100] carried out in special rooms built around scientific instruments, and on 'experimental farms'.[101] Other than vaccines and sera, the majority of products manufactured by the pharmaceutical companies that responded to the CNRS survey consisted in traditional plant-based remedies, and in 'spécialités' (see Table 2.2).[102]

As Table 2.3 shows, in the field of organic synthesis, but not exclusively so, innovation often depended on the connections they maintained with academic scientists, and on co-operation with other companies.

Links with research institutions were often maintained by part-time scientific personnel, as in the case of the Laboratoires Auguste Lumière, but also at the Laboratoire R. Droury in Marsac (Creuse), where out of three

Table 2.2 Products Manufactured by Small/Medium Pharmaceutical Laboratories in France Prior to World War Two

Products	Numbers of Firms making them	Percentage
Vaccines and sera:	14	(19%)
Galenicals, and other plant-based remedies:	12	(16%)
Other specialties:	12	(16%)
Creams, ointments, tablets, hypodermic solutions:	10	(14%)
Synthetic organic chemicals:	7	(10%)
Other biological products (bacteriophage, etc...):	5	(7%)
Organotherapeutic (or 'opotherapeutic'):	4	(5%)
Antiseptics:	4	(5%)
Bandages and other surgical equipment:	4	(5%)
Homeopathic:	2	(3%)

Classification based on the information in the CNRS survey, in ANC 800284, 16–22.

Table 2.3 Connections and co-operation in the French pharmaceutical industry

Company	Instruments	Products	Staff	Consultants	Other links
Dausse	unknown	galenicals	unknown	unknown	Givaudan-Lavirotte
Delamare	calorimeter	pharmaceutical extracts	1 scientist, 1 technician	unknown	David-Rabot
Cooper	microscopes	unknown	4 scientists, 2 technicians	unknown	Cooopérative Pharmaceutique
Fournier Fr.	microscopes	biological	3 scientists	Dr. A. Fournier	Dr Fournier's laboratory
Givaudan-Lavirotte	microscopes	organic chemicals	2 scientists, 4 technicians	unknown	Air Liquide, Dausse, etc.
Lambarène	microscope	phytotherapy	1 scientist, 7 technicians	M. Delaville	400 correspondents
Liposeptine	unknown	organic chemicals	2 scientists	M. Lespagnol	Givaudan-Lavirotte, Sténé, etc.
Lip-Saporex	none	antiseptics	1 scientist, 2 technicians	unknown	Bleu-Guimet
Nyco	microscope	organic chemicals	3 scientists, 3 technicians	unknown	Adrian, Kodack
Organotechnie	microscope	opotherapy	1 scientist	unknown	Cooperative Pharmaceutique
Progil	unknown	malt extracts	unknown	unknown	Ministère de l'Agriculture
R.-G.	unknown	ointments	3 scientists	Naval Res. Stn, Toulon	Navy, Paris City Council
Société Normande	unknown	organic chemicals	1 scientist	unknown	SUCR
Sténé	unknown	vaccines	3 scientists, 1 technician	unknown	Liposeptine
Yzol	unknown	antiseptics	1 scientist	M. Thiroux	unknown

Source: ANC 800284.

scientists, two came in only once a week (including E. Droury, probably a relative of the founder, and a veterinary doctor in charge of the veterinary range of products made by the company).[103] At the Lambarène laboratories (Eure), M. Delaville was included in the personnel list with the title of 'head of the research division', a post he combined with the directorships of the Biological Chemistry Laboratory of the Ecole Pratique des Hautes Etudes, and of the laboratory of the hospital Henri Rousselle.[104] Liposeptine in Lille followed the scientific 'advice' of M. Lespagnol, Professor of Chemistry and Pharmacy at the University.[105] The R.G. laboratories (Eure), specialising in ointments and creams, collaborated with the Naval Research Centre in Toulon.[106]

The physical proximity between many pharmaceutical laboratories and hospitals also suggests that they exchanged services. While firms made their laboratory facilities available to the hospital, for medical analyses for instance, they benefited from the captive market for medicines which the hospital provided.[107] Through such collaborations, companies gained access to scientific and clinical expertise, which made up for limited research within their own laboratories.

Another form of co-operation crucial to the pharmaceutical industry was that between companies, of which there are several examples in the survey. The most important network was organised along the axis Lille-Paris-Lyon, comprising Liposeptine in Lille, Février-Decoisy and Dausse in Paris, and Givaudan-Lavirotte in Lyon, and is represented in Figure 2.5.[108] These cities are important industrial centres (in particular for the chemical industry) as well as centres for the production of scientific knowledge.

Other smaller networks could also be seen, such as the one formed around the Co-opérative Pharmaceutique Française in Melun (including the Cooper lab in Paris and L'Organotechnie in Melun), or around the Etablissements Nyco in Aubervilliers, including the Société Adrian (for pharmaceuticals) and Kodak-Pathé-Kuhlmannn (for chemicals).[109] Some may have been family networks, for instance the link between Liposeptine (directed by Jean Lemoine) and Sténé (directed by Georges Lemoine), or between Givaudan-Lavirotte (for pharmaceuticals) and Louis Givaudan & Cie (for organic chemistry).[110] The importance of outside collaboration was indicated by J. Lepeut of the Laboratoire Biologique, when he wrote that in peacetime their correspondents numbered 400 medical colleagues and pharmaceutical companies.[111]

In this context, co-operation with government through the CNRS seemed like a natural extension of the normal activity of pharmaceutical companies. The mobilisation of laboratories for the war effort provided them with the opportunity of gaining government contracts and financial support, and of acquiring instruments necessary to develop their research-base. The fear of gas warfare created a window for many of the smaller firms, which offered their laboratory facilities for testing toxic gases. For example R-G,

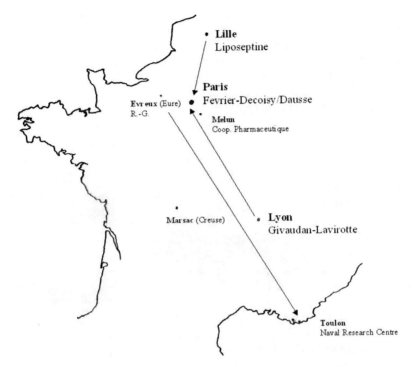

Figure 2.5 Networks of small/medium pharmaceutical firms.

which in peacetime had collaborated with the Naval Research Centre at Toulon, began working for the Navy Ministry and the Paris City Council on problems of neutralisation of vesicants. However, by 1939, many of the smaller laboratories were threatened with closure because of the mobilisation of scientific and technical personnel and the breaking up of collaborations: 'all our collaborators are mobilized or charged with special missions (by the government)' complained the director of a Paris laboratory late in the year.[112] Some of the larger laboratories were commissioned by the Health Ministry to produce quantities of vaccines and other remedies. As the German army pushed into France, many of them moved their equipment to annexes in the provinces (in the case of some Paris or Lille-based companies).

The war provided opportunities for these small and medium laboratories, but it also presented risks. One of these was the growth of state intervention. It was perhaps as a result of the survey carried out by the CNRS, that in 1941 the Vichy government decided to tighten the regulations governing the pharmaceutical industry. It passed a law on 11 September, which limited the number of pharmacies, created special inspectors, and established a monopoly of pharmacists, thus preventing herbalists from dispensing medicines, and imposing pharmacists as directors of pharmaceutical laboratories.[113] The era of government intervention in this sector of the French economy had begun.[114] The effects of this law, combined with the war, were drastic, causing the closure of numerous laboratories, and bringing the French pharmaceutical industry closer to the concentration levels in Britain, and even Germany.[115]

Some small and medium firms survived, albeit at the cost of their independence, as subsidiaries to foreign groups, but also to larger French companies, to French groups with diversified activities, or within financial holdings. Thus, the Produits Scientia became a subsidiary of the American Richardson Merrell; Fournier Frères became part of the Pechiney-Ugine-Kuhlmann group; Givaudan-Lavirotte, together with the Institut Mérieux, were acquired by Spécia, and became part of the group Rhône-Poulenc (now Sanofi-Aventis); Dausse and Robert et Carrière joined the group Synthélabo (also Sanofi-Aventis).[116]

The pooling of information, as well as agreements on raw materials and prices, were not unusual features of the pharmaceutical industry in the 1930s. Nevertheless, it is somewhat a surprise to find such close and extensive collaborations in France, which has been described (and has often perceived itself) as non-co-operative compared with Germany, America, and also Britain.[117] It reveals the 'private' side of French science, which has long remained hidden, but has begun to be uncovered by historians.[118] In pharmaceuticals, it was characterized by a collaborative culture, in which academic and industrial researchers participated, independently of government.

In sum, by allowing the collaboration between Fourneau and Rhône-Poulenc to develop, and by providing a model for many academic and industrial laboratories, the Pasteur Institute did *not* inhibit the expansion of an indigenous pharmaceutical industry.[119] It trained the future staffs of several small and medium industrial laboratories, and enabled the transfer of its research methods towards the leading French pharmaceutical company. Furthermore, the relationship between Fourneau and Rhône-Poulenc, because of its importance, fostered a culture that was becoming established in the French pharmaceutical industry: a culture of collaborative research.

The next section shows that the British experience shared many features with the French. However, in addition, the British side was characterized by an attempt by government (through the MRC) to control industry, according to Jonathan Liebenau.[120] Did government intervention inhibit the growth of R&D in the pharmaceutical industry? On the contrary, the MRC adopted a policy of encouragement of industrial research. It did so by collaborating with industry. Such collaborative relationships were common in inter-war Britain at a grass-roots, as well as government level.

B. THE BRITISH EXPERIENCE

One of the major differences between Britain and France was the greater involvement of government in the funding of science. Consequently, in Britain, a distinct group of scientists, working in government laboratories, was also included in academic-industrial collaborations. The co-ordination of academic and industrial research by government bodies, such as the DSIR and the MRC, was therefore more common in Britain than in France. This created a climate in which academic-industrial co-operation was part of the public, as well as private face of science and industry. The sources I have consulted make it possible to examine this public face. Nevertheless, at the private or grass-roots level, research collaborations occurred much as they did in France.

The next section studies Dale's important role as scientist and public administrator, and compares the impact of his relationship with Burroughs Wellcome, with that of Fourneau and Rhône-Poulenc. The following section examines the part played by the MRC, through episodes such as the organisation of insulin production in the 1920s.

1. Henry Dale and the WPRL

The relationship between Henry (later Sir Henry) Hallett Dale (see Figure 2.6) and Burroughs Wellcome was in many ways different from the one

Figure 2.6 Henry Dale as a young man (with permission from the Wellcome Trust).

Figure 2.7 Scientific staff of the WPRL ca 1914 (with permission from the Wellcome Trust).

between Fourneau and Rhône-Poulenc, in that after Dale had left the company it did not involve any consultancy agreement, and that it was more public than private. However, its impact on the British pharmaceutical industry was comparable. In her thesis on Dale's early career, Tilli Tansey has written that, thanks to the link forged between Dale and Wellcome when Dale worked at the WPRL between 1904 and 1914 (see Figure 2.7), 'there never developed in Britain the overt hostility to industrial pharmacology that occurred in America'.[121] There, by contrast, under the influence of John Abel of Johns Hopkins Medical School, the American Society of Pharmacology excluded investigators from industry.[122] In this section, I develop this analysis further, by arguing that in his later career, when he was Director of the NIMR, member of numerous MRC committees, Chairman of the Wellcome Trust, and President of the Royal Society,[123] Dale exerted a considerable influence over the pharmaceutical industry as well as the biomedical sciences in Britain. More specifically, he encouraged the development of a co-operative relationship between the two, and helped to place it at the centre of British medical and scientific policy.

Like Fourneau, who had gone to Germany at the beginning of his career with Poulenc Frères, Dale went to work in Paul Ehrlich's laboratory in 1903–4 before joining the WPRL. Dale and Fourneau both left industry for academic posts, on the eve of World War One. However, unlike Fourneau, Dale was trained not in pharmacy, but in medicine, having studied physiology at Cambridge. His first career move to a pharmaceutical laboratory was most unusual, according to Tansey. It was not only unusual for a medical man to go into industry, it was also unusual for a British pharmaceutical company to employ a medically trained scientist. However, Dale was well suited to Henry Wellcome's plans for his new laboratory, and to his efforts at creating the illusion of a distinction between research and production within his company.

The WPRL was one of the first laboratories of its kind in Britain. It followed the building of the Wellcome Chemical Laboratory (WCRL) in 1896, and was an indication of the growing importance of research within Burroughs Wellcome.[124] Dale later told the story of the creation of the WPRL, which he had first heard from Charles Martin, then Director of the Lister Institute. Henry Wellcome had offered to sell diphtheria and tetanus antitoxins on behalf of the Institute, but the latter had declined his offer:

> Charles Martin used to tell me that a great opportunity had thus been lost. Lord Lister himself took the view that the Institute was a purely charitable organisation, and did not wish to make any profit out of its activities, or involve itself in any commercial selling agency. As a result, Wellcome felt obliged to establish the laboratories in connexion with his business, of which, eventually, I was to be, for some years, the Director, while the Lister felt itself bound, in the end, to accept a business agency, but from Allen & Hanburys who, having no immunological activities in their own business, were not particularly efficient agents.[125]

Thus, Dale explained the creation of the first pharmaceutical research laboratory in Britain in terms of the Lister Institute's incapacity to reconcile its scientific and industrial vocations, but also its reluctance to collaborate with industry, which in 1961 he felt able to criticize.

However, the creation of the WPRL had more complex origins. Tansey has shown that it was a direct result of the legal constraints on British serum manufacturers after the Cruelty to Animals Act was passed in 1876.[126] The company's first response to the Act was to make contracts with individual scientists who tested their main product, diphtheria antitoxin, on behalf of the company, for instance T.J. Bokeham at St Batholomew's Hospital. In addition, Wellcome sold the first batches of antitoxin below production cost in order to make his product more attractive to the medical profession.[127] However, in 1896, a *Lancet* report on the relative strengths of diphtheria antitoxins showed that Wellcome's product was considerably weaker than others.[128] Therefore, when in 1899 new purpose-built laboratories were built in South London, it is likely that they were created, not only to keep abreast of therapeutic developments, but also to regain the confidence of the medical profession.

In his application to register the new premises, Henry Wellcome thought it important to stress that there existed a clear separation between the laboratories and the 'works and business departments' of his company:

> These laboratories are entirely separate and distinct from the works and business departments of Burroughs, Wellcome and Company. They are under independent direction and are conducted as strictly professional institutions. They are not carried on as a source of profit but are maintained at heavy cost by funds derived from other sources, and like the Wellcome Chemical Research Laboratories (6 King Street, Snow Hill, London E.C.) have been designed and equipped for research work. At the present time, however, this research work is fettered and hindered by the need to carry out necessary physiological experiments.[129]

However, Tansey has questioned the true extent of this separation between the research and manufacturing departments of Burroughs Wellcome. To begin with, they were administered directly from the company headquarters, their staff were all employees of the company, and the diphtheria antitoxin they produced was commercialized by Burroughs Wellcome. The separation between laboratory and factory was, in fact, more illusion than reality.

Such were the circumstances of Dale's appointment as supervisor of routine production and standardisation of anti-toxins. Medically trained, he served both a practical and rhetorical function. His practical role was similar to that of Bokeham before the creation of the WPRL. He also helped, more easily perhaps than if he had been a chemist, to foster the illusion of a separation between the research laboratory and the production facilities, and therefore to enhance the WPRL's academic standing. At this he succeeded perfectly well for, just before leaving the WPRL for the NIMR, he was elected Fellow of the Royal Society in 1914, which was a first for a scientist associated with a pharmaceutical manufacturer and was a signal of acknowledgement by his peers in academe.[130] As the Obituaries and Biographical Memoirs of Fellows of the Royal Society testify, his example would be followed by many more.

2. From the WPRL to the NIMR

Dale's other roles, once he became Director of the WPRL in 1906, were to manage the staff of the laboratory and to maintain and extend the relationship between the laboratories, Henry Wellcome, and the company. This early experience would prove invaluable in the later phases of his career, not only from a managerial, but also from a scientific point of view. At the WPRL, he developed research techniques and interests, which he later transferred to the NIMR. He was given considerable freedom to carry out research as he wished, with better facilities than those available to scientists in academic laboratories. The research he made on ergot provided the experimental base for all his future work. He isolated and physiologically characterized histamine and acetylcholine, began his study of anaphylaxis,[131] and identified substances that either mimicked, or blocked stimulation of the sympathetic and parasympathetic nervous systems.[132]

Furthermore, this early experience would guide him in his future dealings with the pharmaceutical industry, as adviser on the Pharmacopoeia, as member of numerous MRC committees, including the Committee on Biological Standardisation, and of advisory committees of which he was the Chairman (such as the Cinchona Derivatives of Malaria, Chemotherapy, and Hormones), and later as one of the first Trustees of the Wellcome Trust. When the MRC were given the patent rights on the production of insulin in Britain, an experience that was to set the pattern for future dealings between the Council and the pharmaceutical industry according to Liebenau, Dale was closely involved.[133] He personally worked on improving the manufacturing process, before being given the task of contacting firms to be entrusted with the manufacture of British insulin. The firms he selected eventually formed the MRC's group of 'reputable' companies, and later constituted the nucleus of the TRC to which the MRC turned for the production of penicillin during World War Two.

There is no evidence that Dale ever consulted for industry. However, he often gave them informal advice, as he did to other scientists or government officials.[134] The MRC files also reveal numerous examples in which Dale acted as mediator between the different camps. He would often be asked to advise on how best to deal with pharmaceutical firms, and would be able to explain their point of view — sometimes sympathetically, but occasionally critically also.[135] Dale played this role with great skill, based on his experience of working in industry, and with an authority conferred upon him by his membership of the scientific élite. However, his experience in industry, if unusual for a medical man, was not unusual for a British scientist.

3. Blurred boundaries and mobile careers

Like Fourneau and his colleagues Blaise or Delépine, Dale belonged to a generation of scientists for whom the boundaries between academia and industry were fluid. As a result, their careers were characterized by a great mobility between the two spheres of activity. Dale's presence at the WPRL had enabled Wellcome to attract other members of a pre-existing network of promising young scientists from Cambridge.[136] When Dale moved to the NIMR, having been recommended by a member of the MRC Executive Committee, the Cambridge biochemist Frederic Gowland Hopkins, he took with him P.P. Laidlaw and A.J. Ewins,[137] and re-joined there George Barger. Barger had left the WPRL for Goldsmith's College as Head of the Chemistry Department in 1909, moved to the Royal College of Science in 1913–4, and then onto the staff at the MRC at the beginning of the First

World War, retaining a consultative connection with the WPRL for a few years longer.[138] Harold King, who had joined the WPRL in 1912 where he worked under Barger and in collaboration with Ewins, moved in 1915 to the WCRL where he worked on the development of aspirin. In 1919, he too left for the MRC, where he was to pursue his interests in chemotherapy (see Chapter 1).[139] As to Joshua Burn, who had arrived at the WPRL on 1 January 1914, that is to say seven months before Dale's departure, he enlisted in the army and registered as a medical student in October that year. Being required to resume his studies in 1917, he left the army and returned to England. After graduating in 1920, he was convinced by Dale to join his staff at the MRC, before obtaining the post of Director of the Pharmacological Laboratories of the Pharmaceutical Society of Great Britain in 1925, and then the chair of Pharmacology at Oxford University in 1937.[140]

Staff from the WCRL were also lost, but mainly to other British pharmaceutical companies. In 1920, Alfred Bacharach left for Joseph Nathan & Co., a food producer and forerunner of Glaxo, where he played a key role in the firm's entry into the field of vitamins and diversification into pharmaceuticals.[141] As to Francis Carr, having succeeded in setting up Burroughs Wellcome's manufacture of Salvarsan at the beginning of the First World War, he was then poached by Boots. He left with five of his WCRL colleagues: W.F. Thompson, S.C. Fidler, H.E. Wilson, F.C. Chapman, and W.H. Porter, and took with him an extensive — and largely secret — knowledge of alkaloids and synthetic drugs, thus helping to develop the company's capabilities in synthetic chemistry.[142] From there, once again taking with him a number of his colleagues, Carr moved to BDH, which he was instrumental in transforming into a firm with modern manufacturing facilities, capable of producing insulin on a large scale in the 1920s, an achievement that made it one of the leading fine chemical companies in Britain.[143]

The special circumstances of war help to explain May & Baker's success in luring Arthur Ewins, Dale's former colleague at the WPRL, who like Laidlaw had also followed him to the NIMR, back into industry in 1916. However, Dale wrote in his obituary of Ewins that he also found in industry a position well suited to his ability and character:

> He had not, I think, the academic type of mind, with its insatiable desire to penetrate to the theoretical roots of a problem, or the pioneering instinct for penetration into really new scientific territory. He certainly had, on the other hand, qualities which were likely to be of greater importance for success in the main part of his career, namely, an exceptional promptitude in recognizing possibilities of practical developments from new discoveries made elsewhere, and an instinctive readiness to give his colleagues a full share in the interest and initiative required for such developments, and rather more than a full share in the public presentation of the results.[144]

To Dale, therefore, the main distinction between academic and industrial science lay in the personality of the scientist. Whereas the academic scientist was characterized by a propensity for theory and novelty, the industrial scientist showed qualities of promptitude and self-effacement.

Dale gave two examples of Ewins's promptitude, the first with the diamidines, whose anti-trypanosomal action he investigated even before it became widely known, which led to the development stilbamidine and pentamidine; the second with the sulphonamides, which produced sulphapyridine. In both instances, his close contacts with the academic world contributed to the commercial lead the company gained under him. In the first case, up-to-date information was obtained from the scientific literature – perhaps facilitated by Ewins's previous collaboration with the inventor of the diamidines, Harold King -, and in the second, from co-operative research with Sir Lionel Whitby at the Middlesex Hospital and, indirectly, with Fourneau's team at the Pasteur Institute.[145]

Although departures on such a scale weakened Burroughs Wellcome, whose innovative record subsequently dipped, they placed it in a privileged position in its relations with the MRC, and would enable the firm to continue attracting scientists of high caliber.[146]

However, mobility between the academic and industrial spheres was not confined to the pharmaceutical sector. In her thesis on the British food industry, Sally Horrocks has cited the examples of two scientists who moved from industry into universities: the industrial chemist T.P. Hilditch, and the biochemist Harold Raistrick.[147] Raistrick is of particular relevance to us, as he became involved in research on penicillin at two different stages in his career. After obtaining a D.Sc. from Leeds University for research carried out at Cambridge under F.G. Hopkins, in 1920 Raistrick was appointed Director of Research of Nobel's Explosives Company (later amalgamated into ICI).[148] There, he began work on the production of glycerol (a bi-product of the explosives industry, required for the production of soap) and methane by fermentation methods. A programme of pure research followed, in which Raistrick investigated the possibility of manufacturing organic compounds by means of fermentation. For this, he chose to study moulds. In 1929, he left ICI to take up the University Chair of Biochemistry at the London School of Hygiene and Tropical Medicine, where he continued his research on the biochemistry of micro-organisms. In the 1930s, he became involved in investigations of the mould *Penicillium*, and identified the strain described two years earlier by Alexander Fleming correctly as *notatum* (and not *rubrum* as Fleming had originally believed). He discovered two features that were to be important for the later development of the drug: that the substance could be produced on a synthetic culture medium, and that it was extractable from the aqueous medium into ether. However, its instability was proving to be a major stumbling block, and he abandoned the study. During the war, he was contacted by the MRC, and became involved in the development of the antibiotic. Later, as a consultant to ICI, he collaborated on the development of the antifungal griseofulvine. Although Raistrick's career was characterized by a continuous interest in moulds, he moved back and forth between the academic and industrial spheres, and appeared to do so with utter ease.

Like the practice of *cumul* in France, British professional mobility, as illustrated by the careers of Dale, Carr and Raistrick, created bridges between different areas of science and industrial sectors. By allowing the transfer of knowledge and expertise between them, it laid the ground for future developments, for instance in anti-malarial and antibiotic research during and after World War Two. However, these later developments were firmly rooted in the pre-war scientific community.

To conclude, through the respective careers of Fourneau and Dale, once more the similarities between Britain and France appear to outweigh the differences. Both began their careers in industry after a period of training in Germany, which introduced them to organic chemistry. Both transferred their knowledge, in part acquired in German laboratories, and then in the first pharmaceutical laboratories to be built in their respective countries, to medical research institutions, where they obtained academic posts around the time of World War One. From there, they fostered the development of collaborative research with industry during the war and inter-war period.

These similarities lead us to the following question: did Dale and Fourneau both move from industry, into an 'industry-based science', to use a term coined by Wolfgang König?[149] When Fourneau and Dale first went to industry, they took with them an important academic package. They had university qualifications, which included 'codified' knowledge, but also research skills and problem-solving abilities.[150] Industry provided them with an opportunity to put these skills into practice. Industrial research complemented and enriched their academic training, without ever replacing it. Therefore, it was the whole of their accumulated knowledge and experience, first academic and then industrial, which they later took with them into academic posts. It is possible that such a close intermingling of academic and industrial careers were a feature, which Britain and France shared with each other, but not with Germany. It is also possible, as König has suggested, that the description of 'industry-based science' fits the electrical-engineering sector at the turn of the century, better than other industrial sectors and other time-periods.[151]

Or could it be that quantitative studies such as König's, which rely on a clear distinction between science and industry, underplay the fluid boundaries between the two domains? Qualitative studies, which focus on actors and their networks, may be better able to assess the importance of human resources for technological innovation and the production of new knowledge. Applying a qualitative approach to the study of Britain, the next section describes the MRC, the DSIR and the firms with which they developed a collaborative relationship. This relationship became crucial for medical science and medical industry in the period between the wars, and would later provide a model of government-sponsored and co-ordinated research for other countries, such as France.

4. The MRC, the DSIR and collaboration with industry

In Britain, as in France, the Great War boosted the development of co-operative relations between scientific research institutions and pharmaceutical companies. However, unlike France, Britain retained many of the government structures that were established during the conflict, and were to play an important part in academic-industrial relations between the wars. These included not only the MRC, but also the DSIR, established at roughly the same time as the MRC, and whose main purpose was, in the words of the White Paper that led to its creation, to 'promote and organize scientific research with a view especially to its application to trade and industry'.[152] It was to accomplish this by 1) assisting individual industries in setting up co-operative research institutions (known as Research Associations, or RAs); 2) providing support to students and research staff in universities, particularly in areas seen as needing such support, for instance chemistry; and 3) endowing DSIR research establishments.

Writing about Research Associations, the former Secretary to the Committee of the Privy Council for Scientific and Industrial Research, Sir Harry Melville, commented that by 1939 'the corner had been turned', and their continued support by industry was thereafter assured. RAs were a uniquely British phenomenon, and Melville contrasted this institutional approach to co-operation with the American company-based practice of collaborating only on specific research problems, and sponsoring individual scientists in universities or other institutions.[153]

The simultaneous adoption of research practices and co-operative behaviour, which Melville described as having taken place in British industry in the period between the wars, was in part attributable to the government's efforts via bodies like the DSIR. It was also the product of changes occurring in industry, independently of government. Gerrylynn Roberts has illustrated this in her history of ICI's Research Council,[154] which was launched in 1927, and was largely responsible for the company's decision to enter the pharmaceutical field in 1936. It counted eminent scientists such as the chemist Robert (later Sir Robert) Robinson, and the physicist F.A. Lindemann (later Lord Cherwell, Winston Churchill's chief scientific advisor from 1932).[155] Through this Council, defined as 'essentially a branch of high-level public relations', ICI entered the public arena of science.[156] However, Roberts has indicated that the scheme was, in fact, based on a long-enduring, personal link between ICI and F.G. Donnan at University College London (UCL), which began when he was appointed generalist chemical consultant by Brunner, Mond after World War One, and continued after the company was amalgamated into ICI in 1926.[157] She has explained the ultimate failure of the scheme, abandoned in 1936, and ICI's subsequent return to their usual practice of supporting individual researchers in universities, such as Robert Robinson and Alexander Todd,[158] by two key factors. First, by the growing dissension between the different company divisions, which resented the central control exerted by the Council.[159] Second, by the belief that it no longer filled a useful purpose, as by then it duplicated the role of the DSIR, which had become quite effective at creating an open forum for research. Added to these factors was Donnan's departure from UCL and the end of the personal ties underlying the scheme.

The ICI episode illustrates the 'cult of science' that developed within British industry in the 1920s and 1930s.[160] Although the example of ICI has been dismissed as an exception, because its founders, Brunner, and Mond, inherited their model of research directly from Germany,[161] other examples can be found, suggesting that the growth of research in general, and of cooperative research in particular, was an important aspect of the history of the British pharmaceutical industry before World War Two. Liebenau has mentioned the case of Evans Medical Co., whose co-operation with scientists at the Liverpool University Medical School spurred the growth of their own research facilities.[162] Glaxo carried out its research in collaboration with the Lister Institute and NIMR, and received the advice of a consultative committee of external scientific advisers, which provided the firm with access to the chemical departments of the country's top universities.[163] Even Beecham, the patent drug manufacturers, after setting up a research laboratory in 1924, hired two eminent scientists as consultants, Jack (later Sir Jack) Drummond and Charles (later Sir Charles) Dodds, and endowed the Beecham laboratory at the Royal Northern Hospital in London for drug testing and R&D in 1937.[164]

In addition to its encouragement of industrial research, to which several British companies responded positively, the DSIR co-ordinated scientific research to avoid an overlapping of activities between laboratories.[165] Thus, from the start, the DSIR and MRC collaborated closely with each other. They did so within the framework of quarterly meetings between their secretaries and, after the war had ended, through a less formal arrangement, within the framework of ad hoc committees.[166] One of these was the Oxygen Research Committee (1920–4), set up at the very time when the MRC was searching for a means of collaborating effectively with drug companies for the production of insulin (1922–4).[167] It is therefore likely that the Council was influenced, at least in part, by its interaction with the Department and by the way in which it dealt with industry.

5. The MRC's network of 'reputable' firms[168]

Jonathan Liebenau has identified the MRC's experience with insulin as the source of its ambivalent, if not distant attitude towards industry.[169] In this section I argue that his interpretation does not sufficiently take into account the role of previous experience, of key individuals such as Henry Dale, of institutions such as the Royal Society and the DSIR, which provided positive models for the Council, and of collaboration in other fields, such as chemotherapy. The company files in the MRC archives suggest that the Council took on a role that was not only one of regulation, which Liebenau has tended to focus on, but of encouragement of industrial research, similar to the role adopted by the DSIR. The following statement by Dale, in relation to an application by Burroughs Wellcome to the Therapeutic Trials Committee (TTC) for a report on the cardiac stimulants digoxin and digitalinum verum, indicates that the relationship between the MRC and the pharmaceutical industry was far more complex than the one suggested by Liebenau:

> It is useful that we should have, once in a while, a report which ought to be definitely favourable to the practical use of one at least of the substances submitted; and that will probably be felt as an encouragement by the manufacturers. At the same time, we are doing a useful service to them, if we can get reports of investigations as soundly scientific as this one, even if the results are adverse to the value of the substances submitted.[170]

Apart from simply encouraging industrial research, Dale saw the MRC's function as a role-model for industry in terms of scientific procedure. This was a function which could only be fulfilled if the relationship between the MRC and the pharmaceutical industry was a close one. Clearly, the personal connections existing between many of the NIMR researchers and their colleagues in industry made such a close relationship possible.

In what follows, I show how a network of research-based companies, with which the MRC interacted more and more frequently in the 1920s and 1930s, gradually became established.[171] This network of trusted firms was to form the back-bone of the British pharmaceutical industry, and its experience of collaborating with the MRC would guide it in its dealings with government during and after World War Two. Co-operation between British drug companies and the state has been described as an outstanding feature of the post-war period.[172] However, it emerged earlier, as a result of the need to replace German chemotherapeutic remedies in World War One, and develop new biologicals between the wars. This early experience laid the foundation for later schemes to develop penicillin, and even later cortisone (see Chapter 6).

World War One had set an important precedent for the interaction between a government or scientific body and the pharmaceutical industry.[173] In November 1914, the Royal Society formed a Chemical Sub-Committee (later re-named the Drugs-Sub-Committee) in order to replace imported synthetic drugs.[174] The Society was responsible for co-ordinating the production of chemicals (either as finished products or intermediate substances) in academic laboratories. It was 'hoped that manufacturers (would) take full advantage of the scientific help which (was) freely offered them' in the shape of technical advice, as well as benefiting from the products themselves.[175]

The first academic laboratory to be enlisted was the Organic Chemistry Laboratory at Imperial College in South Kensington. Many others followed, in all major university towns throughout the country.[176] The names of Henry Dale, H.B. Baker, and Robert Robinson appeared in connection with the work, which was concerned with the synthesis of drugs such as Novocaine and Eucaine. Several firms were contacted: Boots, the Abbey Chemical company and Burroughs Wellcome for Novocain; Boots, Abbey Chemical, Strange & Graham, and Parke, Davis & Co for Eucaine.[177] When the substances had been produced in large enough quantities, the National Health Insurance Commission was notified, and was asked to inform the leading firms of the availability of the products.[178] By the end of the war, supply was able to meet demand for these drugs. Such success was attributed to the co-ordination between the Commission and the Department, made possible by the joint committee.[179] It was also attributed to the steady supply of trained chemists, who had worn 'war badges', which had saved them from active service on the front. After the war, an important concern of government departments such as the DSIR was that the flow of trained chemists should continue.[180] The Great War had been the chemists' war.[181] The DSIR felt that chemists should lead the country into peace, and became instrumental in ensuring their training in research methods in the period after the war.

The experience of participating in a scheme involving scientific-industrial collaboration in World War One therefore set a significant precedent for the MRC. One of its principal functions in 1916 had been to test British Salvarsan, a task for which Ewins was hired, and which involved two commercial firms: Burroughs Wellcome and May & Baker.[182] The MRC's regulatory role had worked so well in the case of Salvarsan, that Dale described it later in terms of 'moral control', which eventually replaced the specific wartime controls imposed by the Committee on manufacturers.[183] The MRC preferred to exert such moral authority and to establish a relation of mutual trust with producers of pharmaceuticals, allowing for self-regulation on the part of the industry. It was a role which, in the light of the experience with Salvarsan, the MRC knew to be effective, and wished to re-enact with insulin.

In 1920–2, insulin was developed on a small scale in the Physiology Department of the University of Toronto by Banting, Best, and MacLeod. The MRC were offered the patent rights for this important new diabetes medication, in a way that was to be comparable to the arrangement made with Eli Lilly for large-scale manufacture and distribution of the pancreatic extract in North America.[184] Dale and H.W. Dudley, who visited the University of Toronto and other sites for the production and testing of insulin, became familiar with the problems of potency and yield, which tended to drop when processes developed in the laboratory were scaled up. Consequently, they saw their role primarily as 'facilitators towards more effective production', and were directly involved in the work carried out at the NIMR.[185] There, they brought improvements to the existing process, by increasing the average yield of insulin from pancreases in a shorter production time, while reducing the amount of alcohol used and developing a new method of heat sterilisation, which at the same time provided companies with a standard method of preparation.[186]

Throughout this project, the MRC occupied a key position. This enabled them to impose on industry and clinicians their dual role as controller of the producers and co-ordinator of research. Dale held discussions with the representatives of ten principal firms. Other than Burroughs Wellcome, which had the best research facilities, Allen & Hanburys, BDH, Glaxo and May & Baker were selected as being most likely to be able to produce insulin under licence.[187] The arrangement proved satisfactory to all, and by 1923 production of British insulin was under way (see Figure 2.8). The NIMR's contribution made it possible for producers to lower costs, which soon fell below the level set by Eli Lilly. In 1924, clinical trials were organized nation-wide.

This successful outcome made insulin a model of co-operation between academic and clinical researchers and the pharmaceutical industry, in a formal project co-ordinated by a government body, the MRC. In France, the first project of this kind was to develop the large-scale manufacture of penicillin after World War Two. According to the terms binding together the MRC and pharmaceutical firms, the Council regarded themselves 'as being in co-operation with any firms to which they may grant a License' and to which they offered 'scientific help and information'.[188] Public funds were to be used in order to support research and development in industry. In exchange for this support, the MRC expected royalties to be waived by the firms involved in the scheme.[189] The scheme occasionally needed to be adapted, to suit the informal arrangements made between firms and clinical researchers, as in the case of Boots, who had a prior agreement with Professor MacLean at St Thomas's, whom they supplied with small quantities of insulin. The presence of a Boots employee, named Brett, in MacLean's department, caused what Dale described as 'a slight embarrassment'. The matter was resolved by obtaining that Boots 'make no use at this, or any future time, for purposes of advertisement or propaganda, of information which (MacLean) may so give them through Brett'.[190] A few years later, however, Boots had to be brought back into line, when an advertisement made claims which the MRC deemed 'extravagant and not warranted by facts'. However, the relationship established between the Council and the company was secure enough to be carried forward into other projects, such as the development of harmol-hydrochloryde and amyl-meta-cresol for therapeutic use in 1931–3.[191]

To pharmaceutical companies, the arrangement with the MRC was 'something in the nature of a partnership agreement, in which it is not attempted to cover every contingency, but it is anticipated that each side

Figure 2.8 Burroughs Wellcome advertisement for insulin (with permission from the Wellcome Trust).

will work in a spirit of mutual trust and co-operation'.[192] Through such partnership agreements companies had already gained experience of co-operation, and they applied this experience to their new relationship with the MRC, and with other companies for the purpose of producing insulin. BDH entered into an agreement with Allen & Hanburys, which involved sharing supplies of raw material (pancreases) as well as combining their research and manufacturing facilities. A few years later, when liver extract was used for the treatment of pernicious anaemia, BDH entered into a partnership with Burroughs Wellcome and Boots.[193] But in this case, the collaborative scheme failed, because Boots were in a position to monopolize the help of J.F. Wilkinson of the Department of Clinical Investigation at Manchester University (probably because of prior consultative arrangements) and were reluctant to share information with other companies.[194] Despite the failure of this scheme, the MRC remained in contact with the companies and scientific researchers working on pernicious anaemia, and provided an informal link between them. Many other informal links flourished in the 1930s as a result of the creation of the TTC, through which the Council wished not only to regulate, but also encourage industry in its research work.[195]

As a collaborative project, insulin had been successful because of the links that already existed between industry and academic researchers, and increasingly also between the companies themselves. Co-operation was in the interest of most of the parties involved, most of the time. The MRC benefited from its fruitful interaction with the pharmaceutical sector. The speedy transfer from laboratory process to large-scale manufacture and the standardisation of insulin production, which the Council had helped to bring about, were necessary if distribution of the drug as well as the treatment of diabetes were to be rationalized. The MRC's contribution to public health policy helped to strengthen its position within government, at a time when the relationship between the Council and the Ministry of Health (MoH) was vaguely defined, in terms of pure research which the MRC was supposed to focus on, while the MoH dealt with the applied side.[196]

There can be little doubt that the pharmaceutical firms selected by the MRC for the production of insulin also benefited from their association with a scientific and government body. At the same time, it was strengthened by the activities of professional bodies such as the ABCM, which fostered the interests of the industrialists they represented, for instance by securing medical co-operation through the MRC, and later the Therapeutic Trials Committee.[197]

A symptom of British industry's growing effectiveness at achieving public representation, which was associated with increasing co-operation and commitment to research, was the succession of surveys of industrial laboratories carried out under the auspices of the Federation of British Industries (FBI, later the Confederation of British Industries, CBI). This served a similar function to the survey carried out by the CNRS in 1938–40. However, unlike the CNRS survey, little is left of the firms' original responses, which were processed and used to draw up reports, the first one in 1943. Unfortunately, this makes a direct comparison between the two impossible. Nevertheless, it is useful to say a few words about the FBI surveys and their implications for the history of collaboration in the pharmaceutical industry.

6. The FBI's survey of industrial research laboratories

Like the ABCM, created in 1914, the FBI, founded in 1916, reflects the considerable impetus World War One gave in Britain to the development of representative apparatus for industry at the highest level.[198] Throughout the 1930s and 1940s, it carried out a series of surveys on industrial research. From 1942 onwards, these were done under the auspices of the Industrial Research Committee, whose purpose was, in the words of its chairman Sir William Larke:

> [...] to issue a report giving a correct impression of the part played by industrial research in the development of British industry and stressing the desirability of making still further efforts in the direc-tion of research, particularly regarding the necessity for the develop-ment of new products in view especially of the vital need for postwar exports.[199]

Its purpose was, therefore, to help with the post-war reconstruction of the country, in which industrial research was to play a key part, and for which accurate, quantitative data was required, such as the number of laborato-ries and qualified staff, and the level of research expenditure. However, a sign of the times, and a drawback for historians of the pharmaceutical industry, drug firms were not treated separately, as they would be later. Hence, firms with pharmaceutical laboratories can be found in Food and Drink (including Glaxo and Vitamins Ltd.), although the largest number is in Chemicals (Beecham Research, BDH, Boots, ICI, May & Baker, and the Wellcome Foundation).[200]

Like the CNRS survey, the FBI surveys show that companies hoped to gain commercial advantage by being seen to collaborate with government. A list was drawn up of firms that had 'co-operated with the Press Depart-ment on wartime and other achievements', and counted May & Baker and Vitamins Ltd..[201] It also shows that co-operation and research were consid-ered by the FBI to go hand in hand. Ten out of twenty-five questions were concerned with sharing research facilities with other firms, employment of outside consultants, relations with universities and technical colleges, endowment of fellowships, and policy regarding publication of research results and exchange of scientific and technical information.[202]

However, unlike the CNRS survey, the fact that the results of these sur-veys were published in the form of a report in 1943, became the subject of a conference in 1946,[203] and were used by industry in its dealings and negotiations with government in the period of post-war reconstruction,[204] emphasizes the greater continuity between the periods before, during and after the war in Britain, compared with France. In France, it was not until the need for similar survey was felt, no longer in connection with mobilization for war, but with economic planning in the 1960s, that the French government ordered another survey, this time specifically on the pharmaceutical industry, which acquired heightened importance in the era of the Welfare State. However, this survey was carried out without any knowledge of the 1938-40 CNRS survey of industrial laboratories, reflecting the sharp break — the war had created in French research policy.

D. CONCLUSION

In the first part of this chapter, I have argued that the Pasteur Institute did not inhibit the growth of the French pharmaceutical industry. Similarly, in the second part, I concluded that government intervention, through bodies such as the DSIR or the MRC, did not prevent, but on the contrary encouraged the growth of research in the British pharmaceutical industry.

Although there was a greater visibility of government and professional associations in Britain, collaborations occurred in much the same way in both countries. An early impetus for the development of collaborative networks came from industrialists like the brothers Poulenc, or Henry Wellcome, who employed academic scientists in their research laboratories. The evolution towards greater co-operation between scientists and companies continued when the directors of institutes (such as Roux in France), and the medical élite (represented by the MRC in Britain) turned to industry as a source of chemical expertise to develop the new field of chemotherapy. The interruption of supplies of German chemicals, including drugs, in World War One stimulated the growth of collaborative networks, and the exceptional circumstances of war facilitated the mobility of scientists between industry and academia. In the inter-war period, the development of new biological remedies helped to consolidate these networks. Such an evolution was possible because of the existence of a close community of scientists for whom the boundaries between industry and academe were fluid, and because of increasing co-operation amongst pharmaceutical companies, for which partnerships were a response to economic recession and growing competition.

In spite of the structural differences pointed out in Chapter 1, in chapter 2 I have shown that the growth of a co-operative culture accompanied the expansion of research activities in association with novel chemotherapeutic and biological drugs. In both countries, this culture satisfies the definition of co-operation given in the Introduction (see p. 8), and fulfills many of the criteria contained in the literature. These are listed below in four separate points:

1. In Britain and France, there developed a co-operative relationship between scientists and pharmaceutical companies. This relationship was reciprocal,[205] in that it brought costs and benefits to both parties, as with the MRC and its network of reputable companies, or Fourneau and Rhône-Poulenc.
2. It was based on trust, because of prior acquaintance (as between Dale and Burroughs Wellcome), and sometimes even long-lasting friendship (as between Fourneau and Blaise). However this trust was not blind. Although reputation helped to secure it,[206] it had to be earned, and was strengthened by the experience of collaboration.[207]
3. The prospect of long-term interaction, linked to drug development and the expansion of research activities in the medical sciences and the pharmaceutical industry, led to a stable relationship.[208] This, in turn, encouraged the creation of trust and the dissemination of a co-operative culture.
4. The collaboration between scientists and companies took on a great variety of forms, from informal advice, to salaried consultancies, part-time work in pharmaceutical laboratories, or research carried out in co-operative schemes involving government. These different forms of collaboration cannot easily be reduced to any of the categories of consultancy defined by Swann for America,[209] but can be described as collaborative networks and collaborative relationships.[210]

The evidence presented in this chapter urges historians to re-examine assumptions about the backwardness of the pharmaceutical industries in Britain and in France.[211] There was no lack of co-operation between scientists and pharmaceutical companies in either Britain or France before World War Two.[212] In both countries, pharmaceutical research was, essentially, collaborative. The collaboration between companies and scientists outside the industry, and also between the companies themselves, allowed them to compensate for their relatively small size and lack of modern research facilities. Hence, they blossomed in the field of new biological remedies, and were beginning to develop an expertise in the field of chemotherapy, which had taken root in two companies, Poulenc Frères in France, and Bourroughs Wellcome in Britain, and been transferred to institutes of medical research at the time of World War One. However, it was not until World War Two and the development of penicillin and other antibiotics, which combined the two traditions in pharmaceutical research, the biological and chemical, that a whole-hearted commitment to chemotherapy was achieved by many British and French companies. This would bring them up to a par with, and in some cases enable them to overtake, for a time at least, their rivals in Germany.

Part I

Conclusion

Collaborative networks were well established before the Second World War in Britain as well as in France. They had arisen at the turn of the century within a small cluster of institutions and companies.[1] Led by figures such as the Poulenc brothers, Ernest Fourneau and Edmond Blaise in France, and by Henry Wellcome and Henry Dale in Britain, and inspired by examples from abroad, particularly Germany, the community that formed these networks shared similar values, including a belief in the importance of research and of co-operative behaviour. The relationship between science and industry, which they fostered, tended to be informal rather than formal, and relied upon professional solidarity, involving mutual trust and self-regulation. Stimulated by World War One and the interrupted imports of German synthetic drugs, it began to transform not only the drug industry, leading to the expansion of research within firms, but also medicine, giving rise to novel approaches to the treatment of disease, especially chemotherapy and replacement therapy, which following Salvarsan and insulin gained ground in the inter-war period.

This evolution was common to Britain and to France. However, there were significant differences between the two countries' experiences. At a national level, medical research was more centralized in France than in Britain. It essentially took place within one institution, the Pasteur Institute in Paris, and its relationship with satellite institutions and pharmaceutical companies epitomized French collaborative research in the field. In Britain, by the time of World War Two, an extensive network of academic, government and industrial laboratories was in place. It was loosely coordinated by the MRC, which had begun to play the role of co-ordinator of research in World War One for the purpose of developing synthetic organic chemicals, and then between the wars insulin and other drugs. At an institutional level, their organization and style of leadership was also different. French hierarchical structures and autocratic style of leadership contrasted with a more democratic organization and consensual leadership in Britain.

The idea that weak ties, such as those that exist between individual scientists, act as bridges that hold the larger system in place, i.e. the institution or nation, is helpful for understanding the links which existed between these different levels.[2] My evidence suggests that although at the grass-roots, that is to say at the level of individual researchers and their personal networks, Britain and France both had strong co-operative cultures, at the national level co-operation mirrored the institutional level, and in time this would lead to two distinctive national systems of innovation.

This distinctiveness was due to different cultural geographies, in particular the relationship between the centre and periphery, or Metropolis and Province. In France, the existence of a Metropolis-Province dichotomy as a result of the centralisation of the Napoleonic State had created a hierarchical network of academic institutions and their provincial subsidiaries.[3] In Britain, the balance achieved between London and the counties achieved at the time of the Industrial Revolution had led to a broad network of interconnecting academic institutions.[4] And yet, if the British and French experiences are compared with those of the United States and Germany, they still seem very close to each other.

In the scientific, cultural and organisational spectrum, France occupies a place between Britain and Germany, and Britain, between France and America.[5] Which of these distinctive national systems was more amenable to change? In his comparison of the Pasteur Institute in Paris and Robert Koch's Institute in Berlin at the end of the nineteenth century, Paul Weindling has argued that the pluralistic model of the Pasteur and the federalist relationship it entertained with its satellite institutes was better able to adapt to change than the unitary hierarchy of the Koch and the rigid centralized state system within which it operated.[6] Thus, the more consensual, decentralized British system might be expected to be more adaptable than the French system.

About the relationship between hierarchy and creativity in chemistry, J.A. Johnson has asked: 'If strong hierarchies promote stability and productivity in science (...) and if weak ones open the way to change, is not change more likely when the social context in which the hierarchies exist is disrupted?' (for example war, revolution, economic crisis).[7] French hierarchies in the inter-war years produced stability and did not promote change. On the other hand, loose British networks, once mobilized for war, produced paradigm shifts, of which penicillin is a key example. The changes and shifts brought on by war are the subject of Part 2.

Part II

Collaborative Networks in War and Peace

INTRODUCTION

Penicillin was a 'massive innovation' that brought about a cascade of changes, not only in science, technology and medicine, but also in society, the economy and politics.[1] Focusing more particularly on change in science, technology and medicine, Part 2 explains how penicillin came to embody a shift in therapeutic approach.[2] Although the concept of antibiotics as a new class of chemotherapeutic agents had gained ground with the sulpha drugs, by offering a biological alternative to synthetic remedies, penicillin played a special role in helping to resolve the immunotherapy-chemotherapy debate that had been an obstacle to the development of chemotherapy in countries without a strong synthetic chemical industry, such as Britain and France.

The effects of this debate are reflected in the ten-year gap that separated Alexander Fleming's initial observations from the development of penicillin as a drug by Howard Florey during World War Two. Nevertheless, conditions in Britain were favourable to the development of penicillin. On the one hand, the British physiological-pathological tradition provided a fertile ground for the development of biological remedies; on the other, once mobilized for war, the loose collaborative networks that had blossomed in the inter-war period were propitious to the development of radical innovations. Together, these conditions formed a unique 'interlocking pattern', which characterizes the British context for the wartime development of penicillin.[3]

In Chapter 4, I contrast the French with the British experience. The disruptions of war were greater in France, and presented French institutions and companies with an opportunity to reorganize and forge new networks and alliances, the legacy of which would be felt in the post-war period. There were also similarities between the British and French experiences. Like penicillin, Rhône-Poulenc's synthetic anti-histamines, which were not only the result of accumulated scientific knowledge and technical know-how, but also the product of long-established collaborative relations, helped to seal the victory of chemotherapy in France. However, because these had been developed under the very difficult circumstances of German Occupation, penicillin, rather than the anti-histamines, would be held up as a model of co-operative research to be emulated in the post-war period.

3 Mobilizing for War
Making Pennicillin in Britain and the United States

A. INTRODUCTION

After the war, when the British pharmaceutical industry had built up its research capabilities and taken over the collaboration with scientists, it nevertheless continued to receive criticism for lagging behind and having failed to meet the challenge of penicillin.[1] However, industry was not the only scapegoat. British scientific élites were also blamed for the loss of this miraculous discovery. Howard Florey was accused of having handed penicillin to the Americans 'on a platter',[2] and Edward Mellanby, then Secretary of the MRC, was criticized for his old-fashioned attitude to patenting.[3] Thus, penicillin became at once an 'icon' of success and of failure: success at discovering, failure at developing.[4] Robert Bud has shown that one of the most enduring myths surrounding penicillin was that of its 'theft' by the Americans, and that this myth reveals the ambiguous feelings of the British nation towards its changing status in the post-war world.[5]

This chapter describes how penicillin was developed in wartime. Digging deep into the 'mine' of antibiotics history,[6] it fills a gap between Bud's post-war study of penicillin and Chen's analysis of Alexander Fleming's construction of penicillin as a laboratory tool for the production of vaccines.[7] Using the laboratory notebooks, diaries, and correspondence of the Oxford researchers as well as the MRC's penicillin files,[8] it describes how Florey also constructed penicillin, first as a new kind of chemotherapeutic agent to be used in war, and second as a pure scientific fact.[9] Moreover, it examines how penicillin became a massive 'experiment in collaboration', bringing together academic scientists, firms, and government agencies from the two main wartime allies, Britain and the United States, an aspect largely overlooked by histories of penicillin.

The identity of penicillin changed, as it moved from the Inoculation Department at St Mary's Hospital to the Sir William Dunn School of Pathology, from the laboratory to the factory, and from wartime to peacetime. At the same time, the collaborative practices associated with its development evolved, from teamwork, to informal collaboration with individual companies, to national and international co-operative schemes involving government agencies. These practices, tried and tested in war and associated with the major medical breakthrough that was penicillin, would serve as a blue-print for subsequent collaborative projects and transform the relationship between scientists and the pharmaceutical industry in the post-war period.

B. CROSSING BOUNDARIES: FROM ST MARY'S TO THE DUNN SCHOOL, AND FROM IMMUNOTHERAPY TO CHEMOTHERAPY

The use of fungi in medicine goes back to ancient times. However, early ideas about bacterial antagonism, or 'antibiosis', appeared at the end of the nineteenth century. An early observation of the 'struggle for life' between bacteria and the *Penicillium* mould was made by the physicist John Tyndall in 1876. This was followed by Louis Pasteur and Jules Joubert's study of the antagonism between bacteria and the anthrax bacillus. Although they considered applying the phenomenon they had observed to medicine, their ideas centered on immunity, rather than on direct antibacterial action.[10] The word 'antibiosis' was invented by Vuillemin in 1889, but was rarely used until 1928, when it was given more precise meaning by G. Papacostas and J. Gaté in their book on the use of microbes in therapy: *Les Associations Microbiennes: leurs applications thérapeutiques*.

   Therefore, Fleming's chance observation, in 1928, that a colony of staphylococci had been dissolved as a result of contamination of the culture plate by a mould, happened against a background of long-term studies of bacterial antagonism. The culprit was later identified as *Penicillium notatum*, and Fleming named the antibacterial substance it produced 'penicillin'. Fleming's observations took place in the inoculation department at St Mary's Hospital, London, where the manufacture of vaccines provided the focal point for all research.[12] Shaped by Almroth Wright's disbelief in the value of chemotherapy in medicine, the institutional context helps to explain the time gap between these observations and the development of penicillin as a chemotherapeutic agent. By shifting from one institutional and therapeutic domain to another, penicillin would contribute to the resolution of the immunotherapy-chemotherapy debate in which it had remained buried for ten years.[13]

1. Fleming's discovery: penicillin as a laboratory tool

Wai Chen has described how penicillin's first identity was that of a diagnostic reagent used for the isolation of *B. Influenzae* (against which it had no inhibitory effect) grown for the production of the influenza vaccine.[14] Although Fleming had considered the use of penicillin in local applications, for the treating of wounds, his vision of the mould's therapeutic potential was limited by the function of his laboratory. Even in 1939, as the Oxford penicillin project was gathering pace, Fleming expressed reservations about the usefulness of chemotherapy:

> At the present moment vaccine therapy is, in practice, having something of a setback in that medical practitioners have become chemically minded because of the sensational results obtained in certain infections by sulphanilamide and its allies. These drugs have an extraordinary effect on a small number of bacteria which infect the human body, and they are being used to treat all manner of bacterial infections whether or not there is any substantial evidence that there is a likelihood of their being successful. However it is certain that before long the limits of the new chemotherapy will be better understood, and I hope later to produce evidence that the best results in the treatment of certain bacterial infections will be obtained by a combination of vaccine therapy with the new chemotherapy.[15]

Back in 1928, Fleming had studied penicillin within the framework of Wright's campaign against chemotherapy and the 'German method' of assessing the efficacy of drugs in experimentally-infected animals.[16] Thus, in order to investigate the properties of the mould, he used *in vitro* tests, in particular the slide-cell test, which had been developed to study the behaviour of antiseptics in blood. It showed that they destroyed not only bacteria, but also the white blood cells, which according to Wright played the most important role in immunity. However, as well as having the desired effect of emphasising the defects of antiseptics, the slide-cell test also tended to obscure their therapeutic value. This is what happened with penicillin. Fleming found that the activity of penicillin in blood was only half its activity in a bacteriological medium, and he concluded that something in the blood must cause it to be inactivated. He confirmed his *in vitro* observations by injecting penicillin into a rabbit and showing that, after less than thirty minutes, it had disappeared from the blood stream (probably because of rapid excretion by the kidneys). Comparing the fate of penicillin with that of the yellow dye flavine, which although non-toxic like penicillin had been found to be useless therapeutically, Fleming developed serious doubts concerning penicillin as a therapeutic agent.[17] His interest in the mould waned and, as a result, his two younger colleagues, Ridley and Craddock, abandoned their biochemical work on penicillin without publishing their results.[18] Several of the facts they established about the mould were rediscovered ten years later in Oxford. Meanwhile, penicillin remained confined in the laboratory, as a diagnostic reagent and 'bacterial weed-killer', used for eliminating unwanted bacteria from microbial cultures.

Nevertheless, Fleming's extensive network of contacts meant that penicillin was commonly found in the 1930s in bacteriological laboratories across the world. As a result of this widespread acquaintance with the substance, other cases of short-lived interest in penicillin arose in the early 1930s. Harold Raistrick, who was Professor of biochemistry at the London School of Hygiene and Tropical Medicine, began research on penicillin as part of a wider programme on micro-organisms. His findings were published in a joint paper in 1932, after which research on penicillin was, again, abandoned.[19] Cecil G. Paine used crude penicillin in the treatment of several cases of ophthalmia at the Royal Infimary in Sheffield.[20] In 1930, having obtained a sample of the mould from Fleming, whose bacteriology classes he had attended while a medical student at St Mary's, he grew penicillin and used the crude filtrate to irrigate his patients' eyes, curing all the cases he treated in this way. In 1932, he discussed his results with Howard Florey, the new Professor of Pathology at Sheffield, but neither of them chose to pursue the question at that moment. This highlights the importance of the historical context in the development of penicillin as an antibacterial drug. Florey's penicillin project was spurred on by the discovery of the sulphonamides (1935) and by war (1939–45).[21] However, its scientific roots lay in an older project, which had also originated in Fleming's laboratory: lysozyme.

2. From lysozyme to penicillin

In 1921, before his observations on penicillin, Fleming had 'discovered' lysozyme, an enzyme with antibacterial properties present in mucus, while working on a vaccine against influenza.[22] As a newly established scientific fact, and as a substance that might hold the key to natural immunity, lysozyme also stimulated interest in other laboratories. In 1930, Florey published a paper on the antibacterial properties of mucus with Neil Goldsworthy at Cambridge.[23] After moving from Cambridge to Sheffield, and then on to Oxford where he succeeded George Dreyer in the chair of Pathology, Florey pursued his lysozyme project first in collaboration with E.H.A. Roberts, a student of Robert Robinson, Waynflete Professor of Chemistry at the Dyson Perrins Laboratory and his neighbour in South Parks Road, for whom they obtained a two-year grant form the MRC, and then with Ernest Chain, who in 1935 had come from Cambridge recommended by Frederic Gowland Hopkins.[24] In 1939, Florey's lysozyme project reached its conclusion. Chain had succeeded in purifying and elucidating its chemical nature, as well as identifying its substrate (the component of the bacterial cell-wall under attack by the enzyme), a nitrogenous polysaccharide, thereby providing an answer to the question of the mechanism of its antibacterial action. However, to Florey, this conclusion was a 'physiological dead-end', for lysozyme seemed unlikely to lead to any significant advance in the search for natural antibacterial substances.[25] In a grant application to the Rockefeller Foundation, Chain explained that one of the aims of the lysozyme project had been to clarify the relationship between the bacteriolytic substance and the phenomena of natural immunity.[26] In another application, presumably to the MRC, which began funding his research from 1937,[27] he wrote: 'Although chemically ideal for use as an antiseptic *in vivo*, its practical application was limited by the fact that its action was almost entirely confined to non-pathogenic organisms'.[28]

Florey then turned his attention towards micro-organisms with antibacterial properties, in what Macfarlane has described as an 'unexpected diversion'.[29] However, the passage from one project to the other was neither abrupt nor fortuitous. Fleming had believed that penicillin, like lysozyme, exerted a bacteriolytic action upon bacteria. As the lysozyme project was wound down, Florey turned to substances that were thought to have similar action, but unlike lysozyme might be useful in therapy. The connection between understanding the mechanisms of antibacterial action and developing an effective antibacterial drug, that is to say between the pure and applied aspects of the lysozyme project, was also present in the study of penicillin. By adopting the same research strategy to pursue the same questions, continuity and the transfer of knowledge and expertise from one project to the next was assured.

3. Florey's invention:[30] penicillin as a chemotherapeutic agent

Penicillin was only one of several candidates selected for study. Florey and Chain proposed to 'obtain purified preparations of the substances and to study their antiseptic action *in vivo* '. They anticipated that the substances may, by their action against *streptococcus* and *pneumococcus*, make it possible to reduce the large doses of the sulphonamide drugs used in the treatment of infections and therefore avoid some of their toxic side effects.[31]

At the very beginning, therefore, the project intended to find an adjunct to sulphonamide therapy. In fact, penicillin would become a competitor of the sulphonamides, before eventually supplanting them, and one of Florey's main challenges would be to convince the medical community of its superiority as a naturally occurring chemotherapeutic agent in preference to synthetic dyes.[32]

After preliminary tests had been carried out, penicillin alone was kept for study, although the other two micro-organisms became the subject of later studies.[33] At the time Florey was busy with other research projects, and left Chain to begin the work. The latter wrote, in a retrospective account of the facts:

> [...] if I had been working, at that time, in aim-directed surroundings, say in the laboratory of a pharmaceutical firm, it is my firm belief that I would never have obtained the agreement of my bosses to proceed with my project to work on penicillin.[34]

However, Chain still needed to convince Florey of the importance of penicillin, as opposed to his other projects. In March 1940, Chain, who did not hold an animal licence, asked J.M. Barnes to inject a crude preparation of penicillin into a mouse.[35] There were no toxic effects, and he showed his results to Florey, who from then on became more committed to penicillin. Only then did he begin running the penicillin team according to the research strategy formulated earlier, in his grant applications.[36]

This team, initially gathered for other projects, was unusual in inter-war Britain, yet is often considered to have held the key to Florey's success with penicillin.[37] Its origins are pertinent to this book, for the team represents the first level of collaboration involved in the development of the antibiotic, so they are analysed next.

4. Penicillin from multi-disciplinary research programme to research team

Although Florey's approach to running a pathology department reflected the aim of the British reforming élite to modernize medicine through research and teamwork,[38] his multi-disciplinary research strategy was also a practical response to the weakness of central funding for the sciences, especially in Oxford.

His biographers have stressed that, when Florey arrived in Oxford to take up Dreyer's chair, the Dunn endowment had virtually disappeared. Florey had to 'make the rounds of the money dispensers': the Nuffield Foundation, the MRC, the British Empire Cancer Campaign, the Rockefeller Foundation.[39] To attract funding from such disparate sources, Florey applied for several projects simultaneously, and chose different researchers with complementary skills to carry out various aspects of the programme. Florey's strategy was well adapted to the fragmented nature of his funding. With the penicillin project, he was hoping, furthermore, to obtain a long-term grant that would give him and his department some respite from the seemingly endless rounds of grant applications.[40]

Having started at Oxford on a University grant, Chain's first approach to the MRC was turned down. Florey then turned to the biochemical section of the Rockefeller Foundation. In a covering letter to Chain's proposal, he expressed his wish to foster the importance of biochemistry in relation to pathology and bacteriology, and they were awarded the sum of £600 to pay for a fully-qualified biochemist for the period of one year.[41]

Florey conceived the penicillin project as a three-pronged research programme. In the laboratory notebooks, the experiments were recorded under the headings: 'biological', 'chemical', and 'production' work.[42] Although there were overlaps between the different parts of the project, which created frictions between some of the researchers, Ernst Chain and Norman Heatley in particular, the chronological order in which the experiments were carried out reveals a definite order of priority between them. Production work was assigned to Heatley and began first, for without it, there could be no research. Then came the biological experiments, which Florey performed with the help of his laboratory assistant Jim Kent. According to Wainwright,[43] with these experiments, Florey hoped to convince himself of the therapeutic value of penicillin, that he had 'gold in his pan, not pyrite'.[44] Finally, the chemical work began, but only once the mouse experiments (see Figure 3.1) had been carried out.[45]

Thus the nature of the penicillin project, as well as the funding difficulties, helps to explain the tensions that arose between the Oxford workers.[46] These conflicts suggest that, like penicillin itself, the penicillin team was gradually constructed in the laboratory.

5. R&D in an academic laboratory

Although the project had begun earlier, it received major impetus from the war. Firstly, because it prevented Norman Heatley, a biochemist specialized in micro-methods, who had joined Chain from Cambridge to work with him on cancer and was ideally suited to the task of producing penicillin, from leaving for Denmark to work with Linderstrøm Lang. Secondly, because it was to provide a strong focus for the experiments and early clinical trials.

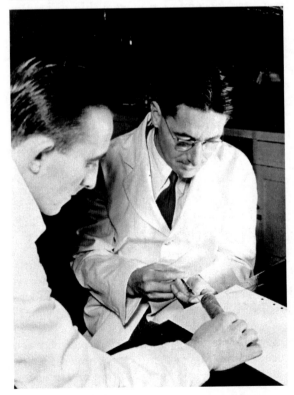

Figure 3.1 Howard Florey and Jim Kent injecting the tail vein of a mouse (courtesy of the Sir William Dunn School of Pathology, Oxford).

In Heatley's laboratory notebooks, the penicillin project opened with the words: 'September 3rd 1939, War declared by Great Britain against Germany'.[47] On 30 September, he wrote in his diary:

> Down to the lab where I saw the Professor. He asked me if I would like to help him design apparatus. Naturally I jumped at the opportunity, and he said that he could probably get me a Nuffield grant at £300 p.a. for six months.[48]

He became Florey's personal assistant and their close relationship reflected not only the compatibility between their characters,[49] but also the close link between the research and production of sides of the penicillin project.[50]

Heatley's first task was to devise an assay method. In the early stages of most investigations of new physiologically active substances, a fundamental problem needs to be solved. Since it is only through their biological effects that their presence can be detected and their concentration estimated, a rapid method of assay is of crucial importance.[51] Not only was this essential for the biological work, but also for the investigation of the different factors influencing the production of penicillin.[52] Heatley was faced with a choice between two different methods: the serial dilution method used by Fleming to measure the lowest concentration of penicillin to prevent growth of the test-organism in broth, or the diffusion technique used by Florey in his study of lysozyme. Heatley chose to adapt Florey's technique, more practical than Fleming's, and devised the plate-cylinder method of assay (see Figure 3.2). This enabled inhibition rings to be measured, at first semi-quantitatively, later more precisely, as the penicillin solution diffused outward from holes drilled in a Petri dish in which agar had been seeded with bacteria.

The new method was first tested with lysozyme on a culture of *M. lysodeikticus*, and then with a solution of penicillin. The results proved conclusive, and it was described in the *Lancet* article of 1941,[53] and later in the collective volume *Antibiotics*, together with alternative assay methods.[54] However, the Oxford method (as the plate-cylinder assay became known) was eventually retained. The Oxford unit of penicillin developed in connection with it also became the standard unit of penicillin required to inhibit bacterial cultures.[55]

The production and extraction of penicillin was Heatley's next task. The extraction of penicillin fell within two areas of study: the production work, which was clearly his province, and the chemical work, which was Chain's. Because of the sensitive nature of penicillin, two options were available to the team. These were the mildest of separation processes in use at the time: back extraction (i.e. the separation of a substance between two immiscible solvents, such as ether and water), and chromatography. Heatley suggested back extraction of the crude preparation into ether, and

Figure 3.2 Norman Heatley performing a plate-cylinder assay (courtesy of the Sir William Dunn School of Pathology, Oxford).

made his first trial of the method on 9 March 1940.[56] Chain then proposed back extraction into amyl-acetate, which is less amenable to decomposition than ether. Chromatography, which became an important stage in the purification of penicillin, was added later to the process by Edward Abraham, another student of Robert Robinson, who moved to the Dunn School from the Dyson Perrins laboratory to work with Chain on lysozyme, before focusing on penicillin.[57] The whole process, developed jointly by the team in the laboratory, was eventually passed on to industry without any major changes. It consisted of eight basic stages, as seen in Table 3.1.

Early in the penicillin project, Heatley had been able to study ways of increasing yields by altering the composition of the medium. For instance, he found that by adding yeast extract to the Czapek-Dox medium he was able to promote growth of the mould.[59] Production was then still a small enterprise, which was intended solely for the biological experiments. However, by the end of 1940, the pressure to produce larger quantities of

Table 3.1 Processes of penicillin production[58]

1) Preparation of medium (Czapek-Dox, later replaced by corn steep liquor)
2) Sterilization and cooling of medium
3) Preparation of spore suspensions and inoculations
4) Incubation
5) Harvesting (or extraction)
6) Concentration
7) Drying (later freeze-drying)
8) Packing

penicillin for human trials was increasing and Heatley's investigation of factors influencing yields came to an end.

6. The biological experiment

The second phase of the project, the biological experiments, became possible once the assay method had been devised and a small amount of penicillin was available for injection. It included curative and toxicity tests. Both had a 'demonstration value', aimed at convincing first Florey, and then his potential audience of the uses of penicillin. The curative tests identified the value of penicillin as a chemotherapeutic agent, and were performed first. They were inspired by the procedure adopted by Gerhard Domagk (director of experimental pathology at the IG Farben research complex in Elberfeld) for testing Prontosil, a procedure itself modeled on Ehrlich's method for testing Salvarsan.[60] They established the field of action of penicillin not only in relation to the sulphonamides, but also in relation to war.

Beginning in May 1940, Florey tested the substance in experimentally infected mice. He infected eight animals intraperitoneally with *Streptococcus*. One hour later, he injected four of the animals with penicillin, administered subcutaneously in order to demonstrate a true chemotherapeutic effect. All the control animals died, but the others survived.[61] In the next few days, he conducted further tests with *Staphylococcus*, against which the sulphonamides had no action.[62] He later went on to infect the mice with other pathogenic organisms, such as the clostridia that cause gas gangrene. Through these early experiments, Florey targeted the treatment of staphylococcal infection, a common cause of septicaemia, but also, more importantly, he targeted the treatment of war wounds. The results of these curative tests, later referred to as the 'mouse-protection experiments', were remarkable, and were published in a joint paper in the *Lancet*, on 24 August 1940, the first paper to present penicillin as a new kind of chemotherapeutic agent.[63]

Less well known than the curative tests, the toxicity tests nevertheless present great interest, for just as Ehrlich's work served as a model for subsequent chemotherapeutic research (for instance at IG Farben), they show the influence of Wright and Fleming's work in the initial stages of the Oxford research.[64] Florey designed experiments that compared penicillin, sulphanilamide, and the synthetic dye proflavine in terms of their toxicity in blood. Between June 1940 and December 1941, he carried out *in vitro* tests comparing the effect of different dilutions of penicillin with those of the sulphonamides or proflavine on the motility of leucocytes in blood, and their ability to perform phagocytosis.[65] These tests were an adaptation of Fleming's slide-cell technique, modified to suit Florey's purpose, which was to demonstrate the anti-bacterial power of penicillin.[66] Hence, Florey advocated the use of serum, not whole blood, because the white blood cells present in whole blood would help to destroy bacteria, and therefore conceal the antibacterial action of penicillin.

In his description of the toxicity tests, Florey referred to C.G. Paine's technique for examining leucocytes in serum, but did not mention Fleming. However, the tests themselves reveal that Fleming's work, and the immunotherapy-chemotherapy debate that had framed it, were present at the beginning of the Oxford penicillin project.[67] As the project developed, this debate was brought to a close. The *in vitro* tests were soon replaced by a new series of tests performed *in vivo*. On 12 December, Florey performed both *in vitro* and *in vivo* tests in mice, but from then on he retained the *in vivo* tests as the sole measure of the substance's toxicity. Subsequently, he would continue to test various commercial preparations of penicillin on mice and rabbits.[68]

The toxicity tests were carried out after the mouse protection experiments had begun. They helped to establish a correspondence between the animal and human models, and aimed at facilitating the passage from laboratory experiments to clinical trials. However, for the trials penicillin was needed in a pure form (whereas that used in the mouse experiments was brown in colour and impure), as well as in large quantities. Florey took a risk concerning the purity of penicillin.[69] Between 12 October 1940 and 5 June 1941, he carried out a limited human trial with a relatively impure preparation obtained in his laboratory, although because of its high antibacterial activity, it was credited with being much purer.[70] These first ten cases were described in the *Lancet* article of 1941.

7. From mouse to man: the first ten cases

The risk was a measured one, but it represented an act of faith on Florey's part. Following the mouse protection experiments and the first toxicity tests, he had become convinced of the non-toxic nature of penicillin. Although the first few cases displayed mild reactions, it was clear to him from the first attempts at extraction that they were due to impurities still present in the penicillin, and not to the penicillin itself.

Florey's decision to carry out these early human trials remains contro-versial. It has been suggested that it was caused by his disappointment at the slow response of British pharmaceutical companies to the publication of the first *Lancet* article.[71] And yet J.W. Trevan, Director of the WPRL at Beckenham, had visited Florey in Oxford on 15 July 1940 (even before the publication of the 1940 *Lancet* article), accompanied by his head biochem-ist Pope, showing an interest in penicillin.[72] After their return to Becken-ham, Pope began some experimental work. Ten days after their visit, they wrote to Heatley asking for details about his assay method. At the end of the month, they sent some penicillin samples to test, and the Oxford team and Trevan kept in contact, exchanging samples of penicillin. Neverthe-less, several months elapsed before any other commercial manufacturers showed an interest in penicillin. The 1940 *Lancet* article had appeared as the war took a turn for the worst, after Europe fell to the Nazis and before the United States entered the war (in December 1941). British industry was under siege, having to contribute to the war effort substances such as vac-cines, antitoxins, blood plasma, sulphonamides, and they were unable to commit major resources to new ventures.[73]

Another, perhaps more likely motive for Florey's decision to carry out early human trials was the sluggish reaction of the medical community to the first *Lancet* article. Although the results of the mouse experiments had attracted the attention of scientists such as Fleming and the Secretary of the MRC, Edward Mellanby, clinicians saw penicillin as a newcomer. Its benefits still had to be proven in relation to other remedies. Until the mouse experiments, Mellanby himself had not 'had much time — or money — for naturally occurring bacterial inhibitors after the advent of the sulphon-amides'.[74] Although he was persuaded by the first *Lancet* article, the rest of the medical community, especially army doctors, needed to be convinced.

Consequently, the small-scale clinical trial in the autumn of 1940 had both an exemplary and experimental value, by ascertaining the dosage needed to treat infections in man and to ensure the successful conduct of large-scale clinical trials. Although he believed in the non-toxic nature of penicillin, Florey was not yet wholly convinced of the applicability of his mouse experiments to humans. Like Fleming before him, he thought that something might inactivate penicillin inside the human organism.[75] The small-scale trial was, therefore, the first stage in Florey's effort at translat-ing his laboratory model into the field.[76]

To carry out his first trial, Florey stepped up the production of penicillin and mobilized his network of friends and colleagues in clinical medicine. Charles Fletcher, Nuffield Research Student at the Radcliffe Infirmary, and the son of the first Secretary of the MRC, Sir Walter Morley Fletcher, was especially useful. He identified cases that were suitable for treatment with penicillin, that is to say those for whom the sulphonamides had proved ineffective. Such a case came into the Infirmary in May 1941 and was described by Florey as 'an ideal case'. He was 'a boy with suspected staphylococcal septicemia, on which sulphathiazole etc have had no effect' (case 4 in the 1941 *Lancet* article).[77] Florey asked Heatley: 'Could we possibly get enough stuff to treat this case?', to which Heatley replied that he thought they could, and he began work on increasing production.[78]

C. CROSSING BOUNDARIES: FROM THE LABORATORY TO THE FACTORY

Florey realized that commercial production depended on clinical proof, and that clinical proof depended on increased production.[79] To break this vicious circle, he had to step up production inside his laboratory, before turning to the private sector for help.

1. The laboratory as a factory

Heatley devised several pieces of apparatus that enabled him to increase the number of batches produced in the laboratory. He designed a rolling apparatus for speeding up the assay of penicillin, and demonstrated it to Fleming and two collaborators (H.J. King and MacLean from the Lister Institute) when they visited the School of Pathology in May 1941.[80] However, it was his continuous countercurrent extractor that was to play a key

Figures 3.3 a) and b) Penicillin plant and countercurrent apparatus (courtesy of the Sir William Dunn School of Pathology, Osford).

role in the large-scale production and purification of penicillin (Figure 3.3b). The original model constructed by Heatley was kept until November 1941, when it was replaced by a new production plant constructed by Gordon Sanders, with Jim Kent's help, while Heatley was away in America.

The laboratory soon began to resemble a factory. Heatley directed several technicians, including George Glister and five young women recruited locally (see Figure 3.4). They were funded by the MRC, worked in the cold room, and received the nickname of 'the Oxford Penicillin Girls'.[81]

The layout and organisation of the School of Pathology were altered to accommodate the project, and reflected the increasing division of labour between members of the team. Heatley summarized the year that had passed in the 31 December 1940 entry in his diary:

> What a year!... The latter part of the year I have left research entirely, and have been concentrating on the production of P on a large scale. Now, with the help of George Glister, Ruth Callow and Claire Inayat we are beginning to grow P on nearly one thousand times the scale on which I was growing it a year ago.[82]

As the research progressed and the different roles assigned to the team members became more clear-cut, conflicts such as those that had occurred early on between Chain and Heatley became less common. While Florey

Figure 3.4 Oxford penicillin girls (courtesy of the Sir William Dunn School of Pathology, Oxford).

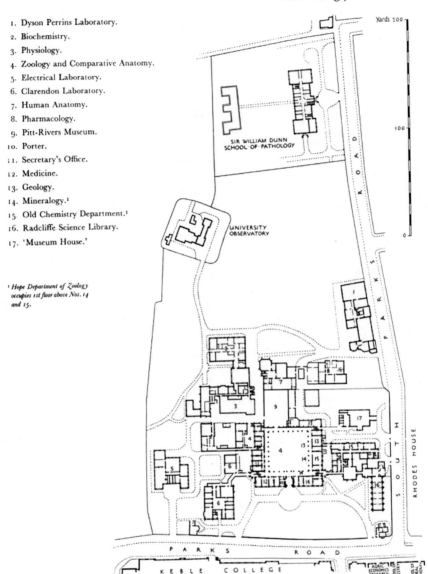

1. Dyson Perrins Laboratory.
2. Biochemistry.
3. Physiology.
4. Zoology and Comparative Anatomy.
5. Electrical Laboratory.
6. Clarendon Laboratory.
7. Human Anatomy.
8. Pharmacology.
9. Pitt-Rivers Museum.
10. Porter.
11. Secretary's Office.
12. Medicine.
13. Geology.
14. Mineralogy.[1]
15. Old Chemistry Department.[1]
16. Radcliffe Science Library.
17. 'Museum House.'

[1] *Hope Department of Zoology occupies 1st floor above Nos. 14 and 15.*

Figure 3.5 Oxford Science Area (with permission from the Bodleian Library).

prepared the human trials, Heatley concentrated on production. As soon as the chemotherapeutic value of the substance had been established by the Oxford group (with the 1940 article in the *Lancet*), Chain and Abraham began work on the purification of penicillin and started their search for its chemical structure, in collaboration with chemists from the Dyson Perrins laboratory (see Figure 3.5).[83] Both were achieved almost simultaneously: penicillin was produced in pure crystalline form in the summer of 1943, and in October Chain and Abraham proposed the beta-lactam ring as its structure, which was confirmed in 1945 by their neighbour in Inorganic Chemistry, the X-ray crystallographer Dorothy Crowfoot (later Hodgkin), against the competing oxazolone ring structure put forward by Robert Robinson.[84]

The purification work, however, was of more immediate relevance to Florey, and until the summer of 1943, in time for the North African campaign, much of Chain's and Abraham's efforts went towards solving the problem. Apart from practical experience with lysozyme, earlier publications about penicillin (in particular Raistrick's) paved the way for the Oxford team's efforts at purification, which involved numerous successive chemical manipulations. A series of thirty-four experiments were conducted between 23 July 1942 and 19 October 1943, for which penicillin was extracted either directly from brew or from urine (indicating that penicillin excreted by an early case was being recycled for research purposes).[85] The aim was twofold: to establish the chemical properties of the antibacterial substance produced by the mould *Penicillium*, and to produce it in a pure form. Inactivation of the substance was avoided by working at low temperature. Because penicillin was also inactivated by acid, alkali and many chemical reagents, purifying had to be restricted to either of two processes: partition or adsorption. In the end, both methods were combined in succession. The final solution was stable, and could be stored several months in an ice-chest. If freeze-dried, it could be stored in a laboratory desiccator, a necessary precaution as the powder was hygroscopic.

The whole process developed at Oxford was later copied by the commercial houses.[86] However, Florey had no thought yet of promoting large-scale industrial production. He envisaged co-operation with industry as a purely academic exercise that would enable him to move onto the next stage of his project, that is to say large-scale clinical trials.[87]

2. Co-operation with industry

The attitude of some pharmaceutical firms towards full-blown co-operation matched Florey's: there was no expectation of continuous collaboration. A traveling salesman for May & Baker visited Oxford in May 1941, revealing that the company had been growing penicillin on a small scale and was waiting for the School to publish before stepping up production.[88] As to Florey, he only began to plan entrusting the large-scale production of penicillin to industry after the first human case showed that penicillin could be successfully applied to man in 1941.

He then turned to fellow scientists who entertained good relations with industry. As well as providing him with chemists to work on the structure of penicillin, Robert Robinson was to be particularly important in this respect (see Figure 3.6). He was senior consultant for two firms that became involved in the production of penicillin: Kemball Bishop and ICI.[89]

Figure 3.6 Oxford chemists: E.P. Abraham, Wilson, E.B. Chain, Robert Robinson (courtesy of the Sir William Dunn School of Pathology).

Florey also turned to Henry Dale. In March, helped by Dale, he approached the Wellcome Foundation (the firm that succeeded Burroughs Wellcome) and discussed plans for large-scale production.[90] This revived the contact made with Trevan almost a year before. In April, Florey and Heatley visited Burroughs Wellcome to study the spray-drying apparatus that would be used for drying penicillin, and Heatley felt it might 'mark a new era in the penicillin work'.[91] After Florey's visit, Wellcome contacted the firm of Kemball Bishop, specialists in fermentation processes, to propose that they should produce large quantities of penicillin brew to be processed at Oxford. Eventually in 1942, penicillin brew would be made available, by Kemball Bishop and also by ICI.[92]

Interest in the large-scale production of penicillin grew rapidly. In May, senior representatives of ICI's Dyestuffs Division visited Florey and made an informal agreement to exchange information and material. Heatley recorded that on 2 June Drs Thurlow and Martin of ICI spent all day in the laboratory, where they were shown how penicillin was grown and extracted. Heatley commented: 'Martin and Thurlow certainly were alert'.[93] A small production unit was established at Blackley, North of Manchester, and by December 1941, ICI began sending preparations of penicillin for pyrogen tests at Oxford.[94] On 3 June 1941, Dr Hobday from Boots visited Heatley's 'penicillinarium', the room where penicillin was grown and worked up. The following day, he saw other processes and talked with Abraham.[95]

Therefore, by the time Florey and Heatley left for America on 26 June, the British pharmaceutical industry had shown real commitment to the project. ICI, who have been reported not to have even begun to invest in production facilities before April 1942,[96] were in fact producing penicillin at Blackley by December 1941. A few other companies were also producing penicillin on a small scale in the first half of 1941. The transfer of penicillin technology from the School to the pharmaceutical industry had begun.

Nevertheless, Florey considered the United States as another source of support, for he felt that penicillin's efficacy in the treatment of systemic cases had only been proven in a modest way. The wording of the second *Lancet* article in August 1941 was still cautious: 'Enough evidence, we consider, has now been assembled to show that penicillin is a new and effective type of chemotherapeutic agent, and possesses some properties unknown in any antibacterial substance hitherto described'.[97] In view of the uncertainties that remained, Florey strengthened his chances of being able to move on to large-scale trials by searching for new allies in America.

In this, he followed his own inclination, but also Mellanby's advice,[98] given at a time when Britain was seeking U.S. support through the Lend-Lease agreements.[99] Discussions to secure American loans had begun in 1940, after Dunkirk. An important aspect of these discussions was co-operation on scientific projects.[100] The Lend-Lease bill was finally signed by President Franklin Roosevelt on 11 March 1941, allowing supplies to reach Britain from America, but with the expectation, in exchange, that the United States would be able to join in any British cartels.[101]

A few days later, in April, Florey and Heatley 'had a most stimulating interview with Warren Weaver of the Rockefeller Foundation about P on a large-scale'.[102] They would benefit from the wide network of contacts provided by Florey's earlier experience of America as Rockefeller Fellow and grantee. On 26 June, they left England with manuscript copies of the first *Lancet* article, with Heatley's laboratory notebooks describing the extraction methods and, most importantly, with his personal knowledge of the plate-cylinder method of assay.[103] They also took with them samples of dried penicillin, some of which had been sprinkled on their clothes in the event of their capture.[104]

Hitler had just begun his invasion of the USSR (on 22 June). His campaign was meeting with success, and tensions were running high. Penicillin was 'offered' to the Americans as pressure was mounting on the British war effort. Florey's requirements for his project coincided with the country's needs at this particular juncture, and he was a man well able to make the most of this opportunity.

3. Extending interests from Britain to America

When Florey and Heatley arrived in America, work there had begun on penicillin as a result of the 1940 *Lancet* article. Merck were already attempting to produce the drug, and Henry Dawson of Columbia University had given the first dose of penicillin to be administered systemically to man.[105] Thus Florey and Heatley were able to tap into the American research networks that were beginning to form around the substance.

They met first with Ross G. Harrisson of the National Research Council (NRC), whose ultimate objective would be the chemical synthesis of the drug, but for the time being envisaged all possible routes to its production.[106] On hearing of their quest, Harrisson therefore sent Florey and Heatley to the U.S. Department of Agriculture, to see Charles Thom, who had spent some time working on penicillia.[107] Thom then took them to Percy Wells, who had been on the team that developed a deep-fermentation process for the manufacture of gluconic acid, and was now responsible for the Department's four regional research laboratories.[108] Predicting that submerged culture would 'facilitate commercial preparation' of penicillin, he sent Florey and Heatley to the Department's Northern Regional Research Laboratory (NRRL) at Peoria, south of Chicago, where, on 14 July, they met Robert Coghill, director of the Fermentation Division. Unlike Merck, the NRRL had no experience in pharmaceuticals, knew little about penicillin,[109] and — as Thom had predicted — Coghill at once suggested a deep-fermentation process for its manufacture. The agreement he reached with Florey was threefold: as well as investigating the possibility of growing the mould in submerged culture, the NRRL would search for a culture medium and a strain of the mould capable of increasing the yields of penicillin.[110] In exchange, he asked that Heatley stayed behind, and showed them the techniques, particularly the assay method, developed in Oxford.

At Peoria, Heatley worked with Andrew J. Moyer for about a month, and together they found that penicillin yields increased tenfold when the mould was grown on corn steep liquor, a waste product for which the laboratory, situated in the heart of the American corn belt, had the mission of finding a use. After Heatley's departure, Coghill's department also began searching for new strains of *Penicillium* that would grow well in submerged culture (whereas Fleming's *P. notatum* produced its best yields in surface culture). After special treatment, a mutant strain of *P. chrysogenum* was eventually chosen for culture in deep-fermentation tanks.

Although the results of this research, which were made freely available, still needed to be converted into commercial production, the NRRL therefore achieved three of the four major steps that were to lead to the large-scale production of penicillin:

1. The development of the corn steep liquor-lactose medium
2. The observation that continuous vigorous agitation of the culture medium (such as that used for gluconic acid) enabled the penicillin-producing organism to grow in submerged culture
3. The isolation and development of higher penicillin yield-producing strains of the organism

Interestingly, according to Gladys Hobby, the fourth — and perhaps most important step — had been Heatley's quantitative procedure for the assay of penicillin solutions.[111] Thanks to his prolonged stay, the tacit knowledge associated with penicillin, as well as the codified knowledge of the notebooks and *Lancet* article, was effectively transferred from Oxford to the NRRL, and later to other U.S. laboratories.

Meanwhile, on 7 August, Florey had a meeting with Alfred N. Richards, with whom he had worked briefly in 1925, and who had recently become Chairman of the Committee of Medical Research (CMR) at the Office of Scientific Research and Development (OSRD).[112] Then, together with Heatley, he crossed the border into Canada to visit the Connaught laboratories which, although officially a part of the University of Toronto, relied on the sale of biological products such as vaccines and insulin to help finance their research. His project to develop penicillin on a large scale met with little enthusiasm there, and they returned to the United States for a tour of pharmaceutical companies.[113]

Despite the doubts and uncertainties that surrounded penicillin at this early stage,[114] the companies Lederle, Squibb, and Pfizer had been working on penicillin for several months. However Merck, which had the most advanced research programme to study micro-organisms in collaboration with Selman Waksman, their consultant since 1938, had made the greatest progress with the substance.[115] On two occasions, in September 1941, Heatley visited their laboratories, and in October went to see their new pilot plant for penicillin-extraction being built in Rahway, New Jersey. In return, Merck also visited Peoria, to see the research being done there.[116] As a result of these contacts, Heatley was invited to spend six months advising Merck on the Oxford techniques, showing them in particular how to use his assay method, and helping them in their efforts to scale-up the extraction process, both of which were crucial for increasing their penicillin yields.[117]

Spurred by Florey's earlier visit, Richards convened a meeting of interested parties on 8 October 1941, at which, as well as Vannevar Bush, Director of the OSRD, Charles Thom, standing in for the NRRL, representatives of the four companies Merck, Squibb, Lederle and Pfizer were present.[118] This had the effect of transforming what until then had been a sporadic effort by American academic institutions and pharmaceutical companies into a co-ordinated research programme under the auspices of the OSRD. The question of co-operation between academic researchers and pharmaceutical firms, and of patents, arose during the meeting. However, the exchange of information was to be kept informal until December 1943, when the investigation of the chemical structure of penicillin, under the scientific leadership of Hans T. Clarke of Columbia University began, and as a result the collaboration became formalized.[119]

The meeting also prompted Merck to invite Heatley to assist them in their efforts at scaling up production.[120] At first Merck and the other firms had been encouraged simply to produce enough penicillin to enable its clinical evaluation. However, the attack on Pearl Harbour, which took place only a few days before Heatley's arrival in Rahway, meant that the U.S. penicillin programme took on a new urgency.[121] The American government urged industry to manufacture penicillin as quickly as possible for the treatment of battle casualties. The four companies were joined by others, including Abbott Laboratories, Winthrop Chemical Co., Upjohn & Co., and also Wyeth Laboratories, Parke Davis, American Cyanamid Co. (Lederle) and Hoffmann-La Roche, which were to participate in the project to synthesize penicillin.[122]

At first, production was to be done by surface culture, for there was no certainty that deep fermentation would succeed.[123] As late as 1943, there remained doubts whether submerged fermentation would replace surface culture of the mould.[124] For the purpose of war, the method of production that had been developed at Oxford appeared the surest way of obtaining results. However, the seeds for future development by submerged culture had been sown.

4. The MRC/TRC collaboration

Meanwhile in Britain, the risk Florey had taken in starting the first trials of penicillin in man had paid off, by generating a wider interest in penicillin. His open-door policy to researchers from academic institutions and industry eventually resulted in the mobilisation of industry and government to further the penicillin programme. Both responded to the pressing need for increased production in order to scale up the trials.

In 1941, the pharmaceutical companies that had formed an informal network for the production of insulin (see Chapter 2) — Boots, BDH, May & Baker, the Wellcome laboratories, three of which had already been in direct contact with Florey's laboratory — plus Glaxo, joined together to constitute the TRC.[125] It was a spontaneous association, whose objective was the pooling of information on any new research initiative, but by 1942, penicillin had taken precedence over all other projects. A Penicillin Sub-Committee was created, later renamed the Penicillin Producers' Conference when ICI and other workers joined the scheme.

Pooling information also meant sharing different areas of expertise. While BDH, Glaxo and the Wellcome laboratories were experienced in the production of biologicals, Boots and May & Baker had a greater experience of synthetic chemical drugs. Later, companies outside the field of pharmaceuticals, but familiar with fermentation processes, such as Kemball Bishop, or with chemical processes on a large scale, such as ICI, also became associated with the scheme.[126] The Lister Institute, which developed an expertise in drying blood plasma that could be applied to penicillin, joined in the project as well.

The TRC was set up with encouragement from the MRC. At this early stage of the penicillin programme, the MRC adopted the role of mediator between academic and industrial interests, which was related to one of its main functions, as stated by its Secretary, Mellanby:

> [...] the purpose of the Council is to stimulate chemotherapeutic research in this country and to ensure that any substances resulting from such research are freely available to the public in this country at reasonable prices.[127]

Although Mellanby's words had been uttered in connection with anti-malarials, another of the great collaborative projects of the Second World War, for which the MRC made special arrangements to co-operate with ICI,[128] penicillin soon became an essential part of the Council's mission to develop chemotherapy in Britain (see Chapter 1).

The MRC-TRC collaboration overlapped with personal collaborations, in particular those established between Florey and Kemball Bishop or ICI. These two levels of co-operation, the official level, and the more personal and informal level, co-existed throughout the war. The role of informal contacts, such as those described in Heatley's diary, was crucial. Thus, the extraction process developed at Oxford could be transferred directly from the laboratory to the factory, where it was scaled up and in large part mechanized.[129] Florey's estimates of the quantities required to treat cases of septicaemia were sent as a guide to the industry in its production effort. In exchange, he hoped that the superior manufacturing capacity of industry would accelerate the setting up of clinical trials, and the weekly production rates of penicillin were circulated by the various parties concerned. In October 1942, these figures were: 1.0 million units per week at Oxford; the same quantity was produced by Kemball Bishop; 1.5 million units were produced by ICI, and 2.5 million by BDH (around 32 000 units would be required for the treatment of one person for a week).[130] Such information was particularly important to Florey once it became clear that he would not be able to count on American penicillin in the immediate future, for the U.S. were now at war and were keeping their production to satisfy their own needs. He wrote:

> You can imagine my irritation, after telling the yanks every single thing we knew on the understanding that they would give us some penicillin

to do some more cases, to find that they have kept the whole lot for themselves.[131]

This experience coloured his general impression of American industry, and his disparaging comments suggest that he was not kept fully informed of the progress taking place across the Atlantic:

> I have now had a very thorough lesson with all these commercial firms. They have been of practically no help to us and I could give you a very snappy judgment on the incompetence we have met almost everywhere; however I can do nothing about that.[132]

However, news of greater yields of penicillin obtained in the United States by deep fermentation instead of surface culture soon began to reach Britain.[133] British industry sought information about the submerged process, both through official and unofficial channels. By the end of 1942, BDH were experimenting with the production of penicillin by submerged culture, but found that yields of penicillin were inferior to those they obtained by surface culture.[134] Evidence shows that ICI were also developing deep-fermentation methods at that time.[135]

The TRC did not enter into full co-operation with government until the autumn of 1942, when a formal government body, the General Penicillin Committee, was created in order to boost penicillin production. Alexander Fleming, who had seen the Oxford installation at first hand and knew one of Churchill's ministers, Sir Andrew Duncan, the Minister of Supply, had managed to stir interest in penicillin among government circles.[136] On 25 September 1942, six ministry officials, two senior officers from the Army Medical Directorate, Fleming, Florey, and Raistrick, as well as representatives from industry, met in London. Florey had recommended that Kemball Bishop should be present, in anticipation of their being able to undertake fermentation of the crude material for processing at Oxford, where Heatley's extractor was running at overcapacity at the time. ICI, who had a privileged relationship with the Oxford group, were also represented. The TRC, of course, came in force.

The purpose of General Penicillin Committee created as a result of this meeting was to 'increase and accelerate the production of penicillin, to effect the pooling of information, and to ensure that the material produced was put to the best possible use.'[137] It met regularly at the office of the Wellcome Foundation in Euston Road, which was also the headquarters of the TRC. It was later joined by Robert Robinson, Ian Heilbron of Imperial College, and Alan Drury, Director of the Lister Institute. Four more committees were created to cover various aspects of the scheme. With so many committees, according to Clark, 'private enterprise and public policy appeared at times to be inextricably entwined'.[138] What is more, Anglo-

American relations added to the complexity of the interaction. However, amidst the confusion, the MRC played a pivotal role, mediating between private and public interests, in Britain and abroad.

5.   The MRC between private enterprise and public policy

This section focuses on the MRC's crucial role in relation to the production of penicillin in Britain, and to the research on its chemical structure. From the beginning of 1942, it studied problems of production.[139] From 1943 onwards, it also turned its attention to the question of organic synthesis through the Penicillin Synthesis Committee (later followed by the Penicillin Synthesis Publication Committee).[140] It formulated agreements with commercial firms, especially in connection with patents emerging out of the collaborative research which the Council had fostered.[141] Finally, once the international production of penicillin was under way, the MRC dealt with penicillin standardisation.[142]

The MRC advised government on the needs of industry. Early in 1942, problems of supplies were such that it had to intercede in favour of Wellcome for the allocation of material judged indispensable to the production of penicillin. Mellanby's argument was based on his belief in the future importance of the drug:

> [...] all the clinical indications at present go to show that penicillin is likely to be of enormous importance in the treatment of infection, probably of greater importance than the sulphonamide compounds now being used in the treatment of this condition [...] Many of the clinical trials are being held up for want of material because of difficulties of making it in sufficient quantities at present. Here we are in competition with many of the large manufacturing firms in America, and for this reason also we must not hold back, as penicillin was entirely a British medical discovery.[143]

The MRC acted as the representatives of the medical community, and of firms of a 'similar reputation to Wellcome', which deserved special consideration. To convince government, the Council argued that international competition required their intervention. The MRC defended British industrial interests, while assuming a role of moral authority over industry in away that shows continuity with the experience of insulin, described in Chapter 2. ICI initially refused to co-operate with the TRC, and this refusal was seen as a major impediment to progress. Florey wrote to Mellanby:

> It seems to me it is eminently desirable for everyone in this country and the States to collaborate on a substance, which, I think, there is enough evidence to show, would be of very considerable help in the treatment

of all types of sepsis. It would seem to me what is needed in the first instance is to break down the purely commercial outlook such as ICI appear to have.[144]

The attitude of ICI towards the TRC changed when an important contribution to the development of penicillin was made by one of its members. Pope, the biochemist from the WPRL who had been the first industrial visitor to the School of Pathology in 1940, improved the culture medium and the method of extraction, which resulted in higher yields. The information was pooled into the TRC, and the provisional specifications of the process (i.e. the first step towards a patent) were handed over to the MRC.

ICI's commercial interests then motivated the firm into joining 'the ring'.[145] Such a change of heart may also have been eased by the creation of a pharmaceutical selling company within ICI. Although the chemical group was without a Pharmaceutical Division until 1944, it set up a selling company (ICP) in 1942 to manage sales of sulphonamides and other drugs, and this, probably helped it to identify with the outlook of the TRC.[146] Having been drawn into the pool, weekly production rates increased from 5 to 6 million units, which were made freely available to the MRC as well as to Florey for the clinical trials.[147]

On the other hand, Kemball Bishop still had no intention of joining the collaboration. They had been applying the information supplied to them directly by Florey and were making steady progress with their production (which reached 6.3 million units per week in March 1943). They preferred to remain out of the ring in order to safeguard their trade secret concerning the use of citrates in the process.[148] Nevertheless, through their close contact with Florey, they still hoped to benefit from the information circulated among academic circles.

The MRC proved invaluable in helping Florey to further his goals. However, there was a price to pay for turning to outside help. Florey viewed the MRC's Clinical Trials Committee with considerable suspicion.[149] It competed with the new set of clinical trials, which he was planning with the penicillin produced at Oxford, and threatened to divert the additional supplies promised by ICI. It was essential for Florey, if he was to ensure the successful transfer of penicillin from the laboratory to the public domain, that he should continue to oversee its development. It was also important for the survival of his team. The increasing involvement of external collaborations and the growing publicity surrounding Fleming's role in the discovery of penicillin threatened to divert funding away from his group at Oxford.[150]

Therefore, Florey made arrangements to take part in clinical trials in North Africa, which involved him personally, in co-ordination rather than in competition with the MRC trials.[151] Thus, war would be Florey's ultimate theatre of proof.

6. Penicillin and the theatre of war

The 1943 field trials enabled Florey to attract and retain a large amount of the penicillin produced in Britain and in the United States. Between the end of March and June 1943, 42 million units produced by ICI were sent directly to Florey (which was roughly the whole of their production over a two-month period); the Americans, anxious to use their penicillin installations at full capacity in order to satisfy the commercial interests concerned, were now prepared to commit supplies of the drug to Florey.[152] About two thirds of the total British production was sent to the Army, an additional small amount was sent to the RAF and the Navy; the rest of the British production was distributed by the Penicillin Clinical Trials Committee to three hospitals in the London area.[153]

Florey did not go to the battlefield unprepared. He devised and then rehearsed a method for the treatment of wounds using penicillin in local military hospitals, even before being sent to the front. Among the first British servicemen to receive penicillin were the RAF fighter pilots treated at the Princess Mary Royal's Hospital in Holton, near Oxford. This, and the use of penicillin at the 101st General Hospital of the RAMC in Oxford, enabled Florey to build contacts with military surgeons.[154] He perfected novel surgical techniques that were compatible with the small amounts of penicillin initially available. Thus, he recommended closing wounds, instead of leaving them open as was customary among military surgeons, and applied the drug locally, through tubes inserted into the wound.

Along with his wife Ethel who took part in this trial of around 200 servicemen, two colleagues helped Florey to convince the military of the benefits of penicillin associated with this novel technique: Hugh Cairns and Ian Fraser. Cairns, an old friend and colleague of Florey's who was to join him in North Africa, ran a Military Hospital for Head Injuries at the Radcliffe Infirmary. Ian Fraser, before being put in charge of a small research unit to investigate the use of penicillin on the battlefield, spent two weeks in Oxford to become acquainted with the substance and the technique.[155] When the research unit could be set up, the invasion of Sicily had begun, and it was transferred to Salerno.

At first, penicillin and the sulphonamides were used complementarily, or even sometimes combined. Florey objected to this practice, which made it impossible to compare penicillin with the sulphonamides. The merits of penicillin were not in themselves obvious, and the military needed to be won over to it. Bickel has quoted a report from the RAMC files that read:

> There is no doubt that even after viewing the wonderful results that penicillin can achieve, most surgeons and most administrators, if forced to choose between penicillin and the sulphonamides, would say: "Give us sulphonamides every day".[156]

However, the appearance of a sulphonamide-resistant strain of gonococcus in a North African military hospital provided what Florey had hoped for, the opportunity to prove the superiority of penicillin over sulphanilamide as a non-specific, systemic chemotherapeutic agent.[157]

By 1944, a special issue of the *British Journal of Surgery* advocated the use of penicillin not only in the treatment of war wounds, but also as 'the most effective and least harmful agent yet discovered, both as a systemically-administered drug and as a local antiseptic'.[158] There is little doubt that Florey's personal involvement had helped to convince military surgeons of the usefulness of the substance.

Florey displayed great talent as a scientist-entrepreneur by convincing the medical community of the superiority of penicillin.[159] He exploited the wartime context, which provided a focus for his research, and enabled him to mobilize government and industry. However, peacetime presented a very different challenge for both Florey and penicillin, and this transition, from war to peace, is studied next.

D. PENICILLIN FROM WAR TO PEACE

Chemists discovered that the strain of penicillin used in Britain had a different structure to the strain used in the United States. These different strains, and the different methods of production, were suited to different contexts. British penicillin was eventually abandoned in favour of the American strain because of a changing rationale for penicillin production.

1. Different penicillins for different contexts

Penicillin's identity changed when the context for its use changed. *P. notatum* (Penicillin I in Britain, or F in the U.S.) did best in surface culture. It was the dominant strain in Britain, where it was produced in sufficient quantities for clinical trials and war. By the end of 1943, Glaxo, for instance, claimed to be able to produce it at a rate of 20–50 million units per week as shown in Table 3.2.

Trevan explained the stages:

Table 3.2 Expected Production (in millions of units per Week)

End 1943	Future in stages		
	A	B	C
Glaxo 20-50	100	500	2000
Belmont (Wellcome) 3.5	50	200	2000
Beckenham (only plans so far)			

Source: PRO FD1 6834: Trevan to MRC (Nov. 1943).

The production expected labelled A should eventuate in a month or two. B in 6 months, perhaps less; C depends on the degree of drive the government department can get behind it.[160]

Although production levels were still erratic, the TRC estimated that in the later stages of war it would reach billions.[161] If these estimates were correct, then Glaxo were reaching a level that was comparable to Squibb, who were producing 25 million units per week at about the same time.[162] On the other hand, if these figures were inflated, as the conflicting evidence might suggest, then they revealed a great deal of optimism and self-confidence, not unlike that of their American counterparts.[163] This indicates that dynamism and entrepreneurship were not lacking on the part of the British pharmaceutical industry, at least from 1943 onwards, when several other British firms were also meeting the challenge of penicillin.[164] Contrary to what is often believed, Britain manufactured enough penicillin using surface culture to satisfy British military needs for the Sicilian campaign in July 1943, and to provide limited allocations to the MoH for hospitals.[165]

P. chrysogenum (Penicillin II in Britain, or G in the U.S.), on the other hand, did best in deep-fermentation tanks. Although developed early in the war, the deep-fermentation method became predominant in America only in 1944, in preparation for mass distribution to the civilian population.[166] For the purpose of clinical trials and the treatment of battle casualties, surface culture had offered a satisfactory method of production. It was the extension on a larger scale of a method that had been tried and tested in the laboratory, and did not carry the same risk of contamination as submerged culture. The first American penicillin produced by Merck and Squibb had been intended for clinical research, and was done in shallow layers. Both companies had banked on the early synthesis of the drug, and were therefore late in changing their production from surface to submerged culture.[167] Even Pfizer, who had the necessary expertise for deep fermentation, continued to produce penicillin using surface culture until 1943, when they produced it both by surface and by submerged culture, until finally switching over to deep fermentation in 1944.[168] Their factory, set up near Brooklyn, was the first commercial plant to manufacture penicillin by submerged culture on a large scale. As a result, their output rose sharply from just under 7 billion Oxford units in 1943, to over 700 billion in 1944.[169] Today one of the largest pharmaceutical firms in the world, its success can largely be traced back to these developments.[170]

However, even in 1944, when the success of deep fermentation seemed assured, Coghill recommended:

While the production of penicillin in surface culture will eventually be superseded by the deep tank method, this report is confined to the former method for several reasons. In the first place, it is the only sure method for those who have not had very extensive experience in the operation of vat fermenters under absolute pure culture conditions. In the second place, it is possible to begin modest commercial operations with a minimum of equipment, expense, and time. Therefore it is recommended that those new to the venture begin their operation in surface culture while they experiment, if they desire, with the operation of vats.[171]

The consensus achieved under pressure from the U.S. government was that, 'although the synthesis may be accomplished at any time, such an event could not be relied on and the only possible course for war purposes was to develop the known methods of production'.[172] Consequently, as Pfizer and others were converting to the mass production of penicillin by submerged culture, the American War Production Board asked the mushroom company Wyeth to maintain surface growth to guarantee a steady supply of the drug.[173] The large-scale destruction of *Penicillium* through contamination in early attempts at deep fermentation posed a risk, reduced once sterile conditions were introduced but, more importantly, deemed worthwhile only once the distribution to the civilian population was anticipated in the later stages of war.

2. From surface culture to submerged culture

In June 1943, Joshua Burn (MRC liaison officer in the United States) wrote to Mellanby from Washington contrasting 'the attitude about penicillin production at home with that here. At home everyone assumes that penicillin will not be available for the general public for a long time'.[174] A few weeks later, a telegram was sent to Florey in North Africa notifying him that American production of penicillin was being stepped up in preparation for eventual peace.

By contrast, British wartime rationale, shaped by shortages, reliance on American supplies, and full employment policies, appeared more deeply ingrained.[175] Furthermore, the resistance to technological change was even greater in Britain than in the United States. The laboratory skills related to penicillin production had been developed since Fleming's discovery in 1928 and through the 1930s. The substance had first been produced in academic laboratories, in Oxford, London, and Edinburgh.[176] The technology was successfully transferred from the laboratory to the factory thanks to close contacts between academic experts and companies. When British pharmaceutical firms became involved in 1942, large-scale surface culture was the logical step up from this laboratory production. It also provided continuity with a strong tradition in industrial bacteriology, in contrast with the agricultural and food industries, which had a greater influence over the early development of American penicillin.[177] Rather than being the victims of failure, could the British have been the victims of their success in developing penicillin?

Without abundant supplies of the agricultural by-products necessary for deep fermentation (in particular corn steep liquor), the British pharmaceutical industry may also have relied more heavily on achieving the synthetic alternative to the biological production of penicillin. The commitment to the synthetic paradigm, and its effects on ICI, are studied in the next section.

3. ICI and the synthetic paradigm

ICI were contacted by the Ministry of Supply (MoS) in 1942, and asked to begin working on the manufacture of penicillin at their main dyestuffs factory. The penicillin plant created at Trafford Park thus became an 'agency factory'.[178] At first, penicillin was produced by surface culture in glass bottles. Later on, in 1944, these were replaced by trays.[179] However, as early as 1942, ICI had also begun experimenting with deep-fermentation methods in their biological research laboratories at Blackley.[180]

In 1943, the chemical and biological teams working on penicillin were transferred from Blackley to Trafford Park. They were installed in new laboratories, in order to bring penicillin research closer to the problems of production, in what was to become the Fermentation Department of the Pharmaceutical Division.[181] Their contacts with Florey and his team gave them confidence in their ability to succeed with their research.[182] However, their belief in the eventual production of penicillin by synthetic means, coupled with their lack of expertise in fermentation methods, hampered their progress.

On the one hand, ICI actively pursued research on the synthesis of penicillin in collaboration with Robinson (who was one of their long-standing consultants) and other members of the Penicillin Synthesis Committee. On the other, mechanical breakdown and contamination plagued their early attempts at submerged culture. Unlike American manufacturers, who had been carrying out this type of work for twenty years, British chemical engineers were relatively inexperienced at handling such problems, and this led to delays.[183]

Nevertheless, as the end of the conflict drew near, economic considerations and criteria for meeting the U.S. 'standard' of production forced ICI to replace their existing surface culture plant with facilities for the deep fermentation of penicillin.[184] The switch to deep fermentation answered short-term, commercial imperatives, but went against the grain of ICI's synthetic paradigm. ICI's objective remained the development of 'a good antibiotic which could be prepared synthetically (even an antibiotic which was toxic might be of value if a non-toxic related compound could be derived from it)'.[185] Such was the strength of this paradigm, according to an ICI employee who wrote many years after the event, that it weakened ICI's commitment to submerged culture at this time.[186] This interpretation is confirmed by the archives. Reports on the experimental work with deep fermentation ceased after April 1944, and did not start again until the end of 1945, suggesting that ICI's efforts in the field were interrupted for a crucial eighteen-month period, when by contrast most firms in the United States, and several in Britain, such as Glaxo, turned towards deep-fermentation methods to mass produce penicillin for the civilian population.

The decision to switch over to submerged culture was therefore taken after some hesitations, which would cause the group to fall behind its competitors. In October 1945, the advantages of surface culture were weighed up against those of deep fermentation. Although in good conditions the rate of production by surface culture was higher, deep fermentation made it possible to produce crystalline penicillin at a cheaper price:

> If crystalline penicillin becomes available at a cheap price, it will soon dominate clinical practice because it can be used in much the same way as any other pure drug. It is safe to say, therefore, that in a few years' time there will be little or no market for surface culture penicillin unless it can be produced at a very cheap price, and there seems little likelihood that surface culture will, in fact, be cheaper to operate than deep culture.[187]

The authors therefore concluded that: 'The need for high potency clinical penicillin increases makes it almost imperative to use deep fermentation.'

The switch to submerged culture finally took place in 1947, when the Pharmaceutical Division gained control of Trafford Park. Even so, ICI maintained surface culture for experimental purposes, in the 'pursuit of fundamental knowledge' on substances such as streptothrycin, streptomycin, aspergillin, polyporin and helvolic acid. Moreover, when a decision had to be made whether or not to buy a U.S. licence to use submerged methods of production, it seemed likely that British firms making penicillin under licence would have to pay royalties to American companies, which was becoming a serious diplomatic issue between the two governments. Hence ICI decided to build on the experience they had acquired during the wartime experimental phase, and develop deep fermentation methods on their own, thus maintaining the special place they had gained in relation to government.[188] In addition, ICI's freedom to enter into licensing arrangements with other firms, such as Squibb, was restricted by their Patents and Process Agreement with the U.S. group Du Pont de Nemours, which was signed in 1929, lasted until 1949, thus leading to further delays.[189]

The case of ICI illustrates the importance of scientific paradigms, of networks of academic collaborators, and of relations with government and between firms, in innovation. ICI, who were strongly committed to the synthetic paradigm, retained the surface culture of penicillin until 1947, even though they had begun experimenting with deep fermentation as early as 1942. Long after ICI had changed over to submerged culture, the Fermentation Products Department at Trafford Park continued to represent a unique part of the company's activities, in that 'chemicals were produced there by the use of living organisms rather than the more conventional chemical syntheses', and penicillin remained its principal product, a legacy of wartime activities.[190] By contrast, Glaxo, whose background was not in synthetic chemistry, and whose research culture was different to that of ICI, decided to buy the rights to the submerged process directly from Merck, thus making huge strides with penicillin production and soon overtaking their competitors.[191] This manufacturing prowess would help to lay the foundations of their post-war development.[192]

4. Towards penicillin synthesis

The production of penicillin by synthetic means was predicted by companies like Merck and ICI, academic scientists, and government officials on both sides of the Atlantic. Research to uncover its structure began as early as 1942, in order to gain a head-start over Germany, whose mighty chemical industry loomed large over the Allies. However, to carry out the chemical manipulations required to discover the structure of penicillin, it was necessary to have enough material.

In the early stages the Oxford group had an advantage over their American colleagues. Heatley wrote to Florey from the Merck research laboratories at Rahway on 16 January 1942:

> Meyer seems to have done some fine work, and with a small amount more of material he should get the structure. That is why in some ways I think it would be unfair to send the information to you; you have the penicillin on hand, and you could cut in and probably do the finishing touches in a short while, whereas he is held up by lack of material. Actually he has done all his work with far less material than has been available to the Oxford chemists. Possibly it would be a fair arrangement if anyone getting the structure of penicillin with Meyer's data, [...] which he is not allowed to publish, [...] was to make a very frank acknowledgement of his work. Maybe you would prefer not to be told of his work, so that there will be no recriminations should you get the structure first [...] On the other hand, if the information is to be made available to commercial firms here, and it certainly will be, I think you should have it too.[193]

Abundance of material for research and familiarity with the substance worked in favour of the British contingent at the beginning of the project. However, by 1944, the situation was reversed: thanks to deep-fermentation methods, the Americans had large quantities of material both for therapeutic use, and for chemical study.

The lure of penicillin synthesis cemented the relationship between the Oxford group and ICI. Florey agreed to work on the chemical structure with ICI on condition that they supply his team with material, and together they formed a powerful alliance.[194] Chain and Abraham were joined by Wilson Baker and Robinson himself at the beginning of 1943, and almost immediately by Heilbron and his group at Imperial College.

The Oxford team's data suggested that the synthesis of penicillin was feasible. As researchers were on the brink of uncovering the structure of penicillin in 1943, Robinson requested that the exchange of information should be formalized. He recommended the creation of a committee under the aegis of the MRC, stressing the urgency of the situation.[195] His call was heard, and the next day the Penicillin Synthesis Committee was formed with the agreement of Chain and Heilbron.

An important concern of the committee was the question of the assignment of patents to the MRC. For this, the model of the OSRD (to which U.S. firms were expected to hand over patent rights) was considered.[196] A few days later, at a meeting of the TRC, it was suggested that a national trustee be set up, to whom patents taken out by the MRC and academic workers might be assigned.[197] However, the idea did not become reality until the creation of the National Research and Development Corporation (NRDC) in 1948 (see Chapter 6). Meanwhile, the question of patents remained a source of tension, leading the MRC to issue specific conditions under which it would collaborate with manufacturing firms.[198]

Following a ban on the publication of the chemical work, American chemists worked independently of the British until May 1944. Nevertheless, information circulated between the two groups led to a formal agreement to exchange data between the Penicillin Synthesis Committee of the MRC and the CMR. Before long it became clear that industrial interests could not be excluded from the collaboration. In Britain, representatives from industry sat on meetings of the Committee. They were described as 'gate-crashers' by Robinson, who saw them as outsiders and potential competitors.[199] They were W. Bradley (from BDH), D.A. Peak (from Boots), G. Newberry (from May & Baker) and Dr Carrington (from ICI). After initially objecting to their presence, Robinson changed his mind and argued that 'the four gentlemen' were all active in research and had submitted programmes of considerable merit. They were welcomed to the meetings, and once more the MRC provided a link between academic and industrial researchers in Britain and in the United States.

Unlike the co-operation that characterized the production programme, the project to unravel the chemistry of penicillin led to intense competition between academic researchers and industrialists. The chemical project was dominated by academic scientists, and a peace time rationale which accentuated scientific rivalries. These were aggravated by the fact that British scientists feared losing the science of penicillin to American industrialists, who dominated the situation there.[200]

The openness of British industrialists was in stark contrast to the scientists' reserve:

The industrial representatives declared their willingness to lay all their information on the table; the attitude of the Oxford workers was less clear. Florey and Wilson Baker, speaking for themselves and for Robinson, said that they would report 'any significant advances' to the Committee. The impression left was that they (particularly the chemists) would be unwilling to discuss work which was projected or even still in progress.[201]

Tensions arose between academic scientists and industrial researchers concerning the publication of results: whereas the latter were keen to publish, the former were reluctant to do so in view of the ban on publication imposed on Americans, which prevented a reciprocal exchange.[202] Eventually, Robinson's position softened, and he gave permission to ICI to publish their results, with the remark that so much had already been published.[203] However, the end of the war spelled the end of the co-operative venture, and publications were held up until a collaborative monograph on the chemistry of penicillin was produced.[204]

By the end of 1945, the chemical structure of penicillin was known, the beta-lactam ring structure proposed by the Oxford team having been confirmed by X-ray analysis by Dorothy Hodgkin, but a practical method of synthesis had not yet been developed. In 1946, the TRC firms lost interest in the question. By then, they were busy changing their surface plants into submerged culture installations, turning to American companies for apparatus and expertise. A decade later, the synthesis of penicillin was finally achieved, leading to the development of a new class of antibiotics, the semi-synthetic penicillins, but the production of penicillin by biological means was never superseded.[205]

With the end of the war, formal collaborations were dismantled, although at an informal level many of the links survived, such as that between Florey and ICI. A symbol of these loosening ties, penicillin underwent yet another transformation: it became a pure scientific fact. The next section describes this transformation.

5. Penicillin from applied to pure science

Fleming, Florey and Chain were awarded the Nobel Prize for medicine in 1946. In his Nobel lecture, Chain wrote that, out of this applied project, came an answer to 'one of the major problems in biochemistry', that is to say 'the nature of chemical linkages, by which naturally occurring peptides acquire their specific and often very pronounced biological properties', in this case the bacteriolytic action of penicillin.[206] Many years later, he wrote: 'the possibility that penicillin could have practical use in clinical medicine did not enter our minds when we started our work'.[207] This transformation, from an applied project to a pure scientific fact, was therefore gradual.

Florey's penicillin project stemmed from a conviction that substances produced by nature were akin to the substances produced by the body which play an active role in immunity, and consequently were better able to combat disease than the products of synthetic chemistry.[208] The link between the pure and applied aspects was apparent in early applications for funding, but was omitted from later accounts. When Florey contacted the Rockefeller Foundation in the hope of obtaining support for the penicillin project, he added in a covering letter: 'It may also be pointed out that the work proposed, in addition to its theoretical importance, may have practical value for therapeutic purposes'.[209] In the 1940 article in *the Lancet*, much vaguer terms were used, which glossed over the connection between pure and applied:

> Following the work on lysozyme in this laboratory it occurred to two of us (E.C. and H.W.F.) that it would be profitable to conduct a systematic investigation of the chemical and biological properties of the antibacterial substances produced by bacteria and moulds. This investigation was begun with a study of the substance with promising antibacterial properties, produced by a mould and described by Fleming (1929). The present preliminary report is the result of a co-operative investigation on the chemical, pharmacological and chemotherapeutic properties of this substance.[210]

After the war, their objective achieved, the importance of the applied aspect of the penicillin project was altogether denied by Florey and his collaborators.[211]

The construction of penicillin as a pure scientific fact was related to Florey's long-term research programme in experimental pathology. His brief, when moving to Oxford, had been to rejuvenate a moribund department through the experimental method. He brought a scientific approach to medicine by studying substances with practical applications, both because these applications attracted funding, and because they served as investigative tools of basic biological mechanisms.[212] Thus, at the end of the project, penicillin could be returned to the laboratory without reference to its applications. As well as an instrument of mass medical care and post-war reconstruction, it became an important tool for the study of bacterial metabolism.[213] Its messy origins, between immunotherapy and chemotherapy, and between the laboratory and the factory, were obscured, leaving an account in which the two domains, of science and industry, were separated by clear boundaries, and had distinct roles to play in drug development.[214]

For the School of Pathology to continue to fulfill this distinct role, defined in relation to basic research, a grant of £50,000 was made by Lord Nuffield to pay for the salaries of three members of his team, Abraham, Heatley and Sanders, who became 'penicillin fellows' at Lincoln College.[215] The grant ensured the survival of Florey's team beyond the war. Other than Chain who left for the Istituto Superiore di Sanità in 1948, disillusioned with Oxford, but also attracted to Rome by Daniel Bovet and Filomena Nitti whom he had met at an international congress in Liège in 1945,[216] they would remain together for thirty years. For Florey and his team, penicillin had more than fulfilled its promise. They not only found the long-term security Florey had been hoping for at the start of the penicillin project, ensuring a continuous flow of funding from a variety of British and American public and private sources,[217] but they built on the knowledge and expertise developed in connection with penicillin, and went on to develop a new antibiotic, cephalosporin C, which unlike penicillin was patented, and helped to bring prosperity to Oxford University in the second half of the twentieth century (see Chapter 6).

E. CONCLUSION

In the process of developing penicillin, both science and industry, and the relationship between the two, had changed. The one-to-one relationship that had been predominant before the war was replaced by a triangular relationship with government. Although British companies were criticized for being less co-operative than their American counterparts, Liebenau has observed that British co-operation was different from the U.S., where state control was much stronger. Despite persisting disagreements between British companies, he has argued that the British attained a 'high degree of co-operation'.[218] This study has shown that British pharmaceutical firms were lacking, neither in entrepreneurship, nor in co-operative spirit. Although different in character, and resting on different organisational structures, the co-operation of British industry was as great as that of its American counterpart, and the evidence provided by this chapter fully supports this view.

As to the MRC, rather than acting from suspicion, it adopted a role of mediator, between public and private interests, and between scientific and industrial expertise. This role was possible because of the co-operative tradition that had become established before the war. War had introduced elements of formality and hierarchy through the collaboration between the MRC and TRC as official representatives of research institutions and pharmaceutical companies. It created a precedent that had important implications for the relationship between scientists and pharmaceutical companies in the post-war period.

Penicillin was a model 'experiment in collaboration' that would be referred to many times afterwards. However, it was itself constructed from previous knowledge and experience, gradually accumulated between the wars.

4 Collaboration and Resistance
Developing Penicillin and the Synthetic Anti-Histamines in France

A. INTRODUCTION

The threat of invasion and aerial bombings disrupted British society, causing the dispersal of staff and equipment of government departments, and of cultural and scientific institutions.[1] However, according to Marwick's four-tiered model, in which war affects society: 1) by its destructive aspects; 2) by the test it provides of a society's structures; 3) by its encouragement to participate in the war effort; and 4) by its psychological impact, the disruption to French society was greater still.[2]

Thus, France's centralized structure was shattered by the German invasion. It no longer had one capital, Paris, but several, in the South with Vichy, and abroad with Algiers and New York, where many intellectuals sought refuge from Nazi Occupation.[3] Defeat and occupation were interpreted as a sign of the failure of the French political system, and the authoritarian Regime of Vichy arose partly in reaction against the Third Republic that had led the country into war. Unlike in Britain, where the encouragement to participate in the war effort was sustained without interruption between 1939 and 1945, in France, between the periods of mobilization and the Liberation, participation was subjugated to the German war effort. Although the psychological impact of World War Two was considerable in both countries, the experience of crushing military defeat and humiliating foreign occupation made it more traumatic in France.

War provided France, more than Britain, with an opportunity for a break with the past and for radical change. In this chapter, I argue that the disruptions caused by the conflict presented French research institutions and pharmaceutical companies with a chance to reorganize and form new alliances that would contribute to the reconstruction of French science and industry once the war was over.[4] Indeed, they stimulated the movement for reform at the Pasteur Institute, and led Rhône-Poulenc to increase its commitment to pharmaceutical R&D. The Pasteur Institute and Rhône-Poulenc both lost touch with their subsidiaries: overseas Pasteur Institutes were cut off from the *maison-mère* in Paris; May & Baker lost contact with, and became independent of Rhône-Poulenc.[5] At the same time, the

collaborative relationship between Fourneau's laboratory and Rhône-Poulenc became looser, reflecting the growing difficulty in maintaining normal
channels of communication. Once the war was over, these loosened ties
never fully regained their former character or strength. However, in the
meantime new ties had been formed these would have lasting impact on
medical science and medical industry in the second half of the twentieth
century.

Despite such disruptions, this chapter also highlights continuities in the
French experience. Until Robert Paxton's book on Vichy France, Vichy had
been presented as little more than a parenthesis in French history.[6] Since
then, several authors have shown how the Regime constituted an active
project to reform French society by dismantling the causes of the collapse
of 1940, and paved the way for the post-war reconstruction of the country.[7]
Thus, Jean-François Picard has argued that it took the authoritarianism of
Vichy to resolve the opposition between social and liberal medicine that had
prevented the development of a workable health policy in France between
the wars.[8] This was achieved by a series of measures taken in 1940–1: the
creation of the Ordre National des Médecins (replacing the doctors' professional organization outlawed by Vichy) in October 1940, followed by the
founding of the Ministry of Health in August 1941; the establishment of
a new law governing the practice of pharmacy in September; the creation
of the Institut National d'Hygiène in November; and finally the passing of
a law creating a modern statute for hospitals in December.[9] While these
measures stemmed from a desire to control the professions and regulate
the economy, they also resulted from a need to ensure the good health of
the public against a background of food shortages, the sale of black-market
drugs, and the export of medicines outside France.[10]

By focusing on the relationship between science and industry that was
central to mobilization, Vichy, and reconstruction,[11] I not only recog-
nize the legacies of the wartime period, I also emphasize the continuities
between the 1930s and 1940s. I show how pre-war projects were pursued
under the difficult circumstances of German Occupation, but also how
new skills and practices, which contributed to the renewal of French science and industry after the war, were learnt.[12] Thus, in association with the
Pasteur Institute, Rhône-Poulenc developed a small, semi-clandestine production of penicillin, which was destined for the Leclerc division and was
stepped up in 1944. The production of antibiotics remained as a legacy of
the firm's role at the time of the Liberation. Like British penicillin, French
penicillin acquired a symbolic value, first as a weapon of the Resistance
and later of the Liberation, helping to place France in the winning camp
at the end of the war. However, the synthetic anti-histamines, rather than
penicillin, represent a genuine French wartime development. Although the
continuation of a research project begun in Fourneau's laboratory, they
were developed independently by the company under the watchful eye of

IG Farben, and therefore unlike penicillin were tainted by suspicion of collaboration with the Occupant.[13]

In his obituary notice of Fourneau, Marcel Delépine stressed the fact that anti-histamines were a French discovery in which industry had played a major part, at a time of severe hardship:

> We would not wish for it to be forgotten that, although the concept of anti-histamine has spread all over the world, it originated in France, and its birth place was the laboratory of Fourneau at the Pasteur Institute; its first steps were guided by Bovet, Miss Staub, Halpern and their collaborators; its first practical applications emerged from the factories of the Rhône-Poulenc company, in the harshest phases of the German Occupation.[14]

Before turning to synthetic anti-histamines as an example of French wartime innovation, I will first describe the conditions under which this research was accomplished, beginning with the Pasteur Institute.

B. THE PASTEUR INSTITUTE DURING THE WAR: FROM COLLABORATION WITH INDUSTRY TO COLLABORATION WITH GERMANY?

The Pasteur Institute, like the capital, was to some extent isolated from the rest of the country. Passage between the northern Occupied Zone and the southern Free Zone remained restricted until 1943.[15] Like the rest of French science, research at the Pasteur Institute was focused on applications, with the production of vaccines and sera being given top priority, and suffered from shortages of raw materials and controls imposed by the Vichy government, exacerbating the effect of demands made by German authorities.

1. The winds of war: from mobilization, to defeat, and Occupation

The financial situation of the Pasteur had been very healthy on the eve of World War Two. As a result of the Spanish Civil War and increased orders from the French government, which had passed a new set of laws on the compulsory vaccination of sections of the population in 1938 and 1939, exceptionally high sales of vaccines enabled the Institute to draw in large profits.[16] War was good for the Institute's business. Its participation in the National Defence scheme required that it stepped up production, and much of its resources were directed towards Garches, where, as well as Ramon's Serumtherapy department, the toxin department and later the vaccine department were relocated. Because of the need to rationalize production for maximum efficiency, a clear separation between research and production appeared for the first time in the history of the Institute, an experience that would influence the course of later reforms under the directorship of Jacques Monod.

The Pasteur's links with the military intensified when the research department of the Ministère de l'Armement was placed in the Institute. In April 1940, a new research laboratory was built at Garches to study wartime surgery.[17] However, in May, a research station in Angers was opened to accommodate some of the Institute's laboratories, which relocated there as the German troops advanced towards Paris. The Hôpital Pasteur was moved to Rambouillet. Anarchy spread through the Institute. The effects of the German advance were compounded by the fact that many of the reforms advocated in the 1937 report had not been implemented (see Chapter 1). There were still no inventories, no archives, and no personnel lists. Different departments continued to have separate accounts, for instance Salembeni's vaccine department had its own budget and bank account; Labpasteur (for veterinary products) and Serpasteur (for human products), which should have merged, continued to function as separate commercial ventures.

The anarchy of the Institute reflected the state of disarray into which the country was plunged in the spring of 1940. René Martin, the Director of the Hôpital Pasteur, was later criticized by members of the Council for being the first to abandon his post when the Germans arrived in Paris.[18] The Institute therefore elected Ramon, whose tight control over Garches had created an impression of strong leadership, to be its new Director in May 1940.[19] His election reflected the growing importance of the manufacturing role of the Institute, but also its wish for reform. With the signing of the armistice, and with the establishment of the Vichy Regime, the opportunity to implement the reforms advocated by Pasteur Vallery-Radot and others before the war seemed, at last, to have arrived.

2. The winds of reform

However, like the rest of the country, the Institute became divided. In October 1940 Alfred Lacroix, President of the Conseil d'Administration, resigned, and was replaced by Pasteur Vallery-Radot. Two months later, Ramon himself resigned, claiming that his administrative responsibilities were incompatible with his work at Garches and that the distance between Garches and Paris prevented him from effectively combining the two.[20] In fact, his six months in office had been punctuated by a series of devastating reports on the state of physical and moral dereliction of the Institute and by violent arguments with his colleagues.[21] With the backing of Pasteur Vallery-Radot, Jacques Tréfouël was appointed in his place, in the hope that he would be more conciliatory in his relations with the Council and uncompromising in his relations with the German authorities. Furthermore, it was hoped that he would implement the long-awaited reforms.

The time was ripe for such measures to be taken, and the first consisted in the creation of a strict administrative hierarchy, in January 1941. Although the 1937 report had emanated from a group identified with the left and later with the Resistance movement, these reforms also coincided with a Petainist view of efficiency, using the professions to establish a new social order.[22] Researchers were no longer to interact directly with the Director, but via their 'chefs de service' (heads of department).[23] This was intended to ensure the efficient running of the Institute, and to open the way for further changes. The hierarchy was reinforced by a new salary scale for the scientific and administrative staff: from the 'chef de service de première classe' earning 75,000 FF, to the 'assistant de troisième classe' earning half as much; and from the Directeur earning 100,000 FF, to the Secrétaire Général (a new post created to facilitate links with the outside, in particular with the Ministry of Hygiene, and filled by Dujarric de la Rivière) earning 72,000 FF.[24]

At the same time, the Conseil Scientifique was reinstated. Its purpose was to ensure smooth communication between researchers, the Conseil d'Administration and the Director.[25] Departments were merged, reducing them to five, so that investigations pertaining to related disciplines could be better co-ordinated. Thus, immunology was grouped under the direction of Ramon; chemistry under Fourneau. As a result of the merger of the chemistry sections, Fourneau was admitted into the Assembly for the first time as a new member in 1941, at the age of sixty-nine.

War, therefore, but even more so Occupation, provided an opportunity for transforming old departments and for creating new ones in response to scientific advances. However, the rationale for reform was not only scientific, it was also economic. The Conseil d'Administration was aware that the financial health of the Institute, that is to say the success of its commercial ventures, depended on the strength of its scientific reputation.[26]

For this, the Council stressed the need to increase co-operation between different departments. Such co-operation would not only be beneficial to the Institute's research, it would also help the reforms. However, the amount of real control the new administration acquired over individual researchers is questionable. Nitti, for example, began working on penicillin in 1942, in collaboration with Rhône-Poulenc, without any knowledge or interference from his superiors, retaining an independence that was reminiscent of the 'old ways'.

As conditions changed under German Occupation and the demand for Pasteur products declined (not only vaccines and sera, but also products from Lemoigne's Fermentation department),[27] fears arose concerning the survival of the Institute. These were fuelled by new laws passed by Vichy on 11 July 1941 that allowed the dissolution of associations whose activities were judged contrary to the nation's interest. In view of such threats, Pasteur Vallery-Radot requested a permanent pass to meet public health authorities in the South ('afin d'assurer une présence continuelle de l'IP dans la Zone non-occupée'), and seems to have made use of this to become involved in the Resistance.[28]

The Institute faced added pressures when IG Farben sent one of their representatives to negotiate with the Director in June 1941. His requests were listed in the Minutes. The IP was asked 1) to deliver vaccines and sera in bulk for the benefit of IG; 2) to collaborate on all biological questions, including the standardisation of vaccines and sera, and reciprocal price agreements; 3) to make available additional supplies for export towards external (i.e. German) markets, and in case of epidemics. The Institute was even asked to collaborate on research concerning the potato! Fears of becoming a mere production annex of IG Farben were expressed. These were not unfounded, for a similar fate had befallen the Pasteur Institute of Lemberg in Poland.[29]

Tréfouël's reply to these demands was non-committal. The Institute was ready to place all vaccines and sera at the disposal of the German government, but other requests would have to be dealt with by the French government.[30] However, in time, Tréfouël would come to play a double game with the German authorities, helping to conceal stocks of medicines and other supplies on behalf of the medical service of the Resistance, which had been set up by Pasteur Vallery-Radot, in the basement of Institute.[31]

3. From Occupation to Liberation

On 29 May 1942, the IG representative returned, acknowledging the legitimacy of the Institute's reservations. Plans to collaborate on vaccines proceeded nonetheless. In 1942, a new department was created for the production of a typhus vaccine developed by Paul Giroud. While it was still at an experimental stage, the Council decided that the Institute should supply the vaccine free of charge until it was definitively and regularly adopted.[32] In December, a special plant was completed at Laroche-Beaulieu in the Dordogne for its production. It was to be linked with a complex network of SS and other German medical organisations, which included using concentration camps as some of their testing stations, although it is not clear how much of this was known to the Pasteur's researchers at the time.

The financial balance of the Institute remained positive despite an apparent drop in production of diphtheria antitoxin.[33] Nitti, as the chief bacteriologist helping with the production of vaccines and sera at Garches, was assigned the task of righting the situation, assisted by Noël Rist.[34] In order to improve the efficiency of production methods, a small number of horses were brought to Paris for experiments, and the Council had to reassure Ramon that the numbers were too small for the Institute to compete with Garches and threaten its monopoly on production.[35]

During Occupation, priority was given to vaccines and sera for preventive purposes. However, in May 1944, a change of policy occurred. The production of therapeutic sera and antitoxins was stepped up as war drew near and preparations were being made for mounting numbers of casualties.[36] As the end of conflict came within sight, the sensitive question of the profits made out of the war was raised by the Council. It cited the fact that supplies had been sold to the Assistance Publique and the Army at prices below the production costs as proof of the disinterested nature of the Institute's business.[37] In the context of a future change of regime, it also felt that the Institute's privileged status, benefiting from dispensations from various taxes on commercial transactions, should be clarified.

Months later, after Paris had been liberated and the Provisional Government installed, the Institute was caught up in the wave of trials of collaborators. With Pasteur Vallery-Radot, who since September 1944 was back as President of the Council after a short spell as General Secretary for Health, and Tréfouël overseeing the proceedings, a Comité d'Epuration headed by Nitti started drawing up the cases against members of the Pasteur Institute. Emmanuel Leclainche, who had replaced Pasteur Vallery-Radot as President of the Council when he was driven underground by his involvement with the Resistance in 1943, was blamed for holding secret meetings with the German authorities, in a way that had 'compromised the independence and dignity of the Institute'.[38] Several members of the Assembly were also accused of collaboration, including Ramon and Fourneau. Ramon was accused of visiting a German centre for the production of a vaccine against foot and mouth disease, which he hoped to imitate on French soil. The accusations against Fourneau were at once more diffuse and more serious. His empathy with German culture was interpreted by the Council as a collaborationist attitude.[39]

As a result of these accusations, control of Garches was handed over to the Director of the Institute, and Ramon was eventually allowed to return to his researches. Fourneau's fate was quite different. Accused of collaboration for his role in the Comité France-Allemagne since 1938 and for his close relations with German intellectual and political milieux (in particular Otto Abetz, the German ambassador to Paris whom he had met at the 1936 Olympic Games in Berlin), which had led him to being entrusted with the censorship of French scientific publications, he was arrested by the police and sent to the Tourelles prison in October 1944.[40] He owed his release two months later to a petition organized by the former resistant, and his brother-in-law, Marc Tiffeneau, and signed by his colleagues, despite the many enemies he had made as a result of his often disparaging comments towards some of them.[41]

On Philippe Burrin's gradual scale of collaboration, Fourneau and Ramon both probably correspond to 'deliberate political accommodation'.[42] Therefore, their different treatment at the hands of the Comité d'Epuration needs to be explained.[43] Fourneau's involvement in the very German discipline of chemotherapy (as opposed to immunotherapy) may have tainted him with an indelible stain in the eyes of his enemies. At the end of the war, parallels were drawn between the synthetic chemotherapeutic approach and German aggression in World War Two, which were contrasted with the more natural, peace-loving approach that led from Pasteur to the development of penicillin:

> Looking back on the brief but turbulent story of chemotherapy, we can readily see the conflict between two schools of thought. Here is Ehrlich who represents the proud conviction of German science that man's intellect overcomes every natural obstacle on the road to success. We can visualize his obstinate faith in the magic bullet, the super-chemical that will destroy all and every microbe. As we can see now, in the fanatic fervor of his belief, he was inclined to minimize the role of our natural defense mechanism.
>
> On the other side we see Pasteur and his disciples, the men who represent the down-to-earth common sense of the French nation, who firmly believe that medical science should follow the road of research designated by those natural forces that dominate and control the human organism. [...] The work of these men was based on a true consideration of the importance of the defense forces.[44]

However, the key argument that resulted in Fourneau's release was that of his overriding concern, as a scientist and inventor, with competing against German therapeutic products.

This argument was put forward by his colleagues of the Pasteur Institute and the Academy of Medicine and was supported by Rhône-Poulenc, who prepared a document entitled: 'Exposé chronologique du rôle de M. Fourneau dans le développement de la chimiothérapie en France et dans la lutte contre l'hégémonie allemande en matière de produits pharmaceutiques'.[45] Therefore, like other elderly prisoners, Fourneau was promptly let out of prison. After the Liberation, the mood was for consensus about the resistant nature of the French people under German Occupation, and the evidence provided by his friends and colleagues in science and industry was accepted as a sign of Fourneau's patriotism.[46] He was able to return to the Pasteur Institute and in 1946 began making plans for a new laboratory which Rhône-Poulenc were building for him in the rue Jean Goujon (studied more closely in Chapter 5).

At the same time, the Institute was involved in plans to scale up a penicillin plant in the rue Cabanel, and the name of this drug, which became associated with the Resistance and Liberation of France, was for the first time mentioned in the Minutes of the Council.[47] The Institute's role in the production of French penicillin will be returned to later in the chapter. To conclude this brief history of the Pasteur Institute in wartime, as a whole it was neither fully collaborationist, nor actively resistant, but preoccupied with survival through adverse conditions. These circumstances provided the Institute with an opportunity to make changes that paved the way for post-war reconstruction. The history of Rhône-Poulenc, which is studied next, presents many similar features.

C. RHÔNE-POULENC: FROM COLLABORATIVE NETWORKS TO 'RÉSEAUX' OF THE RESISTANCE?

Scientific collaboration was reduced from pre-war levels because of secrecy restrictions, shortages of research materials and paper, and controls on publication, but survived nonetheless. The sparse correspondence exchanged between Fourneau and Blaise (who died in 1939), and then Raymond Paul (research director from 1942), conveys an impression not only of the hardship endured by the two laboratories, but also of their loosening connection.

1. The Therapeutic Chemistry Laboratory

The Therapeutic Chemistry Laboratory had been mobilized for war, as were the Rhône-Poulenc factories. Fourneau was commissioned to carry out research work for the Service des Poudres (a department of the War Ministry). New recruits included mostly organic chemists, apart from Viviane Hamon, a physicist put in charge of the analytical laboratory. However, after 1939, the pace of activity slackened considerably.[48]

Fourneau described the wartime vocation of his laboratory no longer as chemotherapeutic, but rather pharmacological, although he continued to pursue 'the great chemotherapeutic questions of trypanosomiasis, malaria and syphilis', as well as the study of synthetic anti-diabetic substances, an offshoot of the sulphonamide research programme.[49] Discussing the subject of antibacterial chemotherapy in 1941, he reckoned that a radically new approach needed to be found.[50] There is no evidence that Fourneau knew anything about the development of penicillin, and his remark may simply have denoted a general sense, drawn from his own experience, of the direction in which the discipline was moving at the time. However, he did not contemplate following this new direction himself, but was content to walk down well-trodden paths.

Therefore, despite continuing relations between Fourneau and Rhône-Poulenc, the two laboratories drifted apart. This was due to practical difficulties in maintaining contacts, and the need to shield the firm's activities from both the Occupant and the State in order to remain independent. It was also the result of a change in the company's research policy, spurred on by war.

2. Pharmaceutical research and the business of war

The new laws passed under Vichy, which required drugs to have novelty for pharmaceutical visas to be granted, as well as the uncertainties of Occupation, led Rhône-Poulenc to place a greater emphasis on research and innovation.[51] Thus, the firm reaped the benefits of earlier investments made in the pharmaceutical laboratories at Vitry-sur-Seine, and in research projects such as the synthetic anti-histamines. Therefore, with the exception of synthetic fibres, pharmaceuticals became the main beneficiary of this new wartime emphasis. On the other hand, production levels slumped, a sign of the heavy pressures exerted on the company by Vichy and the Occupant.[52] The government's attempts to rationalize production placed bureaucratic constraints on industry, hindering the normal inter-play of market forces, while the Occupant's demands drained firms' resources, closing off many of their export markets.[53]

For Rhône-Poulenc, as for the Pasteur Institute, survival was as major preoccupation and meant preserving as much of its independence as possible. However, for a group with factories located mostly in the southern, unoccupied Zone, it was relatively easy to escape the attention of the authorities. During the débâcle, the principal pharmaceutical research laboratories were moved from Vitry to St-Fons near Lyon, where they remained for a time. Then, the firm established new contacts with clinicians and academic laboratories in the Free Zone, in order to conceal from the Occupant information about the products being developed and tested, but also to reap the benefits of the growth of experimental medicine in the provinces, and prepare for the post-war expansion of the company.

My interpretation, based on of the archives of the Direction Scientifique, matches Pierre Cayez's description of the period, but contradicts more extreme conclusions reached by other historians who have seen in Rhône-Poulenc and other firms' dealings with the occupier an enthusiastic response to collaboration.[54] Numerous negotiations took place with IG Farben, continuing a trend begun before the war. During the 1930s, the German and French chemical industries had been exchanging patents and participating in reciprocal agreements that helped to establish personal contacts between firms. As Cayez put it:

> Rhône-Poulenc became accustomed to having to soften the impact of German economic pressure, and to negotiate and refrain from commercial attacks. The protagonists were the same in peacetime as in wartime, and the negotiations that took place in 1940 were, to some extent, the continuation of those that had occurred before.[55]

Therefore, when relations became more cordial between Rhône-Poulenc and IG after 1943, it was partly the result of previous contacts, but also in anticipation of continuing interaction when the conflict was over — something that became easier to imagine after the German Army's capitulations at Stalingrad and El Alamein.

3. Dealing with the enemy

The main objective of the negotiations that began at the end of 1940 with IG was to determine the fate of the pharmaceutical activities of Rhône-Poulenc, which owed many of its products to German discoveries. However, the agreements signed between the two parties extended beyond those products that were derived from such discoveries. They covered Gardenal, Moranyl or Novarsenobenzol, which owed little to Bayer's patents or technological know-how, and for which Spécia found itself obliged to pay 5% of sales to the German group. Paying a percentage of sales, even though it weakened the company, was a way of avoiding an administrative takeover by IG: 'plutôt payer que d'accepter des administrateurs allemands'.[56] A similar kind of reasoning seems to have underpinned the decision to make Théraplix a joint Rhône-Poulenc-Bayer enterprise, with 49% of shares each going to the two companies, and 2% to Faure-Beaulieu, who led the negotiations.

In March 1941, an agreement was reached with IG to exchange scientific information. Internal notes were circulated to decide on which pharmaceutical products to discuss at meetings with the German group. At first, it was felt that the anti-histamines should be kept secret, because there remained uncertainties about their medical applications, and no patent had yet been taken out for them. Similarly, May & Baker's newest products (in particular the trypanocidal diamidines against kala-azar, which Rhône-Poulenc had heard about from Arthur Ewins in December 1939)[57] were concealed from IG, so as to protect the interests of the British subsidiary, as well as out of consideration for the British government, which had organized the clinical trials:

> These products undoubtedly present considerable interest, but as they originated in England, as the trials have so far been almost exclusively carried out by the English, partly in connection with their government, it would seem to us improper and inappropriate to mention them now to the IG.[58]

However, as time went by, the risk that Rhône-Poulenc might be cut out of crucial wartime research programmes such as those on nylon, or might be denied licenses to manufacture important new products, put representatives of the company under great pressure to offer interesting information to IG and appear worthy of what was hoped would become an equal partnership. At a tense meeting in Frankfurt on 5 July 1941, Messrs. Bô and Clouzeau (of the Administrative Council of Rhône-Poulenc) strove to save the company, like the rest of France, from being relegated — as they explained to their German counterparts — to the role of 'agricultural labourers'.[59] Eventually, they decided to reveal the progress made with anti-histamines so as to protect French priority over the discovery as well as the company's commercial interests.[60]

After these somewhat fraught beginnings, by 1943 communications appeared to flow more easily. Information on pharmacological and clinical tests, and product samples were freely exchanged. In October, plans for a joint research programme, which involved estimates of labour requirements and resources, were being made. The tone of the letters was cordial, perhaps because of a growth in self-confidence on the part of the French, and the wish to preserve good relations with the German group after the war.[61] The papers of the Direction Scientifique contain few testimonies of the troubled period that lay ahead, other than a photograph showing American soldiers standing beside the ruined HQ of IG Farben at Leverkusen, received in June 1945. A report about the pharmaceutical research carried out by IG during the war was sent to Rhône-Poulenc in February 1946, in which — interestingly — nothing was said concerning penicillin. By July 1948, the French group were contemplating reorganising IG Farben's research, in collaboration with French academic institutions.

As Pestre has remarked in a paper on the relationship between France and Germany in physics, contacts based on strong pre-existing collaborative networks were re-established after the conflict.[62] The pharmaceutical industry followed a similar trend. Rhône-Poulenc made plans to continue some form of co-operation with Bayer. The group had gained the experience of collaborative research with another as a direct result of the war, much as British industry had done through the penicillin programme, and they carried this experience with them into the post-war period.

Such was the economic and political context in which Rhône-Poulenc pursued its wartime projects. Although the company passed on information to IG Farben about its own research activities, there were hardly any references to external laboratories such as Fourneau's. The German group was eventually informed of the synthetic anti-histamines. However, nothing, according to my sources, was revealed about the penicillin work. Rhône-Poulenc's main contribution to therapy during the war was in the field of anti-histamines, which broke new ground in the understanding and treatment of allergies, therefore I describe these first, before moving on to antibiotics.

4. Synthetic anti-histamines

The substances developed first by Fourneau's team, and later by Rhône-Poulenc, allowed the firm to develop its own expertise, independently of the academic laboratory with which it had collaborated for thirty years, and paved the way for the first neuroleptic drug, chlorpromazine.

The anti-histamine work had begun as part of a broader project to investigate the mechanism of action of substances, both natural and synthetic, by studying their metabolism and formulating likely hypotheses about their activity. At first, this project involved almost exclusively Daniel Bovet (see Figure 4.1), who tested the substances synthesized by Fourneau, in particular those with either sympathomimetic or sympatholytic properties (substances that either mimic or counteract stimulation of the sympathetic nervous system by adrenaline and noradrenaline).[63] The first sympatholytic compound studied by Bovet (883 F) had been synthesized by Fourneau in search of an anti-malarial drug. Noting that the chemical structures of adrenaline and other biogenic amines — such as acetylcholine and histamine — were similar, and reasoning that, just as there were compounds capable of antagonizing the effects of adrenaline, there might be antagonists of histamine, Bovet therefore began searching for such compounds.

Histamine had been isolated in ergot by Dale in 1910, and in 1911 Dale and Laidlaw had shown that it could cause anaphylactic contractions in smooth muscle. However, in the 1930s, there was still no definite proof of a link between histamine, anaphylactic shock, and other allergic reactions. Hence, the question was pursued by Anne-Marie Staub, who was doing a Ph.D. under Bovet, and in her thesis coined the term 'anti-histamine'.[64] Staub and Bovet found that a compound, which had been synthesized earlier by Fourneau, thymoxyethyldiethylamine (929 F), was capable of stopping histamine-induced anaphylactic shock in guinea pigs.[65] Another

Figure 4.1 Daniel Bovet (courtesy of the Pasteur Institute).

compound, a phenylethylenediamine derivative, also synthesized by Fourneau (1671 F), showed even greater activity. Unfortunately, neither could be used in the clinic, for they were both too toxic at the high doses required for them to be effective. Nevertheless, they provided Rhône-Poulenc with valuable leads, and in 1938 the firm undertook the synthesis of further phenylethylenediamine derivatives.

The research of the TCL, which had reached a dead-end, was therefore passed on to Rhône-Poulenc, where it was taken on by Bernard Halpern and his assistant France Walthert. Halpern was born in 1904 in Galicia, which later became part of Poland. In 1926, he moved to Nancy, where he began a medical degree, and from there to Paris, where he worked as an assistant for Professeur Gautrelet (research director of the Experimental Biology Laboratory at l'Ecole Pratique des Hautes Etudes) while studying towards his doctorate. At the same time, he carried out tests on behalf of pharmaceutical laboratories. This allowed him to supplement his income of 1,100 FF per month, bringing it up to 1,800 and even 2,000 FF.[66] On 28 June 1935, he visited Rhône-Poulenc in the hope of being able to continue his research there, while maintaining his link with Gautrelet. The internal note that was circulated about Halpern concluded that he was a first-rate candidate, but probably a foreigner, and also a Jew.[67]

Naturalized in 1935, Naftali-Ber Halpern became Bernard Halpern,[68] and despite earlier reservations about him being Jewish, he was offered a position as pharmacologist at the Direction Scientifique des Recherches Pharmaceutiques in Vitry, beginning in January 1936, so that he would have the time to complete his doctoral thesis.[69] During 1936 he was allowed to spend ten afternoons in Gautrelet's laboratory, but on condition that he revealed nothing of the research carried out at Rhône-Poulenc, or did not publish without the firm's consent.

Gautrelet had studied the properties of histamine after working with acetylcholine, and it is therefore likely that it was in his laboratory that Halpern developed an interest in antagonistic substances.[70] In a talk given at the Medical Faculty in Paris on 24 January 1945, Halpern described how the study of anti-histamines had grown out of the study of sympatholytics:[71]

> The histamine theory of allergy has been subjected to the same vagaries as the theory of chemical transmitters, which is accepted today as a certainty. What allowed the problem of neurotransmitters to progress, was that the physiologist had at his disposal antagonistic substances of great specificity: atropine for acetylcholine, and sympatholytics for adrenaline. Because of the difficulties involved in isolating these active substances, their antagonists were therefore used to characterize particular actions, as either caused by acetylcholine, or by adrenaline. Nothing of the kind existed for histamine, until the discovery of the synthetic anti-histamines.[72]

As with penicillin, the anti-histamine project included, therefore, both an applied and a fundamental aspect from the very beginning. There are also interesting parallels between the study of the antibacterial action of lysozyme, which led to the study of penicillin, and the search for antagonists of adrenaline, which led to the development of synthetic anti-histamines.

Thus, around 1938, having broken new ground in the understanding of the role of histamine in allergies, but without leading to practical applications, the anti-histamine project was transferred to the research laboratory in Vitry, which could synthesize a far greater number of derivatives. There Halpern and Walthert began by adopting a fundamental approach to the problem. They returned to the series investigated earlier by Staub and Bovet, and re-examined the basic premise of the correspondence between their anti-histaminic and anti-allergic properties by means of systematic pharmacological tests.[73]

However, Halpern soon had to interrupt his research.[74] What happened between 1939 and 1942 is somewhat unclear, but from biographical notices and retrospective accounts it is possible to reconstruct a picture of events.[75] Mobilized and then caught up in the Débâcle, Halpern fled South, where for a time he found work as a doctor in the Ardèche. Then, in 1941, the anti-Jewish laws drawn up by the Vichy government led him to accept Rhône-Poulenc's offer of a post in the research laboratories of the SCUR in St-Fons.[76] There, once again with the assistance of Walthert, he began a study of the phenylethylenediamine derivatives made by Rhône-Poulenc's chemists. The most active compound, even at low doses, was N-dimethylaminoethyl-N-benzylaniline (2339 RP – the 'RP' standing for Rhône-Poulenc, reflecting the switch to an industrial locus for drug discovery), which had been synthesized earlier by M. Mosnier.[77] Clinical tests showed that at low doses it was both active against certain types of allergies and well tolerated in man. It was marketed by Spécia in 1942 under the name Antergan.

However, as described in the previous section, under their agreement with IG Farben, before launching Antergan, Rhône-Poulenc found themselves compelled to let the German group know about their progress.[78] Moreover, in April 1942, Halpern's results were published in the *Archives Internationales de Pharmacodynamie et Thérapie*. This was to have unfortunate consequences for Halpern, bringing him to the attention of the German authorities, which moved into the Southern Unoccupied Zone in November 1942.[79] In a poignant understatement, Halpern described the turmoil that followed: 'events forced us to abandon our laboratory and seek refuge (in order to escape from the massacre)'.[80] To avoid the Gestapo and the first convoys of racial deportees, he left for Switzerland.[81] The story of the epic journey he made across the border, accompanied by his wife and children, and assisted by a number of individual Frenchmen and women and of réseaux of the Resistance along the way,[82] was later told on the occasion of his election to the Academy of Sciences.[83]

The Rhône-Poulenc Santé archives reveal the close links Halpern maintained with the group even after leaving St-Fons, a fact that has been omitted in biographical and retrospective accounts. It suggests that the border between occupied France and neutral Switzerland was fairly porous, and that despite the risks and obstacles, information circulated nonetheless.[84] After arriving in Geneva, Halpern joined Professor Roch's service at the Hôpital Cantonal, where he kept in touch with the Direction Scientifique of Rhône-Poulenc via a number of channels: the company's factory at La Plaine (between Geneva and the French border); the Etablissements R. Barberot, an agency contracted to sell Rhône-Poulenc's products; and Dr Sciclounoff's contacts at the Bulgarian delegation in Vichy.[85] In letters circulated internally, Halpern was given an alias, and was referred to as Dr Bernard, or later on as D. Schaffhauser, to prevent the authorities from discovering his true identity, had the documents fallen into their hands.

In Geneva, one of Halpern's roles was to assess the responses of the Swiss medical community to the various products marketed by Spécia (for instance 'Dagenan', the name for M&B 693 in France), as well as to the products of their competitors in Switzerland, which included Hoffman-La Roche, Ciba, and Geigy. Halpern also studied Swiss fashions in therapy and described them for the company. For instance, he noticed that to avoid the toxic reactions associated with chemotherapeutic treatment, in particular with the sulphonamides, Swiss physicians gave large doses of vitamin C ('Redoxon') to their patients. However, Halpern was more than just a passive observer. By keeping a close eye on the tests being carried out in the Geneva clinics, he helped to promote Rhône-Poulenc's commercial interests. Thus, in 1943, he was able to warn the Direction Scientifique about the trials and imminent launch by Ciba of a new sulpha drug, Sulphamidopyrimidine. He also helped to introduce Antergan in Switzerland, and for that he asked for samples and literature to be sent from Paris.

Information about Antergan had reached Geneva by April 1943, and Halpern was surprised at the amount of knowledge displayed by Swiss doctors concerning its experimental use. He attributed this to an article in the journal *Paris Médical*, which like other French journals reached Geneva several months after publication. Hence, in October 1943, he could write in a report:

> Antergan's reputation in Geneva seems well established. Doctors often test it on members of their own families. The fact that Professor Bickel has placed Antergan on the programme of the first congress on therapeutics ([which] has [...] the aim of informing the Swiss medical profession of recent developments in therapy), and that he has decided to deal with the question himself, underlines the importance that medical circles in Geneva attribute to this new form of medication.[86]

By June 1944, he was able to add that Antergan had conquered not only the medical community in Geneva, but the whole of Switzerland. He attributed this to his active lobbying in favour of Rhône-Poulenc's drug.[87]

Whilst serving Rhône-Poulenc's interests, Halpern also pursued his own in collaboration with Professor Roch, developing a method for the treatment of asthma using aerosols. He hoped to apply the method to the treatment of tuberculosis with sulphonamides, for which he requested Rhône-Poulenc's support to purchase a compressor.

Meanwhile, Bovet had moved to Vitry, and an agreement was reached between Jacques Tréfouël and Raymond Paul concerning the conditions under which he was to remain there until the end of the war.[88] Assisted by Simone Courvoisier, he pursued various pharmacological questions, including the synthesis of curare and derivatives, which was to contribute to his Nobel Prize in 1957, and lead Rhône-Poulenc to their muscle relaxant Flaxedil.[89] He also resumed the anti-histamine work, which had been interrupted by Halpern's departure. A letter written by Bovet in December 1942 suggests that, although he did not seem to know why or where Halpern had gone, he was aware of the considerable impact his leaving would have on the research project:

> Last Tuesday, there was a farewell party on the occasion of Dr Savonnat's retirement [...] His departure coïncided with Halpern's, who has left Lyon for some foreign country. The latter will be rich in consequences; indeed Halpern's assistant, Miss Walthert, and Mr Fournel, will move from Lyon to Paris, bringing back with them the wealth of laboratory apparatus he had taken there.[90]

Together, Bovet and Walthert turned to the study of new compounds, which had been prepared by Rhône-Poulenc's chemists by substituting a pyridine nucleus for the aniline nucleus present in the series of phenylethylenediamines. Among these, one compound in particular showed a superior activity to Antergan, mepyramine maleate. It was launched under the name Néo-Antergan, and was quickly to replace Antergan in the clinic.[91]

Halpern concluded his 1945 lecture to the Medical Faculty in Paris by expressing his belief in the promises of chemotherapy, confirmed by the sulphonamides and strengthened, according to him, by the anti-histamines:

> The discovery of the synthetic anti-histamines heralds the advent of the chemotherapy of allergies [...] Following the handsome successes achieved by the sulphonamides, therapeutic chemistry is now tackling a new group of diseases. The potential of chemotherapy, and I shall end by expressing this firm belief, appears infinite.[92]

Thus, the anti-histamines played a similar role in France to that of penicillin in Britain. Following the success of the sulphonamides, they helped to convince the French medical profession of the value of the chemotherapeutic approach. However, the parallels between the two drugs do not end there. Both underwent a similar fate after the war. What had begun as an applied project was transformed into a pure one. In the case of anti-histamines, it was to be concerned with the biology of the immune system, as illustrated by Halpern's subsequent career.

At the end of 1944, he returned to Vitry and began working with the phenothiazine amines that had been synthesized by Paul Charpentier in search of anti-malarials, and were found to have anti-histaminic properties in the pharmacological screens in use at the time. Halpern identified the most active and least toxic compound for further development, prométhazine (3277 RP), which was marketed as Phénergan, and soon displaced Néo-Antergan.

Exhausted by the traumas of war, but rendered professionally attractive by his achievements with Antergan and Phénergan, Halpern left Rhône-Poulenc in December 1945, and joined Pasteur Vallery-Radot at the Hôpital Broussais, where he later became Director of the Institute of Immunobiology. At the same time, he occupied the posts of research director at the CNRS and head of laboratory at the Medical Faculty. By 1958, he was also practising medicine, treating cases of allergy, in particular asthma. In 1948 he began to receive funding as a consultant for Rhône-Poulenc, a position he retained almost until his death in 1979, despite the tensions that arose between him and the firm about the credit for the anti-histamine work, and were caused by his propensity to downplay the contribution of the pharmaceutical team in his accounts of the discovery.[93]

His justification for renewing contact with the firm in 1948 had been that, although he wished to work in an academic environment, he also wished to free himself from preoccupations of a financial nature.[94] In memory of their past collaboration and in order to retain contact with him, the Direction Scientifique agreed to pay him 50,000 FF per month, leaving him total freedom to choose his research topics, but trusting him to show discretion concerning the new products he would be testing on behalf of the company. Two years earlier, Pasteur Vallery-Radot himself had been hired as consultant by Rhône-Poulenc. Together, Halpern and Vallery-Radot represented the scientific élite in the field of allergy in France, and the decision to hire them both as consultants made sound commercial sense. However, it is also a sign that the company was opening up to external collaborations. In the next chapter, it will become clear that World War Two was a turning point for Rhône-Poulenc, whose interactions with other laboratories, both academic and industrial, expanded greatly after the war, but lost the close, personal nature they had had with Fourneau.

5. The expansion of wartime collaborative networks

The decision by Rhône-Poulenc to forge new alliances was, it seems, a direct result of the Occupation and the growth of medical research in the provinces, especially in the Southern Unoccupied Zone, which the firm actively encouraged. Thus, in 1941, Rhône-Poulenc began making plans for the creation of a centre for clinical research in the Free Zone. In order to investigate the possibilities of creating such a centre, Philippe Decourt, a clinical consultant to Spécia who was helping the firm to organize clinical trials of synthetic anti-malarials in North Africa,[95] was sent to provincial capitals in the South: Montpellier, Perpignan, Lyon, Toulouse, Marseille, and Nice.

Decourt had already served a similar function before the war, acting as a go-between between Spécia and Jean Reilly, who while working at the Hôpital Claude Bernard had become interested in the influence of the nervous system on immunity, and saw similarities between the accidents resulting from the use of chemotherapeutic drugs (arsenical drugs as well as the sulphonamides) and anaphylactic shock.[96] A conclusion of Decourt's report, written in 1937 and sent to the Direction Scientifique, had been that it was imperative to develop substances that were antagonists of histamine, and this may well have stimulated Rhône-Poulenc's efforts in the field.[97]

Through his clinical contacts, Decourt not only learnt about novel approaches in therapy, but also became convinced of the need to pursue parallel research projects in different centres, for not all clinicians were of the same high caliber as Reilly. The provinces provided a fertile ground for establishing co-operative networks that included both clinicians and academic scientists, as he explained in a report written in January 1941 after he had visited Montpellier and Perpignan:

> The firm needs [...] to decentralize its research activities in order to exploit the possibilities offered by the provinces, as well as be able to increase the number of tests which it can control. However, it is also important to realize that if the physicians capable of carrying out tests are plentiful, good experimentalists are rare. Moreover, the provinces have an advantage over Paris, in that physicians there usually have more free time for research. Because the different sites in which they work are more concentrated (because of the smaller size of provincial cities), clinicians are also often more willing to return to their hospital department in the afternoon (something they do not do in Paris) and are more likely to work in collaboration with the laboratories directed by the chairs of medical faculties. Sometimes, on top of their clinical appointment, they can also occupy one of these chairs.[98]

The war gave Decourt the opportunity he wished for on behalf of the company. The Free Zone provided a novel testing ground for Rhône-Poulenc's products. Thus, Decourt's principal aim in going to Nice was to have tests carried out with 2168 RP (against kala-azar) by general practitioners, for Nice did not as yet have a medical faculty. However, in an interview with the mayor of the city, Jean Médecin, it became clear to him that Rhône-Poulenc could extend their area of influence beyond the mere testing of drugs, and beyond their two traditional centres of Paris and Lyon. Indeed, Médecin, whom Decourt described as a 'great administrator', expressed the wish to raise the profile of his city by creating a research centre on Mediterranean biology and pathology. This, he hoped, would complement the 'Centre Universitaire Méditerranéen' founded recently by Paul Valéry. For his project, he hoped to attract funding from industry, which helped to explain the presence of a representative of the chemical firm Kuhlmann at the interview with Decourt. Nice eventually acquired a medical faculty after the war, and the scientific decentralisation associated with the period of Occupation appears to have benefited not only Nice, but many other provincial centres.

Thanks to their increased contacts with clinicians, Rhône-Poulenc were kept informed of the results of their experience at the bench or bedside, which could lead to novel, off-the-label uses for their drugs. This happened for instance in 1942, when A.L. Loubatières, a CNRS researcher based in Montpellier, was consulted by his colleague Janbon. The latter had noticed that 2254 RP, a new sulpha drug he had been asked by Decourt to try in patients suffering from typhoid fever, lowered blood sugar levels. Loubatières, who had carried out an experimental study with insulin a few months earlier, promptly made the connection between the activity described by Janbon, and the effects of insulin he had observed himself. Between 1942 and 1946, he carried out a systematic study of the physiological action of 2254 RP, at the end of which he became convinced of the usefulness of sulphonamides in the treatment of diabetes mellitus.[99] At the same time, he obtained the help of Bovet and Dubost in Vitry, who performed pharmacodynamic tests that established the relation between the chemical structure and hypoglycaemic activity of a large number of compounds, with a view to identifying the most promising among them (in 1955, it was still 2254 RP!). Loubatières continued to work with Rhône-Poulenc after the war, and remained their 'collaborateur scientifique' (i.e. their consultant) well into the late 1950s. A similar development occurred when the clinical use of anti-histamines (phenothiazines in particular) led to observations of the effects of these drugs on the central nervous system, and eventually to the development of chlorpromazine in 1952. This will be addressed in greater detail in the next chapter.

War, therefore, represented a crucial turning point in the history of the relationship between Rhône-Poulenc and academic laboratories. It forced the company to free itself from its almost exclusive relation with Fourneau and expand its links with provincial laboratories. The group experienced scientific collaboration in a much wider sense than before: with clinicians in hospitals, and with another group, IG Farben, even if this was under the constraints of the Occupation. However, the almost independent development of penicillin during the war would be used to emphasize its participation in the resistance to, rather than collaboration with, the enemy.

D. FRENCH PENICILLIN

In his fifth report from Switzerland, Halpern wrote about penicillin:

> I recently gave a talk on penicillin to the doctors at the hôpital canton-
> nal in Geneva. The question is absolutely fascinating, and I believe that
> your laboratories should at once be actively pursuing its study, which
> opens up unsuspected perspectives in chemotherapy.[100]

However, there is evidence that, even before Halpern had sent this information, Rhône-Poulenc had been alerted to the existence of penicillin. At
the end of 1942, the company obtained 'English technical reports' describing the preparation and dosage of the substance (these were probably the
1940–1 *Lancet* reports).[101] Scientific information was, therefore, circulating more or less freely via neutral countries, at least from 1942 onwards,
following a complex network of scientific and industrial contacts.

1. Penicillin as a weapon of the Resistance?

To work on penicillin, the firm got in touch with its collaborator at the
Pasteur Institute, the bacteriologist Federico Nitti (see Figure 4.2).

By then, he had moved out of Fourneau's laboratory, and, as shown
earlier, was focusing on the production of vaccines and sera. It is significant that he was chosen for the project, rather than Fourneau, even though
Fourneau had sensed that the chemotherapy of bacterial infections was
taking a fresh turn.[102] There were important similarities between vaccine
production and the penicillin work (see Figure 4.3), and Nitti, being a bacteriologist, had the necessary expertise to handle a micro-organism.[103]

He was also well known to the company, having collaborated on the sulphonamides (see Chapter 2). Finally, being the son of a famous Italian com-
munist who had fled from the Fascist Regime with his family to France in
the 1930s, his political views made him more likely to be discreet. After the
war, stories were told about an incident in which, having been approached
by a German military officer, Nitti surrendered a sample of penicillin he
knew to be inactive.[104] This gesture was, with hindsight, interpreted as an
act of resistance against the Occupant. Although it is not clear from the
Rhône-Poulenc archives whether Nitti really knew the sample to be inactive, Raymond Paul, remembering him, thought it believable.[105]

The penicillin files in Rhône-Poulenc Santé archive open with a warning
from Paul addressed to Nitti. An article in the German journal *Klinische
Wochenschrift* on 17 April 1943, suggested that the Germans were already
on the trail of penicillin.[106] Hence, he urged Nitti to study the question so
that they would not fall behind in what he called the 'penicillin race'.[107] The
motive behind Rhône-Poulenc's decision to embark on penicillin research
was therefore industrial competition, rather than resistance against the

Figure 4.2 Federico Nitti
(courtesy of the Pasteur
Institute).

Occupant, although it would later be presented it in this way to throw a
favourable light on the firm's wartime activities.

Professor Hörlein of IG wrote to the French group, offering some information on penicillin, and, for a brief moment, a reciprocal arrangement
was contemplated between them. But nothing came of this plan. In 1943
the course of the war changed, and the priorities of the German scientific and industrial complex lay elsewhere. In 1944, Raymond Paul told the
American Medical Intelligence Mission, on a visit to Vitry, that he thought
'Wichaus' in Gottingen had been working on penicillin. He also told them
that Dr Schlonsberg had taken from the Pasteur Institute a penicillin sample that was not Fleming's (and therefore may have been inactive, hence the
story about Nitti?).[108]

At first, Nitti worked on his own. He found a sample of *Penicillium
notatum* that had been given to the Pasteur Institute by Alexander Fleming
during one of his visits to Paris.[109] After successfully growing the mould,
Nitti gave Vitry two batches of penicillin juice: the first on 1 October 1943,
and the second, which was found to be more active than the first, on 6

Figure 4.3 Vaccine preparation at the Pasteur Institute (courtesy of the Pasteur Institute).

October. However, Nitti's subsequent attempt to step up production failed. Consequently, Vitry began its own production of penicillin juice in the second half of October 1943.[110] From it, penicillin was extracted in solid form, and this was returned to Nitti for testing, in order to establish scientific priority ('pour une prise de date dans les milieux scientifiques'). At a meeting of the Association de Microbiologie de Langue Française on 25 October, Nitti communicated the results of his experiments on mice, which had been infected with *Staphylococcus aureus*. He described penicillin's 'remarkable activity' on the pathogenic organism *in vivo*.

During November, the quality of the mould kept at Vitry deteriorated and Nitti was asked for a fresh sample. The growth medium and other conditions (such as temperature) were improved, and the resulting penicillin showed an increased activity, up to 20 units per cc. The first clinical tests took place at the beginning of 1944. Dr Cosar at the Hôpital Pasteur treated eye infections with the penicillin extracted at Vitry. This was followed by more extensive tests carried out by Professor Abram at the Hôpital Broussais, where he treated a serious case of staphylococcal infection of the face.[111] However, all in all, these first faltering steps required few man-hours and few resources, as shown by Table 4.1.

Table 4.1 Cost of Penicillin Research at Rhône-Poulenc in 1943–4

Year	Month	No. working days	Cost per day
1943	September	4	1,555.10 FF
	October	15	
	December	7.5	2,003.90
1944	January	15	
	May	36	2,412.90
	June/July/August	124	2,391.90
	October	57	2,522.80
	November	60	2,118.45

Table 4.1 indicates that, at first, Rhône-Poulenc invested a modest number of man-hours in the penicillin project: between seven and fifteen days per month from October 1943 — when they took over the production of penicillin from Nitti — until May 1944, when the efforts were stepped up in connection with D-Day.

In this second phase, Rhône-Poulenc increased their commitment to the penicillin project, which from then on became associated with the liberation of Europe. After the method had been tried in a pilot plant (Figure 4.4), a factory for the production of penicillin by surface fermentation (using bottles, like Boots in England) was constructed in 1944. When the transfer of the science and technology of penicillin began in earnest after the Liberation, although it was known that American submerged culture would eventually replace surface culture in Britain, a conscious decision was made to develop both methods, partly through contingency, for in 1944–5 France was plagued by problems of supply, and partly in order to develop a French method of production, by re-enacting its history on French soil.

2. Penicillin as weapon for the Liberation of France

The end of the war created disruptions that hindered further development of the drug. The factory suffered power cuts and, after the Liberation, the Service de Santé Militaire took charge of penicillin production. This was a period of transition, from war to peace, when a wartime rationale dominated the research and development of the antibiotic. The overriding concern of all parties involved was to produce the drug as quickly as possible for the Leclerc division. Rhône-Poulenc was therefore requested by the Provisional Government to erect a plant on their main production site at Vitry for the extraction, drying and conditioning of penicillin, while a pilot plant was being built for the surface culture of the mould in the rue Cabanel,

Table 4.2 Million Units Received (either as urine or mould juice)

Month	Units received urine	Units received juice	Units produced	Bottles delivered
Feb. '45	8.7		2.5	0
March	31.8		42.6	80
April		27.7	74.9	454
May		354.3	204	749
June		428.4	280.5	1,842
July		251.6	140.9	2,648
August		279.5	200	902

close to the Pasteur Institute. This scheme resembled the early arrangement between the Dunn School and Kemball Bishop. The expertise of the Pasteur Institute was required for the culture of the mould, and Rhône-Poulenc, as well as the pharmaceutical firm Roussel-Uclaf, were asked to co-operate in an enterprise that was to be run by military health officers.

The extraction plant at Vitry was ready on 1 February 1945, even before the Centre Cabanel (as it came to be known) had started production. The first task of the plant was, in the absence of mould juice, to extract penicillin from the urine of American soldiers (see Table 4.2).

This 'pipiline', as it was referred to,[117] symbolized the American gift of penicillin to France.[118] Table 4.2 shows clearly that after the Centre Cabanel came into operation in April 1945, mould juice replaced urine as the main source of penicillin for extraction by the plant at Vitry. The number of units received and manufactured from that date rose steeply, and the penicillin delivered to the Leclerc division more than doubled between February/March, when its value represented 154,328 FF, and June, when it reached 374,008 FF.[119]

Meanwhile, the Pasteur Institute had offered its services to the War Ministry to assist in the building of the Centre Cabanel. It not only provided it with scientific personnel and technicians, but also with a network of contacts that included suppliers, manufacturers, engineers, and of course the chemical group Rhône-Poulenc. In March 1945, Nitti wrote to Jacques Tréfouël: 'Nous avons ... mis en relation le commandant Dreyfus et le capitaine Broch avec Monsieur Grillet (directeur des usines Rhône-Poulenc chargées de l'extraction chimique de la pénicilline)'.[120] Capitaine Broch was the main influence behind the Centre. Of him, the journal *Résistance* wrote in an article entitled 'Thanks to the general Leclerc France produces penicillin' ('Grâce au Général Leclerc la France fabrique de la pénicilline'):

After escaping from Spain into Britain, he gathered there all the scientific elements and building plans necessary to accomplish this objective.

As soon as he returned to France, the general Leclerc put at his disposal a small contingent from his division and the material means necessary [for a military center for the production of penicillin]. Thanks to the military technicians of the Pasteur Institute and to private industry [...] this factory is now ready to begin production.[121]

Another newspaper article, this time in *Samedi Soir*, described the centre Cabanel as the most 'intelligent' penicillin plant that ever existed.[122] Fleming paid a visit to the centre, and apparently lost his Anglo-Saxon cool on seeing the French installation, and was reported to have said that he found it more impressive than the American equivalent.[123]

But, in reality, the centre Cabanel was racked by personal and material problems for the whole period of its short history.[124] The role of the Pasteur Institute had been to set up the centre, and then hand over control to the military. However, the military officers had hoped to gain greater autonomy from the very beginning.[125] The misunderstanding was aggravated by the prolonged absence of the members of the Institute, away on a scientific mission to London.[126] Moreover, the scientific hierarchy of the Pasteur Institute clashed with the military hierarchy of the centre. Thus, Nitti would have wished to see Jacques Tréfouël's position as 'Chef de la Mission de la Pénicilline en Angleterre' take precedence over the military, but he found it not to be so. Furthermore, other than capitaine Netick, the military officers showed little understanding of industrial bacteriology, and this made communication difficult between them and members of the Pasteur Institute. Problems with the culture medium (made from oats, which was too easily contaminated) and low production levels added to the difficulties of a more personal nature.[127] The centre suffered delays, which were compounded by the complications caused by the rapidly changing international situation.

On 27 September 1945, an article in the *Figaro* declared that France was increasing its production, but that supplies of it were still short.[128] This put French progress with penicillin into stark perspective. The huge quantities required for the mass treatment of bacterial infections in man made the combined efforts of Rhône-Poulenc, Roussel-Uclaf and the centre Cabanel appear insignificant. France still had to import most of its penicillin from the United States. However, by October 1945, American penicillin production had been made available to the public, and it became clear that French industry was going to have to try to satisfy at least part of the needs of its own civilian population.[129] Rhône-Poulenc and the Pasteur Institute persevered, confident that their endeavour would help them in their relations with the new government. However, by August 1945, guided by what was happening in Britain where the surface production of penicillin was being replaced by deep fermentation methods, Rhône-Poulenc asked the Ministery of Public Health to be released from their obligations towards the government, and be allowed to enter into a contract with Merck.[130]

Figure 4.4 RP penicillin plant (courtesy of Sanofi-Aventis).

The Pasteur Institute and the Service de Santé Militaire initially objected to this request, because in a contract with Merck they saw a loss of prestige for French science, and a danger for French exports. In response to these objections, Rhône-Poulenc argued that, on the contrary, by agreeing to such a contract, the American firm would be paying homage to French science, and French industry would be able to buy the necessary equipment at cheaper rates.

Jacques Tréfouël acknowledged that private industry had advantages over government installations, in that their contacts with American. firms would enable them to obtain licences to produce penicillin quickly, using American methods and material. The role of the centre Cabanel was therefore to be confined to the development of a French method of submerged culture on a laboratory scale (to preserve French independence should the country once more become isolated) and training of technicians involved in penicillin manufacture.[131] Because of the rapid mastery of American production methods by French commercial firms, by 1947, it was in fact relegated to the role of antibiotic research centre.[132]

The company's decision was eventually accepted, and this moment marks the passage, in 1946, from a wartime to a peacetime rationale for the production of penicillin in France. The hope of developing a purely French method of penicillin production had been abandoned, with the consolation that France would soon be in a position to compete with other penicillin producers.

The contribution of France to the penicillin story is significant. Under Occupation, France developed an almost independent production of penicillin. The French experience is therefore one of successful transfer of the 'science' as well as the 'industry' of penicillin, which could be described as the translation of British laboratory practices and, later, of American production techniques in a French context. This achievement was acknowledged when, after the Liberation, the Director of the Pasteur Institute Jacques Tréfouël was the only non-British European representative to be included in the International Conference on the Penicillin Standard, which took place in London in October 1944.[133]

Thus, penicillin helped to situate France firmly in the winning camp at the end of the war. A 'Mission de la Pénicilline' was set up around September 1944, and included members of the CNRS and of the Pasteur Institute, as well as the military officers in charge of the centre Cabanel in Paris. It was attached to the Mission Scientifique Française en Grande-Bretagne, and like this wider Mission, which became a vehicle for the transfer of British models of organisation,[134] it served a dual function: to introduce into French laboratories new practices, together with new techniques and apparatus.[135] It was based on the belief that French organisational structures had been detrimental to the competitiveness of French science and industry before the war. More fundamentally, it was based on the belief that, by changing the structure of institutions, men's behaviour would be transformed. French scientists would become more co-operative if their environment was altered to foster teamwork and collaborative research, and the structures that had enabled Britain and the United States to develop penicillin became a model for them to follow.

3. Learning to co-operate: the model of penicillin

Penicillin provided an example of collaborative practice at three levels: in the laboratory, between institutions and industry, and on an international scale. In Britain, members of the Mission de la Pénicilline visited both academic and industrial laboratories. While Boots, Glaxo, Burroughs Wellcome opened their doors to the French visitors, Duthie at the Lister Institute showed them his apparatus for drying plasma, which could also be used for drying penicillin. According to Pierre Laurent who visited British chemistry departments at the beginning of 1945, the high productivity of academic laboratories, despite their apparent low level of activity, was due to the 'spirit of co-operation' that enabled British scientists to share in the publication of articles:

> English productivity in chemistry appears at first sight to be superior to our own, as much in quality, as in quantity. It is obvious that war has had something to do with this, however even before the conflict it already seemed to be the case. This fact is all the more paradoxical that when one spends quite a long time in a labortory, as I have done at Liverpool, the English give the impression of being less active than we are, and appear to be sometimes slower. One of the reasons for this contradiciton really seems to be their co-operative spirit.[136]

A popular destination for French visitors was Ian Heilbron's Organic Chemistry Department at Imperial College.[137] It was representative of what Britain had to offer in terms of laboratory organisation, for its democratic character served both the needs of science and those of industry. In his report, Israël Marzak wrote that its objective was to provide scientists with the highest education and training, and with instruments suited to the most advanced research in different branches of the discipline, especially those of interest to industry. He mentioned the existence of special committees, which members of industry were able to attend and thereby influence the direction of certain projects.[138] In spite of inferior instrumentation (especially compared with the Americans), and despite the fact that methods employed in the Organic Chemistry Department were rarely original (they were imported from abroad, including France), Marzak described the research pursued on the synthesis of penicillin as being ahead of what was being carried out elsewhere in the world. To him, the causes were organisational:

> To me, the secret of this success lies not only in the great scientific authority of the team leaders, Professors Jones, Heilborn, and Cook, but also in the patient, orderly, and methodical organisation of their laboratories. It is above all the co-ordination of the work, the thread that ties the chemical, physical, physical-chemical, and biological researches. It is the organisation of teams whose members are not asked to be geniuses, but rather consciencious, enlightened workers. Finally, it is the more humble, but no less important organisation of daily life in the laboratory [...] the same attention to organisation allows ICL to train a new generation of well-qualified, disciplined, and enthusiastic researchers.[139]

The responsibility for caring for equipment and instruments was given to individual researchers, who were encouraged in this way to become members of a 'team'. To the French observers of British laboratories, the ability to work in teams and collaborate with industry was due to the co-operative nature of Anglo-Saxon society. By learning about the larger institutional picture and the smaller organisational details of British laboratories, they were hoping to provide French science with a role model.

On the American side, what struck French visitors was the co-ordination or co-operation on a wider scale, at a national level even, involving both academic and industrial laboratories.[140] After a tour of various chemical laboratories in the United States, Marzak used the example of penicillin as the archetypal co-ordinated wartime project (one which France, in her attempts at post-war re-construction, should imitate). He told the story of the transfer of penicillin from Britain to the United States, 'in order to organize as quickly as possible the manufacture of penicillin.' However, he also described how it was not until 1943 that the authorities concerned became convinced of the importance of investing in penicillin production in a big way. The result of this change of heart was the Commercial Solvent factory in Terre Haute, Indiana, which he described with awe: 'One has the impression that the entire factory is made of porcelain, glass, and stainless steel'. [141] He concluded:

> [...] although the organisation of research differs little from that in France [...] it is nevertheless important to note the close relationship between universities and industry that exists in the United-States. These relations, as it was pointed out to me on several occasions, have proven extremely advantageous, not only to the expansion of scientific research, but also to the development of industry.[142]

As the quotation above suggests, French observers were often allowed to see only what the host country wanted them to see, but were perhaps also told only what they themselves wished to hear. Nevertheless, these visits had a considerable influence on the reconstruction of French science and industry after the war. The British and American examples guided French plans to produce French penicillin, with the knowledge that the chosen method might also be applied to other antibiotics in years to come. For that purpose, in 1946, the Société Nationale des Produits Biochimiques (grouping together representatives of the Pasteur Institute, CNRS and all the major ministries) was created by decree. Although it was inspired by the American example of wartime co-ordination, references were also made to the twenty-year-old French model of the Office National Industriel de l'Azote.[143] The main task of the Société was to make the manufacture of new biochemical products, first penicillin and then streptomycin, more extensive, by setting up factories to carry out the production of penicillin, of which the centre Cabanel was to become one amongst many. These factories had the status of public establishment (with certain financial benefits such as tax relief), functioned like industry, but co-existed with private companies pursuing the same objectives.

The two principal factories where the deep fermentation process was being developed under contract from the Direction des Poudres (the French equivalent of the MoS) were in Seclin, owned by the Société Rapidase, and at the Poudrerie de Ripault, near Sisteron, owned by the Société Française des Glycérines, and working in association with Rhône-Poulenc. Military officials wished for surface culture to be maintained, as it had been in the United States and in Britain, until deep fermentation was fully developed, but scientists from the CNRS — Wurmser, Prévost, Fromageot, Aubel, and Terroine — strongly opposed the idea. They threatened to leave any committee, in this case, the Comité Scientifique des Antibiotiques, which supported the principle of surface culture. Although surface culture could be maintained for the study of new antibiotic substances, it was generally felt that deep fermentation alone carried with it the seal of quality that medical doctors had come to expect from American penicillin (at the time, a rumour that the only suitable penicillin for therapeutic purposes was *P. chrysogenum* was circulating amongst the medical profession). If French penicillin was ever to have a chance of competing with the American product, then it had to be manufactured using American methods. What's more, the British example, with the closure of surface culture plants such as that of Wellcome, which shut down barely a year after it had been opened at the beginning of 1945, and with the opening of a government factory at Speke, modelled on the American Distillers factory which used only deep fermentation, guided the French in their decision to concentrate on the development of submerged culture.[144]

Pushing the comparison between wartime Britain and post-war France even further, an international co-operative arrangement like the one between Britain and the Unitd States was envisaged between France and Belgium, where the production of penicillin was under way, like in France. In Louvain, the government had created a center for antibiotic research at the Institute of Bacteriology, where the university collaborated with industry and with financiers; in Genval, the firm Soprolac produced penicillin using a Schenley process.[145] Preliminary steps were taken to explore the possibility of such an arrangement, but nothing seemed to come of it.

Nevertheless, the idea of international co-operation on a scientific project had been sown. Pestre has shown that, with the advent of 'big science', French physicists actively sought collaboration with their old rivals, the Germans, whose country, like France, had been relegated to second rank in the new world order.[146]

E. CONCLUSION

In sum, the centralized structure of French society had been shattered by war. However, from this traumatic experience arose opportunities for creating new structures and new networks. The administration of the Pasteur

Institute underwent reform, and new alliances were forged between Rhône-Poulenc and clinicians in provincial centers, and with IG Farben. These lay the foundation of the company's post-war collaborative networks. Meanwhile, it distanced itself from Fourneau's laboratory, and developed synthetic anti-histamines independently. These substances represented a genuine French wartime development, but at the end of the war, penicillin, rather than the anti-histamines that had been developed under the watchful eye of IG Farben, was adopted as the symbol of successful co-operation between science and industry. Its development was imitated, step by step, in order to learn the co-operative practices that had accompanied it in Britain and the United States.

How long-lasting were the structures developed in World War Two, and for a time adopted as part of post-war reconstruction?[147] Many were long-lived, because they were based on scientists' personal knowledge of models from abroad. Nevertheless, as these models were being adopted, they were also being adapted to suit the French context.[148] Others were short-lived, because of the weight of pre-war structures, and of recent experience. France recovered its centralized structure, French research remained relatively unco-ordinated until the advent of the Délégation Générale à la Recherche Scientifique et Technique (DGRST), and the CNRS acquired a distinctive emphasis on fundamental research, in reaction to its former emphasis on applied research under Vichy.[149]

This distinctive emphasis was possible because of the key role played by scientists in the Provisional Government and the post-war reconstruction of France. The most striking illustration of this can be found in the story of the development of French Atomic Policy after the war, in which David Pace has seen 'continuity through revolution', when a new generation of scientists, some of whom were younger members of scientific dynasties referred to by Spencer Weart as the 'children of l'Arcouest', came to the fore, thus becoming the scientific 'avant-garde'.[150]

Part II

Conclusion

War had provided Britain and France with very different tests of their social structures.[1] Whereas British networks were strengthened by war, the close relationship between Rhône-Poulenc and Fourneau's laboratory at the Pasteur Institute became looser, reflecting the divisions within French society brought on by defeat and Occupation, and the difficulties in maintaining normal channels of communication. In Britain, collaborative practices between scientists and pharmaceutical firms evolved together with the penicillin project, which introduced formality and hierarchy into British networks, and resulted in an international co-operative scheme involving British and American research institutions and drug companies, co-ordinated by government agencies on both sides of the Atlantic.

Meanwhile, war and Occupation provided France with opportunities for more radical change. The Pasteur Institute began its movement of reform, and Rhône-Poulenc developed new contacts with clinicians, especially in the Southern Unoccupied Zone. Some of these changes were to survive beyond the war. Although France recovered its centralized structure, the Institute pursued its agenda for radical reform under Jacques Monod, and the firm maintained its links with researchers in provincial centres and with other companies in France and abroad.

Following Marwick's four-tiered model, the evidence presented in Part 2 therefore suggests that:

1. in World War Two, France suffered greater disruption than Britain;
2. whereas the war provided a negative test of France's social structures, on the whole it provided a positive test of Britain's, especially in relation to science and technology;[2]
3. in Britain, the encouragement to participate in the war effort was sustained throughout the war, whereas in France participation occurred mostly in the period of mobilisation and the Liberation;
4. the psychological impact of World War Two was considerable in both countries, but more traumatic in France because of military defeat and Occupation.

Having compared the French and British experiences of war in the twentieth century, Marwick has concluded that, by the end of World War Two, France had suffered a dramatic change, much as Britain had done by the end of World War One. This provided French élites with the 'mental set' required for radical post-war reconstruction, whereas their British counterparts were lulled into a false sense of security because they had won the war.[3] Judging by the first and fourth tiers in Marwick's model, the impact of World War Two was therefore greater on France than it was on Britain. Nevertheless, the second and third tiers suggest that it was considerable on Britain as well, because of the large-scale participation of its scientists and industrialists in the war effort.

The evidence presented in Part 2 shows that Marwick's analysis could also be applied to the medical sciences and the pharmaceutical industry, but only up to a point. As well as contrasting the two countries' experiences of war, I have highlighted important similarities between them. Continuities between mobilization, war and post-war reconstruction occurred in France as in Britain. Wartime developments, such as penicillin and synthetic anti-histamines, depended not only on the long-term accumulation of scientific knowledge and technical know-how, but also on pre-existing relationships between scientists and pharmaceutical companies. However, in war, powerful new links were established with government agencies and with clinical researchers, which to a large extent would continue after peace had returned, leading to what is sometimes referred to as a 'biomedical complex'.[4]

Despite these continuities, war therefore presented opportunities to break with the past, in rhetoric as well as in practice. As war was replaced by peace, accounts of the recent past began to arise. These were often negative accounts:[5] British failure was contrasted with American success at developing penicillin; French inability to carry out collaborative research was contrasted with the Anglo-Saxon spirit of co-operation that had won the war.

Historians have sometimes reproduced these accounts without questioning them. Thus, it has been said that French science was revived as a result of the new era of international co-operation that began after World War Two.[6] It is also often believed that the French learnt the value of teamwork in that period.[7] Yet, as I have shown in Chapter 2, teamwork and co-operation had existed in France, at least in the pharmaceutical sector, long before Word War Two. Similarly, co-operation and enterprise were not lacking on the part of the British pharmaceutical industry, and these held the key to Britain's success with penicillin, as shown in Chapter 3.

Hence, the question remains what of the origins of such negative discourses. Perhaps they emerged in order to obscure painful memories: in Britain memories of penicillin being 'lost' to (or stolen by)[8] the Americans because of economic hardship, and in France memories of collaboration with Nazi Germany, because of military defeat. It is significant that these negative discourses were intertwined with a rhetoric of backwardness and decline. They arose at a time of recognition that Britain and France were no longer first-rank world powers. Their comparable experiences, reflected in development of penicillin and of synthetic anti-histamines, were highlighted in Part 2. In Part 3, I emphasize the different impact the war had on Britain and France, and explain these differences in terms of the two countries' distinct approaches to post-war reconstruction.

Part III

Continuity and Change in Medical Science and Industry after World War Two

INTRODUCTION

After the war, a shift in the meaning of the term co-operation occurred. The former emphasis on a close relationship between science and industry was replaced by a new emphasis on a close relationship with government. Co-operation was seen as a key to modernity, which social reconstruction would help to bring about. However, this happened differently in Britain and France.

In Britain, a return to pre-war models was the preferred course of action, whereas in France, the war represented a sharper break with the past.[1] Paradoxically, although in Britain post-war rhetoric stressed change and modernity, of which penicillin was a potent symbol, on the contrary, the continuity of science and culture was emphasized in France.[2] To highlight this paradox, I have entitled Chapter 5 on France: 'Continuity through revolution', whereas Chapter 6 on Britain is: 'Revolution through continuity'.[3]

Chapter 5 argues that French post-war reconstruction was more radical. It was planned and prescriptive, and led to an uneasy relationship between scientists and companies. Thus, the Pasteur Institute and Rhône-Poulenc went their separate ways, forging new alliances. By contrast, Chapter 6 shows that, despite their attempt to develop stronger links with the representatives of the pharmaceutical industry and introduce formality and hierarchy in the numerous collaborative projects of the post-war period, the MRC maintained a relatively close relationship with individual firms, in a largely *ad hoc* response to each new drug being developed. On the other hand, at the grass-roots level the picture was also complex. Scientists such as Florey, Abraham and Chain present contrasting models of interaction with pharmaceutical companies, the first moving gradually away from industrial applications, the latter retaining a close link with industry. Similarly, the companies or institutions they collaborated with, ICI, the NRDC and Beecham, built up different relationships with their consultants.

As a result of penicillin and the numerous other antibiotics that followed it, many pharmaceutical companies adopted research, more specifically chemotherapeutic research, as a core activity. In doing so, they took over a role, which until then had largely been fulfilled by the institutes of medical research. This shift, from an academic to an industrial context for drug research, is studied principally through chlorpromazine on the French side, and through cortisone, fluothane, cephalosporin and semi-synthetic penicillins on the British side. These were novel 'experiments in collaboration', in which companies and their new — often mainly clinical — networks were now playing a major role.

5 'Continuity through Revolution' in France[1]

A. INTRODUCTION

French reconstruction in biomedicine and pharmaceuticals, like in many other areas of science and industry, presents both radical and conservative features. This was partly attributable to France's demographic situation, as a new generation of scientists, many of whom were associated with the resistance movement, came to maturity at the end of the war.[2] The departure of Fourneau from the Pasteur Institute, followed by his death, symbolized the passing of a generation and, with it, of a close and personal relationship with industry. At the same time, the Pasteur Institute underwent a wave of reforms that eventually led to the separation of its two traditional functions of research and production. It developed its vocation of fundamental research, which enabled it to survive as a scientific institution, but in so doing distanced itself from industry.

Meanwhile, the growth of clinical research, encouraged by a new national system of health care and by the reform of medical education organized by Robert Debré, provided industry with a new kind of collaborator. It was such a collaborator, in the person of the naval surgeon Henri Laborit, who led Rhône-Poulenc to chlorpromazine. Like French post-war reconstruction, chlorpromazine combined radical and conservative features. Although revolutionary in its application to psychiatry, it was derived from the phenothiazine amines, a series of compounds familiar to the company and the fruit of its long association with Fourneau's laboratory. To reflect such continuities, the chapter therefore begins with a description of Fourneau's brief post-war career and the fate of the Therapeutic Chemistry Laboratory after his death.

B. ERNEST FOURNEAU AND THE THERAPEUTIC CHEMISTRY LABORATORY IN THE AFTERMATH OF WAR

The transition from war to peace was doubly difficult for Fourneau. Having been accused of collaboration with Germany and subsequently imprisoned, he resigned from his post at the Pasteur Institute (see Chapter 4). However, he did not leave without preparing his succession. In a letter to Raymond Paul dated 17 June 1945, he suggested that there should be no more contracts linking the Therapeutic Chemistry Laboratory and Rhône-Poulenc, even though financial support should continue 'with which the director should be free to do whatever he wishes'.[3]

1. Fourneau's legacy

Since 1940, the director of the Pasteur Institute was Jacques Tréfouël, an old collaborator of Rhône-Poulenc. Hence these arrangements were unlikely to pose major problems. However, as this chapter will show, loosening the ties between the laboratory and the group in this way would make it easier for Jacques Monod, once he became director of the Institute in 1971, to sever the links with Rhône-Poulenc.

Fourneau recommended that the 'Director's fund', as he called it, should be used for cases like Montézier's, a lab technician who, without any academic qualifications, had little prospect of being able to improve his status or salary. He also recommended that agreements be made on an individual basis with Nitti, Bovet and Funke, and that his letter be torn up so that no trace would remain of his intervention in their favour. This particular wish was thankfully (for historians!) never carried out, although subsequent correspondence shows that Fourneau's other recommendations were implemented by Rhône-Poulenc.[4] Whilst preparing his succession at the Therapeutic Chemistry Laboratory, Fourneau made plans for a brand new laboratory, created for him within the administrative HQ of Rhône-Poulenc in the rue Jean Goujon in Paris. The location of this laboratory was symbolic of the place he had occupied at the heart of the company's corporate image.

Post-war reconstruction offered the opportunity for a fresh start for Fourneau. The bulk of the building work was completed by the beginning of 1947, filling him with high hopes for this 'new domain', where he pictured himself walking proudly, like a Lord ('comme un grand seigneur').[5]

2. The new domain of the rue Jean Goujon

The roles he intended for his new laboratory were: 1) to carry out research independently of the factory; 2) to train the future managers of industrial laboratories; 3) to select and train permanent collaborators; and 4) to welcome French and foreign chemists. His good contacts with research institutions and industrial laboratories, which included the Parfumerie Houbigant (whose methods he considered to be very close to those of a chemotherapeutic laboratory), the Laboratoires Scientia and the Institut Gay-Lussac, provided him with technicians, equipment and chemicals. By 1948, he had gathered an embryonic research team, which for a time included his son

Jean-Pierre, and to which he hoped to add Marc Julia, who had worked in his laboratory at the Pasteur Institute. However, after spending two years in Heilbron's laboratory at Imperial College, Julia chose instead to go to the Sorbonne, before returning to the Institute in 1957 as the new director of the Therapeutic Research Laboratory.[6]

In the rue Jean Goujon, Fourneau's team began an investigation of local anaesthetics. On the whole, rather than tackle theoretical problems such as penicillin synthesis, Fourneau preferred to return to old questions, which he felt had not been answered fully.[7] In a letter to Raymond Paul, he wrote that in his new laboratory he saw the crowning glory of his career.[8] His words suggest that Fourneau may have hoped that an Institute bearing his name, like Pasteur or Mérieux, would be created around his new laboratory. If so, his dream was never fulfilled. In 1949 his health deteriorated rapidly, and after his death, which occurred later that year, the laboratory of the rue Jean Goujon was dismantled.

The dismantling of Fourneau's 'new domain', in which he had invested so much hope, requires an explanation. The correspondence between Paul and Fourneau indicates that the company was losing interest in their collaboration, which no longer seemed to serve any practical purpose. They argued about the status of chemotherapeutic research. Fourneau sensed that the company thought of it as an applied, or 'inferior order' of chemistry.[9] Paul responded by saying that pure chemistry and chemotherapy were different areas of research, and that the company increasingly relied on its collaborators for their insights in pure chemistry, rather than chemotherapy, which was now done in-house. Fourneau objected to this distinction. In his view, all chemistry, whether pure or therapeutic, was a matter of inter-disciplinary research. However, his choice of projects for study suggests that he was no longer at the cutting-edge of science. With penicillin, a new era in chemotherapeutic research had begun, in which he showed little interest. Moreover, his criteria for selecting collaborators were reminiscent of an earlier age, in which science was a gentlemanly (or gentlewomanly) pursuit: 'I need well brought up, well educated people, presentable, and able to accomplish any mission'.[10]

Fourneau belonged to an older generation, whose approach to science was ill-adapted to the post-war context. Furthermore, the time for such a close collaboration as that between Rhône-Poulenc and him had passed. The group had been developing its in-house pharmaceutical research facilities, and the need to maintain a laboratory such as Fourneau's was no longer perceived as essential to its interests. Then why the group had created the laboratory for a man of Fourneau's age, long past retirement, requires even more of an explanation than why it was dismantled upon his death.

Fourneau himself suggested an answer to the question in a letter addressed to Raymond Paul. He voiced the feeling that, through the creation of his new laboratory, Rhône-Poulenc had found a way of expressing their gratitude towards him.[11] This lucid observation on the part of Fourneau, as well as the closure of his laboratory after his death, indicates that it was indeed the case. The new laboratory had been a personal gift, which, if the tone of Fourneau's letters is a faithful reflection of his state of mind, succeeded in making his last few years happy and hopeful.

Meanwhile, the relationship between the Therapeutic Chemistry Laboratory and Rhône-Poulenc had been evolving, independently of Fourneau.

3. The Therapeutic Chemistry Laboratory after Fourneau (1949–1970)

After Fourneau's departure, a small part of his research team was reconstituted in Rome when Daniel Bovet moved with his wife Filomena to the Istituto Superiore di Sanità in 1948. Bovet referred to his new home as the 'capital of pharmacology and biochemistry',[12] and to his new laboratory as Fourneau's legacy.[13] He and Filomena were soon to be joined there not only by Ernst Chain, but also by their former collaborators Albert Funke and Germaine Benoît (who had married Funke) in 1960. This prompted the following reaction from Raymond Paul, expressed in a letter to Bovet:

> [...] this will be perfect for Mr Funke, who in your laboratory will find a position that would probably be difficult for him to obtain at the Pasteur Institute. Moreover, his presence will be of benefit to you, for you know his qualities as an organic chemist, as well as those of Miss Benoît (I mean Mrs Funke), better than anyone. Both have great admiration for you, and this will create a good team in Rome.[14]

At first, there had been uncertainty as to whether or not Bovet would continue to receive Rhône-Poulenc's support after leaving for Rome. In a letter to Fourneau dated September 1947, Filomena stressed that, because of her father, and because of the political turmoil in which Italy was plunged at the time, they certainly had no intention of turning to Italian industry for help.[15] On the other hand, as well as the additional support their laboratory would require, they would welcome the additional income that a consultancy would bring them.[16] Bovet's ties with the French group were soon resumed (with back-payment), and he thereby entered the third and last phase in their association, which lasted until he left Rome:

1. consultancy fee from Rhône-Poulenc : 15 Oct. 1929–1 Dec. 1942 (in Fourneau's laboratory)
2. salaried employee of Rhône-Poulenc : 1 Dec. 1942–31 July 1947 (Pharmaceutical Research Department)
3. consultancy fee from Rhône-Poulenc : 1 Aug. 1947–30 June 1967 (Rome)[17]

Meanwhile in Paris, although the collaboration between the Therapeutic Chemistry Laboratory and Rhône-Poulenc survived beyond Fourneau's and Bovet's departure, a golden age had passed. After a period of transition during which Thérèse Tréfouël ran the laboratory, Germaine Benoît became its new director, working in various areas, including analgesics, from 1950 until her departure for Rome in 1960. This period has been described by Jean Igolen as rather dispersed. It was not until Marc Julia's appointment as the new head of the Laboratory that clear direction was given to the group and that the internal dissensions and divisions that had crippled it after Fourneau's departure ceased.[18] Under Julia's leadership, the laboratory survived not only the economic crisis that beset the Pasteur Institute, but also the first wave of reforms that began the transformation of the Institute, and enabled it to adapt to the new post-war environment.

C. THE PASTEUR INSTITUTE IN THE POST-WAR WORLD

The detailed accounts, as they appear in the minutes of Council, show that, despite the great immunisation programmes against tuberculosis and d-t-polio, and the agreement by the Sécurité Sociale (created in 1945) to cover the production costs incurred by the Institute, growing expenditure created a deficit that threatened its very survival. A first wave of reforms, which was to change its status from a private to a semi-public institution, was instigated with the aim of arresting the crisis. However, this transformation was also to pave the way for more fundamental changes, which in time would contribute to loosening the ties between the Institute and industry.

1. Financial crisis and structural reforms (1945–1965)

Growing demand for its products and a burgeoning scientific staff (in 1947 the Pasteur Institute staff numbered 1050, including 32 'chefs de service', i.e. heads of department) placed it under considerable financial strain. It was caught in a vicious circle, needing to delve into its reserves in order to produce more vaccines and sera to maintain a healthy cash flow.[19] As early as 1948, the Conseil d'Administration envisaged the option of seeking state support for research at the Institute. The Cité Universitaire, which had been allowed to maintain its autonomy and independence thanks to decrees defining its status as a public establishment, was held up as an example the Institute might wish to follow.[20] But resistance to a change in status, and to the loss of independence this might entail, was strong. Arguments for and against were shuffled back and forth at meetings of the Council and the Assembly for a period of almost twenty years, until a compromise was reached, and the Pasteur Institute became a partly state-funded institution, whilst maintaining an element of its former autonomy.[21]

Nevertheless, in the short term, structural reforms, leading to a better adjustment of spending to earnings, was the chosen course of action. At a meeting of the Council held in February 1948, Germain Martin declared that the time for radical reform had come.[22] This involved a reorganization of the accounts, and a reduction in the number of staff in some departments.

With expenditures continuing to soar, and earnings stationary or even decreasing, in 1951 the Council proposed to add four measures to its efforts to control spending. The first was to increase prices — difficult in the highly competitive field of vaccines; the second, to exploit the French market more efficiently; the third, to increase sales in overseas territories, despite the fact that these areas were already being targeted by representatives of French and foreign pharmaceutical companies; and the fourth, to develop exports in general — but there again, the problem was competition from the private sector.[23]

In order to implement the last two measures, the Institute needed help from its overseas subsidiaries. These had been highly profitable enterprises, thanks in part to extensive government subsidies before 1945. However, as the former French Colonial Empire was being replaced by a new form of association: 'l'Union Française', these subsidiaries were subjected to budget constraints. Because of their relatively high ratio of profits to research costs, they were nonetheless in a healthier financial situation than the 'maison-mère.'[24]

Whatever savings were made thanks to the measures listed above, they were offset by salary increases, which were needed for the Institute to compete with the private sector, and also with the public sector, by continuing to attract researchers of high caliber.[25]

2. Growing competition in science and industry

The Pasteur Institute was under growing pressure from rival institutions in both science and industry. The relationship between the Institute and industry remained complex. In 1953, the director defined the function of the Pasteur Institute with the following words:

> [...] what one must expect from the IP in the future, concerning the means of combatting and preventing infectious diseases, is research into natural antibiotic substances and the study of viruses.[26]

Hence, the Institute continued to express its role in terms of the study and therapy of infectious diseases, using a two-pronged approach: prevention (with vaccines) and treatment (with antibiotics). This approach placed it in an ambiguous position, as both a potential competitor and a collaborator of industry, as illustrated by the formal contract that was drawn up to allow members of the Institute to consult for the antibiotic manufacturer, the

Société Industrielle pour la Fabrication des Antibiotiques (SIFA).[27] However, because of the demise of Fourneau's group, although Rhône-Poulenc continued to subsidize projects such as the chemotherapy of tuberculosis under Noël Rist in the Tuberculosis Department, on the whole the Institute and the pharmaceutical industry drifted apart.[28]

Whilst distancing itself from commercial firms, the Institute competed with them, particularly in the field of vaccines. The conflict between the two vocations of the Institute, as a non-profit-making enterprise and as an academic institution, was reflected in the promotion of M. Prévot, which had been decided not only on the basis of the practical importance of his research, but also of its 'high moral value' (by which it was meant that he had received no subsidy from industry).[29] Indeed, Prévot had developed a process for the mass-production of bacteria in large fermenters, probably inspired by his wartime penicillin work, a process that could be applied to the preparation of purified toxins, and therefore benefit the Institute's core vaccine business.[30]

In addition, the Institute's dual vocation placed it in an ambiguous position with respect to other research institutions, with which it had to compete to an extent unprecedented in its history. Like them, the Institute needed state support to pay for a rising research bill, but at the same time vied with them for funds and influence. No longer the only institute for biological and medical research in France, its relationship with the CNRS, which took on biomedical research in earnest after the war, and presided over the creation of numerous new laboratories,[31] was complex. Although the Centre paid for the salaries of several researchers at the Institute, it was felt that the costs incurred were not sufficiently compensated by the support received.[32] The Pasteur Institute also had intricate relations with the Institut National d'Hygiène (INH), a government agency created by the Vichy regime, which after the war transformed its initial aim of data collection and co-ordination of research into a veritable scientific programme, at first focusing mainly on nutrition and reproductive medicine.[33] After becoming INSERM in 1964, its funding increased, and its research programme expanded.[34] By 1971, it provided half of the Pasteur Institute's funds, the rest coming from the sale of vaccines, sera, and laboratory products.[35]

In its dealings with the CNRS and INH, the Pasteur Institute emphasized its academic vocation, hence co-operation with industry increasingly threatened its image as a scientific institution.[36] The term co-operation began to signify, instead, a better integration with the government and its health policies, begun under Vichy, and with its research agenda, pursued after the war via the quinquennial Plans.[37] Between 1942 and 1948, the Institute had provided assistance to the Service Central de Pharmacie at the Ministère de la Santé Publique for testing pharmaceutical preparations. After the creation of the Sécurité Sociale, it dealt with applications for pharmaceutical visas by various small firms on behalf of the Ministry, and helped with the drafting of the Pharmaceutical Codex.[38] It was rewarded for this co-operation when, in 1954, the Commission de la Recherche Scientifique et Technique (CRST) created earlier as part of the 2nd Plan,[39] offered to subsidize its research costs in order to compensate it for the losses incurred after the devaluation of the fund in which private donations were accumulated ('fond de dotation'). The idea behind the offer was to make up for the damage caused to French medical research by this devaluation.[40]

However, having to spend more and more money on research, whilst struggling to keep up with new developments in the pharmaceutical industry, especially in the field of vaccines where it was falling below the standard of its competitors, the Pasteur Institute was under huge strain after the war, and such a situation was clearly untenable.[41] It faced a stark choice: either to relinquish its independence from government interference and become, at least in part, a state-supported scientific institution, like the other institutions with which it was competing for funds, or else disappear, like the Lister a few years later. The combination of new opportunities for collaboration with government under the Fourth and Fifth Republics, and the succession of deep financial crises in the aftermath of war, led the Administrative Council to accept a semi-public status for the Pasteur Institute.

3. The long road from private to public institution (1958–1965)

The path that led the Institute to relinquish its private status was long and protracted. It began in 1958, with an appeal to the newly created Délegation Générale à la Recherche Scientifique et Technique (DGRST), and ended in 1965, when a semi-public status was finally adopted. This was to pave the way for another major change: the separation between research and production. The next two sections describe the transformation of the Institute, from the 1958 appeal, to the final divorce between its two principal functions in 1971.

The Pasteur Institute had always been considered as an Establishment of Public Utility, and as such benefited from government support in the shape of subsidies for research and tax relief on the profits from the sales of vaccines. However, fear of accountability to the state had long prevented it from surrendering its private status. What had changed in 1965, to make it accept such accountability? In 1960 the polio vaccine was proving very profitable, boosted its earnings to the extent that it was beginning to feel exposed to the watchful gaze of the Treasury.[42] However, in the mid-1960s, once again, it began to suffer from serious financial difficulties.

As well as financial crisis, there was another reason for such a change of heart. In 1957, a new government fund, designed to support scientific research, was established by decree. This was followed in 1958 by the creation of the DGRST, with the task of co-ordinating all research, pure *and* applied. Thus, the Institute came fully under its umbrella, in a way that had not been possible under the CNRS, partly because of its post-war emphasis on fundamental research.[43] These two events presented the Institute with fresh opportunities, but also with increased pressure to maintain its standard and status as a scientific institution. The following words consigned to the minute book revealed its awareness that state funding is a two-edged sword:

> As a result [of the fund for scientific research created by the decree of 14 March 1957] the Council is unanimous in its belief that, because of the high standard of its research, the quality of its work, the place it occupies in French scientific research, and its contribution to French culture, which are indisputable, the IP cannot be denied the moral and material support provided by the government fund, created to encourage and reward scientific research carried out for the advancement of science.[44]

State funding brought with it an official seal of approval, which the Institute could ill afford to be without. Therefore, it launched an appeal for support to the DGRST. As an outcome of this appeal, the same conclusion was reached by both the DGRST and the Institute. In order to benefit from state funding, it had to go 'public', and for this, there must be a separation between 'research' and 'production'.[45] Although the Institute could continue to draw income from the sale of Pasteurian innovations in the shape of a percentage, its two functions should become clearly distinct, making government support less problematic.[46] A geographical separation between the production units and the research laboratories was contemplated to facilitate this distinction. Thus, the Institute's decentralization committee ('Comité de Décentralisation') proposed to move the production laboratories to Montpellier, and later to Rambouillet. Perhaps the fact that Gaston Ramon had died earlier that year made it easier to break up the traditional ties that had existed between research and production (le 'cercle de la recherche et de la production', as Jacques Tréfouël referred to it).[47]

Plans to change the status of the Institute and separate its research activities from the production of biological remedies were therefore being considered from 1958 onwards. Nevertheless, it took until 1965 for a semi-public status to be adopted, and longer still for the final divorce between research and production. Why such a long time-lag? The evidence suggests that the reformers faced strong opposition, which had first to be quashed.

Several members of the Council (such as Pasteur Vallery-Radot and Antoine Pinay) were against direct control by the state. Their objections to the 'rapprochement' with government were similar to those expressed vis-à-vis the creation within the walls of the Pasteur Institute of a new institute of molecular biochemistry ('Institut de Biochimie Moléculaire'), believed to threaten its traditional balance between academic subjects. As a result the proposal was rejected.[48] Similarly, the opponents to a change of status felt that state control would destroy the close relationship between pure and applied research that had characterized the Institute since its creation.

Nonetheless, the financial crisis, which was deepening by the mid-1960s, began to erode resistance to change. In what follows, the reformers' campaign is also shown to have played an important role in turning the tide in favour of change.

4. Reforming for science in the modern world

The story of this campaign, victorious in the end, deserves to be told in greater detail than it is possible here, for the post-war transformation of the Pasteur Institute is tied to the rise of the French biomedical complex, and to the emergence of France as a technocratic nation.[49] However, a few words can be said to explain its impact on the relationship between scientists and the pharmaceutical industry.

Among the reformers, Elie Wollman, François Jacob, and later Jacques Monod, were leading figures of the new discipline of molecular biology. They were able to use their strong position within the DGRST and the CNRS,[50] and the prestige gained by François Jacob and Jacques Monod from their Nobel Prize, awarded jointly André Lwoff in 1965, to transform the Pasteur Institute both from within and from without.[51] Their strategy consisted in mobilising their colleagues through the Trade Union of Scientific Personnel ('Syndicat du Personnel Scientifique') established in 1958.[52] In 1964, they formed a commission to study the reform of the Pasteur Institute, and published a booklet that was circulated for ratification by the staff before being sent on to the Director. The main objective of the reform, as laid out in the booklet, was the separation between research and production.[53] However, in order to achieve this objective, it was necessary to overturn the Council, which had become the chief obstacle to reform. Their eventual success in overturning the Council resembled a 'coup d'état,' rather than a revolution as it has sometimes been portrayed, because of the crucial role played by a handful of leading scientists.[54] This, rather than measures imposed from above, was to open up the way for the transformation of the Pasteur Institute into a modern research institution. However, it was not until a member of the select group of radical reformers, Jacques Monod, became Director, that its transformation became complete (see Figure 5.1).

Monod responded as much to what was seen as an obstacle to the transformation of the Pasteur Institute into an institution carrying out fundamental research, as to financial crisis.[55] Since 1965, state subsidies had been disappointingly low, totaling only 19% in 1971, which was interpreted as uncertainty on the part of government as to the Institute's will for reform.[56] However, the words used by Monod to delineate the role of the Institute revealed a radical change since 1953, when it had been defined in relation to therapy:[57] 'the fundamental vocation of the IP: the advancement of biology for the benefit of mankind'.[58] Thus, the separation between research and production at the Institute went hand in hand with what has been

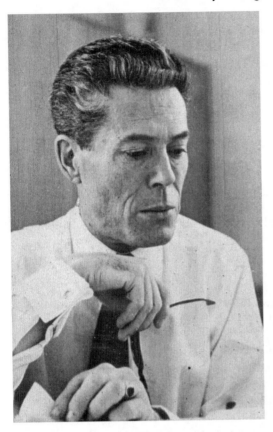

Figure 5.1 Jacques Monod (courtesy of the Pasteur Institute).

described as the 'de-medicalisation' of biology (i.e. the growing separation between biology and medicine), and the 'fundamentalisation' of knowledge (i.e. the increasingly fundamental level of analysis in biological and clinical research) achieved on the national stage by Monod and his colleagues through the DGRST.[59]

The measures taken by Monod were therefore inscribed within an immediate context, that of the financial crisis of the Institute, but also within a long, drawn-out period of reform, at once local and national in character. Many of the changes he advocated, in particular the election of a Director for the Production Centre with industrial experience, had been recommended earlier by the reform committee.[60] However, it is significant that one of his first actions as director of the Pasteur Institute was to close the Therapeutic Chemistry Laboratory, which had collaborated almost sixty years with Rhône-Poulenc. This gesture was of a highly symbolic nature. By aiming for this particular laboratory, which had long been at the heart of the relationship between the Institute and industry, Monod hoped to remove any ambiguity as to the Institute's role as a scientific institution.[61] It was also part of his great plan for the reorganisation of Pasteurian research, reflecting what he saw as the evolution of the biomedical sciences toward basic research. Hence, under this plan, pharmacology was subsumed under the new discipline of cellular or molecular biology.[62]

Whatever were the reformers' motives, their actions meant that the Pasteur survived as research institution. This can be contrasted with the fate of other institutions at around the same time, when the Lister Institute for instance was compelled to close its laboratories: first in Chelsea (in 1975), and second in Elstree (the vaccine and sera laboratories, in 1978). In 1981, the new existence of the Lister as a grant-making body began. In 1982, the Council was disbanded, and the memorandum and articles of the Association were amended.[63]

Meanwhile, the pharmaceutical industry was also having to adapt to the new, post-war context. This is followed through the history of Rhône-Poulenc, which expanded its R&D as well as its research networks at home and abroad, thus sowing the seeds for innovation from the 1950s.

D. RHÔNE-POULENC, THE EXPANSION OF PHARMACEUTICAL R&D AND OF RESEARCH NETWORKS IN THE SECOND HALF OF THE TWENTIETH CENTURY

The expansion of Rhône-Poulenc's in-house pharmaceutical R&D facilities in response to a rising demand for medicines on the home market, and to growing competition on an international market rendered more complex by new advances in science and technology, is characteristic of the French pharmaceutical industry as a whole in this period.[64] Because of its size and the privileged relationship it developed with government, Rhône-Poulenc was also a trend setter. However, the extent to which its example was followed by the rest of the industry, which despite increasing concentration remained fragmented, and until the advent of the DGRST was relatively unco-ordinated in its efforts, is a matter for debate. Another debate, which can only be referred to briefly here, is the extent to which Rhône-Poulenc was able to sustain its post-war momentum to overcome the difficulties that beset the entire industry in the 1970s.[65]

1. Strengthening the links with government: the role of penicillin in particular, and of pharmaceuticals in general

The development of penicillin led to closer links between firms and government, which would culminate in the nationalization of the industry for a short period in the 1970s. Unlike most other drugs, which were placed on a restrictive list of medicines reimbursed by the Sécurité Sociale and were subjected to a stringent price regulation system, penicillin, judged irreplaceable by the Commission for Work and Social Security, was reimbursed in its entirety despite its initial high cost.[66] Moreover, antibiotic producers were encouraged and given special advantages, by a government otherwise largely inattentive to the industry's needs. Thus, thanks to their efforts at the large-scale manufacture of penicillin, and subsequently streptomycin, from 1948 onwards Rhône-Poulenc were able to obtain a series of loans from the Crédit National, at a time when the First Plan showed little interest in the chemical sector as a whole.[67] Similarly, a few years later, the Laboratoires Roger Bellon received two loans of 50 million-francs each from the Crédit National to build an antibiotics factory in Monts (Indre-et-Loire). Then, in 1959, the firm's Alfortville factories were moved to Monts, for which once again it obtained government assistance.[68]

The collaboration of private laboratories, which was offered in support of the government's promise of provision of mass medical care in the years following World War Two, was perceived as an irresistible movement by all concerned.[69] Hence, Rhône-Poulenc chose to invest heavily in pharmaceuticals, a crucial element in its commercial strategy. This was at once a strategy of survival — a legacy of the hardships experienced under German Occupation — and of expansion. Apart from petroleum products, pharmaceuticals not only represented the greatest share of the company's investments, but also the most important increase in the period 1947–52: from 18,28%, they grew to 23,79%.[70] However, this increase can almost entirely be attributed to antibiotics, which represented 4% of total sales in the 1950s, while the sales of other pharmaceutical specialties dropped, partly due to the loss of overseas markets suffered as a result of the war.[71]

High investment in pharmaceuticals went hand in hand with high investments in research. Pharmaceutical R&D, like the medicines that were its products, was presented as a service to the state.[72] Hence, in 1953–4, a new research centre was erected at Vitry-sur-Seine, and named the 'Centre Nicolas Grillet' after the former Director General of the group. Its main purpose was to develop drugs and plant-care products.[73] In this way, the Rhône-Poulenc laboratories acquired their present-day shape (see Figure 5.2). At the same time, Raymond Paul was made director of research for the whole group, and Pierre Viaud became director of pharmaceutical research in Vitry.

As a result of this growing emphasis on research in general, and the recognition of the importance of pharmaceutical R&D in particular, the number of Rhône-Poulenc patents soared in the 1950s. Therefore, despite the late adoption in France of a patent legislation favourable to the pharmaceutical industry,[74] pharmaceutical patents played a significant role in the firm's national and international competitive strategy.[75]

However, the evolution of Rhône-Poulenc owed as much to a continuation of previous trends, as to radical change in the aftermath of war. The group drew from past experience to produce fresh expertise that provided the basis of its post-war expansion (see Figure 5.3).

Figure 5.2 Centre Nicolas Grillet in the 1950s (courtesy of Sanofi-Aventis).

2. A modern company, following tradition

French post-war reconstruction presents a striking blend of modern and traditional features. Thus, the French market for drugs included old-fashioned pharmaceutical preparations as well as innovative drugs that were at the cutting-edge of therapy.[76] Similarly, when presenting itself as a modern company, Rhône-Poulenc tended to stress its contribution to the traditional French research path followed with the synthetic anti-histamines, rather than new developments such as antibiotics. Thus, the anti-histamine project was given considerable publicity after the war had ended. In 1946, the Director of Pharmaceutical Research Pierre Viaud made an announcement on the subject at the 20th Congress of Industrial Chemistry in Paris. In 1947, during a tour of the United States, Daniel Bovet took part in a symposium on anti-histamines, which he described as celebrating 'the glory of France and of Néo-Antergan... the most active and best tolerated (of all antihistamines)'. This led Bovet to write with optimism of the future of European science as a whole, which he contrasted with its American counterpart:

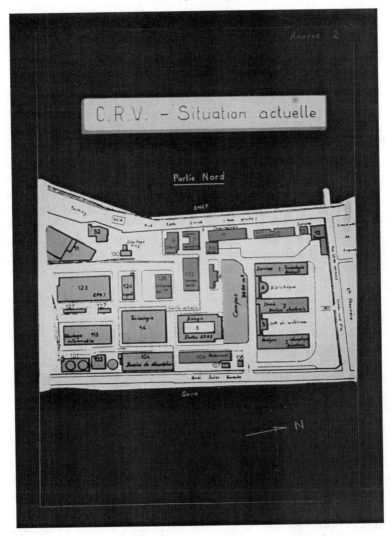

Figure 5.3 Plan of the research Centre in Vitry in the 1980s (courtesy of Sanofi-Aventis).

I have returned fully optimistic that there is plenty of space for us, Europeans, in research. All questions of politics kept aside, the Americans are heading straight for a massive form of capitalism that leaves little room for Latin individualism, personality and genius.[77]

Stressing the latter, in a note to Raymond Paul, Filomena Bovet-Nitti wrote of her husband's negative impressions of the United States:

Daniel thinks the United States are an awful country, and the Americans a people focused on antibiotics and anti-histamines with the principal aim of making lots of money. He writes that there is a whole world to discover, of which they know nothing.[78]

She expressed similar feelings in a letter to Fourneau.[79] In another, she painted a grey picture of post-war Britain, unlike America hardened by wartime privations, but like it spoiled by greed, its only redeeming factor being the congeniality and talent of its scientists, many of whom were refugees from Nazi Germany:

> Even though I detest this country, and it is particularly miserable at the moment, our colleagues there are charming, young and very friendly. In their laboratories they have welcomed a number of German scientists escaped from Nazi Germany, giving them full rights and honours. Such co-operation appears to have borne rich fruits. Thus, we saw Feldberg, Vogt, Schild, who seem to be pharmacologists, much more than they are Germans. I do not like Oxford much, the college in which we lodged was squalid, and the frankly reactionary atmosphere of this nobility based on money is unbearable. It is not like that in our two countries, where intelligent people only accept material domination if it is associated with moral and cultural superiority.[80]

Written at a time when France had to choose between East and West, when the communists were being ejected from government, and the Marshall Plan was being put in place, these comments had a political as well as a scientific dimension.[81] They revealed that a major shift had taken place, from a German to an American model of success in medical science and the pharmaceutical industry. This new model inspired ambiguous feelings in scientists such as Bovet. Like many left-wing intellectuals, he saw the process of Americanisation that accompanied economic aid after 1945 as a threat,[82] and found solace in the birth of the European Community.[83] In this tense international political context, France created itself anew, by forging a French path to central economic planning with the Plan Monnet and its sequels,[84] and by fashioning a French way of doing science.[85]

   This was achieved by following older trails, much as Fourneau had recommended before his death, as well as by developing the newer area of antibiotics. On both accounts, Rhône-Poulenc was innovative, developing drugs that had an impact on therapy and on medical science: spiramycin, and pristinamycin, two new antibiotics invented by the group; the synthetic anti-histamines, to combat the symptoms of allergy; and chlorpromazine, the first of the new class of neuroleptic drugs.[86] The latter was the result of a fresh focus on pharmaceutical research, but was also heir to a long scientific and technological tradition. It stemmed from a continuous practical experience of collaborative research, and from a substance familiar to the chemical industry: phenothiazine.[87]

Phenothiazine, which had been synthesized in 1883 by August Bernthsen in his search for the nucleus of methylene-blue compounds, long remained an important part of the technological arsenal of the chemical industry because of its considerable biological, medical and industrial applications, ranging from pesticides, anti-protozoal remedies, to synthetic fibres.[88] Towards the end of the war, a Rhône-Poulenc chemist, Paul Charpentier, synthesized a new series of phenothiazine derivatives, the phenothiazine amines, in the hope of finding a superior treatment for tropical diseases such as malaria. Unbeknown to him, these compounds had also been synthesized by an American team at Iowa State College, but found useless as anti-malarials.[89] Charpentier therefore persisted in his search, and synthesized prométhazine (Phénergan), which was tested by Halpern and discovered to have anti-histaminic properties (see Chapter 4).

After the war, the expansion of the synthetic textile industry following the discovery of nylon spurred interest in phenol and its derivatives, which became the object of intense research. And it was a phenol compound, more specifically another phenothiazine amine, which had been shelved because of its comparatively weak anti-histaminic activity and powerful effects on the central nervous system (compound 3276 RP),[90] which led to Rhône-Poulenc's great breakthrough in psychopharmacology and psychiatry, chlorpromazine.

These innovations were stimulated by the post-war political and economic context, but also by the new social landscape of post-war France. For Rhône-Poulenc, as for the Pasteur Institute, the term 'co-operation' acquired a new dimension. Shaped by the experience of war and by post-war reconstruction, it signified a better integration with government policies, a greater openness towards other pharmaceutical companies, and a wider network of institutional contacts, at home and abroad.

3. An expanding network at home and abroad

In the post-war era, a new trend developed, influenced by the experience of wartime research projects. Collaboration between university laboratories, government research institutions and industry, which has been described as the 'triple helix',[91] or, by analogy with the scientific-military-industrial complex of the Cold War, the 'biomedical complex',[92] grew in importance. This was accompanied by the formalization of academic-industrial relations, now increasingly underpinned by contracts and reciprocal agreements.

However, in France, the CNRS's new vocation as a basic research institution, later imitated by INSERM,[93] was an obstacle to the development of such open and systematic collaborations.[94] This was soon seen as a problem, which was deleterious to French science as well as industry. An early step to remedy the situation was taken in 1955, when a new commission was formed under the aegis of the Secretariat Technique de la Recherche Scientifique, the 'Commission des Contrats de Recherche'.[95]

The notes prepared for a meeting of the Commission on 3 March 1955 described the current situation:

> Advantages and drawbacks of the current system (or rather of the absence of system):
>
> 1. *Advantages* : flexibility, diversity (to be maintained as much as possible in any new system we will adopt).
> 2. *Drawbacks* : first of all the semi-clandestine nature [of academic-industrial relations], which creates financial difficulties, and has morally unpleasant consequences, such as rumours and suspicions surrounding the activities of some major French laboratories.
> 3. Next, their ill-defined roles, which often leave the different parties concerned feeling that they have both been cheated. (Moreover, on the academic side, after initially under-estimating the work to be done, there can be an over-estimation of the services rendered). Finally, a distraction away from the essential tasks of some laboratories.[96]

After its creation in 1958, the DGRST not only took on the co-ordination of all research, both fundamental and applied, but a dozen years later, identified pharmaceutical research as an area of particular concern, requiring greater co-operation between the public and private sectors, and deserving greater attention from the state. A major step towards this goal came in 1971, with the creation of the Commission de la Recherche Pharmaceutique, targeting academic-industrial relations in the biomedical field.[97] Notes prepared for the first meeting of this Commission suggested that the situation had not much improved since 1955.[98]

However, in the mean time, the pharmaceutical industry had had to make its own arrangements, independently of government efforts. Examples as to how to best remedy such a state of affairs were sought abroad. For instance in Germany, long a model in these matters, a new agency had been created, the 'Vermittlungstelle fur Vertragsforschung', with the aim of facilitating academic research projects carried out under contract on behalf of industry.[99] Because of the intense cross-Channel and cross-Atlantic exchanges that followed the war, examples were also found in Britain and America. Rhône-Poulenc renewed their contacts, which had been interrupted by war, with their British subsidiary, May & Baker. This led to a flurry of activity, including exchanges of letters and numerous trips across the Channel in 1945, through which the scientists and managers of the parent company observed at first hand the fruit of wartime investments in research, especially in new instruments, and heard of the activities of its subsidiary as a member of the TRC.[100] Rhône-Poulenc also learnt about the impact the conflict had had on the collaboration between academic scientists and pharmaceutical firms.

They were told that whereas at one time a move from academia to industry would have been thought to be degrading for the scientist concerned, attitudes had changed among academics. Symptomatic of this was Arthur Ewins's election to the Royal Society. In exchange, industry had started stepping up its support for academic research. Ewins cited the example of ICI's new University Fellowship scheme, through which he felt — somewhat cynically — that the group hoped to gain a number of advantages, listed thus:

1. to guarantee the good will of government and universities;
2. to improve the quality of recruits indirectly, by encouraging chemical education;
3. to ensure good relations with research institutions, which will later make it easier, if necessary, to ask for favours.[101]

In contrast, May & Baker's support was almost solely directed towards the School of Tropical Medicine at Liverpool, where the company funded two research assistants. Although such an arrangement facilitated May & Baker's relationship with the School, the institution retained total control over its own research. Ewins also pointed out the government's growing involvement in the conduct of research, which he believed was a side effect of the war and would diminish once the conflict was over. As to the close relationship between May & Baker and the MRC developed around collaborative projects such as anti-tubercular chemotherapy, he could not reveal much about the firm's activities in this area, hence it was impossible to speak for very long on this subject.[102] Nevertheless, Ewins stressed that the Council's relaxed attitude towards collaboration left companies free to conduct their own research as they wished.

In the aftermath of war, in order to 'catch up' with Anglo-American wartime developments, Rhône-Poulenc also built up new contacts with other British companies, including Boots Pure Drug Co. and ICI. Boots took the initiative to contact Rhône-Poulenc in 1950. The official reason for doing so was their desire to study other firms' laboratories before rebuilding their own, which had been badly damaged by bombs, but in fact the Boots representative admitted over lunch that it was really a good excuse to visit Paris![103] Despite this, the exchange of information between the two firms continued, and lasted at least until 1974. As to ICI, it was Rhône-Poulenc who first contacted them in order to develop a relationship that already existed at a personal level.

The French group informed them, as they had other firms involved in the petrochemical industry, of the work they and their subsidiary Rhodiaceta were carrying out in the field.[104] Through letters and visits between Rhône-Poulenc and ICI representatives, the French group learnt about the

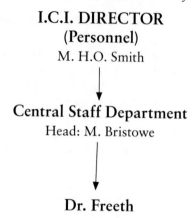

I.C.I. DIRECTOR
(Personnel)
M. H.O. Smith

Central Staff Department
Head: M. Bristowe

Dr. Freeth

Figure 5.4 Raymond Paul's diagram of Dr Freeth's position within ICI.

hierarchical structure of ICI, and about their relations with universities. These involved not only the above-mentioned Fellowships, but also members of staff employed for the purpose, in particular Dr Freeth, a former research director now retired. His role was to encourage and manage these relations, and according to a diagram penned by Raymond Paul and reproduced in Figure 5.4, helping him in this role were the Head of Central Staff Department, M. Bristowe, and above him the Director of Personnel, H.O. Smith.[105]

Raymond Paul described Freeth's functions thus:

1. at the suggestion of research directors, he makes decisions about promoting chemists in the research departments;
2. his mission is to create 'friendly' relations between ICI and English scientists. His purpose is also to create similar links with foreign scientists. As far as France is concerned, for example, he feels that he does not know its scientific milieux well enough. A while ago he invited Champetier to spend a few days in England, and put him in touch with the research departments of the Plastics Division, where Champetier was much appreciated. It is for that reason that he asked me to arrange a meeting with Champetier yesterday afternoon;
3. finally, Dr Freeth is also responsible for the ICI Fellowships, which every year are awarded to about one hundred researchers.[106]

Raymond Paul relayed what he had been told by Freeth, that ICI did not intervene in the choice of candidates. It was left entirely to the universities benefiting from the scheme, i.e. London, Oxford, Cambridge, Edinburgh and a few others located near ICI's different production sites, and involved no discrimination according to sex, nationality, or race. On this, Raymond

Paul commented that this very liberal way of doing things seemed much appreciated by academics.[107] The ICI Fellowships, easier to apply for than similar fellowships offered by the Royal Society or the British government, attracted many researchers, 80% of whom went on to pursue careers in academia. Hence, ten years or so after the scheme had been put place, a large number of British academics could be said to owe ICI a debt of gratitude.

Most important for the growth of Rhône-Poulenc's pharmaceutical business after the war were the links established with the American company Merck. These were facilitated by the existence of earlier ties, strengthened by the appointment as Merck's research director of Randolph T. Major, who had spent some time in Fourneau's laboratory at the Pasteur Institute. In 1921, Poulenc Frères and Powers-Weightman-Rosengarten Co. (a forerunner of Merck & Co. Inc.) signed an agreement to enable the American company to make several Poulenc products, such as Arsenobenzol-Billon (Arsphenamine), and Novarsenobenzol-Billon (Neoarsphenamine), and to sell them in the United States.[108] In 1947, the 1921 contract was renewed, thereby giving Merck access to the synthetic anti-histamines, in which both Drs Major and Molitor (director of the Merck Institute), while on a visit to Paris, declared themselves to be most interested. Subsequently, Merck also acquired the right to sell Flaxedil, a curare-like muscle relaxing agent, drugs against Parkinson's disease, such as Diparcol and Parsidol, and others.[109] In exchange, Rhône-Poulenc could not only manufacture penicillin, and then streptomycin, using deep-fermentation methods under licence from Merck, they were also given details about other Merck drugs, such as vitamin B_{12} and cortisone.[110]

As well as their expertise in synthetic organic chemistry and the legacy of their long association with Fourneau's team, the novel experience of producing antibiotics under licence from Merck was to have a great influence on the French group's post-war expansion in pharmaceuticals, despite the traditional image it projected of itself. Thus, Rhône-Poulenc built up considerable strength in the antibiotic field, going on to develop their own antibiotics, most of which were the outcome of an extensive programme to test strains of streptomyces gathered from all over the world: not only the already mentioned spiramycin and pristinamycin, but also daunorubicin, Rhône-Poulenc's first major drug against cancer, which was isolated in 1958 and underwent clinical trials under the direction of Jean Bernard and Jacquillat in 1964.[111] The French group also tapped into Merck's network of clinical researchers, who tested Rhône-Poulenc's products and facilitated applications to the FDA for approval in the United States.[112] In addition, the group learnt of the crucial role which academic-industrial co-operation had played in the development of antibiotics in America.[113]

However, rather than the need to develop academic-industrial co-operation, which Rhône-Poulenc hardly needed to be convinced of, the main lesson of penicillin for the group was the importance of collaborating with other French companies. Thus, among its network of industrial contacts, in the 1950s it counted Roussel-Uclaf, SIFA, the Laboratoires Fournier, the Institut Mérieux, and the Laboratoires Roger Bellon.[114] Significantly, by 1970, it had acquired two of these firms, Mérieux and Bellon.[115] Several years later, by merging with Hoechst to form Aventis, it would acquire Roussel-Uclaf, by then its chief rival on the French market.

4. Continuing relations with individual scientists

Nevertheless, despite these novel features, ties with individual scientists remained as important as before. The group maintained some of its older contacts with prominent chemists, occupying key positions in the Parisian academic world such as Marcel Delépine (1871–1965), who had joined Poulenc Frères as their Scientific Director of Pharmaceutical Research in 1928 while a Professor at the Faculty of Pharmacy of Paris, before succeeding Charles Moureu to the Chair of Organic Chemistry at the Collège de France in 1930. He remained a close collaborator of Rhône-Poulenc for a total of thirty-seven years. After ceasing to be a Director of Research, he became Scientific Adviser until 1957, and retained contacts with the firm until his death. Apart from giving scientific and technical advice and carrying out tests on substances supplied by the group, one of his principal functions seems to have been to provide Rhône-Poulenc with a scientific voice. Thus, he presented the academic results of the group's research at the Academy of Sciences, of which he had been a member since 1930.[116]

New contacts, less personal and more formal in character, were developed after the war, especially in the 1950s, when the institutional expansion of science in France went ahead in great strides. For instance, Edgar Lederer, at the Institut de Chimie des Substances Naturelles at Gif-sur-Yvette, went against the CNRS tradition by establishing links with Rhône-Poulenc,[117] thereby setting a precedent that would be followed by his successor Pierre Potier, and would contribute to one of Rhône-Poulenc's great discoveries of the later part of the twentieth century, the breast cancer drug Taxotère.[118]

There was also the son of Charles Moureu, Henri, who ran the Laboratoire Municipal de Paris. He had acquired the status of a public hero during the war, when, in 1940, according to a newspaper article, he had been instrumental in transferring stocks of heavy water from France to Great Britain, and, in 1944, had detected the V2 bases aimed towards Paris.[119] Apart from the prestige of having such a collaborator with an impressive scientific pedigree and a link to the Resistance, the focus of his laboratory which focused on the question of tuberculosis, provided a useful connection for the company.[120] However, fifteen years later, when no substance of any great significance had emerged from this collaboration, without much ado the contract was terminated.

Scientists with strong links with the Vichy regime, and even suspected of collaboration with the Germans during the Occupation, were not shunned by the company, especially if they were eminent. Georges Dupont, head of the Chemistry Laboratory at the Ecole Normale Supérieure (ENS), began consulting for the company in 1944, despite the fracas his involvement with Nazi science caused at the time of the purges. His relationship with the chemical group lasted until his death in 1959. On this occasion, his son-in-law, R. Lombard, a chemist working at the Institute of Chemistry at the University of Strasbourg, answered a letter of condolences addressed to his family by Raymond Paul. He expressed his gratitude not only for the condolences, but also for the support Dupont had received from the company, like many other academics, during his lifetime: 'I know how much you have given him in return for his good will, and the help you have given to his students and to his research. I know, since I benefit greatly from it myself, how precious such help is to academics'.[121]

As the quotation suggests, many other researchers benefited from Rhône-Poulenc support in the shape of subsidies to their laboratories, consultancy fees, and often both, for it was in the company's interest to remain on good terms with scientists who were rapidly rising within the academic hierarchy. For instance Marc Julia, who decided to go for an academic rather than an industrial career, first at the Ecole Polytechnique (1950), then the ENS (1956), and finally the Pasteur Institute (1959), at which point his collaboration with Rhône-Poulenc terminated, reflecting the newly-asserted academic vocation of the Institute. While Rhône-Poulenc could not see any harm in personal remuneration (in Julia's case, 70,000 FF per month in 1952), the group rebelled against what it considered to be the government's role, i.e. at having to pay for laboratories:

> We do not wish to play any part in this, for we believe that it is not right that industry should take the place of the state by funding government research laboratories. However, it must be said that, if you decided to give satisfaction to Mr Julia, it would become very difficult for him, if not to leave us, then at least to collaborate with another firm.[122]

Despite these objections, and perhaps in order to strengthen the ties that existed between them, the company therefore chose to give Julia what he asked for: 3.750,000 FF to modernize his laboratory at the ENS. Julia had been a particularly productive scientist, whose research led to patents that were so numerous that they had to be filed in several folders, and he was obviously seen as a good investment by Rhône-Poulenc.

Chemists who played an important part in the reconstruction of French science, for instance Fromageot at the CNRS; Maurice Letort, Professor of Chemistry at Nancy, later President of the CCRST; and Pierre Piganiol, chairman of Saint-Gobain, and subsequently Director of the DGRST, also feature in the post-war files of Rhône-Poulenc.[123] However, these links began even before these scientists occupied such important posts. Although their potential may have been apparent to the company at the time, their position in government cannot have been the cause of the interest they presented for Rhône-Poulenc. In fact, it was probably their links with industry, as well as their talents as scientists, that made them attractive to government, at a time when it was formulating its research policy.

Letort began his interaction with Rhône-Poulenc as Director of the Ecole Supérieure des Industries Chimiques at Nancy around 1946, when the company had shown 'generosity' towards them. It continued after he became Director of the research center of the French Coal Board ('Centre de Recherche des Charbonnages de France') in 1956, until he was elected to the Presidency of the CCRST, otherwise known as the 'Comité des Sages',[124] in 1958, although his RPS file remained open until his death in 1972.

Piganiol had been hired by Saint-Gobain in 1947 to reorganize their research laboratories, and in this capacity he wrote to Rhône-Poulenc, asking them for a sample of penicillin G. The rumour that one of Saint-Gobain's collaborators had been in contact with SIFA led to speculation that the group might be entering the pharmaceutical field, and would therefore become competitors of Rhône-Poulenc. Having obtained reassurances on that point, the two companies reached a co-operative agreement to share the results of their research.[125] This pact of non-aggression was a testimony of Piganiol's belief in the importance of co-operation in overcoming the handicap of small size, typical of the French situation.[126] After Piganiol became Délégué Général (head of the DGRST), which placed him in a key position within government, he remained in touch with the firm well into the 1960s, even after returning to Saint-Gobain in 1962.

An important aspect of this period in the history of Rhône-Poulenc was its growing collaboration with clinical researchers. During the war, the company had strengthened its links with provincial centres, and with clinicians showing an interest in research. After the war, the group sustained its efforts to develop contacts with clinical researchers more widely.

5. Clinicians as collaborators for industry

Rhône-Poulenc's post-war network of clinical researchers included Bernard Halpern, after he had joined Pasteur Vallery-Radot's department at the Hôpital Broussais.[127] Pasteur Vallery-Radot himself, whose laboratory (the 'Clinique médicale propédeutique'), received their support at the rate of 150,000 FF per semester in 1957, became member of the group's administrative council in 1961. Also in Paris, there was Marcel Bessis, who worked at the Centre National de Transfusion Sanguine in the rue Cabanel — an outgrowth of the centre for penicillin production after World War Two. Bessis believed collaboration with industry to be a natural consequence of the reform of medical education in France, and became a consultant for Rhône-Poulenc in 1954.[128] The firm kept him on its books because of his scientific pre-eminence, and as a hedge for the future ('just in case...').

In the provinces, Rhône-Poulenc funded Reilly's laboratory, which received 400,000 FF in 1957,[129] and Loubatières, Professor of Applied Physiology at Montpellier, who had discovered the hypoglycaemic effect of sulphonamides in 1942 (see Chapter 4). This marked the beginning of his long association with the group, but he did not become a paid collaborator until 1946, when he was offered 30,000 FF per month to help the firm develop off-the-label uses for existing drugs.[130] In the 1950s, Loubatières also collaborated with the Laboratoires Servier, and was probably at the origin of the firm's success with Glucidoral, the first hypoglycaemic sulpha-drug to be launched in France.[131] Finally there was Henri Laborit, whom I will return to later.

The growth of medical research after World War Two is a phenomenon shared by a large part of the Western world.[132] Thereafter the two categories of science and medicine became more difficult to distinguish from each other; hence the term 'biomedicine' or 'biomedical' that emerged in the 1960s.[133] However, in France, it had particular significance. The project to modernize French medicine by making it scientific was closely associated with the post-war reconstruction of French society. Instrumental to this was the new generation of French clinicians, which between the 1940s and 1950s came to the fore, many of them quadragenarians who had benefited from Rockefeller support in the 1930s,[134] had joined the Resistance during the war, and emerged from it in positions of political and professional power. They were also assisted and inspired by the reform of medical education, conceived in 1945 by Robert Debré, and realized under the presidency of Charles de Gaulle in 1958.[135]

In addition to this newly found political power at the hands of charismatic leaders, clinicians were able to exploit the niches created by new drugs, in particular antibiotics. The defeat inflicted on infectious diseases allowed them to turn to chronic illnesses such as allergies and diseases of the cardio-vascular system as their prime object of study. As well as opening up new avenues for research, drugs presented them with new tools with which to carry out their investigations and test their hypotheses. By adopting drugs as well as research as a central element in the study of disease, they resurrected the French tradition of scientific medicine created by Claude Bernard almost a century earlier.[136] However, as illustrated by the example of chlorpromazine that follows, this process was neither linear, nor uncontroversial.

6. Chlorpromazine: innovation by accident or by design?

Chlorpromazine was the first of a new class of drugs, which revolutionized psychiatric care and transformed psychiatry giving rise to psychopharmacology.[137] It represented a break with tradition in other respects. It was developed by Rhône-Poulenc's own research team in collaboration with a clinician, the naval surgeon Henri Laborit.

Which side mattered most in the development of chlorpromazine has been debated by two of its historians, Anne Caldwell and Judith Swazey. Whereas Caldwell has leaned towards the demand side in the person of Henri Laborit, and highlighted the importance of serendipitous discovery, Swazey has leaned towards the supply side with Rhône-Poulenc and its research team, and emphasized the importance of design.[138] In fact, both had equal importance. In this section I show that whereas Rhône-Poulenc's earlier breakthrough with sulphanilamide had come from the fundamental approach provided by Fourneau's team, chlorpromazine resulted from the practical experience at the bedside provided by clinical researchers. The firm's growing knowledge of structure-activity relations in particular series of compounds, combined with an expanding therapeutic arsenal, offered opportunities both for accidental discovery and for design.[139]

The path that led Rhône-Poulenc to chlorpromazine is complex.[140] In 1937, Daniel Bovet and Anne-Marie Staub demonstrated the anti-histaminic properties of Thymoxyethyldiethylamine (929 F), a compound belonging to a series of phenolic ether amines synthesized in 1910 by Fourneau. Following this lead, Halpern, working with one of the company's chemists, M. Mosnier, developed phenbenzamine (2339 RP), which became the first clinically useful anti-histamine drug, Antergan (see Chapter 4). Meanwhile, phenothiazine research evolved independently of the anti-histamine work within the Rhône-Poulenc laboratories. Thus, while searching for drugs that were effective against tropical diseases such as malaria and sleeping sickness, in 1944 Charpentier synthesized a new series of phenothiazine derivatives, the phenothiazine amines. However, these were found to be without any significant anti-malarial, anti-helminthic or trypanocidal action.[141] Therefore, other uses for them were sought. In 1945, the phenothiazine and anti-histamine projects intersected when Halpern, together with another company pharmacologist, René Ducrot, turned to Charpentier's series of phenothiazine amines to study their anti-histaminic properties. They identified the most promising among them, and developed Néo-Antergan (compound 2786 RP, mepyramine maleate). However, it was soon replaced by Phénergan (compound 3277 RP, promethazine), which was synthesized by Charpentier in December 1945,[142] and was found to be more active than its predecessor.

Increasing clinical use of synthetic anti-histamines led to observations that they caused drowsiness in patients. Subsequent studies showed that this was due to their action on the central nervous system.[143] Rhône-Poulenc attempted at first to eliminate what they saw as an undesirable side effect. However, after it was realized that this property could be employed to treat the symptoms of Parkinson's disease, as was done with Diparcol (compound 2987 RP, an anti-histamine synthesized in 1945),[144] the company actively started seeking it, with the intention of developing a new class of drug. At first, Rhône-Poulenc searched among compounds that were already on their shelves, but anticipated soon being able to synthesize a novel molecule that would satisfy all their requirements.

Swazey has traced the decision to embark on a new research programme to develop such a drug back to a proposal made by Joseph Koetschet on 3 October 1950.[145] However, the group had already been in contact with Henri Laborit, the naval surgeon who in 1948 came to give a talk to their therapeutic research group on the subject of synthetic anti-histamines in surgery.[146] Laborit was a surgeon in the French Navy, stationed at Bizerte in Tunisia, when he introduced synthetic anti-histamines in surgical therapy. Like the 'spiritual ancestor' of all French surgeons, René Leriche, he believed that a reaction of the sympathetic nervous system caused surgical shock.[147] With the help of his collaborator and friend, the biochemical pharmacologist Pierre Morand, he studied the role of acetylcholine in shock, and became adept at using a cocktail of drugs that included curare to counteract the effects of surgery. Later, his cocktails included Néo-Antergan and Phénergan, because of their activity on the peripheral nerves, but also because of an analogy he saw between anaphylactic shock and surgical shock. With practice, he found that action on both the peripheral and central nerves was desirable in the drugs he used to treat shock. Phénergan, in particular, displayed central as well as peripheral activity, which he found helpful in surgery. Assisted by P. Huguenard, an anaesthetist in Paris and at the time a long-distance collaborator of Laborit, he studied the use of synthetic anti-histamines in conjunction with anaesthetics. He found that they avoided the need for barbiturates and for morphine, deleterious to the post-operative recovery of his patients, and that they enhanced the activity of anaesthetics.

Of his method of approach and his willingness to use drugs as research instruments, Caldwell has written:

> Drugs are for Laborit but instruments to express his ideas and methods merely means to an end: successful therapy. This attitude has perhaps contributed to Laborit's success as a discoverer—it has certainly proved him a great clinician.[148]

Laborit 'discovered' ataraxy, a stable state of the autonomic (sympathetic and parasympathetic) nervous system, which he was able to distinguish from ordinary cortical sedation using drugs, in 1949.[149] Impressed by this discovery, Rhône-Poulenc subsequently followed reports of his work in La Presse Médicale before launching their new programme in October 1950. When Laborit returned later, asking them for a phenothiazine amine with a high degree of central activity, independently of its anti-histaminic properties, his request intersected with this new programme and strengthened it. In December 1950 — a few days before the chlorpromazine molecule was synthesized by Charpentier — Simone Courvoisier began testing synthetic anti-histamines for 'potentiators of general anaesthesia'.[150] After chlorpromazine, such compounds would be referred to simply as 'potentiators of the nerves' ('potentialisateurs nerveux'), and be compared with 4560 RP, which quickly became the team's standard compound for testing activity on the central nervous system.[151]

The moment of departure, when innovation took place, could therefore be situated at either of these two points: at the point of Laborit's request, or further back, at the point of Koetshet's proposal.[152] The drugs themselves were 'in the air', and competitors hot on the heels of Rhône-Poulenc. Merck had been working on a similar project, and there seemed to be a demand for such a drug among clinical researchers.[153] At whatever point innovation might be situated, without the close collaboration that developed between the two sides, chlorpromazine would probably have been discovered elsewhere. The files for a time kept in the Archives of Rhône-Poulenc Santé permit a study of this collaboration.

7. Henri Laborit and Rhône-Poulenc

Rhône-Poulenc's project, launched in 1950, represented a departure from the original anti-histamine programme. However, it was also inspired by it. The research team returned to the phenothiazine series prepared by Charpentier, using the same animal tests, this time seeking central activity in order to enhance it, rather than eliminate it. Compound 3276 RP, which had immediately preceded Phénergan (3277 RP) in the series of derivatives synthesized by Charpentier,[154] but had been shelved because it was useless as an anti-histaminic, remained on the shelves until he picked it up again five years later. Using chemical techniques with which he had grown familiar while working with phenothiazine derivatives, and which enabled him to synthesize compounds for the treatment of Parkinson's disease, in particular 3356 RP (Parsidol, synthesized in 1946),[155] he attached the lateral chain of 3276 RP onto a chloro phenothiazine to accentuate its effect on the central nervous system.[156] The new compound, 4560 RP (one the last compounds synthesized by Charpentier, who retired shortly after his laboratory notebooks ended in 1951), was subjected to pharmacological tests by the pharmacologist Simone Courvoisier and her group.[157] It was then released for clinical investigation under the name chlorpromazine. Therefore, although chlorpromazine was a novelty in that it had been designed, i.e. synthesized with a specific pharmacological effect in mind, it was also the product of routine chemical and pharmacological studies, and an opportunistic response to interest expressed by clinicians, that is to say it was at once a case of serendipity and of design.[158]

Laborit re-entered the stage at this point, by asking Rhône-Poulenc for samples of chlorpromazine. From his new work place at the military hospital of the Val-de-Grâce in Paris, he had started building a scientific and clinical empire based on a new therapeutic approach to the old problem of shock using drugs provided to him by Spécia. Laborit's approach received the name of 'hibernation therapy', as it involved cooling patients down with ice, whilst administering a cocktail of drugs to help them to recover from shock.[159] In 1952, as well as Phénergan, and later Diparcol, he began using chlorpromazine, or Largactil, the name under which it was launched to indicate its wide range of therapeutic effects, which was not restricted to psychiatric disorders, although in time these would become its chief field of application (see Figure 5.5).

L'ANNÉE
1 9 5 3

qui vient de s'achever,

marque une étape importante dans l'évolution de la

Chimiothérapie, par la confirmation, sur le plan

clinique, des activités expérimentales multiples du

4560 R. P.

LARGACTIL

CHLORPROMAZINE

CHLORHYDRATE DE CHLORO-3 (DIMÉTHYLAMINO-3' PROPYL)-10 PHÉNOTHIAZINE

découverte originale

des Laboratoires de Recherches

RHÔNE-POULENC

Figure 5.5 Largactil advertisements (photos reproduced from J.-P. Olié, D. Ginestet, G. Jolles and H. Lôo (eds), Histoire d'une découverte en psychiatrie: 40 ans de chimiothérapie neuroleptique (Paris: Doin, 1992)).

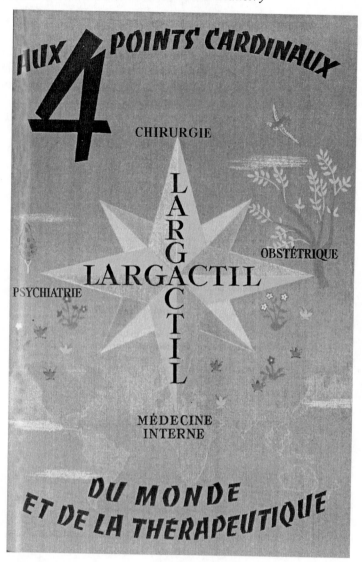

Figure 5.6 Largactil advertisements (photos reproduced from J.-P. Olié, D. Ginestet, G. Jolles and H. Lôo (eds), Histoire d'une découverte en psychiatrie: 40 ans de chimiothérapie neuroleptique (Paris: Doin, 1992)).

As a surgeon, he could see the similarity between post-operative disease and mental disorder. From this new position of medical authority, he therefore helped Largactil to cross the boundary from surgery to psychiatry by introducing it to his colleague Hamon at the Val-de-Grâce. However, it was Jean Delay and Pierre Deniker, at the psychiatric Hôpital Sainte-Anne in Paris, who established what was to become the standard method of clinical application of Largactil, in isolation rather than as part of a cocktail, a method that would facilitated its adoption by psychiatrists across the world.[160]

In association with this method, chlorpromazine was exported, first to Britain, via Rhône-Poulenc's subsidiary May & Baker, and later via Smith-Kline & French, with which Rhône-Poulenc had a special arrangement, to the United States, where it was relatively quickly taken up despite the strength of the psychoanalytic tradition there. The history of the worldwide adoption of the drug is, according to Swazey, a testimony to its success.[161] However, this account underplays the active role played by Rhône-Poulenc in marketing Largactil, by funding Laborit to accompany Deniker in the United States for a round of lectures in 1953, for example,[162] as well as by providing psychiatrists with free samples to encourage their adoption of the drug.[163] Moreover, it ignores the resistance encountered by Laborit, whose fall from grace coincided with chlorpromazine's entry into psychiatry.[164] Once its identity had changed from a 'potentiator of anaesthesia' to a 'neuroleptic drug' (a term coined by Delay and Deniker), after it had been re-appropriated by the psychiatric community, chlorpromazine escaped from Laborit's control, and at the same time he appeared to lose favour with the French medical establishment. Thereafter, support from the company because crucial in enabling him to continue his research.

As a naval medical officer, Laborit had always been an outsider. He did not belong to mainstream medical orthodoxy. Long after he had begun using Largactil in surgery and his theory about its action had been confirmed by the work of psychiatrists such as Delay and Deniker, French doctors remained reluctant to accept his ideas, even though he did have some powerful supporters, in particular Leriche. In 1958, Laborit had a new laboratory created for him with funding from Spécia as well as the Navy at the Hôpital Boucicaut in Paris, and participated in the building of yet another naval laboratory in Toulon, where he developed one of the first emergency and intensive care centres in France.[165]

From 1962, however, he no longer received support from the Navy, his main source of legitimacy until then. They felt that his laboratory was not run according to 'regulations' (probably because his research was seen as too fundamental).[166] As he belonged neither to the CNRS, nor the Faculty of Medicine, nor the University, he was also denied government support. Funding from other sources therefore became all the more crucial to Laborit. To justify providing him with support, a memo was circulated within Rhône-Poulenc, stressing the importance of the legitimacy his research had gained abroad, if not in France:

> His international fame has not ceased to expand. Although never celebrated in France, in 1957 he received the Albert Lasker Prize, the highest scientific honour in America, also known as the 'little Nobel', which 17 Nobel Prize winners received before getting the Swedish

prize. As his work has been systematically rejected for publication by French journals, he has created his own scientific journal: AGGRES-SOLOGIE, which is referred to in every international 'abstract'. Invited abroad each year to deliver academic lectures, he has travelled all over the world, and his laboratory is for ever welcoming foreign visitors, who come and spend a number of years there. This enables him to acquire talented collaborators, for he is of course not allowed to recruit French collaborators through the 'concours' system. He has published 16 books (with Masson & Cie) several of which have been translated into English, Russian, Japanese, German and Spanish.[167]

Consequently, Rhône-Poulenc agreed to continue funding not only his laboratory, but also his new journal *Aggressologie*, although they did not wish to publicize their connection with the journal, so as to protect the scientist's, as well as their own, reputation.[168]

This decision reflects the extent to which the fates of the firm and the clinician were closely interwoven, because of the collaborative nature of the project that had led to the development of chlorpromazine. Both sides had had much to gain from the interaction. Laborit represented a useful ally for Rhône-Poulenc, by encouraging his colleagues to use their drugs, and by facilitating their adoption across disciplinary boundaries. The surgeon's own scientific outlook and career also benefited from contact with the company and by association with their drugs. Not only did support from the group enable him to continue his research, but the success of his research was dependent on the efficacy of their drugs.

Chlorpromazine was hailed as a revolution in psychiatry, akin to penicillin.[169] Both had a unifying effect on medicine. Just as penicillin had helped to bring together biological and chemical approaches to therapy, chlorpromazine helped to unify psychiatry, until then divided between its biological and psychodynamic factions. However, the crucial difference between the two, according to Caldwell, was that penicillin had been 'discovered' by chance, and therefore took longer to develop, whereas chlorpromazine was discovered by design. This chapter has shown that, if it was design, it was because of a growing interest in drugs and research on the part of clinicians as well as industry, and because of increasing collaboration between the two.

Through their new drug, Rhône-Poulenc were able to present an image of themselves that competed with American companies, at a time when France was seeking American aid, but also attempting to maintain its independence.[170] Like penicillin, chlorpromazine therefore acquired a mythical status, laden with political meaning. Just as penicillin became a symbol of the victory of the allies and of modernity, in the wake of the early phenothiazines that 'commemorated the Liberation', chlorpromazine became a symbol of 'the glory of France', in which both science and industry had an important part to play.[171]

E. CONCLUSION

In post-war France, a clearer distinction between science and industry was seen as the key to modernity. Thus, the Pasteur Institute underwent a wave of reforms that eventually led to the separation between its two traditional functions of research and production. It developed its vocation of fundamental research, like the CNRS, and later INSERM. This enabled it to survive as a scientific institution, but led it to distance itself from industry.

Meanwhile, Rhône-Poulenc developed its in-house facilities, taking over the function of chemotherapeutic research laboratory, until then filled by Fourneau's laboratory at the Pasteur Institute, and turning to outside collaborators either for their insights in pure chemistry, or for their experience at the bedside. The growth of clinical research, encouraged by the reform of medical education conceived and implemented by Robert Debré, provided the pharmaceutical industry with a new kind of collaborator. It was such a collaborator, in the person of the naval surgeon Henri Laborit, who led Rhône-Poulenc to chlorpromazine. Like French post-war reconstruction, chlorpromazine presents at once revolutionary and conservative features. Although revolutionary in its application to psychiatry, it was derived from a series of compounds familiar to the company and the fruit of its long association with Fourneau's laboratory, the phenothiazine amines.

The departure of Fourneau from the Pasteur Institute, followed by his death, symbolized the passing of a generation and, with it, of a particularly close relationship with industry. As contemporary analyses suggested, the radical nature of French post-war reconstruction was partly attributable to a new generation who led the country from Liberation to reconstruction, from Debré, to Monod, to Piganiol. In a paper written in 1959, Piganiol thought the task of modernising France depended on a select group of charismatic leaders:

> It will only be in ten years' time that France will recover a certain equilibrium, and that we will have enough working men in relation to those either too young or too old to do the job of a modern country.[172]

In the 1950s, numerous new laboratories were created, with adequate instruments, buildings and even a director, but otherwise, according to Piganiol, 'empty shells'. This institutional expansion, combined with the concentration of power in the hands of a few reformers, resulted in a period of innovation for France, not only in politics, but also in science and industry.

Nevertheless, according to Piganiol, some things, which were cultural in origin, for example a French inability to develop the fruits of research, did not change.[173] He saw modifying the structures of research at a governmental level as the best solution.[174] This idea began to take root under the DGRST, and came to fruition after the 'Loi d'Orientation et de Programmation de la Recherche' of 15 July 1982, by which time it had become associated with the rise of the biotechnology industry in America, and the need to catch up once again in a new field.[175]

However, as the example of Rhône-Poulenc and its networks of collaborators has shown, companies and researchers did not wait for encouragement from the State to collaborate. At the grass-roots level, the incentive to collaborate was so powerful that collaborations occurred nonetheless, independently of government initiatives.

Although similar trends can be observed in Britain, the next chapter describes British post-war reconstruction as a more gradual affair. Pre-war structures were returned to, and adapted to fit the new context. A more pragmatic approach to change, and a more subdued rhetoric characterize the British case, illustrated by the examples of the MRC and its network of reputable companies, of three scientists who represented the British experience with penicillin: Florey, Abraham, and Chain, and of the institutions and companies they consulted for: ICI, the NRDC and Beecham.

6 'Revolution through Continuity' in Britain

A. INTRODUCTION

Before World War Two, pharmaceutical research had often been carried out in collaboration with academic scientists. Afterwards, as companies invested in new R&D facilities and took on chemotherapeutic research in earnest, many also built close relationships with clinical researchers, not only for testing, but also for developing their drugs. As to the MRC, increasingly it interacted with industry through its representatives, first the ABCM, and then the Association of British Pharmaceutical Industries (ABPI), whilst maintaining its ties with trusted companies, especially those it had been able to rely upon for the production of penicillin in wartime they included Glaxo and ICI, who were relative newcomers in the pharmaceutical field, but would gain clear advantages from their participation in the MRC's numerous post-war collaborative schemes.

These changes were comparable with those in France, where the Pasteur Institute and Rhône-Poulenc grew apart, and where hospital clinicians and pharmaceutical companies collaborated more closely than before. However, they were less radical in Britain than in France. The modest and gradual nature of British post-war reconstruction was due, neither, according to Corelli Barnett, to the British élites' 'illusions of grandeur',[1] nor, according to Jean Monnet, to their lack of a vision from within,[2] but rather to their experience of a system that had not only survived the war, but had been strengthened by it. As a result of the intense cross-Channel exchanges that followed, the MRC was imitated in France, where it provided a model for the new CNRS and later for INSERM.[3] British élites were therefore less likely to opt for a radical overhaul of a system that included agencies such as this. Unlike in France, the continuity of British élites and their familiarity with pre-war structures, which they had seen tried, tested, and emerge victorious from the war,[4] meant that their approach to reconstruction was pragmatic, rather than planned and prescriptive.[5]

Penicillin played an important role as an instrument of change — not only at the level of rhetoric, but because of the large-scale mobilization of science and industry for the war effort that had underpinned its development, as a 'model experiment in collaboration' to be referred to and imitated time and time again. Hence, the model of penicillin can be observed at two levels: 1) that of agencies such as the Council, and of pharmaceutical firms now represented by a special body, the ABPI, and 2) the 'grass roots', i.e. individual scientists such as Florey, Chain and Abraham, and the companies with which they entertained special relations, ICI, Beecham and Glaxo.

B. THE MRC AND THE REPRESENTATIVES OF THE PHARMACEUTICAL INDUSTRY

After the war, the MRC developed its interaction with the representatives of the pharmaceutical industry.[6] The ABPI, inspired by the TRC, provided the pharmaceutical industry with a voice that was now independent of its senior partner, the chemical industry.[7] In time, faced with growing government intervention, it would come to play a major role in defending the interests of the industry in its relationship with the state.[8]

The interaction between the MRC and the ABPI reflected a general trend in British government-industrial relations in the post-war period. As the state became more active, so it had to rely more heavily on the ability of industry to speak with 'one voice' and share in the exercise of authority.[9] However, in the case of the MRC and the ABPI, it was also based upon the Council's long experience of dealing with drug companies, and upon these companies' previous experience of collaborating with one another as well as with the MRC, on insulin within the British Insulin Manufacturers (BIM), and on penicillin and synthetic anti-malarials within the TRC.[10]

After the war, the relationship between the MRC and the pharmaceutical industry became a source of strength for the Council, whose quasi unique control over medical research was threatened under the NHS.[11] The tension between the Council and the newly created Ministry of Health is apparent in a letter, in which Edward Mellanby complained about the 'regrettable lack of co-ordination' that had led to a 'gratuitous duplication of activities' between them. He concluded: 'The moral of this story is that when the Ministry invite us to undertake tests of a new remedy they should leave the arrangements, including the negotiations with the manufacturers, in our hands'.[12] However, as well as facilitated by the experience of past collaborations, the relationship between the MRC and the ABPI was facilitated by the Council's changed attitudes towards patents. This led to the creation of the NRDC, with which it was to share the role of co-ordinator of research, as it had done before the war with the DSIR.

1. The MRC and the creation of the NRDC (1948)

Whereas before the war the MRC had been opposed to the patenting of medical discoveries, afterwards it felt more ready to accept them, especially if arrangements could be made with collective bodies rather than individuals. How and why had such a change of heart occurred?

In 1930, faced with the medical profession's persisting objection to the patenting of drugs, associated with the much decried 'patent medicines', the ABCM had proposed a compromise to the Lee Committee, appointed by the National Whitley Council (set up on 4 Dec. 1925) to consider inventions made by Civil Servants. It had suggested that a Medical Patents Trustee be created, which would operate in consultation with an advisory committee representing doctors as well as chemical manufacturers.[13] Under this scheme, the inventor — or his nominee — could receive a free licence to develop his invention and take out foreign patents, or assign this task to the Trustee. The Trustee could then use the resulting royalties to fund medical research. It could also grant low-fee, non-exclusive licences to manufacturers interested in the invention. Although the ABCM's proposal was rejected at the time, by 1939 the MRC's attitude had started to soften, partly as a result of the contributions to chemotherapy made by its own members, for instance Harold King, discoverer of the diamidines. Hence in 1943, as chairman of the War Cabinet's Scientific Advisory Committee on Patents, Henry Dale (see Figure 6.1) was able to revive the idea of a national trustee, which, because of the wartime need to encourage collaboration between academic and industrial scientists, not only in medicine, but also in other fields of research, was received with far greater enthusiasm.[14]

In the context of post-war reconstruction, change therefore became possible, and the MRC lent its full support to proposals for the creation of a

Figure 6.1 Henry Dale as an elder statesman of science (with permission from the Wellcome Trust).

national trustee. In order to articulate this support, it turned to the past for guidance and inspiration. In relation to medical research, the patent law in operation since 1919 was perceived as working 'mischievously', as the author of an MRC memo remarked. Not only did it not achieve its purpose, i.e. to stimulate discovery, 'because it is in fact little used and the incentives to research are other than pecuniary', but the few who used it, mainly 'foreigners', were unduly advantaged by it.[15] Reaching similar conclusions to those of the Lee Committee, the author believed that the best alternative to the abolition of the patent law as it then stood would be to dedicate medical discoveries to a public body 'acting as a national trustee'.

The Lee Committee report, written in 1930, and reprinted in 1944, was re-examined.[16] In this report, it had been observed that World War One had given considerable impetus to innovation:

> Modern war conditions had made prominent the increasing inter-dependence of the military and the civilian population and the close inter-connection between war technique and industry. An invention made by a scientific worker in a Defense department might possess— apart from its military usefulness—a commercial value which might be developed in the national interest.[17]

In 1944, parallels could therefore be drawn between the two world wars. Both had been periods of intense creativity, following which there had been a need to protect inventions and reassert national identities. Nowhere was this felt more acutely than in relation to medical patents, and in the light of the penicillin experience.[18] Penicillin had had both positive and negative lessons for the Council, as well as for the scientists involved in its development. On the one hand, the agreements on the chemistry of penicillin (between the US and the UK, and between academic and industrial collaborators represented by the MRC and the TRC/ICI) had proved that it was possible for the MRC to take out patents — especially if it acted as a single entity and dealt with industry as a body, rather than with individual firms.[19] On the other hand, the failure to take out patents on the early production of penicillin, a failure partly attributable to two of the MRC's most influential figures, Dale and Mellanby, had resulted in loss of potential earnings and in severe criticism of the Council's outmoded attitudes.

Hence, with the penicillin experience firmly in mind, the MRC now put its considerable weight behind the idea of a public body acting as a national trustee, which was pushed forward by the new committee set up in 1946 to examine the question of patents, and led to the passing of the Development and Inventions Bill and creation of the NRDC in 1948.[20] The Bill was followed by the Patents Act of 1949, which made it possible to patent drugs as well as processes, and as such represented an improvement over its predecessor. Significantly, both the Bill and the Act referred to the need to make patents — especially medical patents — respectable, in order to avoid 'another penicillin'.[21] However, as one historian has argued, the dual patenting system that resulted from the Patents Act on the one hand, and the creation of the NRDC on the other, did little to overcome the weaknesses inherent in British patent law, to which the early difficulties of the British dyestuffs and pharmaceutical industries can in part be attributed.[22]

Just as the MRC's position with regards to patents had started to alter even before the war, the attitude of the medical profession towards collaboration with industry had also begun to mollify. Like other scientists, clinical researchers' experience of participating in the war effort reinforced this change in expectations and behaviour.

2. Funding clinical research, organizing trials, and providing new partners for industry

Before the war because of professional prejudices that also made them object to the patenting of drugs, clinicians had been reluctant to make trials of pharmaceutical products on behalf of commercial laboratories.[23] The TTC, set up by the MRC in 1931 with encouragement from the ABCM, was therefore intended to stimulate the testing of new drugs presented by manufacturers to the Chemotherapy Committee (formed by an *ad hoc* joint committee of the MRC and the DSIR in 1927 — see Chapter 1). An outcome of these new structures was that the attitude of the medical profession towards collaboration with industry had begun to alter.

War and the NHS brought two further changes that fostered co-operation between clinicians and pharmaceutical companies: the victory of chemotherapy, experienced at first hand through the use of the sulphonamides, penicillin, and synthetic anti-malarials on the theatre of war as well as on the home front, and the gradual but steady expansion of clinical research within the new, mainly hospital-based, healthcare system.[24] Drugs became the symbol of the contribution of science to medicine, and drug therapy the centerpiece of government healthcare policies, to an extent that it would soon lead to serious concerns about the rising drugs bill.[25] This evolution coincided with the expansion not only of biomedical sciences within government laboratories, universities and research institutions, but also of clinical research. After Harold Himsworth, a practising clinician, had succeeded Edward Mellanby as Secretary of the MRC in 1949, the Council channeled a growing proportion of its funding towards clinical research.[26] Combined with the provisions made to foster research within the NHS, this resulted in the deployment of medical (mainly clinical) research units, which gathered momentum in the post-war period.[27] The clinical evaluation of remedies therefore became more acceptable to clinicians at a time when their numbers were increasing as a result of this new emphasis on clinical research, and the momentum this created precipitated their change in attitude towards collaboration with industry.[28] The switch was such that, although the TTC lapsed during the war years, the MRC felt it unnecessary to reinstall the system once it was over: 'manufacturers were thus enabled to make their own arrangements directly with clinicians'.[29]

Once its earlier mission, which had been to convince pharmaceutical firms to take on the bulk of chemotherapeutic research, was felt to have been accomplished, the Council became freer to devote its energies to fundamental problems.[30] After the war, the NIMR's research programme fell more and more onto the study of the biological aspects of chemotherapy, such as the mode of action of drugs and drug resistance, leading to the fuller understanding of the metabolism of both host and parasite, while 'the purely chemical approach was left to industry'.[31] However, industry participated just as actively in these changes. It, too, had undergone a transformation, and its increased commitment to R&D led it to seek out the collaboration of clinical researchers. Such changes are studied through the development of two drugs: cortisone and anaesthetic halothane.

3. The MRC and pharmaceutical companies: cortisone

The history of the relationship between the MRC and pharmaceutical companies after World War Two is one of tension between two possible approaches to collaboration. The first was based on historical 'precedents': penicillin and insulin, the second on *ad hoc* adaptations to local circumstances. Once a new area for drug development had been identified, the MRC usually began collaborative research projects by dealing, in an impersonal fashion, with the representatives of industry. However, each new drug presented the Council with a fresh set of problems. The pressure to maintain its often ambiguous role between the public and private spheres, and retain control over the 'experiments in collaboration' which it instigated, frequently made the Council resort to exclusive relationships with single trusted companies.

With the growing number of drugs, which formed a cluster often referred to as the 'Therapeutic Revolution', the tension between these two approaches increased. The most significant example of this is cortisone, because it provided the MRC with an opportunity to devise a collaborative scheme that, it was hoped, would serve as a template for future dealings with industry. Cortisone had been isolated by Edward Kendall at the Mayo Clinic, and produced in small quantities by Merck during World War Two.[32] In 1949, Kendall's colleague, the American physician Philip Hench, showed it to be effective in the treatment of rheumatoid arthritis. Under pressure from the MoH, which anticipated considerable demand for the drug, thereby putting great strain on the rising drugs bill, the MRC established a scheme for co-operative research along the lines of penicillin in order to develop cortisone in Britain.[33] Its failure to maintain the scheme in its original form is the subject of the next few paragraphs. In the end, the MRC had to limit its collaboration to a one-to-one relationship with Glaxo, which had a head start over other British companies because of its expertise in fermentation technology, and retained this head start thanks to the privileged position it acquired by collaborating not only with the MRC, but also with the American drug company Merck.[34]

The MRC's cortisone collaborative scheme had a dual purpose: 1) to find 'methods of preparing cortisone other than those covered by existing patents', and 2) to develop 'related compounds with a similar beneficial action in rheumatism and other diseases'.[35] It was felt that the best way to achieve these two goals was to organize a formal collaboration 'between members of the Council's scientific staff, independent workers in University laboratories who are receiving grants from the Council or the Nuffield Foundation, and workers who are employed by, or are in receipt of monetary assistance from interested British commercial firms'. Together with the representatives of these different groups of workers, i.e. the Nuffield Foundation, a charitable organization with an important programme of research into rheumatic diseases, the NRDC and the ABCM, the MRC therefore devised a plan according to which reciprocal agreements between participants would be signed, and two distinct committees would be created. The first would administer the scheme, and the second would advise on the all-important issue of patents:

1. The completion of an agreement between the Council, the Nuffield, the Corporation and any manufacturer who has indicated his willingness to take part in the scheme and his ability to contribute substances to it;
2. The completion of a 'patents pool' agreement, between the Corporation, the ABCM and each industrial participant;
3. The completion of an agreement between the Council, Nuffield or an industrial firm making grants to academic workers and each academic participant;
4. The creation of a joint committee including the representatives of all the different interests to administer the scheme [...];
5. The creation of a patents advisory committee to administer the patents pool, on the initiative of the corporation.[36]

Hope was expressed that the scheme, if successful, would in future 'serve as a prototype for similar schemes of collaborative investigation between government, academic and commercial research laboratories in other fields'. Considering itself to be at the core of this 'triple helix', the MRC willingly took on the role of intermediary, and sent letters to the companies that had shown an initial interest in the scheme, seeking additional information as to the extent of their proposed collaboration. These companies were: Abbott Laboratories, Boots, BDH, British Schering, Evans Medical Supplies, Glaxo, Herts Pharmaceuticals, T&H Smith, Vitamins Ltd., Ward, Blenkinsop & Co. and the Watford Chemical Co.

Unfortunately, by 20 March 1951, only two replies had come back from the manufacturers, T&H Smith and British Schering. Doubt was expressed about whether or not the collaboration proposed by British Schering would be extensive enough.[37] As to T&H Smith, they suggested that their expertise in plant alkaloids would be complementary to the synthetic capabilities of other firms. However, although their newly completed research and analytical laboratories now allowed their research to be centralized, they were not as yet fully staffed.[38]

In the mean time, the labour of academic workers was progressing rapidly. Professor Linnell of the School of Pharmacy at London University, who was a recipient of an MRC grant, published an article in *Nature* on 10 February 1951, on synthetic analogues of adrenal cortical hormones. In a letter to Linnell, J.C.R. Hudson of the MRC expressed relief that the compounds described in this article were unlikely to be adopted in the clinic, for 'once matter has been published it may not be patented and one naturally wishes to avoid a repetition of the case of penicillin, to manufacture which we now have to pay royalties to the U.S. patentees'.[39]

Urged on by the experience of penicillin, and in view of the poor response to their first letter, the MRC sent another circular letter to the managing directors of the firms. This asked them for further details in order to assess the likelihood of a collaborative scheme. Their replies provide an interesting picture of British pharmaceutical companies in the field of hormone chemistry. The findings are arranged in Table 6.1, which includes the names of their research workers, academic workers, or consultants, the nature of their contribution (whether of a chemical or biological nature), the extent of their facilities and whether they were capable of expansion, publications or any patents in the field, and whether they had arrangements with other firms, including foreign parents.

Apart from Glaxo, all companies claimed that their facilities could be expanded, should they be admitted into the scheme. Evans, for example, were willing to engage a highly qualified chemist full-time, in addition to the two part-time researchers employed at the Evans Biological Institute in Runcorn, and to meet the cost of a grant to an academic worker. They also thought that, upon consideration by the board, they would be capable of some expansion. Herts Pharmaceuticals named two consultants: Professor J. Beattie (of the Physiological Laboratory, Cambridge) and F.S. Spring (of the Royal Technical College, Glasgow), who were currently associated with their research. They believed that, although they would be likely to be a relatively junior member of the group, they could nevertheless make a useful contribution, having made considerable efforts in building up their research facilities over the past ten years. As to Vitamins Ltd., they hoped that employing full-time members of the medical profession as well as a full-time veterinarian would weigh in their favour with respect to the Council.

Table 6.1 Pharmaceutical Companies to be Involved in Cortisone Research[40]

Company	Researchers	Consultants	Chemical/Biological expertise	Publications/Patents	Associated Co.
British Schering	unknown	G.F. Marian	Chemical	unknown	Parent co.
BDH	5	0	Chem. and bio	both	free
Herts Pharma.	9	J. Beattie and F.S. Spring	Chem. and bio	Unpublished/no patents	Nivea Pharma.
Evans	2	0	Biological	None/none	free
Vitamins Ltd.	4	0	Chemical	None/none	free
Ward, Blenkinsop & Co.	0	Herrald and Weiss	Chemical	None/none	free
T&H Smith	2	F.S. Spring	Chemical	None/none	free
Glaxo	unknown	Jones, Shoppee and Stacey	Chem. and bio	unknown	Merck

Such a display of enthusiasm denotes a growing interest in research on the part of small and medium pharmaceutical firms, continuing a trend that had begun in the interwar period. Although the number of in-house researchers remained relatively small, research was often carried out collaboratively, with the help of consultants or grant-aided academic workers, as had also happened before the war (see Chapters 1 and 2). Moreover, their enthusiasm reflects the realisation that co-operation with a government body such as the MRC was likely to provide important commercial benefits in an increasingly competitive environment. The Council was well aware of the commercial motives that lay behind the companies' responses, and did not fail to notice the gulf that separated these replies from the lengthy, more detailed, but also more skeptical letter sent by Sir Harry Jephcott, Glaxo's research director. It suggested to the Council that their research on cortisone was already much more advanced than that of the other companies.[42]

Glaxo felt that their principal contribution would be indirect, in the form of subsidies to their academic consultants: Professor E.R.H. Jones in Manchester, Professor C.W. Shoppee in Swansea, and M. Stacey in Birmingham. Otherwise, Jephcott expressed doubt about the validity of the proposed scheme. Jones, at the time of the letter, had reached a promising stage in the synthesis of cortisone from ergosterol (from yeast, used for the production of vitamin D) as a precursor, which it was hoped would provide a cheaper way of producing the drug than bile acids. However, in Jephcott's view, even if Jones's process worked, its commercial exploitation would best be entrusted to Merck, with whom Glaxo had a general agreement, and 'whose huge organisation was much better suited than any in this country to the rapid production of a complex new synthetic substance at an economic price'. Nevertheless, he conceded that the MRC's scheme created a useful precedent, which might be more appropriate 'in respect of other complicated new syntheses in the future.'[43]

However, he voiced the opinion, shared by Glaxo's academic consultants, that the MRC scheme might be more effective if it included the appointment of an overall research director. The TRC, he suggested, 'had perished from inanition in default of such an arrangement.' But the representatives of the Council — Himsworth and Harington — were radically opposed to this:

> [...] the apppointment of such a scientific dictator for a scheme of this kind would certainly be unacceptable to many research workers and [...] the whole object of the joint committee envisaged in the present draft agreements was to achieve a satisfactory measure of co-ordination and direction in a democratic way.[44]

Thus, they feared that the difference the ability of academic and industrial scientists to accept the authority of a research director might generate conflicts, which would undermine a large-scale collaborative scheme. This difference was one of the reasons eventually given for Glaxo's decision to pull out of the scheme in June 1951. The company believed that a great advantage was to be gained from unified control in any programme of research and development, and felt that too much time had already been wasted without such control. Time was 'of the utmost importance', especially when considering the 'much greater experience' and 'numerical importance' of American workers in this field and the unlikely prospect of finding a new route to synthesis.[45]

In fact, as further research has shown, the reasons for Glaxo's decision to pull out were far more complex than those stated to the MRC. These included concerns that the agreement would require them to share their consultants with other firms, and the need to establish a strong patent structure to protect Glaxo's work in the field before embarking on any collaboration, whether with the MRC, or with Merck.[46]

The reactions to Glaxo's defection are nonetheless interesting. Interviewed on the subject, Alexander Todd believed that Glaxo, by refusing to join, had 'completely torpedoed' the scheme, which only had meaning in relation to the first of its stated objectives: to find a shorter, and cheaper route to synthesis.[47] Now that Glaxo had pulled out, it was likely that patents would block any modifications to the established synthetic route. As to the development of analogues, they depended on 'the inspired individual worker' rather than a team, therefore a collaborative scheme, other than that which already existed between academic workers, was unnecessary.

For their part, Glaxo's consultants preferred to keep the collaboration that existed between them and the firm intact. Jones felt that he was freer under the arrangement with Glaxo than if he joined the proposed collaboration with the MRC:

> The collaboration in which we have so far indulged has been an entirely happy one, conducted as it has been on a largely personal basis. The arrangements governing it are almost informal in their nature and are in no way incompatible with complete academic freedom.[48]

Stacey confirmed that nothing needed to be secret about the work he carried out in collaboration with Glaxo. Shoppee offered a slightly different angle to the affair. He would respect his agreement with Glaxo out of loyalty to the company, which had offered him support after moving from Basle University to University College, Swansea in 1943, where his research was not covered by his college grant. Furthermore, he too was happy with the arrangements, which were of a largely personal and informal nature. Hence, Glaxo and their consultants presented a united front to the MRC and the Council was left powerless to restore the co-operative scheme.

However, a year later, the idea of collaboration was revived when a method for the synthesis of cortisone from hecogenin (a by-product of the sisal industry) was developed by J.W. Cornforth and his colleagues at the NIMR. They had worked out a twenty-stage process that competed favourably with Merck's thirty-five-stage synthesis from bile acids.[49] This time, the MRC approached directly both ICI, who showed little interest, and Glaxo, who for the time being preferred to concentrate on Jones' method for producing cortisone from ergosterol, so that they could enter into an agreement with both the MRC and with Merck from a position of strength.[50] Consequently, the Council turned to Herts, which, although small in the way of scientific resources and with little experience of synthetic work, had the backing of the firm Smith and Nephew.[51] After a visit to their company headquarters at Welwyn Garden City, representatives of the MRC described Herts as 'well run on sound commercial lines, with plenty of money available from their "bread and butter" to undertake extensive development in selected fields'.[52]

Nevertheless, following a subsequent meeting with Glaxo that took place in August 1952, by September a collaborative arrangement had been drawn up between the MRC and Glaxo for the synthesis of cortisone from sisal, and this did not include Herts.[53] It was later explained that such exclusive co-operation had been due to exceptional circumstances, in that 'Glaxo were the only firm capable of taking an adequate share of the joint research programme'.[54] This one-to-one relationship was reminiscent not of penicillin, but of insulin, for the production of which the University of Toronto had agreed to collaborate with Eli Lilly, and had justified this exclusive partnership by arguing that 'for humanitarian purposes the manufacture of the said product can be more adequately effected by collaboration with one efficient and reliable commercial firm than by collaboration with several firms'.[55]

It is possible that, shamed by the collapse of the previous collaborative scheme, the MRC felt under pressure to enter into an agreement with industry, even under such restrictive circumstances, in order to show support for the NRDC, which, after all, it had helped to create.[56] As far as Glaxo were concerned, a body such as the MRC represented an important ally within government, as they had experienced in 1951 when the Council's backing helped them to secure approval from the Board of Trade for extensions to their laboratories and factories.[57] With respect to cortisone, it would also help to counterbalance the weight of Merck, whom Glaxo found somewhat overbearing, and would ultimately lead to their dominant position on the British market for corticosteroid (cortisone-like) drugs.[58]

However, two safeguards against monopoly were built into the agreement between Glaxo and the MRC: 1) that the Council, and other parties, should be free to terminate their collaboration after three months' notice, and 2) that any pharmaceutical firm should be free to ask for a licence to produce cortisone using the NIMR method (under clause S. 41 of the 1949 Patents Act). In the event, the collaboration lasted three years, from 1952 to 1955, when the patents for Cornforth's method and an alternative method developed by Glaxo were offered, the first to the NRDC, the second to a holdings company that had both Glaxo and the NRDC as its joint share-holders, GNRD Patent Holdings Co Ltd. Eventually, Glaxo and the NRDC made the decision to end their agreement and develop their own patents independently of each other, which prompted the comments from Harington to Halsbury at the NRDC: 'I am quite gratified to know that for once we have given you a patent over which you are not likely to be the losers.'[59]

The effect of this double approach to collaboration between the MRC and industry, was the creation of a two-tier system, in which grand penicillin-style collaborations were proposed by the Council when smaller, less well known firms were involved, but one-to-one relationships of the insulin type were resorted to when the most respectable and experienced firms came into the project. This happened in the case of cortisone, but in other instances also, such as the development of non-explosive anaesthetics, for which the British Oxygen Company (BOC) was abandoned in favour of ICI.

4. The MRC and pharmaceutical companies: halothane

The Council's association with BOC had begun before the war, within the framework of the Joint Anaesthetics Committee of the MRC and the section of anaesthetics of the Royal Society of Medicine. The collaboration between the Council and BOC had then been confined to specialist assistance, by which the firm helped the Committee with gas analyses and with the construction of various devices. After the war, the search for a safe, all-purpose non-explosive anaesthetic was stepped up as a result of explosions that were related to the increasingly popular use of electrical devices in surgery, such as diathermy apparatus.[60] Hydrocarbon compounds containing one or more fluorine atoms, the fluoroalkanes, which were developed in the 1930s and used as refrigerants, before being used to enable the separation of radioactive isotopes in the Atom Bomb project, offered researchers a fruitful line of research.[61]

Although very volatile, these were stable compounds, and because of their low flammability were prime candidates for the development of non-explosive anaesthetics.[62] In 1953 the MoH, after consultation with the MRC, recommended that studies of fluorinated compounds be carried out by the MRC working on the chemistry and biological side, while the DSIR tackled the electrical and physical aspects of the question, under the aegis of a new committee, the Committee on non-explosive anaesthetic agents, which met for the first time on 11 January 1955.[63]

Invitations were issued to Dr C.G. Harris of ICI and Professor J.H. Burn of the department of pharmacology at Oxford to read a paper 'to acquaint other pharmacologists with the existence of these new drugs in the hope that their interest would be aroused.'[64] The intention was to make the collaboration as wide as possible, and the MRC expressed unease about the close association that already existed between the secretary of the committee, T.H.S. Burns, and BOC: 'while such collaboration is generally to be welcomed, it would be better if it could be between scientists in the University field'.[65] Co-operation between Burns and BOC was allowed to continue nonetheless, and the scope of the scheme was widened, to include other suitable firms, such as Glaxo, ICI, and the Imperial Smelting Co. of Avonmouth. However, at the time the Council thought it preferable that, rather than approach the firms directly, it should ask the ABPI to make nominations.[66]

Despite its good intentions, the Council was never in a position to implement such a grand collaborative scheme, which did not take off. Instead, it was forced into a one-to-one relationship with ICI, as a result of the rapid progress the group had been making with their drug halothane, with the help of the anaesthetist Michael Johnstone at the Manchester Royal Infirmary.[67] Although earlier ICI had approached several anaesthetists in order to define their criteria of selection and identify their target,[68] Johnstone was to play a crucial role by helping to establish a safe anaesthetic procedure associated with the drug. Like Laborit, Delay and Deniker with chlorpromazine (see Chapter 5), Johnstone represented the demand side of innovation, yet he took an active part in the innovation process itself.

The story of the discovery of halothane has been presented by one of its chief protagonists as one of science-based innovation, that is to say one based on the knowledge of the fundamental physical and chemical properties of fluoroalkanes, but also on a quantitative theory of narcosis, which had been formulated by John Ferguson of ICI's General Chemicals Division in 1939.[69] However, the accumulation of — largely empirical — knowledge about these compounds also played an important part in ICI's ultimate success with halothane.[70] Over the 1930s and 1940s, the group had become familiar with fluoroalkanes, which had been developed as refrigerants by researchers at General Motors and later at Du Pont, with whom ICI had an agreement to exchange knowledge and know-how (see Chapter 3). Because of their low toxicity and flammability, the compounds had also been tested as anaesthetics. At ICI, further knowledge of these compounds was gained through the investigation by Ferguson of their potential as pesticides, and through the Atom Bomb project, in which they were used to facilitate the separation of uranium isotopes.[71] An ICI chemist, Charles Suckling, hired by ICI in 1942, studied these substances as a result of the group's involvement in the 'Tube Alloys' project (the code name for the Atom Bomb).[72]

In 1950, Ferguson became research director of General Chemicals, by then part of the Mond Division, and in this new capacity conceived of a project to develop fluorocarbons as anaesthetic agents.[73] For this, he chose Suckling, who was teamed up with the pharmacologist James Raventos (see Figure 6.2), then working in the Dyestuffs Division, which housed ICI's pharmaceutical laboratories before the creation of a separate pharmaceutical research center at Alderley Park in Cheshire in 1957.[74] Because the number of fluorinated compounds was potentially very large, Suckling and Raventos began by defining their target. Their strategy was, in itself, highly innovative.[75] To help them in their task, Suckling and Raventos sought the assistance of anaesthetists, who provided them with criteria for the selection of suitable compounds, that is to say safe compounds, capable of providing rapid and smooth induction, followed by an equally smooth recovery. Translating these criteria first into the desired properties of the gas:[76] volatility, low flammability, stability, and high potency, and subsequently into the required structural features of the molecules, Suckling narrowed down the number of fluoroalkanes to be synthesized,[77] while Raventos carried out pharmacological tests to identify the compounds offering the highest margin of safety, as well as rapid, smooth induction and recovery.[78] The compound that was selected as a result of these tests, and which became known as halothane (marketed under the name Fluothane), was the only one to satisfy the many criteria of selection.[79] This strategy, which led from specific criteria, through testing, to selection of a compound, was described retrospectively by Suckling as an early example of drug design, which he saw as a novelty for the time.[80]

ICI worked on halothane without the help of any university consultants, although they were in loose contact with Professor J.H. Burn in the Department of Pharmacology at Oxford, and with Dr H.G. Epstein in the Nuffield Department of Anaesthetics, also at Oxford. Their principal collaborator

Figure 6.2 Suckling, Johnstone and Raventos (photo reproduced from Carol Kennedy, ICI: the company that changed our lives (London: Hutchinson, 1986), pp. 132-3).

was, in fact, a clinician, the anaesthetist Michael Johnstone at the Royal Manchester Infirmary, who was chosen by ICI to carry out clinical trials, and who visited Raventos's pharmacological laboratory to satisfy himself that the new drug presented enough potential benefits to warrant such trials.[81] He helped to introduce ICI's new drug, halothane, in association with out-of-circuit vaporizers, which made it possible to measure precisely the concentration of the anaesthetic delivered to the inspired mixture.[82]

ICI therefore carefully supervised the design of the apparatus to be associated with halothane. In 1956, they contacted BOC, with whom they had regular meetings to discuss their requirements in terms of design and materials.[83] So as not to be tied to one single industrial partner, ICI also contacted the Longworth Scientific Instrument Company, for whom Epstein was developing an inhaler at the time.[84] Eventually, the British company Cyprane produced the vaporiser which was to become associated with Fluothane, known as the Fluotec (see Figure 6.3 and Figure 6.4).[85]

Secondly, ICI kept close control on the running of hospital trials. Thus, when the question of clinical tests arose, ICI were anxious that Johnstone

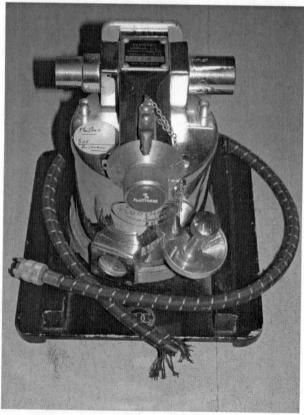

Figure 6.3 The Fluotec mark 1 (with kind permission from the Association of Anaesthetists of Great Britain and Ireland).

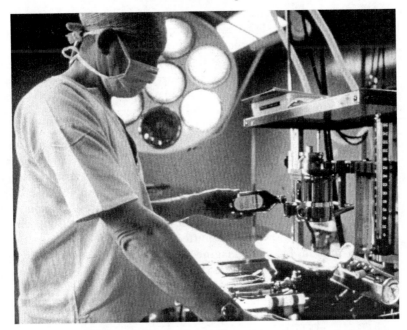

Figure 6.4 The Fluotec in use (photo reproduced from Kennedy)

should be asked to do the first trial. Then, and only then, the firm insisted, could the trial be extended to members of the MRC. Eventually, ICI had their way and a trial was carried out on 310 patients at the Manchester Royal Infirmary, which helped to produce a favourable first impression of the drug.[86]

In his retrospective account of the research, Joseph Artusio felt that the decision by ICI to keep the drug in the hands of a few experts, such as Johnstone 'who were extremely diligent in its use', was a wise one. The adoption of halothane as an anaesthetic agent went hand in hand with that of unconventional out-of-circuit vaporisers. If it had been misused, it could have been lethal and further development would have been stopped.[87] Thus, establishing a safe procedure for testing the drug and controlling the clinical trials by maneuvering their close collaborators into place was an important element in the strategy adopted by the firm, especially when taking into consideration the opposition that was expressed against the drug in the early stages of the research.

The ICI reports received criticism from a member of the Committee, Professor A.E. Pask of the Department of Anaesthetics at the Medical School, King's College, Newcastle-upon-Tyne. He wrote that their conclusions were hasty and provided no clear cut evidence 'that the drug (Fluothane) is notably more potent than chloroform'. He also expressed a wish to see 'more planned pharmacological work' before clinical trials, and suggested that systematic tests be carried out on a limited number of dogs.[88] Although other members of the committee shared Pask's reticence in the face of what they felt were 'over-enthusiastic reports',[89] too severe a criticism of ICI was thought to be dangerous, for it might halt the innovative process and undermine the central role played by the committee. These fears were expressed in Burn's reply to Pask's letter:

> As things are, the work of the Committee has been brought to a standstill by your opinion. It seems to me that this is not only so far as Fluothane is concerned, but also as far as any other anaesthetics are concerned. Professor Stacey, who receives a grant from the MRC for this work, has provided six new substances which are at present in the hands of Dr Burns. If one or more of these proves to be useful in animals, I do not see how the committee will be able to test them in view of your opinion. I cannot imagine that it will ever be possible in practice to test any substance more thoroughly in animals than Fluothane has been tested.[90]

Further, he concluded that, having discussed the matter with Dr Herrald at the MRC, it would be best 'to make an attempt to progress by allowing the clinical members of the committee to test Fluothane as individuals in so far as they may be willing to do so'. These words became the line adopted by the committee with respect to halothane in 1958, when it was decided that 'further work on this drug should be left to individuals while the committee devoted its energies to the production and investigation of other new non-explosive drugs'.[91]

Whatever the doubts expressed about halothane, in the end ICI's reputation weighed in its favour when it was compared with other compounds. The MRC's support of halothane was repaid when ICI promised its support to the committee, by supplying it freely with compounds for research.[92] The 'experiment in collaboration' was therefore safe, even if it survived in a limited form. Such an arrangement was beneficial to ICI through their drug halothane. In their historical introduction to their book, Max Sadove and Vernon Wallace pointed out that some anaesthetists still believed that, because of its multiple effects, it represented a retrograde step in what they saw as progress towards the use of a specific agent or technique for a specific purpose. To others, the undesirable side effects of the drug more than outweighed the desirable effects for which the agent was utilized. Nevertheless, with increased usage, the dominant trend became one of acceptance and even enthusiasm for halothane. Its use spread quickly, first in Britain, and then abroad. In 1956 it reached the United States, and by 1959 was used across the world.[93]

The MRC's co-operative rationale worked in favour of the adoption of ICI's innovation by the community of anaesthetists. Because of ICI's advance in the field (similar to that of Glaxo with cortisone), the Council could do little else but collaborate closely with the company. Otherwise, it was in danger of losing its place at the heart of this 'experiment in collaboration' that might generate new drugs, and also new knowledge. Suckling's 1957 paper had held such a promise: 'We may, at least, confidently hope that the work will contribute to a better understanding of the mechanism of anaesthesia'.[94]

But there was another incentive: continued reciprocal support between ICI and the MRC. ICI had forged a close relationship with the MRC in relation to penicillin, and to synthetic anti-malarials (see Chapter 3).[95] In 1950, ICI had sought the MRC's backing in its attempt to fend off Merck's claims to a retrospective royalty on the production of penicillin by deep-fermentation.[96] In 1953, the Malaria Research Unit in Nairobi, entirely financed by ICI 'with the blessing of the municipality of Nairobi and the Government of Kenya', had also received the approval of the Council.[97]

The drug was a direct outcome of the wishes expressed by clinicians, and was developed in a systematic manner, which actively involved clinicians at two different stages: first in helping the company to set their target, and second in assisting them with the development of the chosen compound from synthesis to market launch, in association with a particular protocol and specific technological device. In their description of the development of halothane, Maxwell and Eckhardt have underplayed the role of clinicians, or indeed of wider collaborative relationships such as those with the MRC.[98] A closer examination of primary sources, which helps to relate the development of halothane to the wider historical context, brings out the role of Johnstone, which is comparable to the role of Laborit, Delay and Deniker for chlorpromazine. This common feature of the development of chlorpromazine and halothane suggests that clinicians played a key role in the rise of rational drug design, by helping to bridge the gap 'between need and science'.[99] However, unlike chlorpromazine, the development of halothane also involved the MRC, which played a central role unparalleled in France.

A considerable interdependence had been created between the MRC and industry. Industry needed the support of the Council for the clinical trials of their drugs. However, the growing research capacity of firms meant that the Council also relied on the expertise of individual firms in order to develop novel therapeutic substances.[100] Its special relationship with industry strengthened its position in relation to the MoH. By supporting large and prestigious companies such as ICI, the Council was able to remain at the centre of the innovative process in biomedicine after World War Two, although it did so at some cost. That cost was having to play an ambiguous role, between public and private, and between science and industry. This ambiguous role is illustrated by the history of the development of the antibiotic cephalosporin, which involved the MRC's Antibiotic Research Station at Clevedon in Somerset, researchers funded by the Council, Oxford University, Glaxo, and the NRDC, for whom this was to be one of their most successful programmes.[101] Over the years, cephalosporin would bring the Corporation £152 million in royalties, which they shared with the inventors, and would in time benefit Oxford University greatly, unlike other often cited missed opportunities for British universities.[102]

5. The MRC between public and private, between science and industry: from cephalosporin to interferon

The MRC had inherited from the inter-war period a sense of mission to support pharmaceutical firms in the face of foreign competition. It had also learnt the lessons of penicillin. The German menace had been replaced by the 'rapacious Americans', against whom it was felt British companies had — once again — to be defended, especially in the emerging field of antibiotics.[103] In this area, the MRC was to play a particularly active role. In 1949, the MRC took control of a small antibiotic research station, which the Navy had set up at Clevedon with the help of Distillers for the purpose of producing penicillin.[104] Clevedon was to play an important part in helping to maintain supplies of, and interest in, cephalosporin, until 1960, when its responsibilities and members of its staff were transferred to the Microbiological Research Station at Porton Down.[105] However, it was not only the MRC which had learnt the lessons of penicillin, but also members of the Sir William Dunn School of Pathology, who with the encouragement of Florey as well as the Council were intent on patenting their discoveries from the early stages of their research on cephalosporin.[106]

The development of cephalosporin, which I will describe in greater detail in the next section, was beset with difficulties, which were only overcome after years of painstaking collaborative research between the School of Pathology, the MRC, the NRDC and industry. Toine Pieters's history of interferon, which was discovered at the NIMR in the 1950s, and was transformed and developed into a new family of biomolecules in the 1990s thanks to a complex web of national and international collaborations, paints a similar picture.[107] Between these two dates, it went through successive cycles of promise and disappointment. After being hailed as the 'new antiviral penicillin', it fell out of favour with researchers in universities, hospitals and industry, until its potential in the treatment of cancer led to renewed interest in the 1970s.[108] However, poor results in large-scale clinical trials brought about another phase of disappointment, after which it underwent one more transformation. This time, it was turned into a new group of genetically engineered drugs, which found uses in the treatment of hepatitis, cancer and multiple sclerosis. As such, interferon heralded not only a new era for drug development, but also a novel approach, that of multi-modal immunotherapy, which thanks to drugs such as interferon would in the latter part of the twentieth century coexist with chemotherapy as part of the physician's therapeutic arsenal.

By then, the MRC's mission had been accomplished, and industrial firms had become close collaborators in research. However, with the rise of the new biotechnology, once again the boundaries between science and industry were to become blurred. Firms, including biotech start-ups, became potentially serious competitors in fundamental research, an area which, since World War Two, the MRC had liked to see as its prerogative.[109]

By lending its support to laws such as the 1949 Patent Act and to organizations such as the NRDC, the MRC took part in the elaboration of a national research policy that fostered a research culture among biomedical scientists and industry, as well as a close relationship between the two. However, as the examples of cortisone, halothane, cephalosporin and interferon suggest, despite this involvement in policy making, the Council's relationship with industry was of a pragmatic nature, adapting to each particular circumstance, and respecting pre-existing arrangements between individual scientists and companies.

The MRC's ruling concerning gratuities was vague, and decisions were usually made on the individual merits of the case. For instance, when Cruikshank, an MRC researcher who was asked to advise Alex Duckham Ltd. and correct a pamphlet the firm had produced on skin disease, wrote to the Council for permission to accept a gratuity,[110] the MRC recognized that the gratuity 'would if anything only help his scientific work by allowing for a little more leisure during the coming months', but insisted that the money should be paid directly to the Council, and then added to Cruikshank's salary. In adapting to the reality of collaboration between researchers and pharmaceutical companies, the MRC made itself a guarantor of scientists' honesty, but also maintained its central position between science and industry.

These individual arrangements were the manifestations of a grass-roots culture, in which relations between scientists and industry owed little to the MRC's, or to the government's actions. In the next section, this grass-roots culture is studied more closely, through three scientists involved in antibiotic research, Florey, Abraham and Chain. They were chosen because of their earlier involvement in penicillin, but also because of their different scientific backgrounds, which led them to follow different paths in relation to pharmaceutical firms. While Florey turned away from research of an applied nature, therefore moving gradually away from industry, Chain maintained his close contacts with drug companies, even constructing his academic career around them. As to Abraham, although he was constantly in touch with pharmaceutical firms at home and abroad, after a brief spell as a consultant to ICI, he was to entertain an even closer relationship with the NRDC, for which he became a consultant in 1958.[111]

Figure 6.5 The Sir William Dunn School of Pathology (courtesy of the Sir William Dunn School of Pathology, Oxford).

C. THE GRASS ROOTS: THE INDIVIDUAL CASES OF FLOREY, ABRAHAM AND CHAIN

Florey epitomizes the basic scientist whose primary purpose was the development of a biomedical discipline through the experimental method. Penicillin represented a parenthesis in his career, albeit a most fruitful one. After penicillin and his brief involvement with cephalosporin, Florey returned to some of the fundamental research topics that had preoccupied him before the war, such as the mechanism of mucus secretion. He also turned his attention to newer topics that were being opened up by advances in clinical medicine, for instance the study of atherosclerosis.

1. Florey, ICI, Abraham, and the NRDC

A complete collection of Florey's offprints, arranged in chronological order and for a time held by the Wellcome Unit for the History of Medicine in Oxford, shows this evolution very clearly. Between 1939 and 1955 his publications were dominated by penicillin and other antibiotics. After 1955, a gradual shift occurred away from antibiotics towards the more fundamental as well as technical aspects of pathology. His biographers explain this gradual shift away from antibiotics by his realisation, after cephalosporin, that the time had passed when scientists such as he could make important contributions in chemotherapy, and that this was best left to pharmaceutical companies.[112] His collaboration with ICI, the only industrial consultancy he ever took, arose as a result of the penicillin experience and had the aim of speeding up the production of cephalosporin. However, in the end it fulfilled little practical purpose, and Florey was reduced to playing the role of a bystander, watching the company carry out its research projects independently of his advice.

The following account of Florey's involvement with the cephalosporin project, which led him to agree to consult for ICI, is drawn from Edward Abraham's personal recollections, and from his papers deposited in the Bodleian archive. In Abraham's own words, 'in the early 1950s an ominous cloud was beginning to appear'.[113] Penicillin-resistant strains of staphylococcus were spreading in hospitals. This prompted a widespread search for new antibiotics.

In 1945, a professor of bacteriology in Sardinia, Giuseppe Brotzu, had found a species of fungus that showed activity against several Gram-negative as well as Gram-positive bacteria (the only antibiotic that was active against Gram-negative bacteria was then streptomycin). Having been unable to interest the Italian pharmaceutical industry in his discovery, he was advised by a British colleague to contact the MRC, which directed him

Figure 6.6 Members of the School (courtesy of the Sir William Dunn School of Pathology, Oxford).

to Florey. In 1948, Florey received from Brotzu a sample of culture of the fungus and a paper in which he described his work. At the School of Pathology, a number of researchers, including Norman Heatley and Edward Abraham, began to study the organism, applying the knowledge and techniques developed in the course of their research on penicillin. However, unlike penicillin, from the very beginning the production of culture fluids was entrusted to others, in this instance the MRC's new Antibiotic Research Station. It would continue to supply the School of Pathology until 1960, by which time industry was both willing and able to take over this role.

The workers at the School of Pathology confirmed that the fungus produced an antibiotic substance, cephalosporin N (later identified as a hydrophilic penicillin, and renamed penicillin N) and that it had a side-chain that conferred upon it its unusual antibiotic activity against gram-negative bacteria, which had been described in Brotzu's paper. However, it was sensitive to penicillinase-producing staphylococcus, and although Guy Newton, a graduate student of the School of Pathology, helped Clevedon to improve its production process, its manufacture never became attractive commercially. At this point, several of the researchers lost interest in Brotzu's fungus.[114] Abraham has not explained why, but it is possible that they were influenced by Florey's agenda, which was to find a penicillin that was active against resistant staphylococci. By 1953, Abraham and Newton were the only two scientists left working on the question.

Abraham was a chemist, therefore his agenda was different from Florey's, and he persisted in his research. He was intrigued by the unusual structure of the substance, and its relation to biological activity against Gram-negative bacteria. Further study of the substance, which thanks to the improved process developed at Clevedon could be obtained in greater quantities and be purified, revealed that it was contaminated by another, with a similar side-chain, hence also active against gram-negative bacteria, but what's more resistant to penicillinase.[115] The work suggested to Florey that, unlike penicillin N, cephalosporin C — as the new substance was called — might be of therapeutic interest. He tested it on mice infected with penicillin-resistant staphylococcus, and although its antibacterial activity was very low, he found it not only to be effective, but also less toxic than benzylpenicillin (by then the most widespread form of therapeutic penicillin).[116]

Florey contacted ICI in the hope of starting production of the substance.[117] Earlier, the NRDC, which had been helping to organize the patenting of the discoveries made by members of the School of Pathology, had tried to involve several firms in the development of cephalosporin, including ICI. However, as had happened with cortisone, ICI decided not to participate in the collaboration (something they later regretted). As to Glaxo, although they had been slow in getting involved, in the end they were persuaded to join the project, thanks in part to Florey's acquaintance with Sir Harry Jephcott.[118] As with cortisone, Glaxo alone showed real interest in the collaboration, and in December 1955 a meeting between the different parties took place, and full technical information was exchanged.[119] However, Glaxo soon struggled in their attempts to scale up production, which not only threatened Abraham and Newton's efforts at unraveling the structure of cephalosporin, but also jeopardized hopes of obtaining enough material for the preliminary clinical trials devised by Florey. Although the structural work carried out at the School of Pathology might pave the way for new derivatives with higher levels of activity, the commercial prospects of cephalosporin C were still in doubt because of the large doses required for intravenous drip, and Glaxo remained somewhat hesitant in their commitment to the project. Therefore once again the involvement of the MRC's Antibiotic Research Station, which continued to provide the Oxford researchers with material for their structural studies, was crucial.

Fortunately, in 1957 Clevedon succeeded in developing a mutant strain that produced higher yields.[120] However, the School's requirements were of 250 mgs of cephalosporin C per year, and Clevedon could only supply them with 100 mgs.[121] Although additional material could also be obtained from Glaxo, who had begun using Clevedon's new strain, it was by no means certain that there would be enough for Florey's trials, and the future of cephalosporin therefore remained uncertain.

At this point a major development occurred, which would not only save the cephalosporin project, but revolutionize the field of antibiotics in general. In 1958, researchers at the Beecham Research Laboratories succeeded in isolating the nucleus of the penicillin molecule, 6-aminopenicillanic acid (6-APA) (see the following section), and a few months later began synthesizing new molecules with different side-chains, so as to confer upon them resistance to penicillinase.[122] As well as 'furore in the press',[123] the publication of the Beecham team's results in 1959 caused a considerable stir among scientific and industrial circles.[124] It was to prove a turning point, giving impetus not only to industry's commitment to cephalosporin, but also to the structural work carried out by Abraham and others.

Glaxo experienced a 'significant change in policy', its Board having agreed to devote a substantial sum to obtain the cephalosporin nucleus by whichever methods might work best, either fermentation or chemical methods.[125] Other firms, including the American company Eli Lilly, began pressing the NRDC for rights to licence under the cephalosporin patents. As to Abraham, although at first he realized that Beecham's discovery meant that cephalosporin C was no longer likely to fulfill its potential as a penicillinase-resistant antibiotic, reasoning by analogy with penicillin, he reckoned that its activity against Gram-negative bacteria might be enhanced if the cephalosporin nucleus could be isolated and new side-chains added onto it.[126] This spurred his and Newton's efforts at isolating the cephalosporin nucleus, named 7-APA (7-aminocephalosporanic acid) followed by the elucidation of its structure.[127]

Although there was to be some controversy about the structure of ceph-alosporin C, just as there had been with penicillin, it was short-lived.[128] Newton and Abraham were soon able to determine it as a ß-lactam-dihy-drothiazine,[129] and this was confirmed by X-ray analysis by Dorothy Hodg-kin and her Ph.D. student Maslem.[130] However, this spelled the end of the Antibiotic Research Station at Clevedon, which had done so much, but now that commercial firms were entering the field was felt by the MRC to have outlived its usefulness. Before too long new chemical procedures developed by Glaxo and by the American company Eli Lilly, which had made pre-liminary approaches to the NRDC in 1959, provided a practical solution to the problem of production, and the first semi-synthetic cephalosporins, cephalothin and cephaloridine, were introduced in 1964.[131]

With these new developments, the range of chemotherapy was extended far beyond that of the original penicillin to include dealing with resistant organisms and with Gram-negative bacteria. Abraham concluded:

> Unlike many antibiotics in clinical use, the penicillins and cephalo-sporins stemmed from research in academic institutions that was not motivated, for the most part, by thoughts of practical application. But their subsequent development would not have occurred without the skill and resources of pharmaceutical companies.[132]

There are strong parallels between the penicillin and cephalosporin stories. The primary motivation for both research projects was academic, according to Abraham, although the applied and fundamental aspects appear inextricably linked in the study of the relationship between chemi-cal structure and biological activity. Abraham had been attracted to cepha-losporin by the chemical properties of the substance. It was an unstable peptide with unusual structural features, similar to an antibiotic named bacitracin, which he had previously studied, and he suspected that these features caused the unusual activity of cephalosporin against Gram-nega-tive bacteria. The researchers encountered an initial reluctance on the part of the pharmaceutical industry, in Britain as well as in Italy, which must have had the effect of 'déjà-vu' on all those involved. And yet, Abraham saw an important distinction between the two episodes. According to him, it marked a radical change in academic attitudes towards the patenting of invention.

Around 1950, Abraham had received a letter from the MRC urging him to patent any discovery of potential commercial value under the NRDC. As a result of this encouragement, he assigned the patents for cephalosporin C and its nucleus to the Corporation. However, he later discovered that the British academic system was unprepared for such a move. Oxford Univer-sity had no policy for receiving royalties, and it looked as if these would go to the inventors themselves. In 1965, when it became clear that royalties on cephalosporin C would be forthcoming, Abraham and his collaborators decided instead to transfer their shares to charitable trusts for the support of biological, medical, and chemical research. However, before this could be done, the researchers needed to clarify their tax position with the Board of Inland Revenue. The lessons of penicillin had been learnt among the 'official world of London', and they were allowed to 'divest themselves of their marketable assets' without risking personal ruin.[133]

Today, several Oxford colleges bear the mark of the shares from royalties on cephalosporin.[134] However, although cephalosporin was to prove most profitable to the University, Abraham stated that early in the 1960s, '... we decided not to attempt to compete with pharmaceutical companies in a search for new semi-synthetic cephalosporins of clinical value'.[135] Instead, Abraham turned his attention to the more fundamental problem of biosynthetic pathways to antibiotics, which, he believed, might in the future find medical applications. As to Florey, he chose to turn his attention to degenerative diseases, which were gaining prominence in medical and pharmaceutical research as a result of the very success of antibacterial chemotherapy and an ageing population.[136]

2. Florey and the antibiotics parenthesis

Penicillin and cephalosporin were a parenthesis in Florey's career. They were also a phase in the development of the biomedical sciences, which, because of his importance within the scientific establishment, was reflected in Florey's research agenda. The penicillin project had secured funding for his department at a time when funding was difficult to obtain in the sciences in Oxford.[137] Moreover, in his attempt to transform the Sir William Dunn School of Pathology, Florey thought that an applied project, involving teamwork and a multidisciplinary approach such as penicillin, was the best way of breathing vitality into a department otherwise described as a 'mausoleum'.[138] With cephalosporin, he may have been pursuing a winning streak, capitalising on the hard-earned gains of the past fifteen years. Even after Florey had ceased working on chemotherapy as such, he continued using drugs as research tools to elucidate fundamental physiological questions, for instance the effect of cortisone on the mechanisms of cell division, or, with the growing use of antibiotics to treat bacterial infections, the biological aspects of antibiotic resistance.[139]

There were also personal gains to be had from applied projects such as penicillin or cephalosporin, for these attracted attention, and honours often soon followed. Although he had been elected FRS before his contribution to penicillin became known, a glance at the titles of his offprints from 1940 onwards suggests that the penicillin work gave him world-wide fame. In the immediate post-war years, he toured the world, from the United States to New Zealand, via France, Spain, Scandinavia, Switzerland, talking about the Oxford penicillin work.[140] As well as helping to ensure continued funding for his department and his group — who were saved from dispersal by a Nuffield Foundation grant — this celebrity must have given him some personal satisfaction, although his biographers have written that he was shy of publicity.

The personal prestige he gained from penicillin also gave him a powerful voice, with which he could attempt to influence government research policy. Thus in the 1960s, as an elder statesman of science (he was knighted in 1944 and became President of the Royal Society in 1960), through lectures and articles published in journals such as *Nature,* he presented his views on twentieth-century science and medicine and on the responsibilities of scientists in the modern world. In an article entitled 'Prestige in academic scientific research', he bemoaned the fact that, despite the considerable progress made in the period since World War Two, on matters of science and technology Britain was lagging behind other great nations, in particular the United States and the USSR.[141] As a result, she was losing political prestige and power. Florey's message to the Parliamentary and Scientific Committee, for whom the paper was originally intended, was that Britain's best scientists and technologists, 'the modern Elizabethans' as he referred to them in what had become a much loved metaphor, were leaving the country for lack of facilities in university laboratories, which he identified as its greatest weakness by comparison with the United States.[142] Drawing an analogy between university research and the coronary artery system, he wrote: 'It will not matter much what we do to the rest of the scientific organisations if the coronary arteries of university research are allowed to thrombose'.[143] He concluded that the state needed to show the same support for university research that it had shown for the research associations, i.e. fund basic as well as applied research.

In another talk, printed in the *Yale Journal of Biology and Medicine,* Florey spoke more generally of medical science in the twentieth century. He reached similar conclusions: much of the progress he identified in his survey was situated in the West, specifically in the United States. The reasons he gave for this were American 'innate vitality', but also the government's support for medical research.[144] He contrasted the situation in the United States with that in Britain:

> It is perfectly true that money will not buy results, but it is quite certain that if insufficient money is put into research, results are much more difficult to obtain, for there is a great waste of energy in finding the wherewithal to carry out research and in making do with less than the best. Perhaps most important, rare original talent becomes much harder to foster than it should be. I am afraid that in many countries, including Great Britain, the money available for medical research still falls short of what could be utilized.[145]

Again preoccupied with the brain-drain to America, and drawing from his own experience as a 'grant-beggar', Florey took the opportunity of his public visibility to put across one fundamental message: that of Britain's decline and backwardness relative to the United States. He, like other scientists, actively participated in the creation of a declinist ideology, which although it had roots far in the past, in the post-war period underwent a resurgence, with the objective of spurring the government into supporting science on a large scale.[146]

Perhaps his attitude to the British pharmaceutical industry should be seen in the light of the ambitions he harboured for British science. Florey had become a consultant for ICI in the hope that he would be able to influence their policy. Instead, he found that he was used to help to build up their scientific image and was reduced to a bystander at their meetings. A letter from Garnet Davey at Alderley Park illustrates the ways in which the company thought Florey might be of use to them as a consultant:

> I think our meeting was most valuable to us because, as I told you, these little gatherings provide an excellent opportunity of *making* our people present a considered reappraisal of particular bits of work. [...] You may think that you did not give much positive help but, to be perfectly truthful, if you were able to do this on every occasion that you visit us I should become seriously perturbed about our abilities.[147]

It is evident from this quotation that the main impetus for research was not expected to emanate from Florey, but from the company's own scientists. However, Florey's 'seal of approval' on ICI's research was still considered to be important, and worth paying for.

Later, in a report on the general situation of the industry in 1974, the following predictions were made concerning the relationship between academic and industrial laboratories:

> [Academic labs], as well as departments of medicine and medical research institutions, will tend [...] to concentrate more on the physiology and biochemistry of the disease process. While the industrial labs will also be working in this more basic field, their contributions to it will be minor compared with those of the academic groups whose discoveries made in this field will give leads to those working in industrial labs.[148]

These comments were undoubtedly based on recent developments in industry. The locus for drug discovery had shifted towards industry, leading to the conclusion that there would be fewer drugs emanating from academic laboratories in the future. Florey's changing relationship with the pharmaceutical industry should therefore also be seen in terms of his changing research interests, moving further away from chemotherapy; in terms of the evolution of the biomedical sciences, towards the study of the fundamental mechanisms of health and disease, and also in terms of changing rationales within industry, with ICI offering the example of a company that had evolved a strategy of depending on its own resources.[149]

Florey was representative of the British scientific élite, and his influence on other scientists was considerable. Chain, on the other hand, was more eccentric, in both meanings of the term. Despite his success with penicillin, he remained on the periphery of British science. He felt himself to have been cast aside by the British establishment and he left for Rome. However, thanks to his relationship with industry and to his contacts with London financiers, he later found a way back to the centre. He was instrumental in turning Beecham's production of tartaric acid into one of the more successful penicillin plants in the country. In return, his academic career, which appeared to have reached a stand-still at the end of World War Two, blossomed.

3. Chain, Beecham and semi-synthetic penicillins

Influenced by the example of his father who had worked as a chemist for the German chemical industry, Chain's model of scientific research, especially where it concerned the patenting of discoveries, was different to the one that was common in Britain at the time.[150] Either because he felt there was an incompatibility between his views and those of the British establishment, or because he was attracted by colleagues such as Daniel Bovet and his wife to go and work at the Istituto di Sanità, where he had at his disposal a pilot fermentation plant (something 'his masters had refused him back in England' according to H.G. Lazell), or else perhaps for both reasons, in 1950 Chain left England for Rome.[151]

According to his biographer Ronald Clark, the ideas Chain developed as a result of his experience with penicillin greatly influenced not only his career, but because of the role he continued to play in antibiotic research, the pharmaceutical industry as well:

> This attitude [of Mellanby and Dale] to the patenting of penicillin became an obsession with Chain, so much so that it played a significant part in his subsequent career and thus in the development of the antibiotics industry in the three decades that followed the end of World War Two. He was influenced first by his dislike of watching Britain pay large sums for developments that had been initiated in Britain — a further indication of his loyalty to the country that had seen him over the hump in 1933. Another factor was his background within the German chemical engineering industry. During the first half of the twentieth-century the links between German academics and their industrial counterparts were of a strength virtually unknown in Britain. To Dale, Mellanby and many others there was a gap between academic research and industry as wide as between gentlemen and players. To Chain, no such gap existed.[152]

This quotation reveals the extent to which post-war rhetoric, in particular with reference to penicillin, has shaped contemporary ideas about the relationship between science and industry. It also reveals the contribution of scientists like Chain to this rhetoric.

According to Clark, the attitudes of men of science like Dale and Mellanby had forced Chain, despite his loyalty to Britain, to emigrate to Italy, where he was to remain fifteen years. It was there that he forged close links with a British pharmaceutical firm, Beecham Research Laboratories. This was a company that had long been making patent medicines, and began hiring scientific consultants before the war, including Charles (later Sir Charles) Dodds. It continued this policy after the war, with people such as Ian (later Sir Ian) Heilbron.[153] Before turning to Chain's collaboration with Beecham, I will briefly sketch the history of the firm.

Beecham's decision to build research laboratories in the immediate post-war period was based on a comparison of current trends in Britain, the United States, Germany and France, which led to the conclusion that the future of pharmaceuticals lay in the development of ethical specialties.[154] It was also based on what Lazell has described as an 'enthusiasm for research', which was in part genuine, but also in part meant to deflect likely attacks from government officials and other 'sectional interests' against the patent medicines business.[155] Before setting up these new laboratories, the company had sought the advice of leading scientists (including Jack Drummond and Charles Dodds), and as a result of their advice the Beecham laboratories were created at Brockham Park in March 1945.

One of the their first goals was to manufacture penicillin. Their first managing director toured the United States in the hope of entering into an agreement with American firms, and of learning American 'know-how', but without any practical results. For many years, the laboratories worked on disparate topics of research, rather disappointingly in Lazell's view. Then, in 1954, Dodds suggested that Chain become their consultant in order to help them set up a fermentation plant for the manufacture of tartaric acid. Chain wished for the terms of his consultancy to be agreed in the presence of his solicitors, including Lord Nathan who had been 'looking after (his) interests for many years'.[156] He subsequently asked for a £5,000 fixed annual honorarium,[157] to be transformed when production began on an industrial scale into a royalty on production value to a minimum of £5,000 (i.e. a maximum of 5% for a production value of up to £100,000). However, he did not wish to receive any remuneration until success was assured. This was, according to him, the 'principle which forms the only acceptable basis of any successful and satisfactory collaboration, that is to say that both parties must benefit'.[158]

Chain proposed that this fermentation plant should also be used to produce penicillin. At a meeting on 19–20 September 1955, which Dodds, Heilbron and Chain attended, his suggestion was taken even further, and the decision was made to concentrate on penicillin manufacture.[159] Beecham employees were sent to Rome 'for indoctrination' into Chain's methods and ideas. Two of the four scientists sent to Chain's laboratory, George Rolinson and Ralph Batchelor, would later be involved in the isolation of the molecular core of penicillin that paved the way to the first semi-synthetic penicillins. By then, the company had strong chemistry and pharmacology departments, smaller bacteriology, biochemistry and physical chemistry departments, to which Lazell attributed Beecham's subsequent success with penicillin. With the discovery as a new bargaining chip, Beecham now turned to Bristol Myers, who were old friends of the company, in the hope of learning from them the large-scale fermentation business. Bristol Myers agreed, and by 1961 Beecham's fermentation factory at Worthing was in place.

Chain's collaboration with industry extended beyond Beecham. He was responsible for establishing co-operative projects between firms, for instance in 1963 between the Laboratoires Roger Bellon, which had sought his advice on fermentation, and Beecham.[160] He was also in close contact with the Rank group (Rank Hovis McDougall Ltd. with whom he had a consultancy agreement from 1965 to 1979) and suggested that they work in collaboration with the NRDC.[161]

However, it was not an industrialist, but Lord Nathan, one of his financial friends, who was instrumental in creating the Institute of Biochemistry at Imperial College, of which Chain became Director in 1965, and which brought him back to England where he stayed until his death in 1979.[162] In his eyes, the Institute was the academic arm of industrial fermentation units such as Beecham, and he hoped that together they would create a powerful British fermentation industry, modelled on Pfizer's collaboration with the biochemical schools at Madison.[163] In the event, not only Beecham, but also Rank Hovis McDougall, as well as the MRC and the Science Research Council, contributed considerable funds to help support Chain's laboratory at Imperial, in a triangular association that was characteristic of the post-war period.[164]

In spite of the differences between Florey and Chain, due to their different scientific backgrounds and upbringing, both maintained that penicillin, which inspired their careers and their lives long after the war had ended, was a fundamental scientific discovery, which had originated in an academic laboratory. They believed that the future lay in ensuring government funding of basic science. Chain wrote that 'academic activities, provided it is of a high standard, serves the country, and industry, best' (*sic*). Like Florey, he concluded that it was the duty of the state, or of research foundations, to finance basic research projects and this, in the long-term, would benefit the country as a whole.[165] Such arguments, echoed in Vanevar Bush's *Science: the endless frontier*, and to some extent shared by companies such as Du Pont,[166] were common among scientists who as a result of the war found themselves in positions of relative power in Britain, and elsewhere in Europe and North America. Although the rhetoric was not new,[167] it constituted an important aspects of the post-war consensus that contributed to the reconstruction of science in the West.[168]

However, it is important to relate this rhetoric to local situations for a more complete picture of post-war collaborations to emerge, in which individual scientists, and individual companies, and the drugs that resulted from their collaborative efforts, still played a major role.

D. CONCLUSION

The transformation of the British pharmaceutical industry had begun in the 1930s (see Chapters 1 and 2).[169] The élites who had overseen its modernization then had also witnessed British structures being tried and tested during the war. Unlike in France, where the 'old guard' was overturned and replaced after the war, British élites were still in place, in science and industry, as well as politics.[170] They provided continuity, and a pragmatic approach to reconstruction.

Change was therefore more gradual in Britain than in France. Continuity can be observed in the relationship between the MRC and trusted pharmaceutical companies, and between Chain and Beecham. Change there was, nonetheless. The experience of penicillin guiding them, the MRC lent their support to the new Patent Law, which encouraged the patenting of medical discoveries, and to creation of the NRDC, which was to share with the Council its role as co-ordinator of research, similar to that of the DSIR before the war. It also developed a stronger relationship with the representatives of industry, much as it had done with the TRC during the war, and in order to maintain its central role at the heart of medical research played an ambiguous role between science and industry.

After the war, many companies developed their R&D facilities, in particular in the field of chemotherapy. This brought them closer to their clients, the clinicians, and led them to develop a new approach to research that was to blossom with the use of computers: drug design. This is an *a priori* approach, made possible not only by knowledge of the relationship between chemical structure and biological activity, but also by the needs articulated by clinicians, whose attitudes towards collaboration with industry had changed, partly thanks to the MRC's efforts, and to the experience of wartime research, and who subsequently became more directly involved in drug development. However, it also drew companies away from some of their previous partners in research, the scientists who, like Florey, were beginning to turn from the applications of their science and in matters of drug development were becoming onlookers rather than active participants.

However, as in France, in the 1980s all this was to change. To respond to the challenge of the emerging biotech industry, and to the increasing globalisation in medical science and industry, Britain's conservative government under Margaret Thatcher emphasized the greater need for co-operation between science and industry. Its drive to cut public spending led to a reduction in funding for universities, thereby encouraging scientists to turn to industry as an alternative source of support,[171] and a return to the 'blurred boundaries' of the inter-war years. It also urged companies to make significant contributions to public education, which many of them objected to, seeing in this a reversal of the state's role of funding basic research.[172] At the same time, it challenged the 'cosy relationship' that had developed since World War Two between pharmaceutical firms and the Department of Health within the 'triple helix'.[173]

Not surprisingly, this decade in which the role of the state was being re-examined and re-modelled, also saw a revival of the declinist literature, as David Edgerton has shown in his recent book entitled *Warfare State Britain*. Such a literature has had the effect, or perhaps even the aim, of rendering invisible an alternative history of Britain, which is incompatible with standard accounts. These have included 'anti-histories of technocracy and state intervention' (i.e. histories that have written technocracy and state intervention out of their analyses), as well as 'welfarist accounts' (i.e. histories either celebrating or criticizing the liberal nature of the Welfare State, in both cases obscuring the part played by technocratic and interventionist governments in shaping twentieth century Britain), and have become important narratives about twentieth-century Britain.[174]

By showing not only how conflicts provided a stimulus for developments such as penicillin, but also how medical science and industry became intertwined with government as a result of two world wars, I have added grist to Edgerton's mill. However, links with the military have tended not to be as powerful and omnipresent in the biomedical sciences and the pharmaceutical industry, as they were in the physical sciences and engineering, on which Edgerton has based his analysis. A comparison between sectors and disciplines would therefore help to refine and develop this analysis further, but it is well beyond the scope of this book. Nevertheless, what I hope to have demonstrated is that a down-up approach to the history of science, medicine and technology, which pays more attention to the 'grass-roots', has as great a potential for challenging standard accounts as a focus on the state.

Part III
Conclusion

In Part 3, I have stressed Britain and France's different approaches to post-war reconstruction. Britain experienced greater continuity because, in the words of Jean Monnet, Britons 'had not known the trauma of wartime occupation; they had not been conquered, their system seemed intact'.[1] Monnet thought that the British had made two essential contributions to civilisation: 'respect for freedom, and the working of democratic institutions', which they 'felt in their bones'.[2] These, and an innate reluctance to change, were, according to Monnet, important elements of their national character that shaped their rather idiosyncratic approach to post-war reconstruction as well as to Europe. My evidence suggests that his view is applicable, but not completely, to the relationship between scientists and the pharmaceutical industry.

The continuation of British élites had encouraged a re-appraisal of, and partial return to, pre-war structures, not because of illlusions of grandeur or any other particular character defect,[3] but because these structures had been successfully tried and tested in war. By contrast, France experienced greater change, caused by the trauma of Occupation and by the almost total overhaul of its élites after the Liberation. Although French centralized and hierarchical structures were promptly returned to, at the hands of a small group of reformers, whose autocratic style of leadership helped to shape post-war France, French post-war reconstruction was more radical than its British equivalent.

Whether the differences between Britain and France were the result of long-established political and economic structures, of national culture, or whether they were the product of history, is a question that this book has attempted to address. In Part 3, I have suggested that, rather than structures or culture, historical events, more especially World War Two, played a crucial role in transforming the relationship between scientists and pharmaceutical firms, and that it did so differently in Britain and France.

In Britain the MRC played a pivotal role between scientific research institutions, pharmaceutical firms and the state, which after the war formed a national innovation system unparalleled in the UK, and may help to explain the success of the pharmaceutical industry compared with other high-tech sectors of the British economy. By contrast, in France, where there was no equivalent for the MRC until the creation of INSERM in 1964, and where the pharmaceutical industry remained relatively fragmented until the 1970s, the 'triple helix' did not arise until later, that is to say until there was a concerted effort by pharmaceutical firms and government laboratories to develop common research objectives and policies.

However, although Britain and France experienced different degrees and rates of change, overall they displayed similar trends. In both countries the close relationships that had existed before the war were replaced by looser, triangular relations involving government. Boundaries were erected between science and industry, and between pure and applied research, in order to encourage large-scale funding from the state.[4] A consequence of this was that a two-tier system emerged, in which co-operative relations became distant at the institutional level, while at the grass roots level the picture was more complex. In Britain the MRC bridged the gap between the two levels, but for this it had to pay the price of playing an ambiguous role between public and private, and between science and industry.

I have therefore argued that the growing separation between academic science (as 'fundamental' or 'basic' science) and industrial research (as 'applied science') was a product of closer links with government. I have also shown that discourses about the importance of pure science, which were common both in Britain and in France (as was its corollary, the two countries' weakness at developing the fruits of research),[5] reflected the 'rapprochement' between scientists and the state, rather than the reality.[6]

This shared, long-term evolution depended on the circulation of the facts and artifacts involved in pharmaceutical research. The post-World War Two era witnessed the growth of biomedicine, characterized by a growing importance of physical instrumentation, and an increasingly fundamental level of analysis, often referred to as the 'the molecularisation' of biology and medicine, reflected in the emergence of new disciplines such as molecular biology.[7] To some extent, this molecularisation was underpinned by drugs, which as well as providing doctors with novel interventive treatments, became tools for clinical researchers to study and understand disease at the molecular level. Part 3 has highlighted the contribution of penicillin to this evolution. Not only did it provide a model for co-operation, but it freed scientists for research into chronic diseases, and provided pharmaceutical companies with opportunities for expansion in chemotherapeutic R&D. Thus, whilst pharmaceutical companies responded eagerly to the mass markets created by the national health services, the fundamentalisation of medicine, in part facilitated by the fruits of their activities, created new niches for clinicians interested in research. In this way, firms and clinicians came to fulfill complementary roles in the era of biomedicine, and the history of their relationship, which in recent years has made the headlines and led to controversy, remains to be told in greater detail.

Conclusion
The Power of Rhetoric, and
a Tale of Two Cultures

1. The power of rhetoric

At key moments in this history of collaborative relationships, the rhetoric has appeared to contradict the reality. Although the Pasteur Institute was rendered relatively prosperous in the 1920s and 1930s by the sale of vaccines and sera, it defined itself increasingly in terms of pure science. Although the British pharmaceutical industry was blamed for being non co-operative and failing to meet the challenge of penicillin, its contribution to the development of penicillin was significant. Although the French described themselves as lacking in co-operative spirit, collaborative relationships were common, both before and during the war. Whereas French post-war rhetoric stressed continuity (through innovations like the synthetic anti-histamines), in Britain it emphasized change and 'modernity' (symbolized by penicillin).[1] Yet, of the two countries, France experienced the greatest change, while Britain experienced the greatest continuity.

Rhetoric, then, has acted as a smoke-screen, and had the effect of obscuring its true object from view. The Pasteur Institute, like several other research institutions before World War Two, relied on business to finance its research.[2] During the war, penicillin was successfully transferred from the laboratory to the factory. By claiming continuity with the interwar period, French élites buried the memory of Vichy and of collaborationism into the subconscious of the nation.[3] By arguing for modernity and change whilst blaming industry for the failure to meet the challenge of penicillin, British élites obscured the memory of penicillin being offered to the Americans due to economic hardship. At times, rhetoric has also acted as a self-fulfilling prophecy,[4] helping to bring about the imagined reality — with the transformation of the Pasteur Institute into an institute of pure research, a British propensity to discover rather than develop,[5] and, as John Krige has pointed out in his recent book, American hegemony in the sciences after World War Two.[6]

The declinist literature which has fed off such rhetoric without first questioning it, thus becoming a veritable 'ideology', has preferred to analyse the evolution of British and French science and industry in terms of the failure of its élites, blinded by self-delusion or a lack of co-operative spirit,[7] rather than as an adaptation to changing local and international contexts. Paradoxically, this literature has had the effect of maintaining the very myth it has endeavoured to demolish, that of the great nation, led down the wrong path by unwise leaders.[8]

Evidence presented in this book has helped to cast doubt upon the objectivity of accusations of backwardness or decline. It has also presented elements for a historical explanation of the problem, which I described in introduction.

2. The agenda of pure science and the rhetoric of backwardness and decline

Chapter 1 suggested that the myth of decline is laden with ideological and political meaning. At the Pasteur Institute, the spectre of decline was brandished by a group of scientists in an effort to mobilize the Administrative Council into reforming the Institute after Emile Roux's death. A connection was established between what was described as its scientific decline under Roux's autocratic and conservative regime, and the confusion between the functions of research and production. This created a precedent for reform, and, eventually, the functions of research and production were separated. However, behind these structural changes there lay a scientific agenda to transform the Pasteur into an institute of pure science, in which scientists had a more powerful voice and in which new disciplines, in particular molecular biology, could find a place.

Scientists who had developed penicillin in the laboratory, such as Florey and Chain, later denied any thoughts of application at the beginning of their research. This rhetoric of pure science, which was associated with an emphasis on the material benefits of pure science symbolized by penicillin,[9] was directed principally at government, from whom it garnered support by brandishing the spectre of decline and the dangers of the brain-drain to the United States. By first building a relationship with industry, and then strengthening their links with government,[10] scientists in Britain and France placed science at the heart of post-war policy, and as well as guaranteeing their professional survival, ensured the large-scale funding of their disciplinary projects, which often went hand in hand with institutional reform.[11]

The rhetoric of pure science has been closely entwined with a rhetoric of backwardness and decline, which has coloured the narratives of contemporary writers and historians on the relationship between science and industry. It was 'an essential component in social change',[12] in that it played an important role in changing the relationship between scientists and pharmaceutical firms in Britain and France. In the paragraphs that follow, I reflect on the power of rhetoric to bring about change.

3. The changing relationship between scientists and pharmaceutical firms in Britain and France

Collaborative networks between scientists and pharmaceutical firms were well developed before World War Two in both Britain and France. They had emerged at the beginning of the century within a small cluster of institutions and companies. Led by key figures such as the Poulenc brothers, Ernest Fourneau and Edmond Blaise in France, and by Henry Wellcome and Henry Dale in Britain, the community that made up these networks shared similar backgrounds and similar values, including a belief in the importance of research and of co-operative behaviour. This belief was inspired by the example of Germany, which was held up as a model of successful interaction between science and industry. Having received considerable impetus from the First World War and the shortage of German synthetic drugs, the relationship between science and industry which they helped to develop therefore began to transform not only the pharmaceutical industry, leading to the growth of research within firms, but also medical science, giving rise to novel approaches to the treatment of disease, including chemotherapy and replacement therapy, which following Salvarsan and insulin were to blossom in the inter-war years.

This evolution was shared by Britain and by France. However, there were significant differences between the two countries. At a national level, medical research was more centralized in France than in Britain. It essentially took place within one institution, the Pasteur Institute in Paris, and its relationship with satellite institutions and drug companies epitomized French co-operation in pharmaceuticals. In Britain, by the time of World War Two, an extensive network of academic, government and industrial laboratories was in place. It was loosely co-ordinated by the MRC, which had taken on the role of co-ordinator of research to help develop synthetic organic chemicals during World War One, a role it pursued in the 1920s and 1930s with insulin and other drugs. At an institutional level also, the two countries' organisation and styles of leadership were distinctive. French hierarchical structures and autocratic style of leadership contrasted with the more democratic organisation and consensual approach in Britain. However, at a grass-roots level, that is to say at the level of individual researchers and their personal networks, collaboration occurred much in the same way in both countries. It was largely informal, relied upon professional solidarity, and was based on mutual trust and self-regulation.

The contrast between these different levels has led me to distinguish between institutional and grass-roots co-operative cultures, and based on the literature on co-operation, to argue that despite their structural differences, Britain and France both had collaborative cultures. However, the ties that connected the different levels together, in time, created distinctive national systems of innovation.

Which of these systems was more amenable to change? On the whole, the more consensual, decentralized British system was more adaptable than its French counterpart. Once mobilized for war, loose British networks produced major innovations and paradigm shifts, of which penicillin, a crucial turning point in the history of collaboration, is a significant example. As a privileged vantage point for analyzing the impact of war on French and British collaborative networks, penicillin is therefore the central case study of this book, which not only examines its development in wartime, but also studies its legacy in the post-war period.

According to Arthur Marwick's model of the impact of war on society, the effect of World War Two was far greater on France than it was on Britain. Nevertheless, it was considerable on Britain as well, mainly because of the large-scale participation of its scientists and industrialists in wartime projects, such as penicillin. Thus Marwick's analysis is applicable to the medical sciences and the pharmaceutical industry, but only up to a point. As well as contrasting the two countries' experiences of war, I have highlighted important similarities between them. Continuities between mobilisation, war and post-war reconstruction occurred in France, and in Britain. In both countries, wartime innovations relied not only upon the accumulation of scientific knowledge and technical know-how, but also on pre-existing networks of scientists and pharmaceutical companies. Nevertheless, in war, powerful new links were established with government agencies and with clinical researchers, and these would transform medical science and medical industry after peace had returned, leading to what is often referred to as the 'biomedical complex'.

Despite the similarities, there were important differences between the French and British experiences of war, which would affect the way in which academic-industrial collaborations were carried out after the war had ended. Whereas British networks were strengthened by war, the close relationship between Rhône-Poulenc and Fourneau's laboratory at the Pasteur Institute became more tenuous, reflecting the difficulties in maintaining channels of communication and the divisions within French society caused by defeat and Occupation. In Britain, collaborative practices between scientists and pharmaceutical firms evolved together with wartime projects, such as the Anglo-American scheme to develop penicillin, which introduced a new formality and hierarchy into collaborative networks. Because of its scientific, medical, and industrial significance, more than any other drug, penicillin became the 'model experiment in collaboration' to be emulated after the war had ended, not only in Britain, but in other countries also.

Meanwhile, despite or perhaps because of the traumas of war and Occupation, France was precipitated into abrupt change. The Pasteur Institute began its movement of reform, and Rhône-Poulenc built up their chemotherapeutic research laboratories independently of Fourneau, developing instead their contacts with clinicians, especially in the Southern Unoccupied Zone, away from IG Farben's close control. These changes were to survive beyond the war. The Institute pursued its agenda for reform under Jacques Monod, and drifted apart from Rhône-Poulenc, which cultivated its new links with researchers in provincial centers, as well as with other companies in France and abroad.

War presented opportunities to break with the past, not only at the level of research practices and co-operative behaviour, but also at the level of discourses. As war gave way to peace, accounts of the recent past began to emerge. These were often negative accounts: British failure was compared with American success at developing penicillin; French inability to carry out collaborative research was contrasted with the 'Anglo-Saxon' spirit of co-operation that had won the war.

It has been written that French science was revived as a result of the new era of international co-operation that began after the conflict, and that the French learnt the significance of teamwork in that period. However, I have shown that teamwork and co-operation existed in France, at least in the pharmaceutical field, even before World War Two. Similarly, co-operation and enterprise were not lacking on the part of the British pharmaceutical industry, both of which held the key to Britain's early success with penicillin.

Why then such negative discourses? They emerged in order to obscure painful memories: in Britain memories of penicillin being 'lost' to, or stolen by, the Americans because of economic hardship, and in France memories of collaboration with Germany because of military collapse. They arose at a time of recognition that Britain and France were no longer powers of the first order, and were entwined with a rhetoric of backwardness and decline. The scientists who became influential as a result of their participation in the war effort or the Resistance played an active role in articulating it, as well as in shaping the post-war reconstruction of their countries.

The comparable experiences of Britain and France, reflected in the development of penicillin and the synthetic anti-histamines, were highlighted in Part 2. On the contrary, in Part 3, I have contrasted the impact of war on Britain and France, and explained these differences in terms of the two countries' different approaches to post-war reconstruction.

Britain experienced greater continuity because, in the words of Jean Monnet, Britons 'had not known the trauma of wartime occupation; they had not been conquered, their system seemed intact'.[13] This, and — according to Monnet — an innate reluctance to change, shaped their idiosyncratic approach to post-war reconstruction. My evidence has suggested that this view is applicable, but only in part, to the relationship between scientists and the pharmaceutical industry.

The continuation of British élites, from inter-war, to war and then post-war, encouraged a re-appraisal of, and partial return to, pre-war structures, not because of any particular character defect, but because these structures had been successfully tested in war. Moreover, unlike France, Britain had not experienced a 'Liberation'. By contrast, France underwent greater change, caused by the trauma of Occupation and by the almost complete overhaul of its élites after the Liberation. Although French centralized and hierarchical structures were promptly returned to, at the hands of a small group of reformers, French post-war reconstruction was more radical than its British equivalent. Thus, rather than culture, which I take here as the grass-roots culture described in Chapter 2, and which remained largely collaborative in both countries, historical events, more especially World War Two, played a key role in transforming the relationship between scientists and pharmaceutical firms, especially at the level of institutions. It did so differently in Britain and France. The conflict created a gap in the two countries' experiences, and contributed to their divergent paths in the post-war period.

4. From divergence to convergence in the second half of the twentieth century

In Britain the war reinforced the pivotal role played by the MRC between scientific research institutions, pharmaceutical firms and the state, which afterwards consolidated into a national innovation system unequalled in the UK, and helps to explain the success of the pharmaceutical sector industries compared with other British high-tech. By contrast in France, where there was no equivalent for the MRC, where unlike in Britain the pharmaceutical industry remained relatively fragmented, and where in reaction to Vichy research institutions were to keep industry at a distance, such a 'triple helix' did not arise until later, in the 1970s. Then, a concerted effort was made by pharmaceutical firms and INSERM to encourage common research objectives and policies, which in response to the challenge of globalisation and the rise of the new biotechnology began to bear fruit in the 1980s.

Thus, since the 1980s, the differences between Britain and France created by World War Two have started to erode, and the two countries have begun to converge. In response to the challenge of the emerging biotech industry, and to the increasing globalisation in medical science and industry, paradoxically France's socialist government under Mitterand, and Britain's conservative government under Thatcher, both emphasized the need for greater co-operation between science and industry. In Britain, Thatcher's drive to cut public spending led to a reduction in funding for universities, thereby encouraging scientists to work closer still with industry, and companies to contribute even more to higher education. It also challenged the comfortable relationship that had developed since World War Two between pharmaceutical companies and the Department of Health. In France, concerns about economic recession, rising healthcare costs, and about falling behind in the new biotechnology, led to interventionist measures from the French government and efforts by industry to respond to the state's encouragement.

Not surprisingly perhaps, this decade, in which the role of the state became a renewed subject of debate and controversy, and in which concerns about falling behind the United States in yet another high-tech sector of the economy, saw a return to the 'blurred boundaries' of the inter-war years, and a revival of the declinist literature on both sides of the Channel.

Therefore, although Britain and France experienced different degrees and rates of change, overall they displayed similar trends. In both countries, the one-to-one relationships that had existed before the war were largely replaced by looser, triangular relationships involving governments. Links with the state led to boundaries being erected between science and industry. In both countries this created a divergence between the grass-roots, where collaborative practices remained relatively unchanged, and the institutions, where a growing separation between fundamental science and applied research occurred. Discourses about the importance of pure science, which were common in Britain and France (as was its corollary: the two countries' weakness at developing the fruits of research), reflected the 'rapprochement' between scientists and the state, rather than the reality.

Underpinning this shared, long-term evolution, was the circulation across national borders of the facts and artifacts, the 'experiments in collaboration' that are drugs, . The post-World War Two era witnessed the growth of biomedicine in the West, often referred to as 'the molecularisation'[14] of biology and medicine, and reflected in the emergence of new disciplines such as molecular biology. To a large extent, this molecularisation depended upon the drugs of the Therapeutic Revolution, which as well as providing doctors with novel interventive treatments, became tools for researchers to study and understand the nature and processes of disease at the molecular level.

Penicillin played a major part in this evolution. Not only did it stimulate drug companies into expanding their R&D facilities and free clinical scientists for research into chronic diseases, increasingly perceived as 'molecular diseases', but it provided a model for co-operation between the principal actors of this molecular revolution in medicine. Thus, whilst pharmaceutical companies responded eagerly to the new, mass markets created by the national health services, the fundamentalisation of medicine, in part facilitated by the fruits of these firms' activities, created new niches for clinicians interested in research. In this way, in the era of biomedicine, drug companies and clinicians have come to fulfill increasingly complementary roles. The history of this relationship also deserves to be told.

Notes

INTRODUCTION

1. '[Faisons] un petit essai de collaboration: un des chimistes de l'usine, par exemple, pourrait se mettre en contact avec moi pour poursuivre les recherches de Monsieur Firmenich, quitte à passer les résultats à ce dernier pour une publication ultérieure'. Rhône-Poulenc Santé, Ernest Fourneau [hereafter RPS] EF1 9704: Fourneau to Blaise (24 April 1929).
2. Public Record Office MRC [hereafter PRO] FD1 354: General chemotherapy of tuberculosis, Harington to Thomson (12 Sept. 1946).
3. Margaret Mead, *Cooperation and Competition among Primitive People*, New York: McGraw Hill, 1937; D. Gambetta, *Trust: making and breaking cooperative relations*, Oxford: Basil Blackwell, 1988; M. Argyle, *Cooperation: the basis of sociability*, London: Routledge, 1991; G. Thompson et al. (eds.), *Markets, Hierarchies and Networks: the coordination of social life*, London: Sage, 1991; R. Axelrod, *The Complexity of Cooperation: agent-based models of competition and collaboration*, Princeton, N.J.: Princeton University Press, 1997.
4. D.J. Prager and G.S. Omen, 'Research, innovation, and university-industry linkages', *Science*, 1980, vol. 379–84; pp. 303–42; R. Stankiewics, *Academics and Entrepreneurs: developing university-industry relations*, London, 1986; P. David, D. Foray and W.E. Steinmueller, 'The research network and the new economics of science: from metaphors to organizational behaviors', in A. Gambardella and F. Malerba (eds.), *The Organization of Economic Innovation in Europe*, Cambridge: CUP, 1999, pp. 303–42. More specifically in relation to drug discovery, see T. Jones, 'The value of academia/industrial links in R&D', in S.R. Walker (ed.), *Creating the Right Environment for Drug Discovery*, Lancaster: Quay Publishing, 1991, pp. 77–84; W. Sneader, *Drug Prototypes and their Exploitation*, Chichester: John Wiley & Sons, 1996, p. 10; J. Chin-Dusting, J. Mizrahi, G. Jennings and D. Fitzgerald, 'Finding improved medicines: the role of academic industrial collaborations', *Nature Reviews Drug Discovery*, 2005, vol. 5, 891–7.
5. Ibid.; A.G. Bearn, 'The pharmaceutical industry and academe: partners in progress', *Am. J. Med.*, 1981, vol. 71, 81–8; D. Blumenthal, M. Gluck, K.S. Louis, M.A. Stoto, and D. Wise, 'University-industry research relationships in biotechnology: implications for the university', *Science*, 1986, vol. 232, 1361–2; R. Ross, 'Academic research and industry relationships', *Clinical and Investigative Medicine*, 1986, vol. 9, 269–72; H. Moses and J.B. Martin, 'Academic relationships with industry; a new model for biomedical research', *J.A.M.A.*, 2001, vol. 285, 933–5; A.C. Gelijns and S.O. Their, 'Medical inno-

vation and institutional interdependence: rethinking university-industry connections', *JAMA*, 2002, vol. 287, 72–7; J.E. Bekelman, Y. Li & C.P. Gross, 'Scope and impact of financial conflicts of interest in biomedical research: a systematic review', *JAMA*, 2003, vol. 289, 454–65; D. Triggle, 'Patenting the sun: enclosing the scientific commons and transforming the university–ethical concerns', *Drug Development Research*, 2005, vol. 63, 139–49.

6. J. Liebenau, 'The MRC and the pharmaceutical industry: the model of insulin', in J. Austoker and L. Bryder (eds.), *Historical Perspectives on the role of the* MRC, Oxford: OUP, 1989, pp. 163–80; J. Liebenau and M. Robson, 'L'Institut Pasteur et l'industrie pharmaceutique', in M. Morange (ed.), *L'Institut Pasteur: contributions à son* histoire, Paris: La Découverte, 1991, pp. 52–61; J. Maienschein, 'Why collaborate?', *J. His. Biol.*, 1993, vol. 26, 167–83; L. Galambos and J.E. Sewell, *Networks of Innovation: vaccine development at Merck, Sharpe & Dohme, and Mulford, 1895–1995*, Cambridge, Mass.: CUP, 1995; J. Goodman, 'Can it ever be pure science? Pharmaceuticals and the pharmaceutical industry in biomedical research in the twentieth century', in J.-P. Gaudillière and I. Löwy (eds.), *The Invisible Industrialist: manufactures and the production of scientific knowledge*, Basingstoke: Macmillan, 1998, pp. 143–65; V. Walsh, 'Industrial R&D and its influence on the organization and management of the production of knowledge in the public sector', in ibid., pp. 298–344; C. Reinhardt and H.G. Schröter, 'Academy and industry in chemistry: the impact of state intervention, and the effects of cultural values', *Ambix*, 2004, vol. 2, 99–106, and other articles in this issue.

7. According to Pinch, this has been one of the models to come out of the 'melting pot of sociology of science and history of technology in the early 1980s'. T. Pinch, 'The Social Construction of Technology: a review', in R. Fox (ed.), *Technological Change: methods and themes in the history of technology*, Amsterdam: Harwood Academic, 1996, pp. 17–35 (22). Important works include M. Granovetter, 'The strength of weak ties', *Am. J. Sociology*, 1973, vol. 78, 1360–80; idem, 'The strength of weak ties: a network theory revisited', *Sociol. Theory*, 1983, vol. 1, 201–33; B. Latour and S. Woolgar, *Laboratory Life: the social construction of scientific* facts, Beverly Hills: Sage, 1979; M. Callon, *La Science et ses réseaux: genèse et circulation des faits scientifiques*, Paris: La Découverte, 1989; J. Law and J. Hassard (eds.), *Actor Network Theory and After*, Oxford: Blackwells, 1999. More specifically in relation to medicine, see I. Löwy, 'The strength of loose concepts – boundary objects, federative experimental strategies and disciplinary growth: the case of immunology', *His. Sci.*, 1992, vol. 30, 371–96; L.J. Jordanova, 'The social construction of medical knowledge', *Soc. His. Med.*, 1995, vol. 8, 361–421.

8. H. Etkowitz and L. Leydersdorff, 'The endless transition: a "triple helix" of university-industry-government relations', *Minerva*, 1998, vol. 36, 203–8. For a critical appraisal of studies of the triple helix, see T. Shinn, 'The triple helix and the new production of knowledge', *Soc. Stud. Sci.*, 2002, vol. 32, 599–614.

9. J.-P. Gaudillière, *Inventer la biomédecine: la france, l'amérique et la production des savoirs du vivant (1945–1965)*, Paris: La Découverte, 2002.

10. For a socio-economic approach to the study of the evolution of co-operation, see R. Axelrod, *The Evolution of Cooperation*, London: Basic Books, 1994. Axelrod has argued that clusters of co-operative individuals can overcome rival strategies better than isolated individuals, p. 21, and pp. 63–6. Although his conclusions are based on the results of a computer tournament, he has applied them to historical situations, for instance the 'live-and-let-live system' which developed between small battalions on both sides of the trenches in

World War I, pp. 75–6. For histories of academic-industrial collaborations in the pharmaceutical industry, see J.-P. Swann, *Academic Scientists and the Pharmaceutical Industry: cooperative research in twentieth-century America*, Baltimore: Johns Hopkins University Press, 1988; idem, 'Universities, industry and the rise of biomedical collaboration in America', in J. Liebenau, G.J. Higby and E.C. Stroud (eds.), *Pill Peddlers: essays on the history of the pharmaceutical industry*, Madison, Wis.: American Institute of the History of Pharmacy, 1990, pp. 73–90; N. Rasmussen, 'The Moral Economy of the Drug Company-Medical Scientist Collaboration in Interwar America', *Social Studies of Science*, 2004, vol. 34, 161–85. For a British case study, see G.K. Roberts, 'Dealing with issues at the academic-industry interface in interwar Britain: UCL and ICI', *Sci. Pub. Pol.*, 1997, vol. 24, 29–35.

11. Cassie Watson has shown that the Nobel Prize winning chemist William Ramsay, whose career as consultant was extensive, was selective in his collection of materials pertaining to that aspect of his scientific career. K.D. Watson, 'The Chemist as Expert: the consulting career of Sir William Ramsay', *Ambix*, 1995, vol. 42, 143–59.

12. For instance, on French scientists see K. Mulholland, 'Introduction', 'French Science since 1945', special issue, *Fr. His. Stud.*, 1991, vol. 17, 1–5; on pharmaceutical firms see M. Wright, 'The comparative analysis of industrial policies: policy networks and sectoral governance structures in Britain and France', Manchester, EPRU working paper, 1991; and J. Liebenau, 'The British success with penicillin', *Soc. Stud. Sci.*, 1987, vol. 17, 69–86 (86). Comparing rates of publication by single and multiple authors, de Solla Price argued that the period following World War II constituted a 'violent transition' towards mass collaboration in most countries, in D. de Solla Price, *Little Science, Big Science*, New York: Columbia University Press, 1965, pp. 88–9. See also P. Galison and B. Hevly (eds.), *Big Science: the growth of large-scale research*, Stanford, Calif.: Stanford University Press, 1992.

13. Axelrod has argued that clusters of co-operative individuals can overcome rival strategies better than isolated individuals, in Axelrod, *The Evolution of Cooperation*, p. 21, and pp. 63–6. More specifically on the role of industrial clusters, see F. Wilson and A. Popp (eds.), *Industrial Clusters and Regional Business Networks in England, 1750–1970*, London: Ashgate, 2003.

14. For a popular account, see J. Le Fanu, *The Rise and Fall of Modern Medicine*, London: Abacus, 1999.

15. Swann, *Academic Scientists and the Pharmaceutical Industry*.

16. Such a reciprocal action is described in relation to technology by W. E. Bijker and J. Law, 'General Introduction', in Bijker and Law (eds.), *Shaping Technology/Building Society: studies in sociotechnical change*, Cambridge, Mass.: MIT Press, 1992, pp. 1–14.

17. Like Callon's engineer-sociologists, they showed an ability to carry out experiments that changed society. M. Callon, 'Society in the making: the study of technology as a tool for sociological analysis', in W.E. Bijker, T.P. Hughes and T.J. Pinch (eds.), *The Social Construction of Technological Systems: new directions in the sociology and the history of* technology, Cambridge, Mass.: MIT Press, 1987, pp. 83–103.

18. Whereas the issue of backwardness has been raised about France, with respect to Britain the main preoccupation has tended to be about decline. D. Edgerton, *Science,Technology and the British Industrial 'Decline', 1870–1970*, Cambridge: CUP, 1996.

19. Stankiewics has seen the main role of academia as a source of innovation for industry, and university-industry linkages as having an important part

to play in ending the recession in Europe, in Stankiewics, *Academics and Entrepreneurs*. See also R. Nelson and N. Rosenberg, 'Science, technological advance and economic growth', in A. D. Chandler, P. Hagström and O. Sölvell (eds.), *The Dynamic Firm: the role of technology, strategy, organization, and regions*, Oxford: OUP, 1998, pp. 45–59.

20. For the traditional view, see D. S. Landes, *The Unbound Prometheus: technological change and industrial development in Western Europe from 1750 to the present*, Cambridge: CUP, 1969. Landes has explained how Germany overtook Britain and France in the third quarter of the nineteenth century because of favourable economic conditions, and because of the quality of German science and the growth of research within firms, pp. 274–6. On the rise of American R&D in the inter-war period, which he has contrasted with the British sluggish response to the needs of modern industry, see pp. 480–5. From the perspective of the sociology of science, but also linking economic prosperity and scientific pre-eminence, see J. Ben-David, *The Scientist's Role in Society: a comparative study*, Englewood Cliffs, N.J.: Prentice Hall, 1971, especially pp. 14–6, 163–5. In Chs. 7/8, he has described the shifting centres of scientific activity from England and France, to Germany and the United States in the late nineteenth and early twentieth centuries.

21. Examples of this declinist literature include M. J. Wiener, *English Culture and the Decline of the Industrial Spirit*, Cambridge: CUP, 1981, and C. Barnett, *The Audit of War: the illusion and reality of Britain as a great nation*, London: Papermac, 1987. Both have analysed the causes of decline as being cultural in origin, and assumed a poorly developed relationship between science and industry. According to Wiener, the cultural values of the English ruling classes prevented fruitful links between scientists and companies from developing to the same degree as on the Continent (especially in Germany), and caused Britain to lag behind its competitors. See Ch. 7, esp. pp. 132–45. In his chapter entitled 'Education for industrial decline', Barnett has argued that a preference for the classics and scorn for scientific knowledge led to Britain's 'accumulated backlog of inferiority', pp. 216–7, and 204–5. Similarly for France, Shinn has turned to the education system and to socio-cultural arguments to explain what he saw as the inadequacy of French R&D until World War II. T. Shinn, 'The genesis of French industrial research 1880–1940', *Soc. Sci. Info.*, 1980, vol. 19, 607–40. Criticising the assumptions contained in this literature, R. Fox and A. Guagnini, 'Britain in perspective: the European context of industrial training and innovation, 1880–1914', *History and Technology*, 1985, vol. 2, 133–50; idem, 'Life in the slow lane: research and engineering in Britain, France, and Italy, ca. 1900', in P. Kroes and M. Bakker (eds.), *Technological Development and Science in the Industrial Age*, Amsterdam: Kluwer Academic, 1992, pp. 133–53. See also: D.E.H. Edgerton, 'Science and technology in British business history', *Bus. His.*, 1987, vol. 29, 84–103. Because French organisational structures were strikingly different from the U.S. model, and in order to explain the French economic miracle of the 1950s, resistance to the declinist ideology appeared earlier in French historiography. For instance, correcting the notion that French entrepreneurs were to blame for France's poor innovation record, Maurice Levy-Leboyer has argued on the contrary that in the 1920s and 1930s they were committed to dynamic, modern industrial development, in 'Innovation and business strategies in nineteenth- and twentieth-century France', in E.C. Carter, R. Forster and J.N. Moody (eds.), *Enterprise and Entrepreneurs in Nineteenth- and Twentieth-Century France*, Baltimore: Johns Hopkins University Press, 1976, pp. 87–135. Also by Levy-Leboyer, 'The large corpora-

tion in modern France', in A.D. Chandler and H. Daems (eds.), *Managerial Hierarchies: comparative perspectives on the rise of the modern industrial enterprise*, Cambridge, Mass.: Harvard University Press, 1980, pp. 117–60. On the French miracle, see F. Caron, *Economic History of Modern France*, London: Methuen, 1979, p. 317.

22. Both Wiener and Barnett have tended to adopt uncritically contemporary views of the situation. For example Wiener, *English Culture and the Decline of the Industrial Spirit*, pp. 129–32, and Barnett, *The Audit of War*, pp. 220–1. Similarly, Shinn has echoed the views of Henri le Chatelier, 'The genesis of French industrial research', 626–7, 632–3. Jean Monnet, as first-hand observer, actor, and writer of memoirs, attributed France's relative backwardness before World War II to a fatalistic attitude to the technological race, and its success since the war to planned reconstruction, in which he played a key role. J. Monnet, *Memoirs*, London: Collins, 1978, Ch. 10, esp. pp. 232–49.

23. According to Liebenau, such modern features were acquired by the German industry even before World War I, and then by the U.S. industry by emulating its German counterpart. Meanwhile, the British industry was being left behind. J. Liebenau, 'Ethical business: the formation of the pharmaceutical industry in Britain, Germany, and the US before 1914', in R.T.P. Davenport-Hines and G. Jones (eds.), *The End of Insularity: essays in comparative business history*, London: Cass, 1988, pp. 117–29; idem, 'Industrial R&D in pharmaceutical firms in the early twentieth century', *Bus. His.*, 1984, vol. 26, 329–46.

24. J. Liebenau, *Medical Science and Medical Industry: the formation of the American pharmaceutical industry*, Baltimore: Johns Hopkins University Press, 1987, Ch. 2.

25. Liebenau has painted a gloomy picture of a British industry slow to modernize, attached to archaic structures, and with little commitment to innovation, in 'The rise of the British pharmaceutical industry', *BMJ*, 1990, vol. 301, 724–33; 'The twentieth-century British pharmaceutical industry in international context', in J. Liebenau et al., *Pill Peddlers*, pp. 123–33. For a similar picture of the French industry, see M. Robson, 'The French pharmaceutical industry, 1919–1939', in ibid., pp. 107–22. In the British case, the 1950s and 60s are often seen as a period of stagnation in relation to other European countries. See R.C.O. Matthews, C.H. Feinstein and J.C. Odling-Smee, *British Economic Growth, 1856–1973*, Oxford: Clarendon Press, 1982, pp. 537–8, 546. On the pharmaceutical industry, see J. Slinn, 'Innovation at Glaxo and May & Baker, 1945–1965', *His. and Tech.*, 1996, vol. 13, 133–47. Caron has interpreted this as a lull, after the process of catching up, but also after the rationalisation which occurred in the 1920s and 30s and was not experienced elsewhere in Europe until after World War II. Caron, 'Introduction', in F. Caron, P. Erker, and W. Fisher (eds.), *Innovations in the European Economy between the wars*, Berlin: de Guryter, 1995, pp. 3–29 (5–8). Idem, *Le Résistible déclin des sociétés industrielles*, Paris: Perrin, 1985, Ch. 7.

26. Caron has expressed regret that the U.S. model was too readily adopted after World War II, especially by France, in ibid. On the British pharmaceutical industry, see T.A.B. Corley, 'The British pharmaceutical industry since 1851', in L. Richmond, J. Stevenson, and A. Turton (eds.), *The Pharmaceutical Industry: a guide to historical records*, Aldershot: Ashgate, 2003, pp. 14–32.

27. A.D. Chandler, *The Visible Hand: the managerial revolution in American business*, Cambridge, Mass.: Harvard Univresity Press, 1977; idem, *Shaping the Industrial Century: the remarkable story of the evolution of the modern*

chemical and pharmaceutical industries, Cambridge, Mass: HUP, 2005, which focuses mostly on the chemical industry, but also has a few pages on the pharmaceutical industry.

28. M. Robson, 'The pharmaceutical industry in Britain and France, 1919–1939', London School of Economics Ph.D. thesis, 1993, p. 343.

29. Swann, *Academic Scientists and the Pharmaceutical Industry*, pp. 51–4.

30. This is one of the possible misuses of the comparative approach, which Peter Burke has identified as ethnocentrism. P. Burke, *History and Social Theory*, Cambridge: Polity Press, 1992, p. 26. See also R. Fox and A. Guagnini, 'Introduction', in Fox and Guagnini (eds.), *Education, Technology and Industrial Performance in Europe, 1850–1939*, Cambridge: CUP, 1993, pp. 1–2.

31. Robson, 'The pharmaceutical industry in Britain and France', p. 345.

32. Ibid., p. 346.

33. J.B. Morrell, 'Professionalisation', in R.C. Olby, G.N. Cantor, J.R.R. Christie and M.J.S. Hodge (eds.), *Companion to the History of Modern Science*, London: Routledge, 1990, pp. 980–9. Arguing that in relation to the sciences, the concept of professionalisation has evolved over time, and is therefore best used as a heuristic tool to study scientists' changing occupational strategies, Morrell has criticized the static approach developed by the sociology of the professions in relation to the medicine. For instance E. Freidson, *Professional Powers: a study of the institutionalisation of formal knowledge,* Chicago: University of Chicago Press, 1986. Linking the issues of the rise of professional and industrial societies, Perkin has attributed British economic decline to the failure of English élites to adapt their social values to what he described as the 3rd Revolution (the professional revolution), and to develop co-operative relations in industry of the kind observed in Germany and in Japan. H. Perkin, *The Third Revolution: professional elites in the modern world*, London: Routledge, 1996, pp. 62–65.

34. L. Hancher, *Regulating for Competition: government, law and the pharmaceutical industry in the United Kingdom and France*, Oxford: Clarendon Press, 1990, p. 6.

35. See Chandler's criticism of Britain's attachment to personal entrepreneurship. A.D. Chandler, *Scale and Scope: the dynamics of industrial capitalism*, Cambridge, Mass.: Belknap, 1990, Part 3. See also Elbaum and Lazonick, blaming Britain's decline on the rigidities of its social and economic institutions, which prevented it from developing effective managerial control of the kind observed in Germany and the USA. Elbaum and Lazonick, 'An institutional perspective on British decline', in B. Elbaum and W. Lazonick (eds.), *The Decline of the British Economy*, Oxford: Clarendon Press, 1986, pp. 1–17 (2). For a more balanced picture, see L. Hannah, 'Visible and invisible hands in Great Britain', in Chandler and Daems (eds.), *Managerial Hierarchies*, pp. 41–76.

36. Here is another danger of the comparative approach: the 'danger of accepting too easily the assumption that societies "evolve" through an inevitable sequence of stages'. Burke, *History and Social Theory*, p. 26. For evidence that historians have begun to question the applicability of the German and U.S. models to the pharmaceutical industry in other, often smaller countries, see R.P. Amdam, 'Professional networks and the introduction of research in the British and Norwegian pharmaceutical industry in the inter-war years', *His. and Tech.*, 1996, vol. 13, 101–14.

37. Chin-Dusting et al., 'Finding improved medicines'.

38. Ibid., 3.

39. M. Blondel-Mégrelis, 'La pharmacie en France 1900–1950, points de repè-res', in C. Debru, J. Gayon and J.-F. Picard (eds.), *Les Sciences biologiques et médicales en France 1920–1950*, Paris: CNRS Editions, 1994, pp. 283–96 (287).

40. E.M. Tansey, 'The early scientific career of Sir Henry Hallett Dale FRS (1875–1968)', University College, London Ph.D. thesis, 1991, p. 419.

41. Robson, 'The pharmaceutical industry in Britain and France'; Wright, 'The comparative analysis of industrial policies'.

42. M.-J. Nye, 'National styles? French and English chemistry in the 19th and early 20th century', in G.L. Geison and F.L. Holmes (eds.), *Research Schools: historical reappraisals, Osiris*, 1993, vol. 8, 30–53 (37–8). See also Ben-David, *The Scientist's Role*, pp. 104–7.

43. M. Bloch, 'Toward a comparative history of European societies', in F.C. Lane and J.C. Riemersma (eds.), *Enterprise and Secular Change: readings in economic history*, London: George Allen & Unwin, 1953, pp. 494–522.

44. L.G. Thomas, 'Implicit industrial policy: the triumph of Britain and the failure of France in global pharmaceuticals', *Industrial and Corporate Change*, 1994, vol. 3, 451–89.

45. Wright, 'The comparative analysis of industrial policies'.

46. Caron, 'Introduction', in F. Caron et al., *Innovations in the European Economy between the wars*, p. 24.

47. On reciprocity as a characteristic feature of collaborative relationships, see Axelrod, *The Evolution of Cooperation*, pp. 69, 118–20. Debating the role of trust in relation to co-operation, E.H. Lorenz, 'Neither friends nor strangers: informal networks of subcontracting in French industry', pp. 194–210 (201–9), and Gambetta, 'Can we trust trust?', pp. 213–37 (220–229), in D. Gambetta (ed.), *Trust: making and breaking cooperative relations*, Oxford: Basil Blackwell, 1988.

48. The classic study of co-operation and competition is Margaret Mead's *Cooperation and Competition among Primitive Peoples*. For a more recent study, see Axelrod: *The Complexity of Cooperation*. See in particular his chapter on disseminating culture, in which he proposes a model of how communities might emerge to form homogenous cultural regions, pp. 145–7, 148–51.

49. Mitchell has argued that culture is not a fixed entity, but that it evolves under the influence of powerful social actors. D. Mitchell, 'There's no such thing as culture: towards a reconceptualization of the idea of culture in geography', *Trans. Inst. Brit. Geog.*, 1995, vol. 20, 102–16. About the different levels of culture within a society, see G. Hofstede, *Cultures and Organizations: software of the mind*, London: McGraw Hill, 1991, pp. 3–19. For an anthropological approach to culture: see C. Geertz, *The Interpretation of Cultures*, London: Fontana, 1993, especially Ch. 1; for an historical approach, see L. Hunt, 'Introduction: history, culture, and text', in Hunt (ed.), *The New Cultural History*, Berkeley: University of California Press, 1989, pp. 1–22.

50. Cambrosio et al. adopted a semi-quantitative approach in order to study collaboration in connection with a specific biomedical technology in A. Cambrosio, P. Keating and A. Mogoutov, 'Mapping collaborative work and innovation in biomedicine', *Soc. Stud. Sci.*, 2004, vol. 34, 325–64.

51. See the seminal study by M.J.S. Rudwick, *The Great Devonian Controversy: the shaping of scientific knowledge among gentlemanly specialists*, Chicago: University of Chicago Press, 1985.

52. T.P. Hughes, *Networks of Power: electrification in Western Society, 1880–1930*, Baltimore: Johns Hopkins Univeristy Press, 1983; Bijker et al., *The Social Construction of Technological Systems*.

53. E. Crawford, T. Shinn and S. Sörlin, 'Introductory Essay', in Crawford, Shinn and Sörlin (eds.), *Denationalizing Science: the contexts of international scientific practice*, Dordrecht: Kluwer Academic, 1992, pp. 1–42. They have argued that in the last 100 years, the dominant trend in science has been towards international co-operation. See also J.N. Cummings and S. Kiesler, 'Collaborative research across disciplinary and organizational boundaries', *Soc. Stud. Sci.*, 2005, vol. 35, 703–22, and other articles in a special issue on scientific collaborations edited by E.J. Hackett.
54. Among work on the collaborative nature of the scientific enterprise, an important body of literature has developed on the hidden role of women, for instance by M.B. Ogilvie, 'Marital collaboration: an approach to science', in P.G. Abir-Am and D. Outram (eds.), *Uneasy Careers and Intimate Lives: women in science, 1789–1979*, New Brunswick: Rutgers University Press, 1987, pp. 104–25; also H.M. Pycior, N.G. Slack, and P. Abir-Am (eds.), *Creative Couples in the Sciences*, New Brunswick, N.J.: Rutgers University Press, 1996.
55. In this respect, trends in economics may be reflecting trends in the economy. See A. Offer, 'Between the gift and the market: the economy of regard', *Econ. His. Rev.*, 1997, vol. 50, 431–45. In this article, Offer has argued that the market economy, as described by Adam Smith, has not completely replaced the gift economy, and is retreating in front of the 'economy of regard', 450–1. This is an economy based on reciprocal exchange, which is often preferred to price-driven market exchange when personal interaction is involved. On the different modes of organisation of economic and social life, see Thompson et al., *Markets, Hierarchies and Networks*. The authors have identified co-operation and trust as the two essential mechanisms of networks, pp. 14–6.
56. For an earlier attempt to bring together the two concerns with society and the economy, see J.H. Kunkel, *Society and Economic Growth: a behavioural perspective of social change*, London: OUP, 1970. Since 1990, the output has dramatically increased. See for instance R.J. Holton, *Economy and Society*, London: Routledge, 1992, and R. Swedberg, *Explorations in Economic Sociology*, New York: Russell Sage Foundation, 1993; idem, *Economic Sociology*, Cheltenham: Edward Elgar, 1996.
57. H.W. Florey, 'Prestige in academic scientific research', *Nature*, 1962, vol. 193, 1017–8. It is worth noting that, to Ben-David, the interplay between co-operation and competition formed the basis of the U.S. model of success, in *The Scientist's Role*, pp. 158–62.
58. For instance Wright, 'The comparative analysis of industrial policies'; and A. Lundgren, *Technological Innovation and Industrial Evolution: the emergence of industrial networks*, Stockholm: Routledge, 1991. Argyle suggested networks as a concept for describing co-operation and cohesion in modern, as opposed to primitive society. M. Argyle, *Cooperation: the basis of sociability*, pp. 76–9.
59. B. Latour, 'On recalling ANT', in J. Law and J. Hassard (eds.), *Actor Network Theory and After*, pp. 15–25 (15).
60. Law, 'After ANT: complexity, naming and topology', in ibid., pp. 1–14.
61. According to Hughes, networks have shared this quality with his own systems approach. T.P. Hughes, 'The seamless web: technology, science, etcetera... etcetera...', *Soc. Stud. Sci.*, 1986, vol. 16, 281–92. Oudshorn has used a network approach to describe pharmaceutical innovation and the role of science, in 'United we stand: the pharmaceutical industry, laboratory and clinic in the development of sex hormones into scientific drugs, 1920–1940', *Science, Technology and Human Values*, 1993, vol. 18, 5–24.

62. Swann, *Academic Scientists and the Pharmaceutical Industry*, pp. 170–81.
63. This is a striking feature of French post-war reconstruction. See H. E. Guerlac, 'Science and French national strength', in E. Mead Earle (ed.), *Modern France: problems of the Third and Fourth Republic*, New York: Russell and Russell, 1964, pp. 81–105. For a more recent study, see G. Hecht, *The Radiance of France: nuclear power and national identity after World War II*, Cambridge, Mass.: MIT Press, 1998.
64. Krige and Pestre, 'Introduction', in J. Krige and D. Pestre (eds.), *Science in the Twentieth Century*, Amsterdam: Harwood Academic, 1997, pp. xxxiii–xxxiv; D. Edgerton, 'Science and War', in Olby et al., *Companion to the History of Modern Science*, pp. 934–45; idem, *Warfare State: Britain, 1920–1970*, Cambridge: CUP, 2006; R. Cooter, M. Harrison and S. Sturdy (eds.), *War, Medicine and Modernity*, Stroud: Sutton, 1998; A. Dahan and D. Pestre, *Les Sciences pour la guerre, 1940–1960*, Paris: Ed. De l'EHESS, 2004. More specifically on the impact of war on the pharmaceutical industry, V. Quirke, 'War and change in the pharmaceutical industry: a comparative study of Britain and France in the twentieth century', *Entreprises et Histoire*, 2005, vol. 36, 64–83.
65. War-like metaphors on the struggle against disease abound in the literature: for example H.J. Parish, *Victory with Vaccines: the story of immunization*, London: E.S. Livingstone, 1968; P. Baldry, *The Battle Against Bacteria: a fresh look. A history of man's fight against bacterial disease with special reference to the development of antibacterial drugs*, Cambridge: CUP, 1965.
66. R. Cooter, *Surgery and Society in Peace and War: orthopaedics and the organization of modern medicine, 1880–1948*, Basingstoke: Macmillan, 1993. Cooter has shown the impact of war on orthopaedic surgery, and through it, on the organisation of the medical profession, Introduction, and Chs. 6/11.
67. A. Marwick, *War and Social Change in the Twentieth Century: a comparative study of Britain, France, Russia and the United States*, London: Macmillan, 1978. Marwick has adopted a sociological approach in order to compare the impact of war on French and British society, amongst others. He begins by identifying their national characteristics, pp. 14 *seq.*, and goes on to evaluate the impact of both international conflicts
68. Miles Weatherall, *In Search of a Cure: a history of pharmaceutical discovery*, Oxford: OUP, 1990.
69. R. J. Wurtman and R. L. Bettiker, 'The slowing of treatment discovery, 1965–1995', *Nature Medicine*, 1995, vol. 1, 1122–5.
70. Hunt, 'Introduction: history, culture and text', in Hunt (ed.), *The New Cultural History*, pp. 6–27; M. Vovelle, *Ideologies and Mentalities*, Paris: F. Maspero, 1982, pp. 228–31.
71. For more on this in the French context, see Gaudillière, *Inventer la biomédecine*; in the British context see for example S. de Chadarevian, *Designs for Life: molecular biology after World War II*, Cambridge: CUP, 2002.
72. According to Ben-David, this weakness was linked to the centralized structures that developed in the course of the nineteenth century. Ben-David, *The Scientist's Role*, pp. 104–7. His analysis may have been based on what French scientists thought of themselves, see Nye, 'National styles?', 37–8. This interpretation has entered the public arena: a French lack of co-operation, linked to the 'French disease', is a recurrent leitmotiv in newspaper articles of *Le Monde*. It is used to explain the relative isolation of French scientists who in terms of discoveries find themselves left behind by the veritable 'task-forces' of American researchers. See 'La note secrète du professeur Escande sur un nouveau traitement du cancer' and 'Les leçons d'une découverte', *Le Monde*

(8 May 1998), 8/14. The co-operation between scientists and companies in France, and more generally in Europe, is seen as the key to redressing the imbalance between Europe and America in areas of new technology, in particular information technology. See 'La recherche au coeur de l'emploi et de la compétitivité', ibid. (14 Jan. 1999), 14. On the French disease, see Alain Peyrefitte, *Le Mal français,* Paris: Plon, 1976.

PART I

1   P. Weindling, 'From infectious to chronic diseases: changing patterns of sickness in the nineteenth and twentieth centuries', in A. Wear (ed.), *Medicine in Society: historical essays,* Cambridge: CUP, 1992, pp. 303–16 (306).

2   For instance R.E. Kohler, *From Medical Chemistry to Biochemistry: the making of a biomedical discipline,* Cambridge: CUP, 1982. On the power of institutions to influence history, see P. David, 'Why are institutions the 'carriers of history'? Path dependence and the evolution of conventions, organizations and institutions', in *Structural Change and Economic Dynamics,* 1994, vol. 5, 205–20.

3   J.H. Warner, *The Therapeutic Perspective: medical practice, knowledge and identity in America, 1820–1885,* Cambridge, Mass.: Harvard University Press, 1986, p. 1. Also W.F. Bynum, *Science and the Practice of Medicine in the Nineteenth Century,* Cambridge: CUP, 1994, Ch. 2.

4   Weindling, 'From infectious to chronic diseases, in A. Wear (ed.), *Medicine in Society,* p. 305. T. McKeown has questioned the true impact of scientific medicine on disease, in *The Role of Medicine. Dream, Mirage, or Nemesis?,* London: Nuffield Provincial Hospitals Trust, 1976.

5   See P. Weindling, *Health, Race and German Politics between National Unification and Nazism, 1870–1945,* Cambridge: CUP, 1989, p. 473.

6   Grey areas remained over what science was to mean exactly to medicine. See Mark Weatherall, 'Scientific Medicine and the Medical Sciences in Cambridge 1851–1939' (Cambridge University Ph.D. thesis, 1994), and T. M. Romano, 'Gentlemanly versus scientific ideals: John Burdon Sanderson, medical education and the failure of the Oxford School of physiology', *Bull. His. Med.,* 1997, vol. 71, 224–48 (209). Christopher Lawrence and George Weisz have pointed out the persistence of a holistic model in inter-war medicine, in C. Lawrence and G. Weisz (eds.), *Greater than the Parts: holism in biomedicine, 1920–1950,* Oxford: OUP, 1998, Chs. 4, 5.

7   J.-F. Picard, 'De la médecine expérimentale (1865) à l'INSERM (1964)', in Debru et al, *Les Sciences biologiques et* médicales, 329–45. For more on this resistance and its eventual erosion, see J.-P. Gaudillière, *Inventer la biomédicine,* 'Introduction'.

8   Quoted in A. Landsborough Thomson, *Half a Century of Medical Research* London: HMSO, 1973, vol. 2, p. 34.

9   Caron, 'Introduction', in F. Caron, P. Erker, and W. Fisher (eds.), *Innovations in the European Economy between the Wars,* p. 27.

10   Nelly Oudshorn has shown that these boundaries can still continue to shift. N. Oudshorn, 'Shifting boundaries between industry and science: the role of WHO in contraceptive R&D', in J.-P. Gaudillière and I. Löwy (eds.), *The Invisible Industrialist,* pp. 345–67.

11   For Britain see by M. Sanderson, 'Research and the Firm in British Industry, 1919–39', *Science Studies,* 1972, vol. 2, 107–51 (114), and *The Universities and British Industry, 1850–1970,* London: Routledge and Kegan Paul, 1972.

For France, see H.W. Paul, *From Knowledge to Power: the rise of the science empire in France, 1860–1939*, Cambridge: CUP, 1985, especially Ch. 4.

CHAPTER 1

1. See for instance A.-M. Moulin and A. Guénel, 'L'Institut Pasteur et la naissance de l'industrie de la santé', in J.-C. Beaune (ed.), *La Philosophie du remède*, Paris: Presses Universitaires de France, 1993, pp. 91–109 (104).
2. Traditional accounts of the history of chemotherapy include: I. Galdston, *Behind the Sulfa-Drugs: a short history of chemotherapy*, New York: D. Appleton-Century Co. Inc., 1943; M.L. Goldsmith, The Road to Penicillin: a history of chemotherapy, London: Lindsay Drummond, 1946; T.S. Work and E. Work, *The Basis of Chemotherapy*, Edinburgh: Oliver Boyd, 1948; H.J. Barber, *Historical Aspects of Chemotherapy*, Dagenham: May & Baker, 1978.
3. J. Liebenau, 'Paul Ehrlich as a commercial scientist and research administrator', *Medical History*, 1990, vol. 34, 65–78.
4. J. E. Lesch, 'Chemistry and biomedicine in an industrial setting: the invention of the sulfa drugs', in S. H. Mauskopf (ed.), *Chemical Sciences in the Modern World*, Philadelphia: University of Pennsylvania Press, 1993, pp. 158–215 (206).
5. On the expanding international networks in science, see Crawford et al. (eds.) *Denationalizing Science*.
6. Ben-David, *The Scientist's Role*, pp. 103–5, and on the superiority of decentralized models of organisation, pp. 171–3.
7. Debru and Gayon, 'Introduction', in Debru et al., p. 17; J. Harvey, 'L'autre côté du miroir (the Other Side of the Mirror): French neurophysiology and English interpretations', in ibid., pp. 71–81; J.-C. Dupont, 'Autour d'une controverse sur l'excitabilité: Louis Lapicque et l'Ecole de Cambridge', in ibid., pp. 83–97. The work of the Cambridge School had important implications for drug development. See Weatherall, *In Search of a Cure*, Ch. 4.
8. Debru and Gayon, 'Introduction', in Debru et al., pp. 9–23.
9. On one of these reformers, Charles Nicolle, and his scientific and political ambitions, see K. Pelis, 'Prophet for profit in French North Africa: Charles Nicolle and the Pasteur Institute of Tunis, 1903–1936', *Bulletin of the History of Medicine*, 1997, vol. 71, 583–622.
10. Picard, 'De la médecine expérimentale', in Debru *at al.*, pp. 332–3. Debru and Gayon note that by the 1930s, the seeds of recovery had been sown in several areas of medical research, 'Introduction', in ibid., pp. 11–12.
11. On Lwoff, see R.M. Burian and J. Gayon, 'Un évolutioniste bernardien à l'Institut Pasteur? Morphologie des ciliés et évolution physiologique dans l'oeuvre d'André Lwoff', in Morange, *L'Institut Pasteur*, pp. 165–86. On his legacy to the French school of molecular biology, see M. Morange, *A History of Molecular Biology*, Cambridge, Mass.: CUP, 1998.
12. See Bovet, *Une Chimie qui guérit: histoire de la découverte des sulfamides*, Paris: Payot, 1988.
13. A.E. Caldwell, *Origins of Psychopharmacology: from CPZ to LSD*, Springfield, Ill.: Charles C. Thomas, 1970; J.P. Swazey, *Chlorpromazine in Psychiatry: a study of therapeutic innovation*, Cambridge, Mass: MIT Press, 1974; E.M. Tansey, '"They used to call it psychiatry": aspects of the development and impact of psychopharmacology', in M. Gijswijt-Hofstra and R. Porter

(eds.), *Cultures of Psychiatry and Mental Health Care in Postwar Britain and the Netherlands*, Amsterdam: Rodopi, 1998, pp. 79–101.

14. For Britain see by M. Sanderson, 'Research and the Firm in British Industry, 1919–39', *Science Studies*, 1972, vol. 2, 114; idem, *The Universities and British Industry*. For France, see H.W. Paul, *From Knowledge to Power*, especially Ch. 4.

15. Weatherall, *In Search of a Cure*, Ch. 5 on 'replacement therapy', and Ch. 7 on 'deficiency diseases'. S. Chauveau, *L'Invention pharmaceutique: la pharmacie entre l'Etat et la société*, Paris: Institut d'Edition Sanofi-Synthélabo, 1999.

16. See V. Quirke, 'Making *British* cortisone: Glaxo and the development of corticosteroid drugs in Britain in the 1950s and 1960s', *Studies in History and Philosophy of Biology and Biomedical Sciences*, 2005, vol. 36, 645–74 .

17. Debru and Gayon, 'Introduction', in Debru et al., *Les Sciences biologiques et médicales*, p. 14.

18. In Great Britain the Lister Institute, in Germany the Kaiser Wilhelm Institute, and in America the Rockefeller Institute. See Picard, 'De la médecine expérimentale', in Debru et al., p. 332. On the different models of research institutions, see W. Bynum, *Science and the Practice of Medicine in the nineteenth century*, pp. 152–7; also P. Weindling, 'Scientific élites and laboratory organisation in *fin de siècle* Paris and Berlin: the Pasteur Institute and Robert Koch's Institute for Infectious Diseases compared', in Cunningham and Williams, *The Laboratory Revolution in Medicine*, pp. 170–88.

19. I. Löwy, 'On hybridizations, networks and new disciplines: the Pasteur Institute and the development of microbiology in France', *Studies in the History and Philosophy of Science*, 1994, vol. 25, 655–88 (662–4).

20. Institut Pasteur Direction Service [hereafter IP DirSer] 49, Pénicilline Divers (2), 1943–6: Tréfouël to the Ministre de la Guerre (22 Feb. 1945).

21. On Nicolle and Roux: see Pelis, 'Prophet for Profit'.

22. On 'L'affaire Ramon', see Picard, 'De la médecine expérimentale', in Debru et al, p. 332.

23. Lecomte du Nouy worked in the physical chemistry laboratory on the physical properties of sera. A. Delaunay, *L'Institut Pasteur, des origines à aujourd'hui*, Paris: France-Empire, 1962, pp. 227, 255.

24. A. Blondeau, *Histoire des laboratoires pharmaceutiques en France: et de leurs médicaments*, Paris: le Cherche Midi, 1992, vol. 1, p. 79.

25. Bovet, *Une Chimie qui guérit*, p. 26; J. Igolen, 'Presque un siècle de synthèse organique à l'Institut Pasteur', *Annales de l'I.P.*, Actualités, 1993, vol. 4, 50–67 (56).

26. Mead observed that cooperation and competition, rather than being opposites, are complementary, and that it might be necessary to add a third category, that of individualism (in the case of cultures where goals are pursued without reference to others), to produce a more complete picture. Mead, *Cooperation and Competition*, p. 16. The individualistic model, as Pestre has suggested in his study of the French physicists' community, might be more suitable in the case of France. D. Pestre, 'Un laboratoire sans équipe: le règne de l'individualisme', in *Physique et physiciens en France*, Paris: Ed. des Archives Contemporaines, 1992, pp. 223–45. However, one should be wary of employing a model that, although well suited to physicists, may not be applicable to other groups of scientists.

27. Mead, *Cooperation and Competition*, p. 16.

28. A.-M. Moulin, 'L'inconscient Pasteurien: l'immunologie de Metchnikoff à Oudin, 1917–1940', in M. Morange (ed.), *L'Institut Pasteur: contributions à son histoire*, Paris: La Découverte, 1991, pp. 144–64 (145–6).

29. A. M. Silverstein, *A History of Immunology*, San Diego: Academic Press, 1989, pp. 305–27.
30. Reflecting the cleavages within immunology and cut off from the production of vaccines, Besredka's programme contributed to moving the Pasteur Institute away from mainstream immunological research. Moulin, 'L'inconscient Pasteurien', in Morange, *L'Institut Pasteur*, pp. 151–3, 156.
31. Pelis, 'Prophet for Profit', 586–90.
32. Bovet, *Une Chimie qui guérit*, pp. 29–39.
33. Studies such as Wiener's and Barnett's have focused on cultural explanations of British decline. See Wiener, *English Culture*, pp. 132–45, and Barnett, *The Audit of War*, pp. 204–17. Shinn has also privileged cultural factors in his study of French R&D between the wars, in 'The genesis of French industrial research', 619–33. Contemporary interpretations also tended to focus on one factor, for instance Jean Monnet in his *Memoirs*, pp. 232–6.
34. J.–P. Gaudillière, 'Catalyse enzymatique et oxydations cellulaires. L'oeuvre de Gabriel Bertrand et son héritage', in Morange, *L'Institut Pasteur*, pp. 118–36.
35. This lack of enthusiasm is mentioned by Bovet, 'Le laboratoire de chimie thérapeutique: de l'arsenic aux sulfamides', in ibid., pp. 207–36 (208).
36. Picard, 'De la médecine expérimentale', in Debru et al., *Les Sciences biologiques et médicales*, p. 331.
37. Such a move brings to mind Pestre's evocation of French physics for the same period, in *Physique et physiciens*, pp. 141–5.
38. On the distinction between 'bacteriology' and 'microbiology', see A. Mendelsohn, 'Bacteriology and microbiology', in J. Heilbron (ed.), *The Oxford Companion to the History of Modern Science*, New York: Oxford University Press, 2003, pp. 75–77.
39. Faure, 'Cent années d'enseignement ', in Morange, *L'Institut Pasteur*, pp. 62–74.
40. The epithet 'Pastorian' was invented by the novelist Fleury to describe the emerging community in the 1890s: Moulin, 'Patriarchal Science: the network of the overseas Pasteur Institutes', in P. Petitjean, C. Jami and A.-M. Moulin (eds.), *Science and Empires*, Dordrecht: Kluwer Academic, 1992, pp. 307–22 (311).
41. Faure, 'Cent années d'enseignement', in Morange, *L'Institut Pasteur*, pp. 68–70.
42. Burian et Gayon, 'Un évolutioniste bernardien à l'Institut Pasteur?', in ibid., pp. 165–85.
43. Gaudillière, 'Les biochimistes français entre légitimité médicale et légitimité biologique, 1930–1960', in Debru et al , *Les Sciences biologiques et médicales*, pp. 265–82 (266).
44. See P. Abir-Am, 'The politics of macro-molecules: Molecular Biology, Biochemists and the Biomolecular Revolution', *Osiris*, 2nd Series, 1992, vol. 7, 164–99.
45. E. Wollmann, 'Succès et limites de la recherche pasteurienne: introduction', in Morange, *L'Institut Pasteur*, pp. 105–7.
46. A.-M. Moulin, 'Patriarchal science', in Petitjean et al , *Science and Empires*, p. 308.
47. IP Conseil d'Administration Registres [hereafter CAReg] 2, III: 21 March 1934.
48. Löwy, 'On hybridization, networks and new disciplines', 676.
49. IP CAReg 3, IV: 6 June 1937..

50. Alexandre Besredka, for example, made private arrangements with industry to produce his 'antivirus' vaccines: Moulin and Guénel, 'L'Institut Pasteur', in Beaune, *La philososphie du remède*, p. 101. Blondeau has mentioned that the Debat company opened a vaccine department at Garches 'thanks to the help and friendship of Professor Besredka', in *Histoire des laboratoires pharmaceutiques,* vol. 1, p. 75.

51. Delaunay, *L'Institut Pasteur*, pp. 250–51; IP CAReg 2, III: 22 March and 22 Nov. 1933.

52. Ibid. (22 Nov. 1933), 439–42.

53. Ibid. (21 March 1934).

54. 'Certes, l'organisation présente de l'IP, qui ne répond plus complètement aux nécessités actuelles, n'a pas eu d'inconvénient graves, en raisons des qualités du personnel. Mais il est à craindre que, dans l'avenir, l'IP souffre d'un défaut d'administration. Tant pour le rendement scientifique que pour l'économie générale de la maison, une gestion rationnelle s'impose'. Ibid., 467.

55. Ibid. (9 May 1934).

56. Term used by Wollman, IP interview (31 May 1999).

57. The resistance to these reforms is described by Kim Pelis in 'Prophet for Profit', pp. 600–19.

58. IP CAReg 2, III: 21 March 1934, 481.

59. P. Ehrlich and S. Hata, 'Die experimentelle Chemotherapie der Spirillosen' Berlin, 1910, translated in H.H. Dale, F. Himmelweit and M. Marquardt (eds., *The Collected Papers of Paul Ehrlich,* London: Pergamom Press, 1960, vol. 3, 'Chemotherapy'. See also Dale, 'Introduction', in M. Marquardt, *Paul Ehrlich*, London: W. Heinemann Medical Books, 1949, pp. xiii–xx.

60. IP CAReg 2, II : Assemblée (9 Nov. 1910).

61. Liebenau and Robson, 'L'Institut Pasteur et l'industrie pharmaceutique', in Morange, *L'Institut Pasteur*, pp. 56–7.

62. On Levaditi, see Delaunay, *L'Institut Pasteur*, pp. 229–31.

63. Bovet, *Une Chimie qui guérit*, pp. 38–39.

64. Bovet, 'Le laboratoire de chimie thérapeutique', in Morange, *L'Institut Pasteur*, pp. 207–36.

65. Bovet, *Une Chimie qui guérit*, p. 26; Igolen, 'Presque un siècle de synthèse organique', p. 56.

66. Letter by Fourneau to Louis Martin, Director (23 March 1936). See Moulin and Guénel, 'L'Institut Pasteur', in Beaune, *La philosophie du remède*, note 84, p. 109.

67. Bovet, *Une Chimie qui guérit*, p. 26.

68. Ibid., p. 31.

69. Lapresle, 'Le rôle de l'hôpital de l'Institut Pasteur dans l'application à la médecine des recherches fondamentales', in Morange, *L'Institut Pasteur*, pp. 45–51.

70. Ibid., p. 48.

71. Weindling, 'Emile Roux et la diphtérie', in ibid., pp. 137–43 (139–40).

72. Delaunay, *L'Institut Pasteur*, p. 247.

73. Picard, 'De la médecine expérimentale', in Debru et al., *Les Sciences biologiques et médicales*, p. 331.

74. Lesch, 'Chemistry and biomedicine in an industrial setting', in Mauskopf, *Chemical Sciences*, p. 164.

75. Weatherall, *In Search of a Cure*, pp. 110–2.

76. Liebenau and Robson, 'L'Institut Pasteur et l'industrie pharmaceutique', in Morange, *L'Institut Pasteur*, pp. 52–61.

77. Löwy, 'On hybridizations, networks and new disciplines', 664.

78. This laboratory was described in a survey of industrial research laboratories carried out by the CNRS in 1938–1940. Archives Nationale Contemporaines [hereafter ANC] 800284, 21: 38 RB. See also W.C. Summers, *Félix d'Hérelle and the Origins of Molecular Biology*, New Haven: Yale University Press, 1999, pp. 158–9, 163, and Ch. 12.

79. Moulin,'Patriarchal Science', in Petitjean et al., *Science and Empires*, p. 308.

80. Weindling, 'Scientific élites', in Cunningham and Williams, *The Laboratory Revolution*, pp. 187–8.

81. Pelis, 'Prophet for Profit', p. 584.

82. On the centralized nature of the French system, see Ben-David, *The Scientist's Role*, pp. 103–5. See also R. Fox, 'Research, education, and the industrial economy in modern France', in *The Academic Research Enterprise within the Industrialized Nations: comparative perspectives*, Washington, D.C.: National Academic Press, 1990, pp. 95–107.

83. Moulin,'Patriarchal Science', in Petitjean et al., *La philosophie du remède*.

84. J. Rosser Matthews, 'Major Greenwood versus Almroth Wright: contrasting visions of "scientific" medicine in Edwardian Britain', *Bulletin of the History of Medicine*, 1995, vol. 69, 30–43 (31).

85. Statistics played a greater role in British medicine than it did elsewhere, particularly France. This point has been made by Gaudillière in *Inventer la biomedicine*, Chapter 6. Contrary to their French counterparts who favoured a general and qualitative approach to physiology, British physiologists leaned towards more quantitative approaches as a means of elucidating the underlying mechanisms of pathological as well as normal conditions. See Debru and Gayon, 'Introduction', in Debru et al., *Les Sciences biologiques et médicales*, pp. 14–7.

86. Matthews, 'Major Greenwood versus Almroth Wright', p. 41. On Karl Pearson and his school, see E. Magnello, 'The introduction of mathematical statistics into medical research: the roles of Karl Pearson, Major Greenwood, and Austin Bradford Hill', in E. Magnello and A. Hardy (eds.), *The Road to Medical Statistics*, Amsterdam: Rodopi, 2002, pp. 95–123.

87. H. Chick, M. Hume and M. Macfarlane, *War on disease: a history of the Lister Institute*, London: Deutsch, 1971, p. 77.

88. Matthews, 'Major Greenwood versus Almroth Wright', p. 42.

89. Chick et al., *War on Disease*; Thomson, *Half a Century of Medical Research*, vols 1 and 2; J. Austoker and L. Bryder (eds.), *Historical Perspectives on the Role of the MRC*, Oxford: Oxford University Press, 1989.

90. Debru and Gayon, 'Introduction', in Debru et al., *Les Sciences biologiques et médicales*, pp. 12–7; see also Abigail O'Sullivan, 'Networks of creativity: a study of scientific achievement in British physiology, 1881–1945', Oxford University D.Phil. thesis, 2002.

91. For a general history of clinical research, see C. Lawrence, 'Clinical research', in J. Krige and D. Pestre (eds.), *Science in the Twentieth Century*, Amsterdam: Harwood Academic, 1997, pp. 439–60. Focussing more on Britain: C. Booth, 'Clinical research', in Austoker and Bryder, *Historical Perspectives*, pp. 205–41.

92. Kohler, *From Medical Chemistry to Biochemistry*, pp. 40–1.

93. For Manchester, see J. Pickstone, *Medicine and Industrial Society: a history of hospital development in Manchester and its region*, Manchester: Manchester University Press, 1985; for Sheffield: A.W. Chapman, *The History of a Modern University: a history of the university of Sheffield*, Sheffield: Oxford University Press, 1955; for Liverpool: T. Kelly, *For Advancement of*

Learning: the University of Liverpool 1881–1981, Liverpool: Liverpool University Press, 1981.

94. On Britain: S. Sturdy, 'Medical chemistry and clinical medicine: academics and the scientisation of medical practice in Britain', in I. Löwy (ed.), *Medicine and Change: historical and sociological studies of medical innovation*, Montrouge: John Libbey Eurotext, 1993, pp. 371–93. On France: see Picard, 'De la médecine expérimentale', in Debru et al., *Les Sciences biologiques et médicales*, pp. 338–42.

95. For Cambridge: Mark Weatherall, 'Scientific Medicine and the Medical Sciences in Cambridge'; for Oxford, M.G. Ord and L.A. Stocken, *The Oxford Biochemistry Department: its history and activities, 1920–1985*, Oxford: Department of Biochemistry, University of Oxford, 1990.

96. See Gaudillière, 'Les biochimistes français', in Debru et al., *Les Sciences biologiques et médicales*, and Picard, 'De la médecine expérimentale à l'IN-SERM', in ibid.

97. Lawrence and Weisz, *Greater than the Parts?*, Ch. 4.

98. Weatherall, *In Search of a Cure*, pp. 69–82.

99. Debru and Gayon, 'Introduction', in Debru et al., *Les Sciences biologiques et médicales*, pp. 17, 23, and Picard, 'De la médecine expérimentale', in ibid.

100. Weatherall, *In Search of a Cure*, p. 129.

101. When it came to biological remedies, Hörlein thought that the strong Anglo-Saxon physiological tradition in medicine presented advantages over the more purely chemically oriented German tradition. Lesch, 'Chemistry and biomedicine in an industrial setting', in Mauskopf, *Chemical Sciences*, p. 168.

102. Z. Cope, *Almroth Wright: founder of modern vaccine-therapy*, London: Nelson, 1966; G. Macfarlane, *Alexander Fleming: the man and the myth*, Oxford: Oxford University Press, 1985, Ch. 7; W. Chen, 'The laboratory as business: Sir Almroth Wright's vaccine programme and the construction of penicillin', in Cunningham and Williams, *The Laboratory Revolution*, pp. 245–92.

103. Chick et al., *War on Disease*, Ch. 4.

104. Ibid., pp. 50–1.

105. Matthews, 'Major Greenwood versus Almroth Wright', pp. 31, 42–3.

106. Chick et al., *War on Disease*, Ch. 2. The Lister was admitted as a school of the University of London in 1905, with responsibilities for teaching, and although in the end, because of a lack of funds, no hospital was constructed, plans were made to connect the Lister to a new research hospital, p. 123.

107. For a study of leadership styles and their influence on the scientific programmes of different schools, see J.B. Morrell, 'The chemist breeders: the research schools of Justus Liebig and Thomas Thomson', *Ambix*, 1972, vol. 19, 2–47.

108. Chick et al., *War on Disease*, pp. 48–9.

109. Contemporary Medical Archives Centre [hereafter CMAC] SA/LIS 5, H15: Sir Ray Lankester, FRS, 'Science from an easy chair: an attempt to manufacture scientific discovery', *Daily Telegraph* (n.d.).

110. Wollman, IP interview (31 May 1999).

111. Chick et al., *War on Disease*, p. 53.

112. CMAC SA/LIS 5, H8: 'Reorganisation 1906'.

113. Ibid., letter from Lord Iveagh to Sir Henry Roscoe (Chairman of the Governing Body) (1906). See also Report of the Committee of the Scientific Members of the Governing Body (Jan. 1906).

114. H. Chick, 'C.J. Martin, 1866–1955', *Biographical Memoirs FRS*, 1956, vol. 2, 173–208.

115. Chick et al., *War on Disease*, p. 161.
116. Ibid., pp. 120–1.
117. CMAC SA/LIS 5, H14: J.L. Pattison to C. Martin (14 Oct. 1914).
118. See Sir Ray Lankester, in SA/LIS 5, H 15. Also, SA/LIS 5, H 10: MG (M. Greenwood) to C. Martin (2 Jan. 1914). Reference to this episode is made by Thomson in *Half a Century of Medical Research*, vol. 1, pp. 110–1.
119. Chick et al., *War on Disease*, p. 122.
120. Ibid., Chs. 15, 16.
121. Gaudillière, 'Catalyse enzymatique et oxydations cellulaires', in Morange, *L'Institut Pasteur*, pp. 131–6 ; Chick et al., *War on Disease*, Chs. 12, 16.
122. Ibid., p. 174.
123. Ibid., Ch. 14.
124. Ibid., pp. 141–2.
125. Ibid., p. 138.
126. C. Dyhouse, *No Distinction of Sex? Women in British universities, 1870–1939*, London: UCL Press, 1995, pp. 167–77. Also: M. and G. Rayner-Canham, 'Hoppy's ladies', *Chemistry in Britain*, 1999, vol. 35, 47–9.
127. Chick et al., *War on Disease*, p. 218.
128. Moulin, 'Patriarchal science', in Petitjean et al. *Science and Empires*. And yet, as Weindling has shown, when compared with the Koch Institute the Pasteur does not appear so hierarchical. Weindling, 'Scientific élites', in Cunningham and Williams, *The Laboratory Revolution*, pp. 187–8
129. Chick et al., *War on Disease*, Chs. 8, 18.
130. Bovet, *Une Chimie qui guérit*, Ch. 2; Picard, 'De la médecine expérimentale', in Debru et al., *Sciences biologiques et médicales*, p. 336.
131. Chick et al., *War on Disease*, pp. 110–1, 142–3.
132. Weatherall, *In Search of a Cure*, p. 54. N. A. Rupke, *Vivisection in Historical Perspective*, London: Routledge, 1990.
133. Robson, 'The French pharmaceutical industry', in Liebenau et al., *Pill Peddlers*, p. 114.
134. Weatherall, *In Search of a Cure*, p. 55.
135. 'The Lister Institute of Preventive Medicine', *Lancet*, 1975, vol. 1, 54.
136. This semi-autonomy, known as the 'Haldane system' after the recommendations of the 1913 Haldane Commission on University Education, became an inspiration for other research councils, in Britain and abroad. See N.J. Vig, *Science and Technology in British Politics*, Oxford: Pergamom Press, 1968, p. 17.
137. Thomson, *Half a Century of Medical Research*, vol. 2, p. 1.
138. Ibid.
139. Ibid., p. 2.
140. J. Austoker, 'Walter Morley Fletcher and the origins of a basic biomedical research policy', in Austoker and Bryder, *Historical Perspectives*, pp. 23–33.
141. Ibid., p. 4. For a more detailed account, see Bryder, 'Tuberculosis and the MRC', in ibid., pp. 1–21.
142. Thomson, *Half a Century of Medical Research*, vol. 2, p. 215; J. Beinart, 'The inner world of imperial sickness: the MRC and research in tropical medicine', in Austoker and Bryder, *Historical Perspectives*, pp. 109–35.
143. Austoker and Bryder, 'The National Institute of Medical Research and related activities of the MRC', in ibid., pp. 35–57.
144. W.S. Feldberg, 'Henry Halett Dale, 1875–1968', *Biographical Memoirs F.R.S.*, 1969, vol. 16, 77–173; also Thomson, *Half a Century of Medical Research*, vol. 1, pp. 115–7.

145. Tansey, 'The Early Scientific Career of Sir Henry Halett Dale'.
146. L.F. Haber, *The Chemical Industry 1900–1930: international growth and technological change*, Oxford: Clarendon Press, 1971, pp. 52–61.
147. On the DSIR see I. Varcoe, 'Scientists and organised research in Great Britain, 1914–16: the early history of the DSIR', *Minerva*, 1970, vol. 9, 192–217.
148. Thomson, *Half a Century of Medical Research*, vol. 2, pp. 45–6.
149. This, and the following quotes are from a 1936–1937 report reproduced in Thomson, *Half a Century of Medical Research*, vol. 2, p. 46. However, Keith Williams has challenged such a view, and argued that between the wars British pharmaceutical companies were much keener to develop chemical compounds than hitherto supposed, which helps to explain the industry's performance in World War Two. K.J. Williams, 'British pharmaceutical industry, synthetic drug manufacture and the clinical testing of novel drugs, 1895–1939' Ph.D thesis, University of Manchester, 2004.
150. Weatherall, *In Search of a Cure*, pp. 152–4. See also V. Quirke, 'From alkaloids to gene therapy: a brief history of drug discovery in the twentieth century', in S. Anderson (ed.), *A Brief History of Pharmacy*, London: Pharmaceutical Press, 2005, pp. 177–201.
151. Thomson, *Half a Century of Medical Research*, p. 50.
152. Williams has stressed the role played by Francis Carr, like Dale formerly of Burroughs Wellcome, and Director of the Association of British Chemical Manufacturers (ABCM), created in 1914. Williams, 'British pharmaceutical industry', Ch. 5. See also Austoker and Bryder, 'The National Institute for Medical Research and related activities of the MRC', in Austoker and Bryder, *Historical Perspectives*, p. 46.
153. 1936–7 report, quoted in Thomson, *Half a Century of Medical Research*, vol. 2, pp. 46–7.
154. Ibid., p. 50. See also Austoker and Bryder, 'The National Institute for medical research and related activities of the MRC', in Austoker and Bryder, *Historical Perspectives*, p. 47.
155. E.M. Tansey, 'The Wellcome Physiological Research Laboratories 1894–1904: the Home Office, Pharmaceutical Firms and Animal Experiments', *Medical History*, 1989, vol. 33, 1–41. On the Institut Mérieux, see Blondeau, *Histoire des laboratoires pharmaceutiques*, pp. 179–91.
156. For example Haber, *The Chemical Industry 1900–1930*; more recently A.S. Travis, H.G.Schröter, E. Homburg and P.J.T. Morris (eds.), *Determinants in the Evolution of the European Chemical Industry, 1900–1939*, and Chandler, *Shaping the Industrial Century*.
157. On the American pharmaceutical industry, see Liebenau, *Medical Science and Medical Industry*; on Britain T.A.B. Corley, 'The British pharmaceutical industry since 1851', in L. Richmond, J. Stevenson and A. Turton (eds.), *The Pharmaceutical Industry*; on France S. Chauveau, *L'Invention pharmaceutique*.
158. V. Walsh, 'Invention and innovation in the chemical industry: demand-pull or discovery-push?', *Research Policy*, 1994, vol. 13, 211–34. Robson, 'The pharmaceutical industry in Britain and France', pp. 330–50.
159. S. Chauveau, 'Entreprises et marchés du médicament en Europe occidentale des années 1880 à la fin des années 1960', *Histoire, Economie et Société*, 1998, vol. 1, 49–81 (60–7).
160. Robson, 'The pharmaceutical industry in Britain and France', Part 1, Ch. 1: 'Introduction'.
161. J. Foreman-Peck, *Smith and Nephew in the Health Care Industry*, Aldershot: Edward Elgar, 1995, p. 29. See also Robson, 'The French pharmaceutical industry, 1919–39', in Liebenau et al., *Pill Peddlers*, p. 111.

162. Robson, 'The pharmaceutical industry in Britain and France', Part 1, Ch. 3.
163. Haber, *The Chemical Industry 1900–1930*. On France's loss of ground in chemical dyestuffs and in the electrical industry, see R. Fox, 'Contingency or mentality? Technical innovation in France in the age of science-based industry', in M. Kranzberg (ed.), *Technological Education- Technological Style*, San Francisco: San Francisco University Press, 1986, pp. 59–68; and on Britain: P. Reed, 'The British chemical industry and the indigo trade', *British Journal of the History of Science*, 1992, vol. 25, 113–25.
164. G. Tweedale, *At the Sign of the Plough: 275 years of Allen & Hanburys and the British pharmaceutical industry, 1715–1990*, London: Murray, 1990, p. 122. For a similar judgment on the French pharmaceutical industry see Robson, 'The French pharmaceutical industry', in Liebenau et al., *Pill Peddlers*, p. 119.
165. Robson, 'The pharmaceutical industry in Britain and France', Ch. 2. More specifically on Britain: Corley, 'The changing structure of the pharmaceutical industry'; C.J. Thomas, 'The pharmaceutical industry', in D. Burn (ed.), *The Structure of British Industry*, vol. 2, Cambridge: CUP, 1958, pp. 331–75; W.D. Reekie, 'Pharmaceuticals', in P.S. Johnson (ed), *The Structure of British Industry*, London: Granada, 1980, pp. 106–30. On France: R. Fabre and G. Dillemann, *Histoire de la pharmacie*, Paris: PUF, 1971; K. Blunden, *Etude sur l'évolution de la concentration dans l'industrie pharmaceutique en France*, Luxembourg: Office des Publications Officielles des Communautés Européennes, 1975; Chauveau, *L'Invention pharmaceutique*, Part II, Ch. 5.
166. M. Cassier, 'Brevets pharmaceutiques et santé publique en France: opposition et dispositifs spécifiques d'appropriation des médicaments entre 1791 et 2004', *Entreprises et Histoire*, 2004, vol. 36, 29–47.
167. On the other hand smaller companies could launch their new remedies without the burden of complicated registration procedures. Robson, 'The French pharmaceutical industry, 1919–1939', in Liebenau et al., *Pill Peddlers*, p. 110. On the role of patents in general, see Liebenau, 'Patents and the chemical industry: tools of business strategy', in Liebenau (ed.), *The Challenge of New Technology: innovation in British business since 1850*, Aldershot: Gower, 1988, pp. 135–50.
168. Chauveau, 'Entreprises et marchés du médicament', p. 58.
169. Ibid., p. 57.
170. E. Homburg, 'The emergence of research laboratories in the dyestuffs industry, 1870–1900', *British Journal of the History of Science*, 1992, vol. 25, 91–111.
171. W.J. Reader, *Imperial Chemical Industries: a History*, London: Oxford University Press, 1975, 2 vols; P. Cayez, *Rhône Poulenc: 1895–1975*, Paris: Armand Colin/Masson, 1988.
172. Citing ICI as his example, Corelli Barnett has argued that the chemical industry was the only sector of the British economy that was not backward compared with Germany at the onset of the Second World War, in *The Audit of War*, pp. 181–3.
173. Robson, 'The pharmaceutical industry in Britain and France', p. 84.
174. Liebenau, *Medical Science and Medical Industry*, pp. 48–56; Galambos and Sewell, *Networks of Innovation*, Ch. 1.
175. G. Macdonald, *One Hundred Years Wellcome, 1880–1980*, London: The Wellcome Foundation Ltd., 1980.
176. Tweedale, *At the Sign of the Plough*, p. 120. See also Liebenau, 'Industrial R&D in pharmaceutical firms', 339.

177. Many of these small pharmaceutical laboratories were described in a survey carried out by the CNRS. Archives Nationales Contemporaines [hereafter ANC] 800284, 16–22.
178. Robson, 'The British pharmaceutical industry and the First World War', in Liebenau, *The Challenge of New Technology*, p. 94.
179. Cayez, *Rhône-Poulenc*, p. 25.
180. Ibid., pp. 66–7.
181. J. Slinn, *May & Baker, 1834–1984*, Cambridge: Hobson's Ltd., 1984, Ch. 5.
182. Ibid., p. 101.
183. On the importance of co-operative learning and inter-war cartels, which spurred on innovation in the chemical industry, see J. Cantwell and P. Barrera, 'The localisation of corporate technological trajectories in the inter-war cartels: cooperative learning versus an exchange of knowledge', University of Reading Discussion Papers in Economic and Management series, Feb. 1996, no. 340, vol. 8, 1–43.
184. Gaudillière has shown that even in Germany, where the pharmaceutical industry was dominated by the chemical industry, different systems of innovation existed, which were often firm-specific. J.-P. Gaudillière, 'Hormones, régimes d'innovation et stratégies d'entreprise: les exemples de Schering et Bayer', *Entreprises et Histoire*, 2004, vol. 36, 84–102.
185. Robson, 'The Pharmaceutical Industry in Britain and France', p. 311.
186. R.T.P. Davenport-Hines and J. Slinn, *Glaxo: a history to 1962*, Cambridge: CUP, 1992, pp. 68–97.
187. Blondeau, *Histoire des laboratoires pharmaceutiques*, vol. 1, pp. 227–39.
188. Chauveau, *L'Invention pharmaceutique*, pp. 55–7.
189. Blondeau, *Histoire des laboratoires pharmaceutiques*, vol. 1, p. 231.
190. Slinn, *A History of May & Baker*, pp. 122–6; see also J.E. Lesch, 'The discovery of M&B 693 (Sulfapyridine)', in G.J. Higby and E.C. Stroud (eds.), *The Inside Story of Medicines: a symposium*, Madison: American Institute of the History of Pharmacy, Madison, Wis., 1997, pp. 101–9.
191. Blondeau, *Histoire des laboratoires pharmaceutiques*, vol. 1, pp. 230–1.
192. Tweedale, *At the Sign of the Plough*, Ch. 7.
193. Robson, 'The pharmaceutical industry in Britain and France', Part 1, Ch. 3.4.
194. Shinn, 'The genesis of French industrial research', 608–19.
195. Homburg, 'The emergence of research laboratories', 111.
196. Caron, 'Introduction', in Caron et al., *Innovations in the European Economy*, pp. 3–29.
197. Liebenau, 'The rise of the British pharmaceutical industry', 727.
198. For Britain see by M. Sanderson, 'Research and the Firm in British Industry, 1919–39', and *The Universities and British Industry*. For France, see Paul, *From Knowledge to Power*, especially Ch. 4.
199. R. Fox, 'An Uneasy Courtship: rhetoric and reality in the relations between academic and industrial chemistry, 1770–1914', IV National Meeting 'Storia e Fondamenti della Chimica' (Venezia, 7–9 Nov. 1991), 4.
200. W. Breckon, *The Drug Makers*, London: Eyre Methuen, 1972, Ch. 1.
201. Bynum, *Science and the Practice of Medicine*, p. 165.
202. Quoted in Slinn, *May & Baker*, p. 22.
203. Tweedale, *At the Sign of the Plough*, p. 52.
204. Blondel-Mégrelis, 'La pharmacie en France', in Debru et al , *Les Sciences biologiques et médicales*, p. 285.

205. M. Ruffat, 1175 *Ans d'industrie pharmaceutique française: histoire de Synthélabo.*
206. Sally Horrocks has discussed the importance of routine scientific work, as well as innovative research, in relation to the food industry in 'Technology and chocolate: research in the British food industry before 1940', in Caron et al., *Innovations in the European Economy*, pp. 131–48.
207. Robson, 'The French pharmaceutical industry', in Liebenau et al., *Pill Peddlers*, pp. 110–1.
208. Tweedale, *At the Sign of the Plough*, Ch. 5; Williams, 'British pharmaceutical industry'.
209. PRO FD1, 923: joint letter Allen & Hanburys and BDH to MRC (May 1934).
210. Robson, 'The pharmaceutical industry in Britain and France', p. 323.
211. Quoted in Blondeau, Histoire des laboratoires pharmaceutiques, vol. 1, p. 75.
212. Cayez, *Rhône-Poulenc*, pp. 122–5.
213. ANC 800284, 16–22. Many of the plans contained in the survey show that pharmaceutical laboratories were constructed so as to reflect the separation between scientific disciplines.
214. Discussed in Liebenau, in 'The rise of the British pharmaceutical industry', 727. See table in Davenport-Hines and Slinn, *Glaxo*, p. 139.
215. For example, A. S. Travis, 'Modernizing industrial organic chemistry: Great Britain between two world wars', in Travis et al., *Determinants in the Evolution of the European Chemical Industry*, pp. 171–98 (173).
216. Ben-David, *The Scientist's Role*, pp. 103–5, and on the superiority of decentralized models of organisation, pp. 171–3.
217. J. Tomlinson, 'Inventing "decline": the falling behind of the British economy in the post-war years', *Econ His Rev*, 1996, vol. 49, 731–57. Tomlinson has argued that the declinist ideology has changed over time, and under different political regimes (in Britain, it has been different under Labour and the Conservatives).
218. Robson and Liebenau, who do not distinguish between the Institute as a whole and Fourneau's laboratory, conclude that the relationship was more distant than similar relationships abroad: Liebenau and Robson, 'L'Institut Pasteur et l'industrie pharmaceutique', in Morange, *L'Institut Pasteur*, p. 61.

CHAPTER 2

1. See for instance Robson, 'The pharmaceutical industry in Britain and France', p. 343.
2. Mowery, 'The organisation of industrial research in Great Britain, 1900–1950', in D.C. Mowery and N. Rosenberg (eds.), *Technology and the Pursuit of Economic Growth*, Cambridge: CUP, 1989, pp. 98–119 (98–9). Mowery has linked Britain's preference for extramural research, reliance on government funded co-operative research, low levels of investment in R&D, and poor economic performance. Yet, he has also described relations between academic and industrial research as 'weak' (p. 99), and contrasted the British experience with what he saw as a more successful American strategy. Idem, 'Industrial Research, 1900–1950', in Elbaum and Lazonick (eds.), *The Decline of the British Economy*, pp. 189–222. See also Ben-David, *The Scientist's Role*, p. 175. Ben-David suggested that Britain's scientific élites,

with excellent political and social connections, were instrumental in design-ing a science policy with little or no benefit to the economy.

3. Edgerton, *Science, Technology, and the British Industrial 'Decline'*; Levy-Leboyer, 'Innovation and business strategies', in Carter et al., *Enterprise and Entrepreneurs in Nineteenth- and Twentieth-Century France*. Foreman-Peck has shown that pharmaceuticals cast a different light on the question of the decline of the British economy, and argued for 'The long run competitiveness of British healthcare businesses' (paper delivered at the Business History Unit Symposium, 'Future Directions in the Business History of Pharmaceuticals', 19 Nov. 1993). According to him, the post-1945 period saw a remarkable shift in British revealed comparative advantage towards pharmaceuticals and healthcare, which can only be explained if it is seen as being rooted in pre-war developments.

4. D.E.H. Edgerton and S.M. Horrocks, 'British industrial research and devel-opment before 1945', *Econo His Rev*, 1994, vol. 47, 213–38.

5. For instance M. Le Roux, 'Evolution des stratégies de recherche d'une grande entreprise française: Pechiney 1866–1975 — le cas de l'aluminium', Ph.D. thesis, Paris IV- Sorbonne, 1994, Parts 1 and 2; S. Boudia, *Marie Curie et son laboratoire: sciences et industrie de la radioactivité en France*, Paris: Ed des Archives Contemporaines, 2001. In his preface to the book, Pestre highlights the fact that, although the Curies played a crucial role in setting up the radium industry in France, industrial consultancies were nevertheless frowned upon. See also S. Weart, *Scientists in Power*, Cambridge, Mass.: Harvard University Press, 1979, chs. 1, 2.

6. See P. Lundgreen, 'The organisation of science and technology in France: a German perspective', in R. Fox and G. Weisz (eds.), *The Organisation of Science and Technology in France 1808–1914*, Cambridge: CUP, 1980, pp. 309–32 (332).

7. See footnotes 21–5 in the Introduction.

8. F. Crouzet, *De la Supériorité de l'angleterre sur la france*, Paris: Perrin, 1985. Crouzet has warned against the dangers of comparing one country's relative economic success with another's failure.

9. M.-J. Nye, 'National styles?', in Geison and Holmes (eds.), *Research Schools: historical reappraisals*, Osiris, 1993, vol. 8, pp. 37–8; Pestre, *Physique et physiciens*, pp. 208–58.

10. Robson, 'The pharmaceutical industry in Britain and France', Part One, ch. 3.4.

11. Blondel-Mégrelis, 'La pharmacie en France ', in Debru et al. *Les Sciences biologiques et médicales*, p. 287.

12. Cayez, *Rhône-Poulenc*, p. 86.

13. M. Delépine, 'Ernest Fourneau, sa vie, son oeuvre', *Bulletin de la Société Chimique de France*, 1950, 1–75 (4). See also M. Delépine, 'Notice sur la vie et les travaux de Ernest Fourneau, 1872–1949', *Bulletin de la Société Chimi-que de France*, 1950, vol. 17, 953–82.

14. Between 1905 and 1914 they wrote at least eight papers. For example: E. Fourneau and M. Tiffeneau, 'Sur quelques oxydes d'éthylène aromatiques monosubstitués', *Comptes rendus*, 1905, vol. 140, 1595; idem, 'Détermi-nation de la constitution des halohydrines par action des amines tertiaires. Iodhydrines dérivées du styrolène', *Bull. Soc. Chim. Fr.*, 1914, vol. 15, 4, 275. The last joint publication was a contribution to the proceedings of a conference : 'Sur les propriétés anesthésiques des alcoxybenzhydrylamines', 12e Congrès de Stockholm, 1926.

15. Delépine, 'Notice', 955.

16. For many of these names, see Blondeau, *Histoire des laboratoires pharmaceutiques*, vol. 1.
17. IP LCT.1, Discours, 'La molécule' (8 May 1929). See also Blondel-Mégrelis, 'La pharmacie en France', in Debru et al. (eds.), *Les Sciences biologiques et médicales*, p. 287.
18. 'Edmond Emile Blaise (1872–1939)', in C. Charle and E. Telkès, *Les Professeurs de la Faculté des Sciences de Paris: dictionnaire biographique, 1901–1939*, Paris: Ed. CNRS, 1989, pp. 40–2.
19. Cayez, *Rhône-Poulenc*, p. 18.
20. IP LCT.1: autobiographical notice (16 Sept. 1944), 1.
21. Bovet, *Une Chimie qui guérit*, p. 25.
22. Emil Fischer (1852–1919) was Professor of Chemistry at the University of Berlin; Theodor Curtius (1857–1928) at Heidelberg; Ludwig Gattermann (1860–1920) at Freiburg; Richard Willstätter (1872–1942) was at Zurich between 1905 and 1912, when he left for Berlin and then Munich in 1916. Poggendorff, *Bio.Lit.Hand.* 1904–22, v–vi.
23. Bovet, *Une Chimie qui guérit*, p. 25.
24. Slinn, *A History of May & Baker*, p. 92.
25. Cayez, *Rhône-Poulenc*, p. 44.
26. IP CAReg 1, II: 9 Nov. 1910.
27. Bovet, *Une Chimie qui guérit*, p. 31.
28. IP CAReg 1, II: 9 Nov. 1910.
29. Bovet, *Une Chimie qui guérit*, pp. 25–6.
30. The term 'administrator' probably meant membership of the Conseil d'Administration of Poulenc Frères, see 1966 copy of an earlier letter by Fourneau in RPS EF 9711: 25 May 1966.
31. Cayez, *Rhône-Poulenc*, p. 44.
32. Moulin and Guénel, 'L'Institut Pasteur', in Beaune, *La Philosophie du remède*, p. 104.
33. Löwy, 'On hybridizations, networks and new disciplines', 677.
34. Liebenau and Robson, 'L'Institut Pasteur et l'industrie pharmaceutique', in Morange, *L'Institut Pasteur*, pp. 59–60.
35. '[...] l'état des choses actuel- qui a fait ses preuves- qui nous donne pleine satisfaction- qui a toute la souplesse désirable et qui est basé sur une confiance réciproque plus efficace que tout contrat [...] J'ai collaboré avec Poulenc depuis 1900. Je continuerai jusqu'à épuisement de mes facultés'. RPS EF 9711: 8 Jan. 1931.
36. Ibid., 'Contrat SUCR Fourneau 16 Février 1932' (3 Dec. 1949).
37. See IP FUR B.1: 'Note (1934)', which states the exact amount paid in salaries by the Institute and by Rhône-Poulenc to Fourneau himself, and to his collaborators in the LCT.
38. RPS EF 9704-11.
39. RPS EF 9711: Fourneau to Paul (4 July 1946).
40. IP FUR Comité de Libération: 'Liste des collaborateurs du prof. Fourneau' (14 Dec. 1944).
41. Pestre, *Physique et physiciens*, p. 223.
42. J.J. Beer, 'The emergence of the German Dye Industry', *Illinois Studies in Social Sciences*, 1959, vol. 44, Ch. 7.
43. Pestre has given three examples of physicists who, unlike the majority of their colleagues between the wars, worked closely with industry: Maurice Ponte, Yves Rocard and J.J. Trillat. In Pestre, *Physique et physiciens*, pp. 238–41. Unfortunately, he has not said whether such a connection led to their laboratories being organized differently. Nevertheless, the extensive

research activity of Ponte's laboratory, which included engineers, technicians and Ph.D. students, suggests an approach to research that was perhaps inspired by industry, and by a model imported from abroad. Ponte had spent time at the Royal Institution in London, where he received training in X-ray crystallographic techniques under William Bragg, who was able to build a research team, unusual for Britain at the time, thanks to a grant from the DSIR, and who from 1928 to 1931 was Chairman of the DSIR Committee on applications of X-rays to industrial research. See J. Hughes, 'Craftsmanship and social service: W.H. Bragg and the Modern Royal Institution', in F.A.J.L. James (ed.), *'The Common Purposes of Life': science and society at the Royal Institution of Great Britain*, Aldershot: Ashgate, 2002, pp. 225–47; also V. Quirke, '"A big happy family": the Royal Institution under William and Lawrence Bragg, and the History of Molecular Biology', in ibid., pp. 249–71.

44. Bovet, *Une Chimie qui guérit*, Chs. 2, 3.
45. Other marital collaborations at the IP included Marguerite and André Lwoff. On the subject of marital collaboration in science: M.B. Ogilvie, 'Marital Collaboration: an approach to science', in P.G. Abir-Am and D. Outram (eds.) *Uneasy Careers and Intimate Lives,* pp. 104–25.
46. See the correspondence in IP FUR B.1, in particular between Daniel and Filomena Bovet and Fourneau.
47. Axelrod has demonstrated that stability is an important element in the development of a co-operative relationship, in *The Evolution of Co-operation*, pp. 95–7, and p. 125.
48. 'A propos de Mme Tréfouël, je vous dirai quelques mots sur ce que je pense des femmes, des femmes travaillant dans les laboratoires bien entendu... Dire que je suis satisfait de cette collaboration féminine est à peine suffisant car je ne vois pas comment je pourrais m'en passer. Du reste, tous ceux qui me font l'honneur de visiter mon laboratoire sont frappés par l'ambiance sympathique qui y règne et qui est certainement due à la présence des jeunes femmes. Ils peuvent se rendre compte qu'il est parfaitement possible de concilier un travail acharné avec une certaine atmosphère esthétique, et que la grâce s'allie parfaitement à la science.' RPS EF 9711: 4 June 1948.
49. IP LCT.1: Ernest Fourneau, interview on Radio Luxembourg, 10 Dec. 1958.
50. RPS Raymond Paul [hereafter RP]: 7 March 1959. And yet, Chauveau has shown that the number of women employed in the industry rose sharply between 1916 and 1936. Chauveau, *L'Invention pharmaceutique*, p. 98.
51. RPS 9720: 15 Oct. 1951.
52. RPS EF 1, 9704: 24/25 June 1930.
53. J.-F. Picard, *La République des savants: la recherche française et le CNRS*, Paris: Flammarion, 1990, p. 36.
54. Of the exchange only Fourneau's letter remains, in RPS EF 9711: 4 July 1946.
55. Bovet, *Une Chimie qui guerit*, p. 26 ; Cassier, 'Brevets pharmaceutiques', pp. 39–44.
56. RPS EF 9711: 25 April 1936.
57. See J. Liebenau, 'Patents and the chemical industry: tools of business strategy', in Liebenau, *The Challenge of New Technology*, pp. 135–50.
58. RPS EF 4, 9707: 8 Aug. 1935.
59. Ibid., (9 Nov. 1935).
60. RPS EF 2, 9705: 15 Jan. 1932.
61. RPS EF 4, 9707: 9 April 1940.
62. RPS EF 2, 9705: 1 May 1931.
63. RPS EF 1, 9704: 27 May 1930.

64. Ibid. (21 Oct. 1930).
65. RPS Daniel Bovet [hereafter DB] "Début à...": 13 June 1932.
66. A. Oliviero, 'Daniel Bovet, 1907–1992', *Bio. Mem. F.R.S.*, 1994, vol. 39, 59–70.
67. Bovet, *Une Chimie qui guérit*, Ch. 10.
68. Lesch, 'Chemistry and biomedicine in an industrial setting'.
69. Robson, 'The pharmaceutical industry in Britain and France', p. 99.
70. Slinn, *A History of May & Baker*, pp. 124–5.
71. RPS EF 4, 9707: 25 March 1937.
72. Ibid. (March/April 1936).
73. Carsten Reinhardt has shown that in the 1920s and 1930s, IG Farben was introducing a basic scientific approach into their laboratories. Reinhardt, 'Basic research in industry: two case-studies at IG Farbenindustrie in the 1920's and 1930's', in Travis et al., *Determinants in the Evolution of the European Chemical Industry*, pp. 67–88.
74. This friendship may also help to explain why Fourneau decided not to add his name to the article published by his team in 1935: J. Tréfouël, T. Tréfouël, F. Nitti and D. Bovet, 'Activité du p. aminophénylsulpfamide sur les infections streptococciques expérimentales de la souris et du lapin', *Société de Biologie*, 23 nov. 1935, 756–8. S. Baverey-Massat-Bourrah, 'De la copie au nouveau medicament: le laboratoire de chimie thérapeutique et Rhône-Poulenc: un réseau alternatif d'innovation', *Entreprises et Histoire*, 2004, vol. 36, 48–63 (61–3).
75. RPS EF 2, 9705: 6 April 1933. Fourneau's views were corroborated by the Germans, who published a pamphlet in August 1939 accusing him of spying during his stay in German laboratories and copying their best products: IP LCT.1: autobiographical note, 14.
76. N. Chevassus-au-Louis, *Savants sous l'Occupation : enquête sur la vie scientifique française entre 1940 et 1944*, Paris: Seuil, 2004, p. 218.
77. Delépine, 'Notice', 956.
78. E. Fourneau and D. Bovet, 'Recherches sur l'action sympatholytique de nouveaux dérivés du dioxane', *Comptes Rendus des séances de la Société de Biologie*, 1933, vol. 113, 388–90.
79. Oliviero, 'Dabiel Bovet', p. 65.
80. H.O. Schild, *Adventures with Histamine*, London: H.K. Lewis & Co., 1962; idem, 'Dale and the development of pharmacology', *Br. J. Pharmacol.*, 1997, vol. 120 (4 suppl.), 504–8.
81. A.-M. Staub, 'Recherches sur quelques bases synthétiques antagonistes de l'histamine', Ph.D. thesis, Faculté des Sciences de Paris, 1939.
82. A.-M. Staub and D. Bovet, 'Action de la thymoxyéthydiéthylamina (929F) et des éthers phénoliques sur le choc anaphylactique du cobaye', *Comptes rendus des séances de la Société de Biologie*, 1937, vol. 125, 818–21.
83. Oliverio, 'Daniel Bovet', p. 66.
84. RPS 9785: biographical notice (15 Feb. 1957).
85. For a study of the importance of basic research in industry, see N. Rosenberg, 'Why do firms do basic research (with their own money)?', *Research Policy*, 1990, vol. 19, 165–74, in which he has argued that in-house research was essential in order to evaluate research conducted outside the firm. Also K. Pavitt, 'What do firms learn from basic research?', in D. Foray and C. Freeman (eds.), *Technology and the Wealth of Nations: the dynamics of constructed advantage*, London: O.E.C.D., 1993, pp. 29–40.
86. Blondel-Mégrelis, 'La pharmacie en France', in Debru et al., *Les Sciences biologiques et médicales*, p. 288.

87. Cayez, *Rhône-Poulenc*, p. 86.
88. RPS 9550.
89. RPS EF 9711: 12 Jan. 1949.
90. This is particularly true for countries hitherto described as having deficient R&D, such as Britain: see S.M. Horrocks, 'Consuming science: science, technology and food in Britain, 1870–1939', University of Manchester Ph. D. thesis, 1993, Ch. 4. For France, see Blondeau, *Histoire des laboratoires pharmaceutiques*, although he does not examine the nature and function of the laboratory in the pharmaceutical industry. See also Chauveau, *L'Invention pharmaceutique*; Ruffat, 175 *Ans d'industrie pharmaceutique française.*
91. This has been done up to 1914 by Fox and Guagnini, in *Laboratories, Workshops and Sites. Concepts and practices of research in industrial Europe, 1800–1914*, Berkeley: Berkeley Papers in History of Science, 1999, vol. 18; and in relation to the food industry by Horrocks, 'Technology and chocolate', in Caron et al., *Innovations in the European Economy*, pp. 131–48.
92. An earlier, and very valuable example of a study of the role of research within the industrial firm in the 1920s–30s, is M. Sanderson's 'Research and the Firm in British Industry, 1919–39'.
93. Picard, *La République des savants*, pp. 15–31. Picard has argued that all research policies are derived from a preoccupation with applied rather than pure science, and therefore result from a rationale that is essentially external to science.
94. Ibid., p. 61.
95. The full quote is 'un bourgeonnement anarchique, un flot de chercheurs individuels et de laboratoires plus ou moins officiels, tous en quête fiévreuse d'un complément de subvention s'offrant à entreprendre n'importe quel problème, mais prêts le plus souvent pour aucun', in ANC 800284: 35 (1939).
96. D.A. Hounshell and J.K. Smith, *Science and Corporate Strategy: Du Pont R&D, 1902–1980*, Cambridge: CUP, 1988; L.S. Reich, *The Making of American Industrial Research: science and business at GE and Bell, 1876–1926*, Cambridge: CUP, 1985.
97. Ibid., 21:113 RB. And yet, these scientists were not considered to be part of a research team, see Blondeau, *Histoire des laboratoires pharmaceutiques*, vol. 2, p. 183.
98. ANC 800284, 48 RB; 241 RB; 8 MX; 11 BA.
99. This point was made by Foreman-Peck, 'The long-run competitiveness of British healthcare businesses', 25–6. British patent medicines, nerve tonics, laxatives, health foods etc... were well adapted to its market. The same thing could be said of France see Robson, 'The French pharmaceutical industry', in Liebenau et al., *Pill Peddlers*, p. 111.
100. For instance, the opotherapeutic remedies 'panbiline' for liver complaints, 'rectopanbiline' for the intestine, and 'hemopanbiline' against anaemia, made by the Docteur Plantier in the Ardèche. ANC 800284, 16: 10 AT.
101. For example, the Laboratoire Homéopathique Moderne carried out research on the manufacture of homeopathic dilutions and looked for new preparations, in ANC 800284, 21: 40 RB; Dausse had an 'experimental farm' for testing and research in galenicals, ibid., 69 RB.
102. It is not clear from the descriptions whether these are 'spécialités commerciales' (destined to the public at large) or 'spécialités médicales' (destined for physicians who alone can prescribe them). On this distinction, see Chauveau, *L'Invention pharmaceutique*, p. 99. However, in the inter-war period it seems that the latter gained ground over the former. Idem, pp. 100–1.
103. ANC 800284, 17: 01 ED.

104. Ibid., 18: 13 ES.
105. Ibid., 19:10 MB. After World War Two, Charles Lespagnol also advised Rhône-Poulenc: see RPS 10019.
106. ANC 800284, 17: 11 ES.
107. For example, when asked about external collaborations, the Licardy laboratory described itself as 'adjoining the communal hospital of Neuilly', in 21: 109 RB; also 10 NH; 5 OD; 113 RB; 186 RB. On the widespread collaboration between firms and hospitals, see Chauveau, *L'Invention pharmaceutique*, pp. 148–9.
108. Ibid., 21: 221 RB. Février-Decoisy became notorious as a result of the Stalinon affair (see Chauveau, *L'Invention pharmaceutique*).
109. Ibid., 233, 259, 358 RB.
110. Ibid., 18: 10/11 MB; 20: 39/40 PF.
111. Ibid., 21: 241 RB.
112. Ibid., 21: 173 RB.
113. Chauveau, *L'Invention pharmaceutique*, Part 2.
114. This intervention has been criticized by J. Servier, *Le Médicament français: une industrie de pointe en voie de liquidation?*, Paris: Institut Economique de Paris, 1986.
115. Blunden, *Etude sur l'évolution de la concentration*; see also R. Fabre and G. Dillemann, *Histoire de la pharmacie*.
116. See Blondeau, *Histoire des laboratoires pharmaceutiques*; Ruffat, *175 Ans d'industrie pharmaceutique française*.
117. Studies of industry in the smaller manufacturing countries have begun to see it terms of networks rather than hierarchies. For example, on Sweden, see Lundgren, *Technological Innovation and Network Evolution*, and on France, see Lorenz, 'Neither friends nor strangers', in Gambetta, also in Thompson et al., *Markets, Hierarchies and Networks*, pp. 183–92.
118. G. L. Geison, *The Private Science of Louis Pasteur*, Princeton, N.J.: Princeton University Press, 1995. The private side of the Curie laboratories is also being unveiled, for instance Boudia, 'Marie Curie et son laboratoire'; M. Pinault, 'Frédéric Joliot, la science et la société: un itinéraire de la physique nucléaire à la politique nucléaire (1900–1958)' Paris I doctoral thesis, 1999.
119. See Pelis, 'Prophet for Profit', 589. Also Moulin and Guénel, 'L'Institut Pasteur', in Beaune, *La Philosophie du remède*, pp. 91–109.
120. J. Liebenau, 'The MRC and the pharmaceutical industry: the model of insulin', in Austoker and Bryder, *Historical Perspectives*, pp. 163–80.
121. Tansey, 'The early scientific career of Sir Henry Hallett Dale', p. 419.
122. J. Parascandola, '"The Preposterous Provision": the American Society for Pharmacology and Experimental Therapeutics ban on industrial pharmacologists, 1908–1941', in Liebenau et al, *Pill Peddlers*, pp. 29–47.
123. Feldberg, 'Henry Hallett Dale', 119–54. On the history of the Wellcome Trust, see A.R. Hall and B.M. Bembridge, *Physic and Philanthropy: a history of the Wellcome Trust, 1936–1986*, Cambridge: CUP, 1986.
124. Burroughs Wellcome was the second industrial firm in Britain to have started a research laboratory after United Alkali, Sanderson, 'Research and the Firm', 110.
125. Royal Society Dale papers [hereafter RS 93HD] 24.3 1–65: Dale to Beaver (25 Jan. 1961).
126. E.M. Tansey and R.M.C.E. Milligan, 'The early history of the Wellcome Research Laboratories, 1894–1914', in Liebenau et al, *Pill Peddlers*, pp. 91–106. Tansey, 'The WPRL', 5–9.
127. Ibid., 4–5.

128. Ibid., 11–3.
129. Quoted by Tansey, in ibid., 20.
130. Tansey has stressed the fact that the election took place before his move from the WPRL was decided. Tansey, 'The early scientific career of Sir Henry Hallett Dale', p. 171.
131. The term 'anaphylaxis' refers to the laboratory-produced condition, whereas anaphylactic shock refers to the natural phenomenon. See L. Unger and M.C. Harris, 'Stepping stones in allergy', *Annals of Allergy*, 1974, vol. 32, 340–60.
132. Barger and Dale coined the term 'sympathomimetic' in G. Barger and H.H. Dale, 'Chemical structure and sympathomimetic action of amines', *J. Physiol.*, 1910–11, vol. 40, 19–59.
133. Liebenau, 'The MRC and the pharmaceutical industry', in Austoker and Bryder, *Historical Perspectives*, p. 171.
134. Dale took his role as advisor very seriously. See Tansey, 'The early scientific career of Sir Henry Hallett Dale', p. 198.
135. For example Dale supported the views of the ABCM that the facilities for proper clinical tests in this country were inadequate. In PRO FD1 2497. Also 'Letter to the editor', *Lancet*, 1930, vol. 2, 1149–50.
136. Williams, 'British pharmaceutical industry', 3.7, p. 133.
137. H.H. Dale, 'Sir Patrick Playfair Laidlaw, 1881–1940', *Obit. Not. FRS*, 1939–41, vol. 3, 427–47; idem, 'Arthur James Ewins, 1882–1958', *Bio. Mem FRS*, 1958, vol. 4, 81–91.
138. H.H. Dale, 'George Barger, 1878–1939', *Obit. Not. F.R.S.*, 1939, vol. 3, 63–85.
139. C.R. Harington, 'Harold King, 1887–1956', *Bio. Mem. F.R.S.*, 1956, vol. 2, 157–71.
140. E. Bülbring and J.M. Walker, 'Joshua Harold Burn, 1892–1981', *Bio. Mem. F.R.S.*, 1984, vol. 30, 45–89.
141. Davenport Hines and Slinn, *Glaxo*, pp. 71–2.
142. Williams, 'British pharmaceutical industry', 4.7.
143. Ibid., 6.5.
144. H.H. Dale, 'Arthur James Ewins, 1882–1958', *Bio. Mem. FRS*, 1958, vol. 4, 81–91 (88).
145. Slinn has highlighted the importance of these networks, in particular May & Baker's indirect connection with Fourneau's team. J. Slinn, 'Research and development in the UK pharmaceutical industry from the nineteenth century to the 1960s', in R. Porter and M. Teich (eds.), *Drugs and Narcotics in History*, Cambridge: CUP, 1996, pp. 168–86 (178). However, Lesch has stressed the delay taken in realizing the significance of the French team's discovery, in J.E. Lesch, 'The discovery of M & B 693 (Sulfapyridine)', in G.J. Higby and E.C. Stroud (eds.), *The Inside Story of Medicine: a symposium*, Madison, Wis.: American Institute of the History of Pharmacy, 1997, pp. 101–19.
146. Williams, *British Pharmaceutical Industry*; also R. Church and T. Tansey, *Knowledge, Trust, and Profit: a history of Burroughs Wellcome & Co. and the transformation of the British Pharmaceutical Industry*, Lancaster: Carnegie Publishing, forthcoming in 2006, Ch. 10.
147. Horrocks, 'Consuming science', Ch. 7.
148. J.H. Birkinshaw, 'Harold Raistrick, 1890–1971', *Bio. Mem. FRS*, 1972, vol. 18, 489–509.
149. W. König, 'Science-based industry or industry-based science? Electrical engineering in Germany before World War I', *Technology and Culture*, 1996, vol. 37, 70–101.

150. See Pavitt, 'What do firms learn from basic research?', in Foray and Freeman, *Technology and the Wealth of Nations*, pp. 29–40.
151. Ibid., p. 33. Pavitt has pointed out that the chemical and drugs industry have traditionally maintained closer links to basic research in the biological sciences. However, a more detailed examination of the contribution of biologists to vitamins and hormones might correct this picture.
152. Quoted in H.W. Melville, *The Department of Scientific and Industrial Research*, London: George Allen & Unwin, 1964, p. 23. See also R. MacLeod and K. MacLeod, 'The origins of the DSIR: reflections on ideas and men', *Public Administration*, 1970, vol. 48, 23–32; I. Varcoe, 'Scientists, government and organized research: the early history of the DSIR, 1914–16', *Minerva*, 1976, vol. 8, 192–217.
153. Melville, *The Department of Scientific and Industrial Research*, p. 93.
154. G.K. Roberts, 'Dealing with issues at the academic-industrial interface in inter-war Britain: University College London and Imperial Chemical Industries', *Science and Public Policy*, 1997, vol. 24, 29–35.
155. C. Kennedy, *ICI: the company that changed our lives*, London: Hutchinson, 1986, pp. 54, 120–1. Also Reader, *Imperial Chemical Industries*, pp. 81–3; 90–1.
156. Ibid., p. 91.
157. Roberts, 'Dealing with issues', 30.
158. Robinson became Professor of Organic Chemistry at Oxford in 1930. Lord Todd and J.W. Cornforth, 'Robert Robinson, 1886–1975', *Bio. Mem. FRS*, 1976, vol. 22, 415–527. See also T.I. Williams, *Robert Robinson: chemist extraordinary*, Oxford: Clarendon Press, 1990.
159. On this, see also Reader, *Imperial Chemical Industries*, p. 91.
160. Sanderson, 'Research and the Firm', 114. He noted that the term 'research' gradually replaced that of 'experiment' during this period.
161. Barnett, *The Audit of War*, pp. 181–2.
162. Liebenau, 'Industrial R&D in pharmaceutical firms', 336–9.
163. Davenport and Slinn, *Glaxo*, p. 86.
164. H.G. Lazell, *From Pills to Penicillin: the Beecham story*, London: Heinemann, 1975; T.A.B. Corley, 'The Beecham Group in the world's pharmaceutical industry', *Zeit. Unternehmensges.*, 1994, vol. 39, 18–30.
165. Melville, *The Department of Scientific and Industrial Research*, Ch. 2.
166. I. Varcoe, *Organising for Science in Britain: a case-study*, Oxford: OUP, 1974, Ch. 6.
167. PRO FD1 4343.
168. The term is found first in relation to the manufacture of insulin in PRO FD1 944 (1922–4) E. Lilly: terms of licence; and second of penicillin in PRO FD1 6878 (Penicillin standardization 1943–4): Hartley to Mellanby (11 Aug. 1943).
169. Liebenau, 'The MRC and the pharmaceutical industry', in Austoker and Bryder, *Historical Perspectives*, p. 180.
170. PRO FD1 2520: Dale to F.H.K. Green (13 March 1933).
171. PRO FD1 922-7 (BDH); 930 (Boots); 919–20 (Burroughs Wellcome); 1456 (Glaxo).
172. Wright, 'The comparative analysis of industrial policies', 3–4; Hancher, *Regulating for Competition*, Ch. 3.
173. My interpretation matches the MacLeods's analysis of the impact of WWI on British industry in general. Using the optical industry as their example, they have argued that science and technology acquired a new prominence in British industry, and British science-based firms were obliged to expand, collabo-

rate, and eventually form part of a great national network as a direct result of the war. R. and K. MacLeod, 'War and economic development: government and the optical industry in Britain, 1914–8', in J.M. Winter (ed.), *War and Economic Development: essays in memory of David Joslin*, Cambridge: C.U.P., 1975, 165–203 (165–6).

174. RS CMB 28 and CMB 36.
175. RS CMB 36 (Nov. 1914), 4.
176. RS CMB 36: report (Dec. 1917).
177. RS CMB 28 (13 Oct. 1916), 2–3.
178. Ibid., minutes (23 Sept. 1915).
179. RS CMB 36 (23 Jan. 1918), 2.
180. RS CMB 28 (31 Jan. 1918), 3. For a study of the impact of the First World War on the profession of chemistry, see C.A. Russell, N.G. Coley and G.K. Roberts (eds.), *Chemists by Profession: the origins and rise of the Royal Institute of Chemistry*, Milton Keynes: Open University Press, 1977, Chs. 12, 13.
181. See R. MacLeod, 'Chemistry for King and Kaiser: revisiting chemical enterprise and the European war', in Travis et al., *Determinants in the Evolution of the European Chemical Industry*, pp. 25–49 (26).
182. Liebenau, 'The MRC and the pharmaceutical industry', in Austoker and Bryder, *Historical Perspectives*, pp. 165–6.
183. Ibid., pp. 169–70, quoting from FD1 1092,15.
184. M. Bliss, *The Discovery of Insulin*, Basingstoke: Macmillan, 1987; see also C. Sinding, 'Making the unit of insulin: standards, clinical work, and industry, 1920–1925', *Bulletin of the History of Medicine*, 2002, vol. 76, 231–70.
185. Liebenau, 'The MRC and the pharmaceutical industry', in Austoker and Bryder, *Historical Perspectives*, p. 168.
186. Ibid., p. 171.
187. Ibid., p. 174.
188. PRO FD1 930: letter to Boots (20 Dec. 1922).
189. PRO FD1 924: MRC to BDH (7 April 1923).
190. PRO FD1 930: Dale to Fletcher (15 March 1923).
191. Ibid., Mellanby to Boots (25 Jan. 1926); files FD1 2516/8. Boots were not alone in trying to take commercial advantage of their collaboration with the MRC. Liebenau has mentioned an episode of industrial spying at Burroughs Wellcome, in 'The MRC and the pharmaceutical industry', in Austoker and Bryder, *Historical Perspectives*, pp. 178–9.
192. PRO FD1 924: BDH to MRC (22 Dec. 1922).
193. PRO FD1 2255: (15 Feb. 1928).
194. PRO FD1 2258: memo (19 April 1934).
195. PRO FD1 2520: Green to Lewis (6 March 1933).
196. Bryder, 'Public health research and the MRC', in Austoker and Bryder , *Historical Perspectives*, pp. 59–83.
197. PRO FD1 2497.
198. M. Wilcox, 'Introduction', in A. Crookham et al., 'The Confederation of British Industry and Predecessor Archives', Coventry: Modern Records Centre Resources Booklet no. 7, 1997, p. 8.
199. Modern Records Centre [hereafter MRC] MSS.200/F/1/1/166: minutes of 1st meeting of the Industrial Research Committee, 17 Dec. 1942.
200. See lists in MRC MSS 200/F/3/T1/127 (e); replies in MSS 200/F/3/T1/127 (c).
201. Ibid.
202. MRC MSS 200/F/3/T1/80a.

203. 'Research in industry: a report of the FBI Committee', *Research and Industry*, 1943, vol. 62, 424–5; FBI, *Industry and Research: the full report of a two-day conference held at the Kingsway Hall*, London: Isaac Pitmona, 1946.
204. S. Horrocks, 'Enthusiasm constrained? British industrial R&D and the transition from war to peace, 1942–51', *Bus. His.*, 1999, vol. 41, 42–63.
205. See Axelrod, *The Evolution of Co-operation*, pp. 69, and 118–20.
206. Ibid., pp. 23, and 150–4.
207. Lorenz has shown that trust could operate both as a precondition, and as a consequence of co-operation, in 'Neither friends nor strangers', pp. 201–9.
208. On the importance of a stable environment for promoting co-operation, see Axelrod, *The Evolution of Co-operation*, pp. 128–9.
209. Swann, *Academic Scientists and the Pharmaceutical Industry*, Chs. 3, 4, 5.
210. According to Frances et al., networks are the most suitable term for models of informally organized coordination: 'Introduction', in Thompson et al., *Markets, Hierarchies, and Networks*, pp. 3, 14–6.
211. Describing the backwardness of the British and French pharmaceutical industries, see Liebenau, 'The rise of the British pharmaceutical industry', and Robson, 'The French pharmaceutical industry, 1919–39'.
212. And yet, according to Liebenau, not only was there little collaboration in Britain between academic scientists and pharmaceutical companies, but British pharmaceutical companies could not avoid competing amongst themselves: 'The twentieth-century British pharmaceutical industry in international context', in Liebenau et al., *Pill Peddlers*, p. 131, a statement which he has contradicted in another article: 'The British success with penicillin', *Social Studies of Science*, 1987, vol. 17, 69–86 (83). On co-operation between French scientists and industry, see Robson, 'The pharmaceutical industry in Britain and France', p. 345.

PART I: CONCLUSION

1. On the importance of clusters in the development of co-operation, see Axelrod, *The Evolution of Cooperation*, pp. 21, and 63–6.
2. Granovetter, 'The strength of weak ties'; idem, 'The strength of weak ties: a network theory revisited'.
3. M.-J. Nye, *Science in the Provinces: scientific communities and provincial leadership in France, 1860–1930*, Berkeley: University of California Press, 1986; R. Fox, 'Research, education, and the industrial economy in modern France', in *The Academic Research Enterprise within the Industrialized Nations: comparative perspectives*, pp. 95–107.
4. I. Inkster, 'Introduction: Aspects of the History of Science and Science Culture in Britain, 1780–1850 and beyond', in I. Inkster and J. Morrell (eds.), *Metropolis and Province: science in British culture, 1780–1850*, London: Hutchinson, 1983, pp. 11–55.
5. See Perkin's 'great arch', of which Britain is the keystone, in *The Third Revolution*, pp. 20–7.
6. Weindling, 'Scientific élites', in Cunningham and Williams, *The Laboratory Revolution in Medicine*, pp. 187–8.
7. J.A. Johnson, 'Hierarchy and creativity in chemistry, 1871 1914', *Osiris*, 2nd Series, 1984, vol. 5, 214–40 (239).

PART II

1. On the power of massive innovations to produce system shifts, see Picon, 'Towards a history of technological thought', in Fox, *Technological Change*, 37–49.
2. See A.I. Markus, 'From Ehrlich to Waksman: chemotherapy and the seamed web of the past', in E. Garber (ed.), *Beyond History of Science: essays in honor of Robert E. Scholfield*, Bethlehem, Penn.: Lehigh University Press, 1990, pp. 266–83.
3. T.I. Williams, *Howard Florey: penicillin and after*, Oxford: OUP, 1984, p. 123.

CHAPTER 3

1. For example: J. Jewkes, D. Sawers and B. Stillerman (eds.), *The Sources of Invention*, London: Macmillan, 2nd edn, 1969, pp. 31–32, 279–79. See also Liebenau, 'The British success with penicillin', *Soc. Stud. Sci.*, 1987, vol. 17, 69–86.
2. L. Bickel, *Rise up to Life: a biography of Howard Florey who made penicillin and gave it to the world*, London: Angus and Robertson, 1972, p. 170.
3. R. Bud, 'Penicillin and the new Elizabethans', *B.J.H.S.*, 1998, vol. 31, 305–33 (320).
4. D. Wilson, *Penicillin in Perspective*, London: Faber, 1976, pp. 3–4.
5. Bud, 'Penicillin and the new Elizabethans', 314–8.
6. D. J. McGraw, 'On leaving the mine: historiographic resource exhaustion in antibiotics history', *Dynamis*, 1991, vol. 11, 415–36.
7. Chen, 'The laboratory as business', in Cunningham and Williams, *The Laboratory Revolution in Medicine*, pp. 245–92.
8. Florey's papers at the Royal Society, Chain and Heatley's papers at the CMAC, Abraham's papers at the Bodleian Library, as well as MRC's files at the PRO. The TRC files have just been moved from Glaxo Wellcome (now GSK) to the CMAC, but have not yet been catalogued and are therefore inaccessible. The Dunn School's research grants journals were also used. Bodleian Library [hereafter BOD] PT 17/1–2.
9. Although many recent histories of penicillin have concentrated on debunking the myth of Fleming, few have examined in depth the myth surrounding the Oxford contribution. See M. Wainwright, *Miracle Cure: the story of penicillin and the golden age of antibiotics*, Oxford: Basil Blackwell, 1990, p. 77. On Florey's role, see his biographers: E.P. Abraham, 'Howard Walter Florey', *Bio. Mem. FRS*, 1971, vol. 17, 255–302; Bickel, *Rise up to Life*; G. Macfarlane, *Howard Florey: the making of a great scientist*, Oxford: O.U.P., 1979; Williams, *Howard Florey*; also V. Quirke, 'Howard Florey — medicine maker', *Chemistry in Britain*, 1998, vol. 34, 35–8. Kevin Brown has reassessed Fleming's role in the light of the more recent historical work on the Oxford group in *Penicillin Man: Alexander Fleming and the antibiotic revolution*, Thrupp, Gloucs.: Sutton Publishing Ltd., 2004, while Eric Lax has emphasized the importance of Norman Heatley in *The Mould in Dr Florey's Coat: the remarkable true story of the penicillin miracle*, London: Little, Brown, 2004. On Heatley, see also C.L. Moberg, 'Penicillin's forgotten man: Norman Heatley', *Science*, 16 Aug. 1991, vol. 253, 734–5.

10. See H.W. Florey, *Antibiotics: a survey of penicillin, streptomycin, and other antimicrobial substances from fungi, actinomyces, bacteria and plants*, Oxford: OUP., 1949, vols. 1 and 2. Also V. Quirke, 'Penicillin', *Encyclopedia of Life Sciences*, London: Nature Publishing Group, 2002, vol. 9, pp. 109–12.

11. E.A. Heaman, *St Mary's: the history of a London teaching hospital*, Montreal and Kingston: McGill-Queen's University Press, 2003. See also Brown, *Penicillin Man*, esp. Ch. 3.

12. The debate is summarized in Chen, 'The laboratory as business', in Cunningham and Williams, *The Laboratory Revolution in Medicine*, pp. 269–72.

13. Ibid., pp. 284–92.

14. A. Fleming, 'Recent advances in vaccine therapy', *British Medical Journal*, 1939, vol. 2, 99–115. As Ilana Löwy has justly observed, when Fleming's paper appeared in July 1939, he did not seem to have 'an inkling as to what the next important therapy for infectious diseases would be'. I. Löwy, 'Biotherapies of chronic diseases in the interwar period: From Witte's peptone to Penicillium extract', *Studies in History and Philosophy of Biology and Biomedical Sciences*, 2005, vol. 36.

15. R. Hare, 'New light on the history of penicillin', *Med. His.*, 1982, vol. 26, 1–24.

16. Ibid., 14–6.

17. R. Hare, *The Birth of Penicillin: and the disarming of microbes*, London: George Allen & Unwin, 1970, pp. 93–101.

18. Ibid., pp. 100–3.

19. Wainwright, *Miracle Cure*, pp. 38–48.

20. On the importance of the wartime context, see E.P. Abraham, 'Oxford, Howard Florey and World War Two', in C.L. Moberg and Z.A. Cohn (eds.), *Launching the Antibiotic Era: personal accounts of the discovery and use of the first antibiotics*, New York: Rockefeller University Press, 1990, pp. 19–30.

21. Chen, 'The laboratory as business', in Cunningham and Williams, *The Laboratory Revolution in Medicine*, pp. 274–84.

22. Williams, *Howard Florey*, p. 58.

23. Ibid., pp. 50–4.

24. Macfarlane, *Howard Florey*, p. 279.

25. CMAC Chain papers [hereafter PP/EBC] 9, B 16 (Nov. 1939).

26. BOD PT 17/1: pp. 44–52.

27. CMAC PP/EBC 9, B 15 (n.d.).

28. Macfarlane, *Howard Florey*, p. 279.

29. On the distinction between 'discovery' and 'invention', see T.S. Kuhn, *The Structure of Scientific Revolutions*, Chicago: Chicago University Press, 2nd edn, 1970, pp. 55–6, 66.

30. CMAC PP/EBC 9, B 15.

31. Bickel, *Rise up to Life*, p. 201.

32. Williams, *Howard Florey*, p. 83.

33. R.W. Clark, *The Life of Ernst Chain: penicillin and beyond*, London: Weidenfeld & Nicolson, 1985, p. 37.

34. Macfarlane, *Howard Florey*, p. 309.

35. Williams, *Howard Florey*, pp. 106–7.

36. 'Penicillin and modern research', *Lancet*, 1950, vol. 1, 76–7.

37. R. Cooter, 'Between playing fields and killing fields: the language and labour of teamwork in medicine, c. 1900–45' (unpublished conference paper, Skills Conference, Wellcome Institute for the History of Medicine, April 1996).

38. BOD PT 17/1-2. See also Bickel, *A Rise up to Life*, p. 48; J.B. Morrell, *Science at Oxford, 1914–1939: transforming an arts university*, Oxford: Clarendon Press, 1996, p. 204.
39. Williams, *Howard Florey*, p. 88.
40. Clark, *The Life of Ernst Chain*, p. 41.
41. RS Florey papers [hereafter 98HF]: Laboratory notebooks.
42. Wainwright, *Miracle Cure*, p. 78.
43. P. Galison, *How Experiments End*, Chicago: Chicago University Press, 1987, pp. 1–4.
44. CMAC PP/EBC, B 36: Nobel lecture.
45. Wainwright, *Miracle Cure*, pp. 102–5.
46. CMAC Heatley papers [hereafter GC/48], A V: 33. See also E.P. Abraham *et al.*, 'Further observations on penicillin', *Lancet*, 1941, vol. 2, 177–89.
47. CMAC GC/48, B4: Diary, 1 (30 Sept. 1939).
48. In interviews, Norman Heatley often pointed out that he did not get on so well with Chain as with Florey, who persuaded him to stay in Oxford by assuring him that he would be responsible to him, and not to Chain. 'Dr Norman Heatley, Hon DM', in interview with Max Blythe, Oxford 28 October 1987 (The Royal College of Physicians and Oxford Brookes University Medical Sciences Video Archive MSVA 029).
49. Norman Heatley, personal communication, 1996.
50. Williams, *Howard Florey*, p. 97.
51. CMAC GC/48, A V, 59.
52. Abraham et al., 'Further observations on penicillin', 178–80.
53. Florey et al., *Antibiotics*, vol. 1, Ch. 3.
54. E. Sidebottom, 'Norman Heatley: last survivor of the team that developed penicillin', obituary, *The Independent* (23 Jan. 2004), 22.
55. Williams, *Howard Florey*, p. 103.
56. Obituary, 'Sir Edward Abraham', *Times* (12 May 1999), 21.
57. A.L. Bacharach and B. A. Hems, 'Chemistry and manufacture of penicillin', in A. Fleming (ed.) *Penicillin: its practical* application, London: , 1946, pp. 24–45. See also D. Perlman, 'The evolution of penicillin manufacture', in A. E. Elder (ed.), *The history of penicillin production*, Chem. Eng. Series, 1970, vol. 66, 23–30. Bacharach, formerly of BW, and Hems, were both Glaxo scientists.
58. CMAC GC/48, A V: 107 (12 Dec. 1939).
59. Bickel, *Rise up to Life*, p. 50.
60. RSA 98HF 9 (2nd Folder): 25 May 1940. See also CMAC GC/48, A VI: 126–129 (25 May 1940)
61. RSA 98HF 9 (2nd Folder): 11 July 1940.
62. E.B. Chain et al., 'Penicillin as a chemotherapeutic agent', *Lancet*, 1940, vol. 2, 226.
63. 'Penicillin: an antiseptic of microbic origin', *BMJ*, 1941, vol. 2, 310.
64. RS 98HF 9 (2nd Folder): 'Leucocytes'.
65. Abraham et al., 'Further observations on penicillin', 181–3.
66. Ibid., 182.
67. RSA 98HF 9 (2nd Folder): 'Leucocytes'.
68. On drug safety regulation in Britain, see E.M. Tansey and L.A. Reynolds (eds.), 'The committee on safety of drugs', in *Wellcome Witnesses to Twentieth-Century Medicine*, London: Wellcome Trust, 1997, vol. 1, pp. 103–35.
69. Williams, *Howard Florey*, p. 105.
70. Williams, *Howard Florey*, p. 114.
71. CMAC GC/48, B4.

72. G.L. Hobby, *Penicillin: meeting the challenge*, Yale: Y.U.P., 1985, pp. 85, 125.
73. Quoted in Bickel, *Rise up to Life*, p. 102.
74. Williams, *Howard Florey*, p. 116.
75. B. Latour, 'Give me a laboratory and I will raise the world', in K. Knorr-Cetina and M. Mulkay (eds.), *Science Observed: perspectives on the social study of science*, London: Sage, 1983, pp. 141–70 (146–9).
76. Abraham et al., 'Further observations on penicillin', 186–7.
77. CMAC GC/48, B4: 8 May 1941.
78. Macfarlane, *Howard Florey*, p. 343.
79. CMAC GC/48, B4: 26 Feb. 1941.
80. Bickel, *Rise up to Life*, p. 118. These penicillin girls are named in BOD PT 17/1: account book for the Dunn School of Pathology (1939–1943), p. 144, and mentioned in a letter written by Florey to Herrald of the MRC (n.d.) asking for another 12 months of MRC funding, to pay for their salaries, for 'we can consider ourselves lucky to have kept them, as they could easily earn a great deal more in other jobs locally'.
81. CMAC GC/48, B4: 31 Dec. 1940.
82. CMAC PP/EBC 9, B 36.
83. G. Ferry, *Dorothy Hodgkin: a life*, London: Granta Books, 1998, Ch. 6.
84. RSA 98HF 9 (Ist Folder).
85. Ibid., Abraham, 'Purification and chemistry of the Penicillins' (March 1946).
86. Williams, *Howard Florey*, p. 117.
87. CMAC GC/48, B4: 21 May 1941.
88. Todd and Cornforth, 'Robert Robinson'.
89. CMAC GC/48, B4: 27 March 1941.
90. CMAC GC/48, B4: 10 April 1941.
91. Williams, *Howard Florey*, pp. 154–6.
92. CMAC GC/48, B4: 2 June 1941.
93. RSA HF9 (1st Folder): 'Penicillin Pyrogen Tests'.
94. CMAC GC/48, B4: 4 and 5 June 1941.
95. Liebenau, 'The British success with penicillin', 75.
96. Abraham et al., 'Further observations on penicillin', 188.
97. Bickel, *Rise up to Life*, p. 135. See also PRO FD11752 (1941).
98. W.K. Hancock and M.M. Gowing, *British War Economy*, London: H.M.S.O., 1949, pp. 224–47.
99. On the Tizard Mission to the USA, see R.W. Clark, *Tizard*, London: Methuen, 1965, Ch. 11.
100. A.P. Dobson, *US Wartime Aid to Britain, 1940–1946*, London: Croom Helm, 1986, p. 41.
101. CMAC GC/48, B4: 14 April 1941.
102. Merck & Co., Inc., Archives: 'Norman G. Heatley', interview conducted by J.L. Sturchio, Rockefeller University, 25 Oct. 1989, p. 6.
103. N. Heatley personal communication 1996; also 'N.G. Heatley', Blythe interview.
104. Hobby, *Penicillin*, Ch. 4.
105. Ibid., p. 94.
106. In fact, a few years earlier, like Rasitrick, he had correctly identified Fleming's mould as *P. notatum*. Ibid., p. 87.
107. Ibid., pp. 89–90, 177.
108. 'Norman G. Heatley', Sturchio interview, p. 7.
109. Hobby, *Penicillin*, p. 95.

110. Ibid., p. 99.
111. Ibid., Ch. 5.
112. Macfarlane, *Howard Florey*, p. 341.
113. Hobby, *Penicillin*, pp. 109–10.
114. Ibid., p. 175.
115. 'Norman G. Heatley', Sturchio interview, pp. 7–12.
116. Ibid.
117. Hobby, *Penicillin*, pp. 104–5.
118. Ibid., p. 94
119. 'Norman G. Heatley', Sturchio interview, p. 10.
120. Ibid., p. 12.
121. Hobby, *Penicillin*, p. 186.
122. Ibid., p. 109.
123. Hobby, p. 183.
124. Liebenau, 'The British success with penicillin', p. 129. At around the same time, the insulin network also was formalized, and the British Insulin Manufacturers (BIM) association was created. GlaxoSmithKline [hereafter GSK] SCS 669: Memo from A. Worlock to Chairman Bd WF Ltd (17 Sept. 1974).
125. R. Bud, *The Uses of Life: a history of biotechnology*, Cambridge: CUP, 1993, Ch. 5.
126. PRO FD1/5341, 677: letter re. ICI collaboration with MRC on antimalarials (22 July 1943).
127. See V. Quirke, 'War and change in the pharmaceutical industry', 68–70.
128. PRO FD1 6831, Penicillin production (1942) I: Florey to Carr (Chairman of the research panel of the TRC) 9 April 1942.
129. Ibid., (13 Oct. 1942).
130. Ibid., Florey to Mellanby (11 Dec. 1942).
131. Ibid.
132. Ibid., J.H. Burn Newsletter 25. Progress with deep fermentation was achieved despite the uncertainties and fears surrounding the process. See Hobby, *Penicillin: meeting the challenge*, Chs. 5 and 9.
133. PRO FD1 6831: letter from Dale to Mellanby (9 Dec. 1942).
134. ICI Penicillin reports [thereafter CPR] 4: 1 (14–26 Sept. 1942).
135. Bickel, *Rise up to Life*, p. 169.
136. Quoted in Clark, *The Life of Ernst Chain*, p. 78.
137. Ibid., p. 79.
138. PRO FD1 6831–4 (1942–4).
139. Ibid., 6835 (1943–51); also 7049 (1944–5): Penicillin Synthesis Committee minutes.
140. Ibid., 6837–42 (1943–57).
141. Ibid., 6878–9 (1943–6).
142. Ibid., 6831: Penicillin Production (1942), Mellanby to Moran, at the Ministry of Food (9 March 1942).
143. bid., Florey to Mellanby (11 Feb. 1942).
144. Ibid., Dale to Mellanby (29 June 1942).
145. Reader, *ICI*, vol. 2, pp. 286–27, 459.
146. PRO FD1 6832: ICP to Mellanby (18Feb. 1943).
147. Ibid., Letter from Kemball Bishop (25 March 1943).
148. Williams, *Howard Florey*, pp. 161–4.
149. Bickel, *Rise up to Life*, p. 197.
150. PRO FD1 6832, Penicillin Production II (1943): General Penicillin Committee (15 March 1943).

151. Ibid., Burn to Mellanby (4 June 1943). Also PRO FD1 6833: Penicillin Production III (1943–5), cable to Florey in Algiers (29 June 1943).
152. PRO FD1 6834: Penicillin Production IV-V (1944), Landsborough Thomson to Rickett (Ministry of Production), 5 Nov. 1943.
153. Williams, *Howard Florey*, p. 162.
154. Ibid., pp. 177–9. Obituary, 'Sir Ian Fraser', *Daily Telegraph* (13 May 1999), 33.
155. Bickel, *Rise up to Life*, p. 201.
156. Williams, *Howard Florey*, 181.
157. 'Penicillin in warfare', *Brit. J. Surgery*, 1944, vol. 32, 124.
158. See V. Quirke, 'Howard Florey- medicine maker', *Chem. in Britain*, 1998, vol. 34, 35–8.
159. PRO FD1 6834: Trevan to MRC (Nov. 1943).
160. PRO FD1 6832 : note for EM (June 1943).
161. Liebenau, 'The British success with penicillin', 77. However, Pfizer were producing much more – see Hobby.
162. Hobby, *Penicillin*, Ch. 9.
163. J.A. Hunt, 'Pioneering penicillin production in Britain', *Pharm. J.* (Dec. 21/28, 1991), 807–10.
164. Liebenau, 'The British success with penicillin', 79–81.
165. On penicillin distribution in America, see D. P. Adams, 'Wartime bureaucracy and penicillin allocation: the committee on Chemotherapeutics and other agents', *J. His. Med. All.Sci.*, 1989, vol. 44, 196–217.
166. P. Neushul, 'Fighting research: army participation in the clinical testing and mass production of penicillin during the Second World War', in Cooter *et al*, *War, Medicine and Modernity*, pp. 203–24. Neushul has shown that the changeover to deep fermentation was imposed on companies by the American government.
167. Gladys Hobby has also suggested that John Smith of Pfizer had personal reasons for persuading his company to switch over to deep fermentation. It was Patricia Malone, a two-year-old girl suffering from staphylococcal sepsis, who made a miraculous recovery after being given penicillin, whereas he had seen his own daughter die from a similar infection a few years earlier. Hobby, *Penicillin*, pp. 189–90.
168. Ibid, pp. 184–5.
169. J.L. Rodengen, *The Legend of Pfizer*, Fort Lauderdale: Write Stuff Syndicate, 1998.
170. PRO FD1 6834: Coghill, report (1944).
171. Ibid., Heilbron and Robinson mission to the USA and to Canada, VIII Chemotherapeutic Topics.
172. Hobby, *Penicillin*, pp. 191–5.
173. PRO FD1 6832: Burn to Mellanby (4 June 1943).
174. C. Ponting, *1940: myth and reality*, London: Hamish Hamilton, 1990; Barnett, *The Audit of War*.
175. Professor T.J. Mackie ran a penicillin production plant at the Bacteriology Department in Edinburgh. PRO FD1 6833: 28 Oct. 1943.
176. Liebenau, 'The British success with penicillin', 75.
177. J.G. Cook (Dyestuffs Division), 'Penicillin at Trafford Park', *ICI Magazine* (Nov. 1947).
178. ICI CPR 4: 1 (1942–6).
179. Ibid., Report (14–26 Sept. 1942).
180. Ibid., 1–27 Feb. 1943.
181. Ibid., dispatch records to Florey and to Robinson.

182. ICI CPR 4, 3: memo PSC/ M3R.
183. Ibid., minutes of the Steering Committee.
184. Ibid., research proposal, Calam (1 Oct. 1945).
185. ICI: G. Driver to P. Cunliffe (24 June 1986).
186. ICI CPR 4, 3: memo (8 Oct. 1945) signed P.H. Gregory and C.T. Calam.
187. PRO FD1 388. Reader, *ICI*, vol. 2, Ch. 24.
188. D.A. Hounshell and J.K. Smith, *Science and Corporate Strategy: Du Pont R&D, 1902–1980*, Cambridge: CUP, 1988, Ch. 10.
189. 'Fermentation Products Department' (Pharmaceutical Division, ICI ltd, Jan. 1972).
190. Davenport-Hines and Slinn, *Glaxo*, pp. 141–9.
191. Ibid. See also E. Jones, *The Business of Medicine*, London: Profile Books, 2001.
192. PRO FD1 6831: Heatley to Florey (16 Jan. 1942). Meyer refers to Karl Meyer of Columbia University.
193. PRO FD1 6831: Florey to Mellanby (11 Feb. 1942).
194. PRO FD1 6833: letter from Robinson (17 Oct. 1943).
195. Ibid., Mellanby to Richards (n. d.).
196. PRO FD1 6834: TRC to Robinson (3 Nov.1943).
197. PRO FD1 6838: Penicillin agreements with commercial firms, vol. II (1944), 19 Jan. 1944.
198. Ibid., Robinson to Mellanby (14 Feb. 1944).
199. PRO FD1 6835: Penicillin Synthesis Committe, Mellanby to Robinson (27 April 1944).
200. Ibid., report of conference between the TRC, ICI and Oxford workers (13 Oct. 1942).
201. Ibid., Robinson to Mellanby (30 March 1943).
202. Ibid., Mellanby to Robinson (30 March 1945).
203. H. T. Clarke, *The Chemistry of Penicillin*, Princeton:Princeton Universitiy Press, 1949.
204. The route to penicillin synthesis, which had defeated chemists since the war, was achieved in 1957 by John Sheehan after he had left Merck to work at MIT. J.C. Sheehan, *The Enchanted Ring: the untold story of penicillin*, Cambridge, Mass.: MIT Press, 1982. At almost the same time (1957–8), the isolation of the penicillin nucleus was realized by researchers in the Beecham Company labs, which had Chain as their consultant, and this led to a veritable patent war between the two labs. See also Lazell, *From Pills to Penicillin*.
205. CMAC PP/EBC, Box 9: B36, Nobel lecture. NB: penicillin was believed at first to have a bacteriostatic action, like the sulphonamides: Abraham et al , 'Further observations on penicillin', 180–2.
206. E.B. Chain, 'Thirty years of penicillin therapy', *Proc.R.S.L.*, B, 1971, vol. 179, 293.
207. N.E. Goldsworthy and H.W. Florey, 'Some properties of mucus with specific references to its antibacterial functions', *B. J. Ex. Path.*, 1930, vol. 11, 192–208.
208. Bickel, *Rise up to Life*, Ch 6.
209. Chain et al., 'Penicillin as a chemotherapeutic agent', 226–7.
210. Florey et al., *Antibiotics*, vol. 2, p. 637.
211. J. Goodman, 'Can it ever be pure science? Pharmaceuticals and the pharmaceutical industry and biomedical research in the twentieth-century', in Gaudillière and Löwy, *The Invisible Industrialist*, pp. 143–65.
212. For a long time, the mechanism of action of penicillin remained misunderstood. This study of penicillin action has continued until quite recently. See

R. Hakenbech, J.-V. Höltje and H. Labischinski (eds.), *The Target of Penicillin: the nurein sacculus of bacterial cell walls, architecture and growth,* Berlin: W. de Gruyter, 1983.

213. See V. Quirke, 'Penicillin and Post-War Reconstruction in Britain and France: science and industry in the balance', in *La Lettre de la Maison Française d'Oxford,* 1997, vol. 6, 87–98.
214. Williams, *Howard Florey,* pp. 348–9.
215. IP FUR B.1: Ernest Fourneau Correspondance France IP: Daniel Bovet à Ernest Fourneau 24 Oct. 1945.
216. BOD PT 17/2: Grant book 1940s–60s. The huge increase in the number and value of grants after the war can be seen by contrasting this with the earlier book, in PT 17/1.
217. Liebenau, 'British success with penicillin', 83.

CHAPTER 4

1. Marwick, *War and Social Change in the Twentieth Century,* pp. 151–83 (158). See also H.L. Smith (ed.), *War and Social Change: British society in the Second World War,* Manchester: Manchester University Press, 1986.
2. Marwick, *War and Social Change in the Twentieth Century,* Ch. 1, esp. p. 11.
3. D. Lindenberg, *Les Années souterraines (1937–1947),* Paris: La Découverte, 1990, Ch. 4.
4. Hecht, *The Radiance of France,* Introduction.
5. In the RPS May & Baker file, there are no communications between the two firms from May 1940 until March 1945.
6. R.O. Paxton, *Vichy France: Old Guard and New Order, 1940–1944,* New York: A.A. Knopf, 1972.
7. J.-P. Azéma and F. Bédarida (eds.), *La France des années noires,* Paris: Seuil, 1993.
8. J.-F. Picard, 'Aux origines de l'INSERM, l'Institut national d'hygiène et la recherche médicale', *Sciences Sociales et Santé,* 2003, vol. 21, 5–30. For an English version, see Picard, 'The Institut National d'Hygiène and Public Health in France', 1940 –1946' (http://picardp1.ivry.cnrs.fr/).
9. The important legacy left by the Vichy regime on French public heath and social policy is an aspect overlooked by Paxton, as noted by the historian Pierre Guillaume. P. Guillaume, *Le Rôle du médecin depuis deux siècles (1800–1945),* Paris: Assocation pour l'Histoire de la Sécurité sociale, 1996.
10. Picard, 'Aux origines de l'INSERM'; Chauveau, *L'Invention pharmaceutique,* Part 2, Chs. 1,2.
11. Hecht, *The Radiance of France,* Ch. 1.
12. On the impact of war on the pharmaceutical industry, see V. Quirke, 'War and change in the pharmaceutical industry'.
13. Chevassus-au-Louis, *Savants sous l'occupation,* pp. 18–19.
14. 'Nous n'aurions pas voulu laisser ignorer que si la notion d'antihistaminique a pris un essor considérable dans le monde, son origine est française et que son berceau fut le laboratoire de Fourneau à l'Institut Pasteur; que ses premiers pas furent guidés par Bovet, Mlle Staub, Halpern et leurs collaborateurs; que les premières réalisations pratiques sortirent des usines de la Société Rhône-Poulenc, aux périodes les plus dures de l'occupation allemande'. Delépine, 'Ernest Fourneau', 1–4.

15. IP CAReg 3, IV (20 Dec. 1940): members of the Conseil d'Administration of the Pasteur Institute who were in the Free Zone were unable to attend a meeting.
16. IP CAReg 3, IV: 10 March 1940.
17. Ibid., (29 April 1940).
18. Ibid., (23 Aug. 1940).
19. Ibid., (15 April 1940).
20. Ibid., (20 Dec. 1940).
21. Chevassus-au-Louis, *Savants sous l'Occupation*, p. 214.
22. J.-P. Azéma, 'Le Régime de Vichy', in Azéma and Bédarida, *Les Années noires*, pp. 151–79. On the continuity between the pre-war and Vichy periods, see R.F. Kuisel, *Capitalism and the State in France: renovation and exonomic management in the 20th* century, New York: Cambridge University Press, 1981.
23. IP CAReg 3, IV:16 Aug.1940.
24. Ibid., (31 Jan. 1941).
25. Ibid., (3 Jan. 1941).
26. 'Les conditions particulières de l'activité commerciale de l'IP subordonnent en grande partie le développement des ventes à l'éclat des travaux scientifiques'. IP CAReg 3, IV: 2 May 1941.
27. Ibid., (28 March 1941).
28. Ibid. In 1940, Pasteur Vallery-Radot contacted the Free French forces. Chevassus-au-Louis, *Savants sous l'occupation*, p. 211.
29. P. Weindling, *Epidemics and Genocide in Eastern Europe, 1890–1945*, Oxford: OUP, 2000, Ch.12.
30. 'Conformément à sa tradition humanitaire (...) l'IP est prêt à mettre à la disposition du gouvernement allemand tous sérums et vaccins. Les autres points seront soumis à la décision du gouvernement français'. IP CAReg 3, IV: 24 Oct. 1941.
31. Chevassus-au-Louis, *Savants sous l'occupation*, p. 211.
32. Ibid., (13 Feb.1942).
33. The balance was positive in 1941–2. IP CAReg 3, IV: 27 March 1942, 2 April 1943.
34. Ibid., Transfer: 31 Jan. 1941; promotion to 'chef de labo de 3e classe': 4 Dec. 1942; reorganisation of production in the diphtheria department: 12 Nov. 1943.
35. Ibid., (12 Nov. 1943).
36. IP CaReg 3,V (1944–50): 19 May 1944.
37. Ibid., (26 May 1944). It is not clear which army this was, although Giroud's anti-typhus vaccine had been sold to the Wehrmacht.
38. Ibid. (22 Sept. 1944). See also Chevassus-au-Louis, *Savants sous l'occupation*, pp. 212–3.
39. IP CaReg 3, V (1944–50): 29 Sept. 1944.
40. Chevassus-au-Louis, *Savants sous l'occupation*, Ch. 5, and pp. 216–9. See also V. Duclert, 'Les revues scientifiques: une histoire de la science et des savants français sous l'Occupation', *La Revue des Revues*, 1997, vol. 24, 161–95.
41. FR IP LCT.1 : 'Pétition à M. le ministre de l'Intérieur pour la libération de M. Ernest Fourneau' (17 Nov. 1944). Fourneau, in particular, thought of Jacques Tréfouël as an 'upstart', detested his wife Thérèse, and despised Pasteur Vallery-Radot whom he considered 'ineffective' and 'mediocre'. Chevassus-au-Louis, *Savants sous l'occupation*, pp. 220–2. To some extent, these opinions were shared by others, particularly Daniel and Filomena Bovet-Nitti. See IP FUR.B1: F. Bovet-Nitti à E. Fourneau, 19 April 1949.

42. P. Burrin, *Living with Defeat: France under the German Occupation, 1939–1945*, London: Arnold, 1995, Conclusion.

43. P. Buton, 'L'Etat restauré', in Azéma and Bédarida, *La France des années noires*, pp. 405–28. Imprisonment was frequently used to protect the accused from potential acts of vengeance. A third of those put in prison was released after a few weeks.

44. B. Sokoloff, *Penicillin: a dramatic story*, London: Allen & Unwin, 1946, p. 123.

45. RPS EF 9711: 'Annexe à la pétition à M. le Ministre de l'Intérieur pour la libération de M. Fourneau' (25 March1945).

46. O. Weiviorka, 'La Résistance', in Azéma and Bédarida, *La France des années noires*, pp. 65–90.

47. IP CAReg 3, V: 8 Dec. 1944.

48. For a study of the effect of war and occupation on another laboratory, that of Antoine Lacassagne, see B. Chamak, 'Un scientifique pendant l'occupation: le cas d'Antoine Lacassagne', *Revue d'Histoire des Sciences*, 2004, vol. 57, 101–33.

49. RPS EF 4: 24 March 1941.

50. 'Dans le domaine de la chimiothérapie antibactérienne, je crois que tout est à créer sur des bases nouvelles'. In ibid.

51. Cayez, *Rhône-Poulenc*, pp. 144–6.

52. See M. Margairaz and H. Rousso, 'Vichy, la guerre et les entreprises', *Histoire, Economie et Société*, 1992, vol. 3, 337–68; Cayez, 'Négocier et survivre: la stratégie de Rhône-Poulenc pendant la seconde guerre mondiale', in ibid., 479–92.

53. Chauveau, *L'Invention pharmaceutique*, Part Two, Ch. 2; idem, 'L'Etat français et l'industrie pharmaceutique: modernism, corporatisme, réquisitions', in O. Dard, J.-C. Daumas, and F. Marcot (eds.), *L'Occupation, l'état français et les entreprises*, Paris: Association pour le Développement de l'Histoire Economique, 2000, pp. 347–60.

54. Cayez, 'Négocier et survivre'. By contrast, see A. Lacroix-Riz, 'Les élites françaises et la collaboration économique: la banque, l'industrie, Vichy et le Reich', in *Revue d'Histoire de la Shoah* (Janvier-Avril 1997), 8–123.

55. 'Ainsi Rhône-Poulenc s'habituait à contenir les effets de la pression économique germanique, à négocier et à limiter les agressions commerciales réciproques. Les interlocuteurs du temps de paix et du temps de guerre furent les mêmes et les négociations qui débutèrent en 1940 furent, en une certaine mesure, la continuation de celles qui avaient eu lieu avant'. Cayez, 'Négocier et survivre', 481.

56. Ibid., 484.

57. RPS 10063: Ewins to Koetschet, 2 Dec. 1939.

58. 'Ces produits ont indubitablement un gros intérêt, mais comme ils sont nés en Angleterre, que les essais ont été jusqu'ici presque exclusivement effectués par des Anglais, en partie en liaison avec le Gouvernement, il nous paraîtrait indélicat et peu correct d'en parler dès maintenant à l'IG'. RPS IG Farben: 18 April 1941.

59. 'M. Bô, devant ce tableau, a demandé à M. Ter-Mer si son idée était que la France, comme les journaux le disent, se confine aux travaux des champs'. Ibid., 5 July 1941. Ter-Mer is probably a misspelling of Friedrich ter Meer (1884–1967), head of IG Farben's dyestuffs group and pharmaceuticals division. See P. Hayes, *Industry and Ideology: IG Farben in the Nazi era*, Cambridge: CUP, 1987.

60. RPS IG Farben: 13 March 1942.

61. Ibid., Bô to Horlein (30 Oct. 1943).
62. D. Pestre, 'From Revanche to Competition and Co-operation: physics research in Germany and France', *Society in the Mirror of Science: the Politics of Knowledge in Modern France* (unpublished conference paper, Berkeley, 30 September–1 October 1988).
63. A. Oliverio, 'Daniel Bovet, 1907–1992', *Bio. Mem. F.R.S.*, 1994, vol. 39, pp. 61–70.
64. A.-M. Staub, *Recherches sur quelques bases synthétiques antagonistes de l'histamine*, thèse de doctorat, Faculté des Sciences de Paris, 1939.
65. A.-M. Staub and D. Bovet, 'Action de la thymoxyéthyldiéthylamina (929 F) et des éthers phénoliques sur le choc anaphylactique du cobaye', *Comptes Rendus de Biologie*, 1937, vol. 125, 818.
66. RPS 9785: internal note (1 July 1935).
67. 'Candidat tout à fait intéressant -Malheureusement, comme le Bulgare du Laboratoire Schaeffer, c'est encore un Etranger et probablement un Juif'. Ibid., 3.
68. Chevassus-au-Louis, *Savants sous l'Occupation*, p. 16.
69. RPS 9785: Grillet to Halpern (31 Oct. 1935).
70. Ibid., 'La Médication Anti-histaminique' (discours présenté à la Faculté de Médecine de Paris le 24 janvier 1945), 2.
71. Ibid.
72. 'La théorie histaminique de l'allergie passe par les mêmes vicissitudes que la théorie des médications chimiques qui est aujourd'hui admise comme une certitude. Ce qui a permis au problème des médiateurs chimiques de faire une avance c'est que le physiologiste disposait de substances pharmacodynamiques antagonistes d'une grande spécificité: l'atropine pour l'acétylcholine, les sympatholitiques pour l'adrénaline. L'isolement des substances actives ayant rencontré les mêmes difficultés, on se basait sur cet antagonisme pour affirmer qu'il s'agit bien d'une action acétylcholinique ou adrénalinique. Il n'existait rien de semblable pour l'histamine jusqu'à la découverte des anti-histaminiques de synthèse'. Ibid., 10.
73. RPS 9785: biographical notice (15 Feb.1957).
74. Ibid.
75. R. Courrier, 'Allocution' (Académie de Paris, 20 March 1965), 43–52, in Institut Pasteur (IP) Rapkine; 'Hommages à Bernard Halpern, 1904–1978' (Paris: Association des Amis de Bernard Halpern, n.d.).
76. For this, Halpern would later help to defend the company chairman, Nicolas Grillet, against accusations of collaboration. AN F 12 9576. Dossier de la Commission Nationale interprofessionnelle d'épuration. Dossier Nicolas Grillet (1871–1947) 8 décembre 1945. Lettre de B. Halpern à N. Grillet.
77. B. N. Halpern, 'Les antihistaminiques de synthèse. Essais de chimiothérapie des états allergiques', *Archives Internationales de Pharmacodynamie et de Thérapie*, 1942, vol. 68, 339–408 (340).
78. RPS IG Farben: 13 March 1942.
79. Halpern had given a copy of his manuscript to March Tiffeneau, on a visit to Lyon for a conference. Tiffeneau then transmitted it to the editor of the Belgian journal, the *Archives Internationales*. However, it is unclear how the German authorities first came to hear of it: either Tiffeneau mentioned it to Fourneau, his brother-in-law, who may have said a word to his friends at the German Embassy, or else the files on Antergan prepared by Rhône-Poulenc for their visa application caught the attention of the authorities. Chevassus-au-Louis, *Savants sous l'Occupation*, pp. 16–9.

80. 'Les circonstances nous obligèrent à quitter notre laboratoire et à chercher refuge (afin d'échapper au massacre)'. RPS 9785: 'La médication anti-histaminique' (n.d.).

81. A description of Halpern's escape can be found in IP Fonds Rapkine: R. Courrier, 'Allocution' (Académie de Paris, 20 March 1965), 43–52, and in Chevassus-au-Louis, *Savants sous l'Occupation*, pp. 19–20.

82. On the attitude of the French population as a whole towards the Jewish community during the Second World War, see A. Cohen, *Persécutions et sauvetages: juifs et français sous l'occupation et sous Vichy*, Paris: Ed. du Cerf, 1993. See also F. Bédarida, 'La persécution des juifs', in Azéma and Bédarida, *La France des années noires*, pp. 129–58.

83. Courrier, 'Allocution'.

84. Halpern later defended Rhône-Poulenc's director, Nicolas Grillet, when he was accused of collaboration by the Comités d'Epuration. Archives Nationales (AN) F 12 9576. Rhône-Poulenc. Dossier de la Commission Nationale interprofessionnelle d'épuration. 13 mai 1949. I thank Sophie Chauveau for letting me have an extract of her notes.

85. RPS 9785: Rapport 4. Dr Sciclounoff, a Bulgarian national, who worked with Roch in Geneva.

86. 'La réputation de l'Antergan à Genève semble être bien assise. Souvent les médecins l'expérimentent sur les membres de leur propre famille. Le fait que le Professeur Bickel a mis la question de l'Antergan à l'ordre du jour du premier congrès de thérapeutique ([dont] le but [...] était de renseigner le corps médical suisse sur les progrès réalisés dernièrement dans le domaine de la thérapeutique), et qu'il a voulu lui-même traiter de cette question soulignent l'importance que l'on attribue dans les milieux médicaux de Genève à cette nouvelle médication.' (28 Oct. 1943).

87. Ibid., Rapport 9 (1 June 1944): 'l'opinion que nous avons pu créer a fait tache d'huile et a fini par gagner toute la Suisse.'

88. IP FUR.B1: D. Bovet à E. Fourneau, 18 Aug. 1943.

89. Oliviero, 'Daniel Bovet', p. 66. For more on this, see Chapter 5.

90. 'Mardi dernier a eu lieu à l'usine la réunion d'adieu à l'occasion du départ du Dr Savonnat qui prend sa retraite [...] Son départ coïncidait avec celui d'Halpern qui a quitté Lyon pour quelque pays étranger. Ce dernier sera riche de conséquences; en effet l'assistante d'Halpern, Melle Walthert, et M Fournel vont venir de Lyon à Paris, et amener avec eux tout le riche matériel de labo qu'il y avait transporté.' IP FUR.B1: D. Bovet à E. Fourneau, 31 Dec. 1942.

91. RPS 9785: Koetschet to Halpern (26 Sept. 1946).

92. 'Il nous semble que par la découverte des anti-histaminiques de synthèse nous abordons la chimiothérapie des états allergiques [...] Après les beaux succès de la sulfamidothérapie la chimie thérapeutique s'attaque à un nouveau groupe d'affections. Les possibilités de la chimiothérapie et nous terminerons sur ce credo, nous paraissent illimitées'. Ibid.

93. Ibid., Paul to Jacquinot, Directeur du CNRS (7 Dec. 1965). Halpern's biased presentation of events also appears to have upset Bovet and his wife Filomena. IP FUR.B1: F. Bovet-Nitti à E. Fourneau, 19 April 1949.

94. RPS 9785: Direction Générale to Halpern (12 July 1948).

95. Weatherall, *In Search of a Cure*, p. 192.

96. See RPS 9542: 29 Dec. 1948. After the war, Reilly became consultant for Rhône-Poulenc.

97. 'Il faut [...] décentraliser les recherches à la fois pour profiter des possibilités d'expérimentation offertes par la province et pour pouvoir multiplier les expériences qui peuvent ainsi être contrôlées; mais il faut se rendre compte

en même temps que si les médecins susceptibles de faire une expérimentation sont relativement nombreux, les bons expérimentateurs sont rares. La province a en outre un avantage sur Paris: c'est que les médecins ont généralement plus de temps disponible pour la recherche et, surtout, que les éléments de travail étant plus centralisés (par la moindre étendue de la ville), les chefs de service repassent volontiers dans leur service l'après-midi (ce qu'ils ne font pas à Paris) et travaillent plus facilement avec les laboratoires officiels des chaires de facultés; ils sont même parfois titulaires d'un de ces laboratoires en supplément de leur service hospitalier'. Ibid., 'Rapport sur les travaux effectués dans le laboratoire du Dr Reilly et sur l'intérêt des recherches pharmacologiques qui s'y rapportent'.

98. Ibid., 'Voyage à Montpellier et Perpignan' (14 Jan. 1941).
99. RPS 10448: A.L. Loubatières, 'Les Sulfamides Hypoglycémiants: historique et développements de la question de 1942 à 1952.' This work is mentioned in Bovet, *Une Chimie qui guérit*, pp. 287–8.
100. 'Nous avons fait récemment devant les médecins de l'hôpital cantonnal de Genève une causerie sur la pénicilline. Cette question est absolument passionnante et nous estimons que vos laboratoires devraient s'occuper activement, dès maintenant, de cette étude qui ouvre des perspectives insoupçonnées en chimiothérapie.' RPS 9785: 16 Dec. 1943, 3.
101. RPS 186, Pénicilline 1: R. P. au Ministre de la Santé Publique (7 Aug. 1945).
102. RPS EF 4: 24 March 1941.
103. RPS186, 1: 11 March 1945.
104. Jean Bernard, *La Pénicilline*, Paris: Corréa, 1947, pp. 32–3.
105. Raymond Paul personal communication, 1996.
106. 'Les allemands sont déjà sur la pénicilline et, d'une façon plus générale, sur les produits antibactériens produits par les champignons'. RPS 186, 1: 5 May 1943.
107. (30 Aug.1943).
108. (8 Sept. 1944).
109. Another version of the story, given by B. Sureau, according to whom André Lwoff had returned from a visit to England in 1936 with a sample of penicillin, and given it to Nitti who cultivated it until he heard about British progress with the drug on Radio Londres, can be found in D. Bovet, 'Le laboratoire de chimie thérapeutique de l'arsenic aux sulfamides', in Morange (ed.), *L'Institut Pasteur*, pp. 221–2.
110. RPS 186, 1: Dr Cosar: 'Débuts de la pénicilline à Vitry' (15 May 1944).
111. (20 Jan. 1944).
112. (18 Jan. 1945).
113. (May 1944).
114. (26 Jan. and Aug. 1944).
115. IP DirSer 49, Pénicilline 1: Direction des Poudres à J. Tréfouël (13 Feb. 1946); also article in *Samedi Soir* (14 Sept. 1945).
116. RPS 186, 2: 12 Sept. 1945.
117. P. Broch, J. Kerharo, J. Netick and J. Desbordes, *Une Expérience française de récupération de la pénicilline*, Paris: Vigot Frères, 1945, p. 9.
118. Catalogue, *Exposition de la pénicilline au Palais de la Découverte* (Dec. 1945–Jan. 1946), esp. 'Documentation française: de Pasteur à Fleming'. RPS 186, 2: Rhône-Poulenc exhibit (30 Oct. 1945).
119. Ibid., note (13 Aug. 1945).
120. IP DirSer 49, 2: Nitti to Tréfouël (19 Mar. 1945).
121. 'Celui-ci, après son évasion d'Espagne, avait réuni en Angleterre tous les éléments scientifiques et les plans de construction nécessaires à la réalisation de

ce but. Dès son retour en France, le Général Leclerc mit à sa disposition un petit détachement de sa division et les moyens matériels indispensable [pour un centre militaire de la pénicilline]. Grâce aux techniciens militaires de l'Institut Pasteur et de l'industrie privée [...] cette usine est maintenant prête à fonctionner'. (11 April 1945).

122. 'La fabrique de pénicilline la plus intelligente qui soit [...] (utilisant) des méthodes nouvelles et entièrement françaises... ils se débrouillent...'. (14 Sept. 1945).

123. 'Il a beau être calme et parler peu, trois Français lui ont fait perdre son flegme [...] C'est plus fort que le système des américains [...] Je n'avais jamais vu ça nullepart'.

124. Gaudillière, *Inventer la biomédecine*, pp. 46–60.

125. IP DirSer 49, 2: Nitti to Tréfouël (19 March 1945).

126. Ibid, 'rapport de la mission de la pénicilline en Grande Bretagne' (February 1945). This 'mission de la pénicilline', which lasted from 25 January to 6 February 1945, included Jacques Tréfouël, his wife Thérèse, and Marguerite Lwoff from the Pasteur Institute, as well the medical officers Pierre Broch and Yvon Dreyfus, and Israël Marszak.

127. RPS 186, 2: rapport du centre Cabanel (25 July 1945).

128. Ibid.

129. (30 Oct. 1945).

130. RPS 186, 1: lettre au Ministre de la Santé Publique (7 Aug. 1945).

131. IP DirSer 49, 1: note meeting (9 Feb. 1946), and letter Tréfouël to the Direction des Poudres (29 March 1946).

132. Gaudillière, *Inventer la biomédecine*, p. 60.

133. IP DirSer 49, 4: 14 Feb. 1945.

134. Picard, *La République des savants*, Chs. 3/4. Also D.T. Zallen, 'Le cycle Rapkine et la Mission Rapkine, le développement de la recherche médicale en France', *Sciences Sociales et Santé*, 1992, vol. 10, 11–23; D. Dosso, 'Louis Rapkine (1904–1948) et la mobilisation scientifique de la France libre', University of Paris VII Ph.D. thesis, 1998, pp. 369–78.

135. On this dual transfer, which also characterized physics, see D. Pestre, 'Les physiciens dans les sociétés occidentales de l'après-guerre: une mutation des pratiques techniques et des comportements sociaux et culturels', *Rev. His. Mod. Contemp.*, 1992, vol. 39, 56–72.

136. 'La production anglaise paraît à première vue dans le domaine chimique comme étant supérieure à la nôtre tant au point de vue de la qualité que de la quantité. Il est évident que la guerre y est pour une certaine part, cependant avant les hostilités, il semblait en être déjà ainsi. Ce fait est d'autant plus paradoxal que lorsqu'on séjourne un temps assez long dans un laboratoire comme je l'ai fait à Liverpool, les Anglais laissent l'impression d'être moins actifs que nous et paraissent quelquefois plus lents. L'une des raisons de base à cette contradiction semble réellement être leur esprit de co-opération'. ANC 800284, 58: rapport 139.

137. A.H. Cook, 'Ian Morris Heilbron', *Bio. Mem. FRS*, 1960, vol. 6, 65–75.

138. IP Dir RR03, Divers: Rapport de Mission Scientifique aux Etats Unis d'Israël Marzak (1944).

139. 'Pour nous, le secret de cette réussite réside non seulement dans la haute autorité scientifique du professeur Jones, Heilbron, Cook, directeurs d'équipe, mais aussi dans l'organisation patiente, ordonnée et méthodique. C'est avant tout la coordination des travaux, le fil directeur qui relie les recherches chimiques, physiques, physico-chimiques et biologiques. C'est l'organisation d'une équipe dont on ne demande pas aux membres d'être des génies, mais des tra-

vailleurs conscients, éclairés, c'est enfin l'organisation plus humble, mais non moins importante de la vie quotidienne du laboratoire [...] le même souci d'organisation permet à l'ICL de former une nouvelle génération de chercheurs qualifiés, disciplinés, enthousiastes'.

140. Thus beginning France's love-hate relationship with the United States. See R.F. Kuisel, *Seducing the French: the dilemma of Americanization*, Berkeley: University of California Press, 1993.
141. ANC 800284, 58: rapport 35.
142. '[...] malgré une organisation de la recherche scientifique peu différente de celle de la France [...] Il est pourtant intéressant de souligner les relations étroites qui existent aux Etats-Unis entre les universités et l'industrie. Ces relations, comme on me l'a indiqué à plusieurs reprises, se sont montrées très avantageuses aussi bien pour l'élargissement du domaine de la recherche scientifique que pour le développement de l'industrie'. Rapport 153.
143. IP DirSer 49, 1: 'Création par décret de l'Office National Industriel des Produits Biochimiques' (1946).
144. IP DirSer 49, CNRS (1945–6): 'Compte Rendu d'une réunion du Comité Scientifique des Antibiotiques' (26 July 1946).
145. IP DirSer 49: J. Tréfouël à la Direction des Poudres (29 March 1946).
146. Pestre, 'From revanche to competition and co-operation'.
147. When the Mission Scientifique was disbanded in November 1945, it was replaced by a Bureau Scientifique attached to the French Embassy in London. ANC 800284,183: note (6 Dec. 1946).
148. See I.M. Wall, *The U.S. and the Making of Postwar France, 1945–54*, Cambridge: CUP, 1991.
149. Picard, *La République des savants*, Chs. 4/5/6. See also Guerlac, 'Science and French national strength', in Earle, *Modern France*, pp. 81–105.
150. D. Pace, 'Atomic energy and the ideology of science in post-war France', *French Science since 1945*, 38–61 (61); S.R. Weart, *Scientists in Power*, Cambridge, Mass.: Harvard University Press, 1979, p. 270.

PART II: CONCLUSION

1. Marwick, *War and Social Change*, pp. 11–3, 64–72.
2. Ibid., p. 68. According to Marwick, war's ability to test social structures includes the testing of 'human reluctance to exploit the full potential of science and technology'.
3. Ibid., pp. 195, 202–5.
4. Gaudillière, *Inventer la biomédecine*, Introduction.
5. Edgerton, *Science, Technology and the British Industrial 'Decline'*, Conclusion.
6. Guerlac, 'Science and French national strength', in Earle, *Modern France*, pp. 81–105.
7. See Mulholland, 'Introduction', *French Science since 1945*, 1–5.
8. Bud, 'The new Elizabethans'.

PART III

1. On the contrast between static structures and axes of change, see J. Agar, 'The new price and place of University research: Jodrell Bank, NIRNS and

the context of post-war British academic science', *Contemp. Brit. His.*, 1997, vol. 11, 1–30 (2).
2. See Bud, 'Penicillin and the new Elizabethans'. Also, Quirke, 'Penicillin and post-war reconstruction in Britain and France'; Jacq, 'Science and industry in post World War II France'; Pestre, 'The moral and political economy of French physicists in the first half of the XXth century'.
3. Pace, 'Atomic energy and the ideology of science in post-war France', p. 61.

CHAPTER 5

1. I have borrowed the title from Pace, 'Atomic energy and the ideology of science', p. 61.
2. Picard, *La République des savants*, Ch. 4.
3. RPS EF 9711: 17 June 1945.
4. (27 Dec. 1945).
5. (25 Mar. 1947).
6. (27 March 1947) and (10 Sept. 1948). J.-P. Fourneau worked for Houdé after leaving his father's laboratory, but Ernest was concerned that he would find it impossible to do research there. About Julia, see Igolen, 'Presque un siècle de synthèse organique à l'Institut Pasteur', 50–67.
7. RPS EF 9711: 4 July and 8 Dec. 1946.
8. 'J'aurai été le prétexte à la création d'un centre nouveau et original [...(et qui)] sera le couronnement de ma carrière'. (8 Dec.1946).
9. (4 July 1946).
10. 'il me faut des gens très bien élevés, d'un physique agréable, susceptibles de remplir n'importe quelle mission'. (21 Jan. 1947).
11. 'Je ne suis pas encore sûr qu'il n'y ait pas eu dans cette création surtout un touchant sentiment de reconnaissance pour ma longue et fidèle collaboration'. (n.d., probably between June and October 1948).
12. RPS DB: Début à ... (12 Feb. 1948).
13. 'Notre labo de Rome est tout plein de vous, de votre enseignement, et nous l'espérons de votre esprit de recherches'. IP FUR.B1: D. Bovet à E. Fourneau (2 June 1948).
14. '[...] ce sera une excellente chose pour M. Funke, car il aura chez vous une situation qu'il pourrait difficilement obtenir sans doute dans le cadre de l'Institut Pasteur. Vous en tirerez d'ailleurs un bénéfice certain, car vous connaissez mieux que personne ses qualités d'organicien, et celles de Mlle Benoît (je veux dire Mme Funke). Ils ont beaucoup d'admiration pour vous, et cela constituera certainement une bonne équipe à Rome'. 'En Cours...' (1 June 1960).
15. IP FUR.B1: F. B-N. to EF (26 Sept. 1947).
16. 'Mais il s'agit de vivre : et nous ne pourrons pas jouer éternellement les universitaires quoique cela nous paraisse plein de charmes pour le moment. Il y a aussi la question des recherches elles mêmes, quoique [...] les moyens matériels de M Marotta soient immenses'. Ibid.
17. RPS 4147: 'Daniel Bovet' (5 Nov. 1973).
18. See correspondence in AIP FUR.B1, especially between Filomena Bovet-Nitti and Ernest Fourneau.
19. AIP CAReg 3, V: 5 Dec.1947. Ten years later, the rapid expansion of the French economy also threatened the financial balance of the IP: AIP CAReg 4, VI: 23 May 1958.
20. Ibid., (4 June 1948).

21. AIP CAReg 4, VI: 18 Feb. 1956/14 June 1957.
22. 'la période des réformes profondes de transformation est maintenant ouverte'. AIP CAReg 3, V: 13 Feb. 1948. G. Martin was responsible for the accounts.
23. Ibid., (19 Oct. 1951).
24. AIP CAReg 4, VI: Ass., 13 June 1952/11 May 1953/ 23 May 1958.
25. Ibid., (8 Oct. 1948). Also 31 Jan. 1958. Between 1954 and 57, salaries increased by 40% to keep up with the public sector.
26. '[...] ce qu'il convient d'attendre de l'IP pour l'avenir, au sujet des travaux sur les moyens de combattre et prévenir les maladies infectieuses, est particuliè-rement l'étude des antibiotiques d'origine naturelle et les recherches sur les virus'. Ibid., (Ass., 11 May 1953).
27. AIP CAReg 4, VII: 17 Dec. 1959 and 9 June 1960.
28. RPS 10598: Noël Rist (1951–68). For more on this project, see J.-P. Gaudi-llière, 'Screening and copying: tuberculosis chemotherapy after 1945', paper presented at the conference on 'Perspectives on 20th-century Pharmaceuti-cals' (St Anne's, Oxford, 14–16 July 2005).
29. IP CAReg 3, V: 27 May 1949.
30. See IP CAReg 4, VI: Ass., 22 June 1956. Prévot had worked on penicillin dur-ing the war, and developed an assay method that was quicker than Heatley's and was used by Rhône-Poulenc at least until 1947. RPS 10285: Rhône-Pou-Lenc to Merck (18 April 1947). A.R. Prévot, 'A rapid Method for the titration of penicillin', in J. Hamburger (ed.), Medical Research in France during the War (1939–1945), Paris: Flammarion, 1947, pp. 231–33.
31. Picard, *La République des savants*, p. 105–7.
32. 'Le CNRS entraîne pour l'Institut Pasteur des dépenses plus qu'il ne lui apporte un appui'. IP CAReg 3, V: 14 Oct. 1949. The quote is by M. Jolly.
33. The directors of the INH and of the Pasteur Institute, Bugnard and Tréfouël respectively, were asked to speak on behalf of the biological and medical sciences on the Conseil supérieur de la recherche et du progrès technique (CSRPT) created by Pierre Mendès France in 1954 to help prepare the 3rd Plan. Gaudillière, *Inventer la biomédecine*, pp. 93–4.
34. J.-F. Picard, 'Poussée scientifique ou demande de médecins? La recherche médicale en France de l'Institut national d'hygiène à l'INSERM', *Sciences Sociales et Santé*, 1992, vol. 10, 47–106 (68) ; idem, 'Aux origines de l'IN-SERM, l'Institut national d'hygiène et la recherche médicale', *Sciences Socia-les et Santé*, 2003, vol. 21, 5–30.
35. AIP, fonds Monod [thereafter MON]: 'Jacques Monod et le redressement de l'Institut Pasteur, 1971–1976' (anon., May 1976).
36. The Pasteur Institute/CNRS/INH trio became central to the state-sponsored biomedical complex in France, Gaudillière, *Inventer la biomédecine*, p. 111.
37. On the history of the plans, see for instance P. Massé, *Aléas et progrès. Entre Candide et Cassandre*, Paris: Economica, 1984, or Henri Rousso (ed.), *De Monnet à Massé: enjeux politiques et objectifs économiques dans le cadre des quatre premiers Plans (1946–1965)*, Paris : Editions du CNRS, 1986.
38. See IP DirSan.
39. Picard, La République des savants, pp. 147.
40. IP CAReg 4, VI: 17 Dec. 1954.
41. IP CAReg 4, VI: 30 Apr. 1954. See also Blondeau, *Histoire des laboratoires pharmaceutiques*, pp. 213–25 (222).
42. 'En raison de sa qualité d'Etablissement reconnu d'utilité publique, [il] ne doit pas accumuler les bénéfices'. IP CAReg 4, VII: 29 Mar. 1960.
43. Picard, *La République des savants*, Ch. 6.

44. 'En conséquence [du fonds particulier à la recherche scientifique créé à l'issue du décret du 14 Mars 1957] le Conseil estime à l'unanimité que l'IP, en raison de la qualité de ses recherches, de la place qu'il occupe dans la recherche scientifique française, de son apport au rayonnement culturel du pays, qui ne sont discutés par personne, ne peut être exclu du bénéfice moral et matériel du fond créé par le Gouvernement pour encourager et récompenser les travaux et recherches scientifiques qui concourent à l'avancement de la science'. AIP CAReg 4, VII: 23 May 1958.
45. Ibid., (7 Nov./ 19 Dec.1963).
46. It would also solve other problems, created by the reform of the Sécurité Sociale. The IP found itself falling into neither one category (that of producer of medicines), nor another (that of research establishment), or rather into both, which made it very difficult to fill in the forms sent by the Service Central de la Pharmacie. See IP DirSan: Tréfouël to Volkringer (9 Dec. 1963).
47. Ibid.
48. AIP CAReg 4, VII: 25 May 1961.
49. Gaudillière, *Inventer la biomédecine*; Hecht, *The Radiance of France*, Ch. 1.
50. X. Polanco, 'La mise en place d'un réseau scientifique: les rôles du CNRS et de la DGRST dans l'institutionalisation de la biologie moléculaire en France (1960–1970)', *Cah. His CNRS*, 1990, vol. 7, 49–90.
51. Ibid., 53–54. Also: AIP Interview with Elie Wollman (31 May 1999).
52. See Picard, *La République des savants*, Ch. 7.
53. AIP: 'Projet de réorganisation de l'Institut Pasteur' (1964–1965).
54. Polanco, 'La mise en place d'un réseau scientifique', note 14, 54.
55. See Lwoff, 'Jacques Lucien Monod', in A. Lwoff and A. Ullmann (eds.), *Origins of Molecular Biology: a tribute to Jacques Monod*, New York: Academic Press, 1979, pp. 1–23.
56. IP MON: 'Jacques Monod et le redressement de l'Institut Pasteur, 1971–1976' (anon., May 1976).
57. See IP CAReg 4, VI: Ass., 11 May 1953.
58. 'La vocation fondamentale de l'IP: le progrès des sciences biologiques au service de l'homme'. IP MON : 'Institut Pasteur: Esquisse d'une politique de développement scientifique à moyen terme (1976–1980)' (n.d., probably 1975).
59. Gaudillière, *Inventer la biomédecine*, pp. 294–304.
60. IP MON : 'Institut Pasteur : Esquisse'.
61. Igolen, 'Presque un siècle de synthèse organique à l'Institut Pasteur', 50–67. In the 1950s, Rhône-Poulenc established individual contacts with a small number of pasteurian scientists, in particular Jean Jacob, Director of the physiological laboratory. See RPS 9903.
62. IP MON: 'Institut Pasteur: Esquisse', 7.
63. See Weatherall, *In Search of a Cure*, p. 55; 'The Lister Institute of Preventive Medicine', *Lancet*, 1975, vol. 1, 54.
64. Chauveau, *L'Invention pharmaceutique*, Chs. 3–5.
65. L. G. Thomas, 'Implicit industrial policy'; Quirke, 'War and change in the pharmaceutical industry'. See also A.D. Chandler, *Shaping the Industrial century*.
66. Chauveau, *L'Invention pharmaceutique*.
67. Cayez, *Rhône-Poulenc*, p. 154.
68. Chauveau, *L'Invention pharmaceutique*, p. 314.
69. AIP DirSan: 23 Jan. 1964. Also L. Roche, J. Sabatini and R. Serange-Fonterme, *L'Economie de la santé*, Paris: PUF, 1982, pp. 34–53.

70. Cayez, *Rhône-Poulenc*, table p.162.
71. Ibid., pp. 172–3.
72. IP DirSan: 24 June 1964.
73. M.J . Marteret, 'Le Centre de Recherche Nicolas Grillet de la Societé Rhône-Poulenc', *L'Industrie Nationale*, 1956, no. 3, 36–45.
74. See for example M. Cassier, 'Brevets pharmaceutiques et santé publique en France'.
75. Cayez, *Rhône-Poulenc*, pp. 174–6.
76. Chauveau, *L'Invention pharmaceutique*, p. 315.
77. 'En ce qui concerne notre point de vue, à nous européens, je suis revenu pleinement optimiste et convaincu qu'il nous reste beaucoup de place dans le domaine des recherches. Toute question politique mise à part, les américains se précipitent tête baissée sur la voie d'un capitalisme gigantesque qui laisse de moins en moins de place à notre individualisme, à la personne et au génie latin'. RPS DB: Début à ... (11 Nov.1947).
78. 'Daniel trouve les Etats-Unis un pays affreux, et les américains des gens polarisés sur les antibiotiques et les antihistaminiques dans le but principal de gagner beaucoup d'argent. Il m'écrit qu'il nous reste un monde à découvrir, auxquels ils ne songent pas'. Ibid., (1 Oct.1947).
79. IP FUR. B1: F. B-N. à EF (26 Sept. 1947).
80. 'Quoique je déteste ce pays et qu'il soit particulièrement triste en ce moment, nos collègues y sont charmants, jeunes et bons camarades, ayant acceuilli dans leurs labos avec tous les droits et tous les honneurs, des savants allemands échappés de l'Allemagne nazie. Cette coopération paraît avoir porté des fruits royaux: ainsi nous avons beaucoup vu Feldberg, Vogt, Schild, qui nous ont paru beaucoup plus pharmacologues qu'allemands. Je n'aime guère Oxford, le collège où nous étions sordide et cette atmosphère résolument réactionnaire d'une noblesse toute fondée sur l'argent me paraît irrespirable. Il n'en est pas ainsi dans nos pays, où nos peuples intelligents ne subissent la domination matérielle qu'accompagnée d'une certaine supériorité spirituelle et culturelle'. IP FUR.B1: F. B-N. à EF (19/8/47).
81. The year in which these letters ere written, i.e. 1947, revealed the fractures that were opening up with the onset of the Cold War. Wall, *The United States and the Making of Postwar France*, p. 63. On the convergence between scientific and political agendas that took place on both sides of the Atlantic, see also J. Krige, *American Hegemony and the Postwar Reconstruction of Science in Europe*, Cambridge, Mass.: MIT Press, 2006, Ch. 5.
82. Ibid., pp. 113–26; Kuisel, *Seducing the French*, Ch. 1.
83. Wall has described the successive strategies adopted by French politicians to deal with the challenges of the postwar period: first of all, the quest for American economic aid, the ensuing struggle for French independence, finally achieved through Europe. Wall, *The United States and the Making of Postwar France*, pp. 113–26. See also Monnet, *Memoirs*, esp. Ch. 10.
84. See J. Bouvier, 'Le Plan Monnet et l'Economie Française, 1947–1952' (EUI working paper 83, Badia Fiesola, Italy, Jan. 1984). Also: P. Mioche, *Le Plan Monnet: genèse et élaboration, 1941–1947*, Paris: Editions de la Sorbonne, 1987; H. Rousso (ed.), *De Monnet à Massé*.
85. Gaudillière, Inventer la biomédecine.
86. These drugs are listed in F. Gambrelle, *Innovating for Life: Rhône-Poulenc, 1895–1995*, Paris: Albin Michel, 1995, pp. 34–5. L. Pasteur Vallery-Radot (ed.), *Les Acquisitions médicales récentes*, Paris: Flammarion, 1951, illustrates the role played by drugs such as penicillin, synthetic anti-histamines, and neuroleptics in the adoption of a scientific approach in medicine.

87. S. Massat-Bourrat has followed the trajectory of these substances in her Ph.D. thesis. S. Massat-Bourrat, 'Des phénothiazines à la chlorpromazine: les destinées multiples d'un colorant sans couleur', thèse de doctorat, Université Louis Pasteur, Strasbourg, 2004.

88. J. P. Swazey, *Chlorpromazine in Psychiatry: a study of therapeutic innovation*, Cambridge, Mass.: MIT Press, 1974, pp. 23–33.

89. P. Viaud, 'Les amines dérivées de la phénothiazine', *Journal de Pharmacie et Pharmacologie*, 1954, vol. 6, 361–89. The Americans' results were published in 1944, but did not reach the French team in time. H. Gilmann and D. A. Shirley, 'Some derivatives of phenothiazine', *Am. J. Chem. Soc.*, 1944, vol. 66, 888–93.

90. Swazey, *Chlorpromazine in Psychiatry*, p. 91.

91. H. Etkowitz and L. Leydersdorff, 'The endless transition: a 'triple helix' of university-industry-government relations', *Minerva*, 1998, vol. 36, 203–8.

92. Gaudillière, *Inventer la biomédecine*, 'Introduction'.

93. With respect to the CNRS, a joint effort at open collaboration with Rhône-Poulenc in 1975 led to furore in the press and to political intervention, and it was therefore abandoned. F. Guinot, 'Chimie d'hier, chimie de demain', unpublished paper, 14/09/06. With respect to INSERM, an attempt to remedy this situation did not occur until the 1980s, which heralded a new era of more open collaborations. INSERM, 'La valorisation sociale de la recherche médicale et en santé': rapport d'un groupe de réflexion (Jan. 1984).

94. Thomas has argued that, compared with Britain, France was handicapped by an over-reliance on government research laboratories, by the persisting fragmentation of the pharmaceutical industry, and by ill-suited government policies. Thomas 'Implicit industrial policy'. See also Chauveau, *L'Invention pharmaceutique*, Parts 2 and 3; Gaudillière, *Inventer la biomédecine*.

95. RPS 9467.

96. 'Avantages et inconvénients du système actuel (ou plutôt de l'absence de système):
a) *avantages*: souplesse, variété des formules. (A conserver autant que possible dans tout système que nous pourrons adopter).
b) *inconvénients*: D'abord semi-clandestinité qui entraîne des difficultés matérielles d'indemnisation et certains aspects moralement désagréables, tels que faux bruits ou suspicions diverses, concernant l'activité de certains grands laboratoires français.
Ensuite, définitions insuffisantes laissant souvent les parties en présence sous l'impression qu'elles sont toutes deux lésées. (Parfois, en outre, du côté Universitaire, une sous-estimation initiale et une sur-estimation du service rendu). Enfin, détournement de certains laboratoires de leurs tâches essentielles. RPS 9467: réunion du 3 mars 1955.

97. ANF 1715: Commission de la Recherche Pharmaceutique.

98. ANF 1715 : Commission de la Recherche Pharmaceutique. 'Note relatives aux modalités possibles d'articulation entre l'industrie, l'université et les organismes publics de recherche' (10 March 1971). To remedy what was seen as the poor relations between academia and industry in France, the creation of a National Institute for Pharmaceutical Research, which would be the equivalent of INSERM, was contemplated. However, this was firmly opposed by representatives of the pharmaceutical industry, including Raymond Paul.

99. RPS 9467: 'La recherche sous contrat en Allemagne' (n.d.).

100. RPS 10063: note MM. Paul and Koetschet (16–26 June 1945).

101. '1 – à s'assurer les bonnes grâces du Gouvernement et des personnalités universitaires

2 – indirectement, à améliorer la qualité de son recrutement en favorisant l'éducation chimique

3 – à s'assurer, dans les Centres de recherches, des relations lui permettant le cas échéant, de demander certains services'. RPS 10063: note MM. Paul et Koetschet (16–26 June 1945).

102. Ibid., 'Visite à la Société May & Baker' (2 Nov. 1945).
103. RPS 9142: 'Visite du Dr Broom a Vitry le 9 février 1950', note de M. Koetschet (11 Feb. 1950).
104. RPS 9811: note de la Direction de la Production à la Direction Scientifique (n.d., but probably late 1949– early 1950).
105. Ibid., 'I.C.I.– visite du Dr Freeth et du Dr Winter', note de R. Paul (26 Sept. 1950). Dr Winter was the controller of research for the entire group.
106. 'A) il décide de l'avancement des Chimistes dans les Services de recherches, sur propositions des Directeurs de ces services.

B) il a pour mission d'établir des relations 'd'amitié' entre l'I.C.I. et les savants anglais. Il s'occupe également de créer de telles relations avec les savants étrangers. Pour la France, par exemple, il estime qu'il ne connaît pas assez les milieux scientifiques. Il y a quelques temps, il a fait venir Champetier plusieurs jours en Angleterre et l'a mis en contact avec les Services de recherches de 'Plastics Division' où celui-ci a été fort apprécié. C'est pour cette raison qu'il m'a demande de lui m'engager une entrevue hier après-midi avec Champetier.

C) Enfin, le Dr Freeth a également dans ses attributions les 'Fellowships' de l'I.C.I. qui, tous les ans, sont attribués au nombre d'une centaine environ. RPS 9811: note de R. Paul, 'ICI – visite du Dr Freeth et du Dr Winter' (26 Sept., 1950).

107. 'Cette façon de faire, extrêmement libérale comme on le voit, est paraît-il fort appréciée des universitaires'. Ibid.
108. RPS 10285: French translation of contract (13 Jan. 1948). Roy Vagelos, former president of Merck, seems to have been unaware of the existence such contracts when he wrote of Merck's 'Not-Invented-Here' mentality. R. Vagelos, *Medicine, Science and Merck*, Cambridge and New York: CUP, 2004, p. 131.
109. RPS 10285: 'Visite des Drs Major et Molitor' (20 May 1948).
110. Ibid., 'Entretien avec Mr Georges de Merck, du 13 Mai 1949'.
111. Direction des Recherches, Rhône-Poulenc Santé, *Rhône-Poulenc 40 years of research in the field of health care*, Besançon: Direction Information of Rhône-Poulenc, 1982, pp. 15–7.
112. RPS 10285: 'Essais cliniques de nos produits chez Merck' (23 Dec. 1949).
113. R.T. Major, 'Cooperation of science and industry in the development of the antibiotics', *Chem. and Eng. News*, 25 Oct. 1948, vol. 26, 3186–91.
114. RPS 186 bis; 10685; Fournier ; 10292.
115. RPS 10685; 'Dépenses de recherche pharmaceutique des grands concurrents pour 1970 – en millions de francs' (note du 27 mars 1972). NB: Roussel-Uclaf, which by then had merged with SIFA, were behind the group Rhône-Poulenc, which included SUCRP + Spécia + Théraplix + R. Bellon + Mérieux + May & Baker + A.E.C. + Poulenc ltd., but ahead of SUCRP + Spécia + Théraplix.
116. RPS 9550. He had trained with Emile Blaise, the first Scientific Director of the group after the amalgamation. Interestingly, Delépine's dual occupation, as Professor at the Collège de France and as Director of Research for a pharmaceutical company, was not mentioned in his 'notice nécrologique', *Annales pharm. franç*, 1965, vol. 23, 61–2.

117. RPS 10014: E. Lederer (1950–65). After 1965, the files came under the name 'Gif-sur-Yvette'. E. Lederer, 'La chimie des substances naturelles', *Cah. His. CNRS*, 1989, vol. 2, 43–54.
118. M. Le Roux, 'Genèse des textes de Pierre Potier, chimiste des substances naturelles', *Genesis*, 2003, vol. 20, 91–125; V. Walsh and M. Le Roux, 'Contingency in innovation and the role of national systems: taxol and taxotère in the USA and France', *Res. Policy*, 2004, vol. 33, 1307–27; M. Le Roux, 'Between academy and industry: the story of an unusual CNRS laboratory: the ICSN, 1960–2000', 5th International Congress on the History of Chemistry, Lisbon, Sept. 2005 (http://5ichc-portugal.ulusofona.pt/paperslist.asp); M. Le Roux, 'Hommage à Pierre Potier (1934–2006)', *Bulletin de L'Association des Anciens Amis du CNRS*, 2006, vol. 41, 5–27.
119. *Le Figaro*, 3 Oct. 1961.
120. RPS 10320.
121. 'Je sais combien vous avez payé de retour sa bienveillance et quelle aide vous apportiez à ses élèves et à ses travaux; je sais, puisque j'en bénéficie largement, combien cette aide est précieuse pour les universitaires'. RPS 9569: 1 Jan. 1959.
122. 'Nous ne voulons pas prendre parti dans cette affaire, car nous trouvons anormal que l'Industrie se substitue à l'Etat pour l'entretien de ses établissements. Nous devons dire, cependant, que si vous décidiez de donner satisfaction à M. Julia, il lui serait certainement très difficile, peut-être pas de nous quitter, mais sûrement d'apporter sa collaboration à une autre société'. RPS 9917: note pour Bô (3 May 1957). Julia had by then joined the ENS.
123. RPS 9720/10020/10438. On their role within government see Picard, *La République des savants*, Ch. 6. Fromageot was also a collaborator of Roussel-Uclaf. See Hagemann, 'Un cinquantenaire de l'époque héroïque de la pénicilline au développement de la microbiologie industrielle', p. 25. After the war, Fromageot moved from his provincial chair in Lyon to Paris, where he became Director of the Biochemistry Laboratory at the Faculté des Sciences. P. Desnuelle, 'Claude Fromageot, 1899–1958', in *Mémorial Claude Fromageot, 1899–1958*, Paris, n.d., 5–27.
124. Picard, *La République des Savants*, p. 161.
125. RP 10438: note pour Bô (10 Feb. 1950).
126. Piganiol, 'Les Gouvernements et la Science', *Publicis*, 1959, vol. 7, 15.
127. Picard named him as one of the reformers of French medicine after the war. See Picard, 'De la médecine expérimentale', in Debru et al, *Les Sciences biologiques et médicales*, p. 339.
128. RPS 9133: report on the structure of medical research in France (29 Nov. 1966). One of the recommendations presented in conclusion was a system of exchange between universities and industry, 24.
129. RPS 9542.
130. RPS10448: Paul to Loubatières (22 Oct. 1946).
131. Chauveau, *L'Invention pharmaceutique*, pp. 405–6.
132. On the growing faith in science, which was crystallized in the national health systems after the war, see D.M. Fox, 'The National Health Service and the Second World War: the elaboration of consensus', in H.L. Smith (ed.), *War and Social Change*, pp. 32–57.
133. Picard, 'De la médecine expérimentale', Debru et al., *Les Sciences biologiques et médicales*, p. 329.
134. D.T. Zallen, 'The Rockefeller Foundation and French research', *Cah. His. CNRS*, 1989, vol. 5, 35–58.

135. H. Jamous, *Sociologie de la décision: la réforme des études médicales et des structures hospitalières*, Paris : Ed. CNRS, 1969, pp. 121–57.
136. Picard, 'De la médecine expérimentale', in Debru et al, *Les Science biologiques et médicales*, p. 342.
137. R.A. Maxwell and S.B. Eckhardt, *Drug Discovery: a casebook and analysis*, Clifton, N.J.: Humana Press, 1990, p. 111; E.M. Tansey, '"They used to call it psychiatry": aspects of the development and impact of psychopharmacology', in M. Gijswijt-Hofstra and R. Porter (eds.), *Cultures of Psychiatry and Mental Health Care in Postwar Britain and the Netherland*, Amsterdam: Rodopi, 1998, pp. 79–101.
138. A.E. Caldwell, *Origins of Psychopharmacology: from CPZ to LSD*, Springfield, Ill: Charles C. Thomas, 1970; Swazey, *Chlorpromazine in Psychiatry*.
139. The term serendipity is derived from the ancient name for Sri-Lanka: Serendip. Horace Walpole (1717–1797) invented the name to signify discovery, either by accident or by sagacity, thus anticipating the phrase coined by Louis Pasteur: 'le hasard favorise les esprits bien préparés'. See I. L. Larson, 'Folklore, druglore and serendipity in pharmacology', in M. J. Parnham and J. Bruinvels (eds.), *Discoveries in Pharmacology*, Amsterdam: Elsevier, 1987, pp. 2–21 (13–8). The close relationship between design and serendipity, and the role played by scientific collaboration, has been made in connection with other innovations, for instance that of polythene: see M.W. Perrin, 'The story of polythene', *Research*, 1953, vol. 6, 111–8 (118).
140. Swazey, *Chlorpromazine in Psychiatry*, pp. 259–75. Caldwell has compared the complex trajectory of chlorpomazine with that of penicillin: Caldwell, *Origins of Psychopharmacology*, note 8, pp. 142–6.
141. Maxwell and Eckhardt, *Drug Discovery*, p. 115.
142. Sanofi-Aventis (hereafter SA), Paul Charpentier, Cahiers de Laboratoire, vol. 15 : 'Diméthylamino 2 propyl 1 thiophénylamine 3277 RP chlorhydrate' remis le 14 déc 45.
143. Bovet had at first conceived the anti-histamine project while working on sympatholytic substances. See Chapter Two.
144. SA, Paul Charpentier, Cahiers de Laboratoire, vol. 13 : Apr. 1944.
145. Koetschet was Scientific Director of SCUR. His research proposal is reproduced in Swazey, *Chlorpromazine in Psychiatry*, pp. 82–5.
146. RPS 10003.
147. See R. Rey, 'René Leriche (1875–1955): une oeuvre controversée', in Debru et al., *Les Sciences biologiques et médicales*, pp. 297–309.
148. Caldwell, Origins of Psychopharmacology, p. 29.
149. Ibid., note 12, 150-2. He discovered ataraxy, in fact, before the term 'ataraxic' was coined (retrospectively, using drugs) by Fabing and Cameron.
150. SA R1/4N15B, conteneur 2121, RP 4400-4599: 4435 RP (synthesized on 21/4/50, tested by Courvoisier on 5/12/50), and 4553 RP (synthesized by Charpentier on 22/11/50 and also tested by Courvoisier on 5/12/50).
151. Ibid., 4534 RP tested by Courvoisier in May 1951, 4583 RP tested by Courvoisier in Feb. 1951.
152. Maxwell and Eckhardt, *Drug Discovery*, pp. 112–3.
153. Ibid.
154. SA, Paul Charpentier, Cahiers de Laboratoire, vol. 15 (Nov. 1945).
155. Ibid., vol. 15 (Apr. 1946).
156. Ibid., vol. 19 : Diméthylamino p propyl chlor phénothiazine. Chaîne chlorée 4560 1 gr remis le 11 déc '50.
157. S. Courvoisier et al., 'Propriétés pharmacodynamiques du chlorhydrate de chloro-3-(diméthylamino-3'propyl)-10 phénothiazine (4560 RP)', *Arch. Int. Pharmacodyn.*, 1953, vol. 92, 305–61.

158. See R. Tissot, 'Découverte de la chlorpromazine et hasard', in J.-P. Olie, D. Ginestet, G. Jollès and H. Lôo (eds.) *Histoire d'une découverte en psychiatrie: 40 ans de chimiothérapie neuroleptique*, Paris : Doin, 1992, pp. 47–53.

159. Leriche saw this as a revolutionary step. See Caldwell, Origins of Psychopharmacology, p. 38.

160. J. Delay and P. Deniker, *Méthodes chimiothérapiques en psychiatrie: les nouveaux médicaments psychotropes*, Paris : Masson, 1961.

161. Swazey, *Chlorpromazine in Psychiatry*, Part 2.

162. RPS 10003.

163. Massat-Bourrat, 'Des phénothiazines à la chlorpromazine'.

164. Ibid., p. 133.

165. RPS10003: 'Dr H. Laborit et le CEPBEPE' (Centre d'Etudes expérimentales et cliniques de Physiobiologie, de Pharmacologie et d'Eutonologie, created for him at the Hôpital Boucicaut) (n.d.).

166. Ibid.

167. 'Cependant sa notoriété internationale n'avait cessé de s'étendre. Jamais couronné en France, il avait reçu par contre en 1957 la plus haute distinction scientifique américaine, le prix Albert LASKER, connu comme le 'petit Nobel', que 17 prix Nobel ont d'ailleurs reçu avant de recevoir le prix suédois. Ses travaux étant systématiquement refusés dans les revues françaises, il avait créé sa propre revue scientifique, actuellement analysée dans tous les 'abstracts' internationaux: 'AGRESSOLOGIE'. Invité chaque année à faire des conférences dans les universités étrangères, il a parcouru le monde entier et reçoit en permanence dans son laboratoire des chercheurs étrangers qui y effectuent des stages de plusieurs années, ce qui l'aide d'ailleurs à trouver des collaborateurs de qualité car un recrutement français basé sur les concours lui est évidemment interdit. Il a publié 16 ouvrages imprimés (chez Masson & Cie) dont plusieurs sont traduits en anglais, russe, japonais, allemand et espagnol.' Ibid.

168. Ibid., D.S. à D.S.Ph. (11 Dec. 1959). In Britain, at around the same time, ICI also funded a journal intended for the wider public: *Endeavour*. One of its main purposes seems to have been to vaunt ICI's contribution to the penicillin project. See R. Bud, 'Penicillin and the new Elizabethans', 324–5.

169. See H. Lôo, 'Une révolution thérapeutique en psychiatrie: la chlorpromazine', and M. Goudemand, 'La situation hospitalière avant et immédiatement après l'introduction de Largactil', in Olie et al., *Histoire d'une découverte*, pp. 13–9 and 19–27; Caldwell, *Origins of Psychopharmacology*, pp. 127-34.

170. Wall, *The United States and the Making of Postwar France*, Chs. 6, 7. On the 'co-production of American hegemony' that resulted from French dependence on, and American willingness to grant aid to rebuild science in France, see Krige, *American Hegemony*, Ch. 4.

171. Caldwell, *Origins of Psychopharmacology*, p. 7.

172. '[...] c'est seulement dans dix ans que la France retrouvera un certain type d'équilibre et que nous aurons suffisamment d'hommes actifs par rapport à l'ensemble des hommes trop jeunes ou trop âgés pour accomplir les tâches d'un pays moderne'. Piganiol, 'Les gouvernements et la science', 7.

173. In another publication, Piganiol mentioned the French patent system which, by not providing adequate protection, handicapped French innovation: 'Sizing up France's science', *Chemical Weekly*, 1962, vol. 91 (no page).

174. Piganiol, 'Les gouvernements et la science', 9.

175. INSERM, dossier de valorisation.

CHAPTER 6

1. Barnett, *The Audit of War.*
2. Monnet, *Memoirs*, p. 452.
3. Picard, 'De la médecine expérimentale', in Debru et al., *Les Sciences biologique set médicales en france*, pp. 336, 343.
4. On war as a test of social structures, see Marwick, *War and Social Change in the Twentieth Century*, Ch. 1 and p. 186. Exploring the notion of war as experiment, see S. Sturdy, 'War as experiment. Physiological innovation and administration in Britain, 1914–1918: the case of chemical warfare', in Cooter et al., War, *Medicine and Modernity*, pp. 65–84.
5. On continuity of the political élites, see J. Saville, *The Politics of Continuity: British foreign policy and the labour government, 1945–46*, London: Verso, 1993, 4. R. Hewison, *Culture and Consensus: England, art and politics since 1940*, London: Methuen, 1995: Hewison has compared Britain's culture of consensus with hegemonic rule on the continent, p. xvi.
6. PRO FD1 2497: notes on Professor Elliott's conference on the history of the Chemotherapy Committee (16 Feb. 1931).
7. For example, PRO FD1 8187: meeting (6 Nov. 1958); also PRO FD1 430.
8. GSK Wellcome Foundation archive [hereafter GSK] SCS 1511 (1976–7). Pricing regulation and Section 41 of the 1949 Patents Act were major bones of contention between the industry and the state, and the ABPI won important victories in both areas of government regulation. See J. Slinn, 'Drug-guzzlers or medicine junkies? Regulating the cost and consumption of prescription pharmaceuticals in the UK 1948–1967', *Business History*, 2005, vol. 47, 352–66.
9. S. Blank, *Industry and Government in Britain: the Federation of British Industries in Politics, 1945–65*, Farnborough: Saxon House, 1973, pp. ix–xii.
10. Both the BIM and TRC resulted from the need to formalize and consolidate relations between firms during wartime. On the BIM, see GSK SCS 284, minute book 3: minute 1144, and *FF*.
11. Thomson, *Half a Century of Medical Research*, vol. 2, pp. 23–6.
12. PRO FD1 430: Mellanby to Darlymple-Champneys (20 May 1948).
13. A. Muhammad, 'Patenting dyes and drugs in Britain, 1860–1960: case studies on the role of patents in chemical science and industry', Ph.D. thesis, University of Manchester, 2004, pp. 163–4.
14. Ibid., Ch. 6, esp. pp. 178–86.
15. PRO FD1 650: MRC memo (n.d.).
16. PRO FD1 650: 'Lee Committee Report'.
17. Ibid.
18. Bud, 'Penicillin and the new Elizabethans', 318–21.
19. PRO FD1 602: Thomson to Vannevar Bush (6 Nov. 1947).
20. On the foundation of the NRDC, see for instance P. Gummett, *Scientists in Whitehall*, Manchester: Manchester University Press, 1980, pp. 35–6. Also, S.T. Keith, 'Inventions, patents, and commercial development from governmentally financed research in Great Britain: the origins of the National Research and Development Corporation'', *Minerva*, 1981, vol. 19, 92–122.
21. Bud, 'Penicillin and the new Elizabethans', 321.
22. Muhammad, 'Patenting dyes and drugs in Britain'.
23. PRO FD1 2497: the ABCM and the MRC (1922–49).
24. C. Webster, *The Health Services since the War, vol. 1: Problems of Health Care: the National Health Service before 1957*, London: HMSO, 1988,

pp. 24–8 (24). On the history of clinical research, see C. Booth, 'Clinical Research', in W.F. Bynum and Roy Porter (eds.), *Companion Encyclopedia of the History of Medicine*, pp. 205–29; C. Lawrence, 'Clinical Research', in J. Krige and D. Pestre (eds.), *Science in the Twentieth Century*, pp. 439–60.

25. Webster, *The Health Services since the War*, vol. 1, pp. 133–83.

26. PRO FD1 300: 1942 memo by Sir Thomas Lewis at Stanborough Hospital, Watford, on the need to create adequate conditions for clinical research to develop. By 1952–3, the MRC felt that their efforts had born fruit. See Thomson, *Half a Century of Medical Research*, vol. 2, pp. 21–3.

27. Between 1950 and 1970, of the 82 newly formed MRC units, 46 were devoted to clinical research. Booth, 'Clinical research', in Austoker and Bryder, *Historical Perpectives*, pp. 233–4.

28. On the impact of the MRC on the expansion of clinical research in Britain, see C. Booth, 'Clinical research', in Austoker and Bryder (eds.), *Historical Perspectives*, p. 232.

29. Ibid., p. 237.

30. Industry also considered the Council to have such a mission. PRO FD1 677: ICI collaboration on anti-malarials.

31. Thomson, *Half a Century of Medical Research*, vol. 2, p. 50.

32. N. Rasmussen, 'Steroids in arms: government, industry and the hormones of the adrenal cortex in the United States, 1930–1950', *Med. His.*, 2002, vol. 46, 299–324.

33. Harry Marks has shown that the American equivalent was not as straightforward an example of co-operation as the British observers might have been led to believe. H.M. Marks, 'Cortisone, 1949: a year in the political life of a drug', *Bull. Hist. Med.*, 1992, vol. 66, 419–39. See also L.B. Slater, 'Industry and academy: the synthesis of steroids', *His. Stud. Phys. Sci.*, 2000, vol. 30, 443–79. On the British contribution, see D. Cantor, 'Cortisone and the politics of drama, 1949–55', in J.V. Pickstone (ed.), *Medical Innovations in Historical Perspective*, Basingstoke: Macmillan, 1992, pp. 165–84; idem, 'Cortisone and the politics of Empire: imperialism and British medicine, 1918–1955, *Bull. His. Med.*, 1993, vol. 67, 463–493.

34. V. Quirke, 'Making *British* cortisone: Glaxo and the development of corticosteroid drugs in Britain in the 1950s–1960s', *Stud. His. Phil. Biol. Biomed. Sci.*, 2005, vol. 36, 645–674.

35. This and the following quotes are in PRO FD1 636: confidential memo MRC 51/146.

36. Ibid.

37. Ibid, Green to Harington (25 March 1951).

38. PRO FD1 637: letter from T&H Smith (8 Feb. 1951).

39. Ibid., Hudson to Linnell (12 March 1951).

40. Table compiled from replies in PRO FD1 637.

41. Quirke, 'Making *British* cortisone', 655–60.

42. Jephcott's voice had much weight in the newly reorganized Glaxo of the 1950s: see Davenport-Hines and Slinn, *Glaxo*, Part 2.

43. PRO FD1 637: Correspondence with academic workers and firms re Cortisone (March 1951).

44. Ibid., (7 June 1951).

45. Quirke, 'Making *British* cortisone', 655–60.

46. PRO FD1 637: (13 June 1951). Alexander Todd, in fact, also became a consultant for Glaxo, and was to join the company's cortisone programme. See Quirke, 'Making *British* cortisone'.

47. PRO FD1 637: Jones to Himsworth (11 June 1951).

48. R.K. Callow, J.W. Cornforth and P.C. Spensley, 'A source of hecogenin', *Chemistry and Industry*, 18 Aug. 1951, vol. 33, 699–700. This process enabled the MRC and companies to operate within the Sterling exchange area. On this, and other constraints over British R&D in the period, see S.M. Horrocks, 'Enthusiasm constrained? British industrial R&D and the transition from war to peace, 1942–1951', *Bus. His.*, 1999, vol. 41, 42–63 (53).

49. Quirke, 'Making *British* cortisone', 656–8.

50. PRO FD1 642: notes of meeting (21 Feb. 1952).

51. Ibid., memo visit to Welwyn Garden City (6 Mar. 1952).

52. Ibid., meeting (12 Aug. 1952); 'Proposed collaboration with Glaxo on the synthesis of cortisone' (1 Sept. 1952).

53. Ibid., memo (14 Nov. 1952).

54. PRO FD1 944: indenture (30 May 1922).

55. See J. Hendry, *Innovating for Failure: government policy and the early British computer industry*, Cambridge, Mass.: MIT Press, 1989, p. 8.

56. PRO FD1 1456: Tizard to Himsworth (16 May 1951).

57. Quirke, 'Making *British* cortisone', 664–6.

58. PRO FD1 642, vol. 2: letter to Halsbury at the NRDC (10 Aug. 1955).

59. J. F. Artusio, 'Rationale and History of the Development of Halothane', in N. M. Greene (ed.), *Halothane*, Philadelphia: F.A. Davis Co., 1968, pp. 2–10 (2).

60. C.W. Suckling, 'The development of halothane', *Manchester University Medical School Gazette*, 1958, vol. 37, 53–4. C. Kennedy, *ICI*, pp. 130–1.

61. Ibid., note 133, p. 3. PRO FD1 8186: report on the preparation of organic fluorine compounds by G. Fuller, M. Stacey and J.C. Tatlow of the Chemistry Department at Birmingham (n.d.).

62. PRO FD1 8181: minutes (11 Jan. 1955).

63. PRO FD1 8182: Pask to Burn (6 April 1956). Burn was valued for his clinical experience as well as his 'unquestioned right to authority in all matters pharmacological'.

64. PRO FD1 8185: meeting (2 Oct. 1957).

65. PRO FD1 8187: meeting (6 Nov. 1958).

66. PRO FD1 8181: Professor Burn visits ICI; in exchange, Dr Raventos (member of the Biological Research at ICI) visits Oxford (12 Dec. 1955).

67. Kennedy, *ICI*, p. 124.

68. C. Suckling, 'The discovery of the anaesthetic halothane: the story of a science-based innovation' (discourse presented on 20 March 1992 at the Royal Institution); idem, 'Some chemical and physical factors in the development of Fluothane', *Brit. J. Anaesth.*, 1957, vol. 29, 466–72.

69. On this see for example F.E. Bennetts, 'The early development of fluorinated anaesthetics', *Proc. A.A.S.*, 1997, vol. 21, 82–8.

70. Suckling, 'Some chemical and physical factors', 466–7.

71. Kennedy, *ICI*, Ch. 6, and pp. 123–29.

72. Ibid., p. 131.

73. Sexton, 'The Research Laboratories'. The role played by teamwork in the discovery of halothane was emphasized in the editorial to a special issue dedicated to halothane: see 'Team Research', *Brit. J. Anaesth.*, 437.

74. Kennedy, *ICI*, p. 131.

75. On translation as a central feature of the social construction of science, technology, and medicine see B. Latour, 'Give me a laboratory and I will raise the world', in K. Knorr-Cetina and M. Mulkay (eds.), *Sciencce Observed*, pp. 141–70.

76. Suckling, 'Some chemical and physical factors'.

77. M.S. Sadove and V.E. Wallace, *Halothane*, Oxford: Blackwell Scientific, 1962, p. 5.
78. Ibid., 4; J. Raventos, 'Action of Fluothane: a new volatile anaesthetic', *British Journal of Pharmacology*, 1956, vol. 11, 394.
79. Sadove and Wallace described halothane as being 'tailor-made' because many of its properties had been predicted from *prior* knowledge of the properties and actions of related compounds, in Sadove and Wallace, *Halothane*, p. 5. On the question of design, see Kennedy, *ICI*, p. 134, and C. Suckling, 'The discovery of anaesthetic halothane'.
80. Johnstone is pictured sitting comfortably, but also somewhat sceptically between Suckling and Raventos in Kennedy, *ICI*, p. 132. See also 133.
81. Had the two — halothane and out-of-circuit vaporizers — not been developed in tandem, there might have been serious accidents, which could have jeopardized future development of the drug, particularly in America, where in-circle vaporizers were more common at the time than in Britain. Artusio, 'Rationale and history of the development of halothane', 7–8.
82. IC (P) Ltd report, Alderley Edge, Manchester, U.K. CPR2: minutes of a meeting of ICI Ltd., Pharmaceuticals Division Development Directors' Conference (20 June 1956).
83. Ibid., minutes of meeting (18 July 1956).
84. Artusio, 'Rationale and history of the development of halothane', 8. Cyprane was later acquired by the American firm Fraser Sweatman, Inc., which was itself later acquired by BOC. F. Bennetts, personal communication.
85. PRO FD1 8181: meeting at Oxford leading to a clinical trial (14 Dec. 1955). PRO FD1 8182: report on the trial (5 May 1956). See also Artusio, 'Rationale and History', 7.
86. Ibid., 7–8.
87. PRO FD1 8182: Pask to Weevil (of ICIP, Wilmslow), 4 Feb. 1956.
88. PRO FD1 8183: meeting (1 Feb. 1957).
89. PRO FD1 8182: proposed reply to Pask, 21 May 1956 (written by Burn?).
90. PRO FD1 8187: meeting (18 Sept. 1958).
91. PRO FD1 8188: meeting (11 June 1959).
92. Sadove and Wallace, *Halothane*, pp. 3–6.
93. Suckling, 'Some chemical and physical factors', 471.
94. PRO FD1 677: 22 July 1943.
95. PRO FD12175: C.M. Scott to Landsborough Thomson (18 May 1950).
96. PRO FD1 1928.
97. Maxwell and Eckhardt, *Drug Discovery*, pp. 297–305.
98. Kennedy, *ICI*, 134. Schueler begins his book on drug design by stressing the importance of the partnership which exists between chemists and physicians 'as the respective originators and final judges of new drugs', in F.W. Schueler, *Chemobiodynamics*, New York: McGraw Hill, 1960, p. 3.
99. PRO FD1 430: Green to Harington at NIMR (24 Nov. 1948).
100. Sir Edward Abraham, 'Penicillin and its successors: a personal view', *Bull. Amer. Acad. Arts and Sci.*, 1985, vol. 39, 8–27; idem, 'Selective reminiscences of β-lactam antibiotics: early research on penicillin and cephalosporins', *BioEssays* 1990, vol. 12, 601–6. Detailed historical accounts, supported by documentary evidence for patenting purposes, can also be found in the Edward Abraham papers held in the Bodleian Library, Oxford. See in particular Bodleian Library [hereafter BOD] EPA C.401: 'Cephalosporin C'. History of early developmt of cephalosporin – to be used as an aide-mémoire in petition to High Court to obtain an extension of UK patent 810,196 ('basic C case').

101. One of these is monoclonal antibodies. See Tansey and Catterall, 'Technology transfer in Britain: the case of monoclonal antibodies', in Tansey et al. (eds.), *Wellcome Witnesses to Twentieth-Century Medicine*, London: Wellcome Trust, 1997, vol. 1, pp. 3–34.
102. PRO FD1 944: term used at a meeting in Mr Duncan's office (13 Dec. 1951). See also PRO FD1 511–516: re clinical trials of anti-histamine drugs.
103. BOD EPA C. 287 (1949–). Williams has written that Florey encouraged the MRC to make such a move. Williams, *Howard Florey*, p. 303.
104. BOD EPA C.336: RHL Cohen to EPA (18 Feb. 1960).
105. This was partly at the instigation of the MRC, who urged them to patent the processes under the aegis of the NRDC, and partly at the instigation of Howard Florey himself. See BOD EPA C.293: EPA to BB Kelly (MRC Antibiotic Research Station, Clevedon) 13 Jan. 1951.
106. Pieters sees in the experience with cephalosporin, rather than that with cortisone, the precedent for the collaborative scheme to develop interferon. T. Pieters, *Interferon: the science and selling of a miracle drug*, London: Routledge, 2005, pp. 60–6.
107. Ibid., pp. 36–9.
108. This helps to explain the frequent accusations that were aimed at companies for their 'showy work'. PRO FD1 430: note by Green and Dalrymple-Champneys with reference to PAS against tuberculosis (7 Oct. 1948).
109. PRO FD1 433: letter to J.R. Squire (MRC Industrial Research Unit, Birmingham).
110. Abraham's correspondence is dominated by his interaction with pharmaceutical companies interested in cephalosporin C and other beta-lactam antibiotics. BOD EPA C. 606 (Beecham) to 963 (UpJohn). His consultancy for ICI, which began in 1955, was brought to an end in 1958, when he started consulting for the NRDC.
111. Abraham, 'Howard Walter Florey', 255–302.
112. Abraham, 'Penicillin and its successors'.
113. Abraham, 'Selective reminiscences', 603–4.
114. E.P.A. Abraham and G.G.F. Newton, 'Isolation of cephalosporin C, a penicillin-like antibiotic containing D-α-aminoadipic acid', *Biochemical Journal*, 1961, vol. 79, 651–8.
115. H. W. Florey, 'The medical aspects of the development of resistance to antibiotics', *Giornale di. Microbiologia*, 1956, vol. 2, 361–70.
116. RS 98HF 194: 1. See 3), A. R. Martin and J. K. Landquist, 'Antibacterial Drugs', submitted by M. Sexton (15 Dec. 1961).
117. Williams, *Howard Florey*, p. 315.
118. BOD EPA C.401: 'Cephalosporin C' aide-mémoire.
119. Williams, *Howard Florey*, p. 303.
120. BOD EPA C.401: 'Cephalosporin C' aide-mémoire.
121. On Beecham's contribution to the penicillin story, see Lazell, *From Pills to Penicillin: the Beecham story*, London: Heinemann, 1975; T. A. B. Corley, 'The Beecham group in the world's pharmaceutical industry', *Zeitschrift für Unternehmensgeschichte*, 1994, vol. 39, 18–30. On the synthesis of penicillin, see Sheehan, *The Enchanted Ring*.
122. BOD EPA C.370: B.J.A. Bard (NRDC) to Abraham (28 Apr. 1959).
123. F. R. Batchelor, F.P. Doyle, J. H. C. Nayler, and Rolinson, 'Synthesis of penicillin: 6-aminopenicillianic acid in penicillin fermentations', *Nature*, 1959, vol. 183, 257.
124. BOD EPA C.401: 'Cephalosporin C' aide-mémoire. Ibid., C.376: Abraham to J. C. Cain (NRDC) (12 Sept. 1959).
125. Abraham, 'Penicillin and its successors', 22–3.

126. The precise chronology is often unclear in retrospective accounts. However, a letter sent by Bloxham of the NRDC to Abraham in July 1959 suggests that the Beecham publication stimulated Abraham's efforts at isolating the cephalosporin nucleus, and the prospect of patenting this spurred Abraham into proposing a chemical formula for it. BOD EPA C.371: Bloxham to Abraham (8/7/59).

127. Abraham, 'Selective reminiscences', 603–5.

128. E.P. Abraham and G.G.F. Newton, 'The structure of cephalosporin C', *Biochem. J.*, 1961, vol. 79, 377–93.

129. D.C. Hodgkin and E.N. Maslen, 'The X-ray analysis of the structure of cephalosporin C', *Biochem. J.*, 1961, vol. 79, 393–402.

130. They were, together with Glaxo, one of the first companies to show interest in cephalosporin. See Abraham, 'Selective reminiscences', 605.

131. Abraham, 'Penicillin and its successors', 24.

132. Ibid., 24–5.

133. The dining hall at Linacre College, for instance, bears a plaque commemorating this benefaction.

134. Abraham, 'Selective reminiscences', 605.

135. Abraham, 'Howard Walter Florey', 273.

136. Morrell, *Science at Oxford*, pp. 204–11.

137. Macfarlane, *Howard Florey*, p. 231; Abraham, 'Howard Walter Florey', p. 261.

138. K.B. Roberts, H.W. Florey and W.K. Joklik, 'The influence of cortisone on cell division', *Quart. J. Exp. Physio.*, 1952, vol. 37, 239–57. Florey, 'The medical aspects of the development of resistance to antibiotics'.

139. Florey talked at the Penicillin Conference of the Palais de la Découverte in 1946; about antibiotic research at a Conference at the Real Academia Nacional de Medicina in Madrid on 17 April 1950.

140. Florey, 'Prestige in academic scientific research', *Nature*, 17 March 1962, vol. 193, 1017–8.

141. Bud, 'Penicillin and the new Elizabethans', 329–31. The term had originally been coined by A.L. Rowse during the Second World War.

142. Florey, 'Prestige', 1018. By then, Florey's attention had shifted away from chemotherapy towards basic problems such as atherosclerosis.

143. Florey, 'Medical science in the twentieth-century', *Yale Journal of Biology and Medicine*, 1960, vol. 33, 212–26 (224).

144. Ibid.

145. On the creation of a declinist ideology in the post-war period, see J. Tomlinson, 'Inventing "decline": the falling behind of the British economy in the post-war years', *Econ. His. Review*, 1996, vol. 49, 731–57. David Edgerton has highlighted the role of scientists in promoting a techno declinist version of British history in the 1950s and 1960s, a version that gained fresh impetus in the late 1970s at the hands of historians such as Martin Wiener and Corelli Barnett. D. Edgerton, *Warfare State Britain, 1920–1970*, Cambridge: CUP, 2006, Chs. 5 and 7.

146. RS 98HF 194–28: D.G. Davey to Florey (3 March 1963). Davey was also the President for the European Society for the Study of Drug Toxicity.

147. RS 98HF 194-55-64 (1974).

148. See Reader, *ICI*, p. 460.

149. Clark, *The Life of Ernst Chain*, pp. 10–1. See also E.B. Chain, 'Penicillin and beyond', *Nature*, 1991, vol. 353, 492–4. Chain himself encouraged this opinion: see Chain papers at the CAMC [hereafter PP/EBC]: 43 G 59, 'Comments on the relationship between university and non-university research institutes in Germany'.

150. Lazell, *From Pills to Penicillin*, 139.
151. Clark, *The Life of Ernst Chain*, 56–7.
152. F. Dickens, 'Edward Charles Dodds', *Bio. Mem. FRS*, 1975, vol. 21, 227–67. Dodds worked for the NRDC as consultant and lent his support to the development of cephalosporin. On Heilbron, see Cook, 'Ian Morris Heilbron'. Heilbron had worked for a short time at the British Dyestuffs Corporation (a future part of ICI) after the First World War, and remained their consultant until 1949, when he retired from his Chair of Organic Chemistry at Imperial College. He then served as first Director of the Brewing Industry Research Foundation until 1958.
153. Lazell, *From Pills to Penicillin*, pp. 46–7 (meeting on 1 April 1942).
154. Ibid., 53.
155. CMAC PP/EBC 29 F 45: Chain to Dodds (23 May 1955).
156. It is interesting to contrast this with the fee paid by NRDC to Abraham, which in 1958 amounted to 350 guineas p.a. BOD EPA C. 368: BJA Bard to EP Abraham (7 Nov. 1958).
157. CMAC PP/EBC 29 F 45: Chain to Heilbron (28 June 1955).
158. Minutes of the meetings in Lazell, *From Pills to Penicillin*, pp. 140–4.
159. CMAC PP/EBC F327.
160. Ibid., F313–4 and F 316.
161. Ibid., G 41–46: 'Landmarks and perspectives in biochemical research': inaugural lecture at Imperial College, published in *BMJ* (Jan. 1965).
162. Ibid., 29 F 46: Chain to Heilbron (28 June 1955).
163. Clark, *The Life of Ernst Chain*, 159–72.
164. CMAC PP/EBC 43 G 59: 'Relations between academic research laboratories and the biologically based industry'.
165. V. Bush, *Science – the Endless Frontier*, Washington, DC.: National Science Foundation, 1945; Hounshell and Smith, *Science and Corporate Strategy*, Ch. 17.
166. See Fox and Guagnini concerning Lyon Playfair, 'Britain in perspective', note 1, 147.
167. On the consensus about the role of 'basic science', which contributed to the 'co-production of American hegemony' in the postwar era, see Krige, *American Hegemony*, Chs. 1 and 9.
168. David Edgerton has argued that war was not the turning point it is often made out to be, in *Science, Technology and the British Industrial 'Decline'*, pp. 37–8.
169. Saville, *The Politics of Continuity*, p. 4.
170. Walsh, 'Industrial R&D', in Gaudillière and Lowy (eds.), *The Invisible Industrialist*, p. 335.
171. See for example GSK SCS 1567: minute 11,553 (4 May 1988).
172. GSK SCS 459: memo by D. Godfrey (23 July 82).
173. Edgerton, *Warfare State Britain*, pp. 303–4.

PART III: CONCLUSION

1. Monnet, *Memoirs*, p. 452.
2. Ibid., pp. 451–2.
3. Ibid. Barnett has, perhaps unwittingly, followed Monnet's interpretation in *The Audit of War*.
4. See E. Lederer, 'La chimie des substances naturelles', 49–51. At the CNRS contacts with industry had to be concealed from the public eye (and yet they

still existed!). On the need to fund basic science, which became the consensus of the post-war period, see V. Bush, *Science: the endless frontier*, pp. 13–5.
5. Bud, 'Penicillin and the new Elizabethans', 305–33. P. Piganiol, 'Sizing up France's science', in *Chemical Weekly*, 1962, vol. 91, (no page).
6. See for example C. Mukerji, *A Fragile Power: scientists and the state*, Princeton, N.J: Princeton University Press, 1989, for America; Gummett, *Scientists in Whitehall*, for Britain; Weart, *Scientists in Power*, for France.
7. On this see S. de Chadarevian and H. Kamminga, *Molecularizing Biology and Medicine: new practices and alliances*, London: Harwood Academic, 1998; Picard, 'De la medicine expérimentale à l'INSERM'; Gaudillière, *Inventer la biomédicine*.

CONCLUSION

1. Bud, 'Penicillin and the new Elizabethans', 320.
2. Chen, 'The laboratory as business', in Cunningham and Williams, *The Laboratory Revolution in Medicine*.
3. R. Frank, 'La mémoire empoisonnée', in Azéma and Bedarida, 'La France des Anne'es noires', vol. 2, pp. 483–514.
4. In his study of culture in organisations, Hofstede has identified self-fulfilling prophecy as a key mechanism by which cultural conditioning occurs, and culturally determined beliefs perpetuate themselves. G. Hofstede, 'Motivation, leadership and organization: do American theories apply abroad?', in D.S. Pugh (ed.), *Organization Theory: selected readings*, London: Penguin, 1997, 4th edn, pp. 223–50 (224).
5. As in the case of monoclonal antibodies, discovered in Britain but developed in the United States. See E.M. Tansey and P.P. Catterall (eds.), 'Technology transfer in Britain: the case of monoclonal antibodies', in Tansey et al., *Wellcome Witnesses to Twentieth-Century Medicine*, 3–34. Several references are made to the experience with penicillin, as the archetypal British experience in science and technology, 5, 19, 22.
6. Krige, *American Hegemony*, Chs. 1, 9.
7. For example: Wiener, *English Culture and the Decline of the Industrial Spirit*; 129–32; Barnett, *The Audit of War*, 220–1; Shinn, 'The genesis of French industrial research', 626–7, 632–3; Monnet, *Memoirs*, pp. 232–49.
8. Barnett has accused the post-war Labour government of leading Britain down the wrong path, in *The Lost Victory: British dreams, British realities, 1945–1950*, London: Macmillan, 1995.
9. Bush's *Science: the endless frontier* provided a model for this rhetoric. It was based on the experience of the war-time penicillin programme: see Hobby, 'Epilogue', *Penicillin*. See also Krige, *American Hegemony*, p. 11.
10. Mukerji has described the dependence of scientists on the state as a two-edged sword, in C. Mukerji, *A Fragile Power*, Princeton, N.J.: Princeton University Press, 1989.
11. See for instance Picard, 'Profession chercheur', *La République des savants*, 167–91. Molecular biology was one of the main beneficiaries of this strategy, as shown for example by de Chadarevian in *Designs for Life*.
12. A.G. Gross, *The Rhetoric of Science*, Cambridge, Mass.: Harvard University Press, 1996, 2nd edn, p. 177.
13. Monnet, *Memoirs*, pp. 451–2.
14. On this see de Chadarevian and Kamminga (eds.), *The Molecularization of biology and Medicine*.

Bibliography

1. ARCHIVE SOURCES

1.1 Public archives

Britain:
Modern Records Centre, Warwick University: Confederation of British Industries and predecessors, MSS.200/F series.
Public Record Office, the National Archives Kew: MRC collection, FD1 series.
France:
Archives Nationales (AN), Fontainebleau: CNRS collection, n° 800284; Commission de la Recherche Pharmaceutique: F 715 ; Rhône-Poulenc. Dossier de la Commission Nationale interprofessionnelle d'épuration. 13 mai 1949. F 12 9576.

1.2 Institutional archives

Britain:
Contemporary Medical Archives Centre, Wellcome Institute, Euston Road, London: the Lister Institute papers (SA/LIS); N.G. Heatley (GC/48); E.B. Chain (PP/EBC).
Modern Records, Bodleian Library: the Dunn School's research grants journals (PT 17/1-2); Edward Abraham papers (EPA).
Royal Society papers, London: Chemical sub-Committee (World War I: CMB files); H.H. Dale (93HD); H.W. Florey (98HF).
France:
INSERM, 'La valorisation sociale de la recherche médicale et en santé': rapport d'un groupe de réflexion (Jan. 1984).
The Pasteur Institute, rue du Dr. Roux: minutes Conseil d'Administration (CA Reg); Direction Services (DirSer); Direction Santé (DirSan); A. Besredka (BES); E. Fourneau (FUR); Laboratoire de Chimie Thérapeutique (LCT); M. Macheboeuf (MAC); J. Monod (MON); L. Rapkine (RAP).

1.3 Private archives

Britain:
GSK Wellcome Foundation archive SCS series (loaned to the Contemporary Medical Archives Centre in 2005 for a project to write the history of Burroughs Wellcome).

ICI: AstraZeneca, Alderley Park, Macclesfield: CPR reports.
Uncatalogued collection of H.W. Florey offprints and incomplete manuscript draft on mucus secretions, formerly in the Wellcome Unit for the History of Medicine, Banbury Rd., Oxford, now CMAC, London.
France:
Rhône-Poulenc Santé, Centre de Recherche, Vitry-sur-Seine: uncatalogued collection, now destroyed.
Sanofi-Aventis, Centre de Recherche, Vitry-sur-Seine: Paul Charpentier, Cahiers de Laboratoire ; fiches de chimie.

2. INTERVIEWS

Archives de l'Institut Pasteur: Interview by Denise Ogilvie with Elie Wollman, 31 May 1999.
Merck & Co., Inc., Archives: 'Norman G. Heatley', interview conducted by J.L. Sturchio, Rockefeller University, 25 Oct. 1989.
The Royal College of Physicians and Oxford Brookes University Medical Sciences Video Archive MSVA 029: 'Dr Norman Heatley, Hon DM', interview with Max Blythe, Oxford 28 October 1987

3. PERSONAL COMMUNICATIONS

Norman Heatley, 1996–8.
Raymond Paul, 1996.

4. PRINTED SOURCES

Abir-Am P.G. and Outram D. (eds.) (1987) *Uneasy Careers and Intimate Lives: women in science, 1789–1979*, New Brunswick, N.J.: Rutgers University Press.
Abir-Am P.G. (1992) 'The politics of macro-molecules: molecular biology, biochemists and the biomolecular revolution', *Osiris*, 2nd Series, 7: 164–99.
Abraham E.P. et al. (1941) 'Further Observations on Penicillin', *Lancet*, 2: 177–89.
Abraham E.P. and Newton G.G.F. (1961) 'Isolation of cephalosporin C, a penicillin-like antibiotic containing D-α-aminoadipic acid', *Biochem. J.*, 79: 651–8.
Abraham E.P. and Newton G.G.F. (1961) 'The structure of cephalosporin C', *Biochem. J.*, 79: 377–93.
Abraham E.P. (1971) 'Howard Walter Florey', *Bio. Mem. FRS*, 17: 255–302.
Abraham E.P. (1985) 'Penicillin and its successors: a personal view', *Bull. Amer. Acad. Arts and Sc.*, 39: 8–27.
Abraham E.P. (1990) 'Selective reminiscences of ß-lactam antibiotics: early research on penicillin and cephalosporins', *Bioessays*, 12: 601–6.
Abraham E.P. (1990) 'Oxford, Howard Florey and World War Two', in C.L. Moberg and Z.A. Cohn (eds.) *Launching the Antibiotic Era: personal accounts of the discovery and use of the first antibiotics*, New York: Rockefeller University Press, pp. 19–30.

Adams D. P. (1989) 'Wartime bureaucracy and penicillin allocation: the committee on Chemotherapeutics and other agents', *J. His. Med. All. Sci.*, 44: 196–217.

Agar J. (1997) 'The New Price and Place of University Research: Jodrell Bank, NIRNS and the Context of Post-War British Academic Science', *Contemp. Brit. His.*, 11: 1–30.

Amdam R.P. and Sogner K. (1994) *Wealth of Contrasts: Nyegaard & Co. — a Norwegian pharmaceutical company, 1874–1985*, Oslo: Ad Notam Gyldendal.

Amdam R.P. (1996) 'Professional networks and the introduction of research in the British and Norwegian pharmaceutical industry in the inter-war years', *His. and Tech.*, 13: 101–14.

Argyle M. (1991) *Cooperation: the basis of sociability*, London: Routledge.

Arthur C. (10 Oct. 1996) 'At breakfast this scientist was rejected for a grant. By lunch he had won a Nobel Prize', *The Independent*, 3.

Artusio J.F. (1968) 'Rationale and history of the development of Halothane', in N. M. Greene (ed.) *Halothane*, Philadelphia: F.A. Davis Co., pp. 2–10.

Austoker J. (1989) 'Walter Morley Fletcher and the origins of a basic biomedical research policy', in J. Austoker and L. Bryder (eds.), *Historical Perspectives on the Role of the MRC*, Oxford: OUP, pp. 23–33.

Austoker J. and Bryder L. (1989) 'The National Institute of Medical Research and related activities of the MRC', in J. Austoker and L. Bryder (eds.), *Historical Perspectives on the Role of the MRC*, Oxford: OUP, pp. 35–57.

Austoker J. and L. Bryder (eds.) (1989) *Historical Perspectives on the Role of the MRC*, Oxford: OUP.

Axelrod R. (1994) *The Evolution of Cooperation*, London: Basic Books.

Axelrod R. (1997) *The Complexity of Cooperation: agent-based models of competition and collaboration*, Princeton, N.J.: Princeton University Press.

Azéma J.-P. (1993) 'Le Régime de Vichy', in J.-P. Azéma and F. Bédarida (eds.) *La France des années noires*, Paris: Seuil, pp. 151–79.

Azéma J.-P. and F. Bédarida (eds.) (1993) *La France des années noires*, Paris: Seuil.

Bacharach A.L. and Hem B.A. (1946) 'Chemistry and manufacture of penicillin', in A. Fleming (ed.) *Penicillin: its practical application*, London: Butterworth & Co., pp. 24–45.

Baldry P. (1965) *The Battle Against Bacteria: a fresh look. A history of man's fight against bacterial disease with special reference to the development of antibacterial drugs*, Cambridge: CUP.

Barber H.J. (1978) *Historical Aspects of Chemotherapy*, Dagenham: May & Baker.

Barger G. and Dale H.H. (1910–1911), 'Chemical structure and sympathomimetic action of amines', *J. Physiol.*, 40: 19–59.

Barnett C. (1987) *The Audit of War: the illusion and reality of Britain as a great nation*, London: Papermac.

Barnett C. (1995) *The Lost Victory: British dreams, British realities, 1945–1950*, London: Macmillan.

Basalla G. (1988) *The Evolution of Technology*, Cambridge: CUP.

Batchelor F.R., Doyle F.P., Nayler J.H.C. and Rolinson (1959) 'Synthesis of penicillin: 6-aminopenicillianic acid in penicillin fermentations', *Nature*, 183: 257.

Baverey-Massat-Bourrah S. (2004) 'De la copie au nouveau medicament: le laboratoire de chimie thérapeutique et Rhône-Poulenc: un réseau alternatif d'innovation' *Entreprises et Histoire*, 36: 48–63

Bearn A.G. (1981) 'The pharmaceutical industry and academe: partners in progress', *Am. J. Med.*, 71: 81–8.

Beaune J.-C. (ed.) (1993) *La Philosophie du Remède*, Paris: PUF.

Beckelman J.E., Li Y. and Gross C.P. (2003) 'Scope and financial impact of financial conflicts of interest in biomedical research: a systematic review', *JAMA*, 289: 454–65.

Bédarida F. (1993) 'La persécution des juifs', in J.-P. Azéma and F. Bédarida (eds.) *La France des années noires*, Paris: Seuil, pp. 129–158.

Beer J.J. (1959) 'The emergence of the German Dye Industry', *Illinois Studies in the Social Sciences*, 44: Ch. 7.

Beinart J. (1989) 'The inner world of imperial sickness: the MRC and research in tropical medicine', in J. Austoker and L. Bryder (eds.) *Historical Perspectives on the Role of the MRC*, Oxford: OUP, pp. 109-35.

Ben-David J. (1971) *The Scientists' Role in Society: a comparative study*, Englewood Cliffs, N.J.: Prentice Hall.

Bennetts F.E. (1997) 'The early development of fluorinated anaesthetics', *Proc. A.A.S.*, 21: 82–8.

Bensaude-Vincent B. (1995) 'Introductory Essay', in B. Bensaude Vincent and F. Abbri (eds.), *Lavoisier in European Context: negotiating a new language for chemistry*, Canton, Mass.: Science History Publications, pp. 1–17.

Bernard J. (1947) *La Pénicilline*, Paris: Corréa.

Bickel L. (1972) *Rise up to Life: a biography of Howard Florey who made penicillin and gave it to the world*, London: Angus and Robertson.

Bijker W.E, Hughes T.P. and Pinch T.J. (eds.) (1987) *The Social Construction of Technological Systems: new directions in the sociology and the history of technology*, Cambridge, Mass.: MIT Press.

Bijker W.E and Law J. (1992) 'General Introduction', in Bijker W. E. and Law J. (eds.) *Shaping Technology/Building Society: studies in sociotechnical change*, Cambridge, Mass.: MIT Press, pp. 1–14.

Bijker W. E. and Law J. (eds.) (1992) *Shaping Technology/Building Society: studies in sociotechnical change*, Cambridge, Mass.: MIT Press.

Birkinshaw J.H. (1972) 'Harold Raistrick', *Bio. Mem. FRS*, 18: 489–509.

Blank S. (1973) *Industry and Government in Britain: the Federation of British Industries in Politics, 1945–65*, Farnborough: Saxon House.

Bliss M. (1987) *The Discovery of Insulin*, Basingstoke: Macmillan.

Bloch M. (1953) 'Toward a comparative history of European societies', in F.C. Lane and J.C. Riemersma (eds.) *Enterprise and Secular Change: readings in economic history*, London: George Allen & Unwin, pp. 494–522.

Blondeau A. (1992) *Histoire des laboratoires pharmaceutiques en France: et de leurs médicaments*, Paris: Le Cherche Midi, vols. 1 and 2.

Blondel-Mégrelis M. (1994) 'La pharmacie en France 1900–1950, points de repères', in C. Debru, J. Gayon and J-F. Picard (eds.) *Les Sciences biologiques et médicales en France 1920–1950*, Paris: CNRS Editions, pp. 283–96.

Blumenthal D., Gluck M. Louis K.S., Soto M.A. and Wise D. (1986) 'University-industry research relationships in biotechnology: implications for the university', *Science*, 232: 1361–2.

Blunden K. (1975) *Etude sur l'évolution de la concentration dans l'industrie pharmaceutique en France*, Luxembourg: Office des Publications Officielles des Communautés Européennes.

Bonta I. L. (1987) 'Folklore, druglore and serendipity in pharmacology', in M. J. Parnham and J. Bruinvels (eds.) *Discoveries in Pharmacology*, Amsterdam: Elsevier, pp. 2–21.

Booth C. (1989) 'Clinical research', in J. Austoker and L. Bryder (eds.), *Historical Perspectives on the Role of the MRC*, Oxford: OUP, pp. 205–41.

Booth C. (1990) 'Clinical research', in W.F. Bynum and R. Porter (eds.) *Companion Encyclopedia of the History of Medicine*, London: Routledge, vol. 1, pp. 205–29.

Boudia S. (2001) *Marie Curie et son laboratoire: sciences et industrie de la radioactivité en France*, Paris: Editions des Archives Contemporaines.

Bovet D. (1988) *Une Chimie qui guérit: histoire de la découverte des sulfamides*, Paris: Payot.

Bovet D. (1991) 'Le laboratoire de chimie thérapeutique: de l'arsenic aux sulfamides', in M. Morange (ed.), *L'Institut Pasteur: contributions à son histoire*, Paris: La Découverte, pp. 207–36.

Bouvier J. (1984) 'Le Plan Monnet et l'Economie Française, 1947–1952', EUI working paper 83, Badia Fiesola, Italy, Jan. 1984.

Breckon W. (1972) *The Drug Makers*, London: Methuen.

Broch P., Kerharo J., Netick J. and J. Desbordes (1945) *Une expérience française de récupération de la pénicilline*, Paris: Vigot Frères.

Brown K. (2004) *Penicillin Man: Alexander Fleming and the antibiotic revolution*, Thrupp, Gloucs.: Sutton Publishing Ltd.

Bryder L. (1989a) 'Public health research and the MRC', in J. Austoker and L. Bryder (eds.) *Historical Perspectives on the Role of the MRC*, Oxford: OUP, pp. 59–83.

Bryder L. (1989b) 'Tuberculosis and the MRC', in J. Austoker and L. Bryder (eds.) *Historical Perspectives on the Role of the MRC*, Oxford: OUP, pp. 1–21.

Bud R. (1993) *The Uses of Life: a history of biotechnology*, Cambridge: CUP.

Bud R. (1998) 'Penicillin and the new Elizabethans', *BJHS*, 31: 305–33.

Bülbring E. and Walker J.M. (1984) 'Joshua Harold Burn, 1892–1981', *Bio. Mem. FRS*, 30: 45–89.

Burian R.M. et Gayon J. (1991) 'Un évolutioniste bernardien à l'Institut Pasteur? Morphologie des ciliés et évolution physiologique dans l'oeuvre d'André Lwoff', in M. Morange (ed.) *L'Institut Pasteur: contributions à son histoire*, Paris: La Découverte, pp. 165–85.

Burke P. (1992) *History and Social Theory*, Cambridge: Polity Press.

Burn (ed) (1958) *The Structure of British Industry*, vol. 2, Cambridge: CUP.

Burrin P. (1995) *Living with Defeat: France under the German Occupation, 1939–1945*, London: Arnold.

Bush V. (1945) *Science: The Endless Frontier*, Washington, DC: National Science Foundation.

Buton P. (1993) 'L'Etat restauré', in J.-P. Azéma and F. Bédarida (eds.) *La France des années noires*, Paris: Seuil, pp. 405–28.

Bynum W.F. (1994) *Science and the Practice of Medicine in the nineteenth century*, Cambridge: CUP.

Caldwell A.E. (1970) *Origins of Psychopharmacology: from CPZ to LSD*, Springfield, Ill.: Charles C. Thomas.

Callon M. (1987) 'Society in the making: the study of technology as a tool for sociological analysis', in W.E. Bijker, T.P. Hughes and T.J. Pinch (eds.) *The Social Construction of Technological Systems: new directions in the sociology and the history of technology*, Cambridge, Mass.: MIT Press, pp. 83–103.

Callon M. (1989) *La Science et ses réseaux: genèse et circulation des faits scientifiques*, Paris: La Découverte.

Callow R.K., Cornforth J.W. and Spensley P.C. (1951) 'A source of hecogenin', *Chemistry and Industry*, 18 Aug., 33: 699–700.

Cambrosio A., Keating P. and Mogoutov A. (2004) 'Mapping collaborative work and innovation in biomedicine', *Soc. Stud. Sci.*, vol. 34: 325–64.

Cantor D. (1992) 'Cortisone and the politics of drama, 1949–55', in J.V. Pickstone (ed.) *Medical Innovations in Historical Perspective*, Basingstoke: Macmillan, pp. 165–84.

Cantor D. (1993) 'Cortisone and the politics of Empire: imperialism and British medicine, 1918–1955', *Bul. His. Med.*, 67: 463–93.

Cantwell J. and Barrera P. (1996) 'The localisation of corporate technological trajectories in the inter-war cartels: cooperative learning versus an exchange of knowledge', University of Reading Discussion Papers in Economic and Management series, 8: 1–43.

Caron F. (1979) *Economic History of Modern France*, London: Methuen.

Caron F. (1985) *Le Résistible déclin des sociétés industrielles*, Paris: Perrin.

Caron F. (1995) 'Introduction', in F. Caron, P. Erker, and W. Fisher (eds.) *Innovations in the European Economy between the wars*, Berlin: de Gruyter, pp. 3–29.

Caron F., Erker P., and Fisher W. (eds.) (1995) *Innovations in the European Economy between the wars*, Berlin: de Gruyter.

Carter E.C., Foster R. and Moody J.N. (eds.) (1976) *Enterprise and Entrepreneurs in Nineteenth- and Twentieth-century France*, Baltimore: Johns Hopkins University Press.

Cassier M. (2004) 'Brevets pharmaceutiques et santé publique en France: opposition et dispositifs spécifiques d'appropriation des médicaments entre 1791 et 2004', *Entreprises et Histoire*, 36 : 29–47.

Cayez P. (1988) *Rhône Poulenc: 1895–1975*, Paris: Armand Collin/Masson.

Cayez P. (1992) 'Négocier et survivre: la stratégie de Rhône-Poulenc pendant la seconde guerre mondiale', *Histoire, Economie et Société*, 3: 479–92.

Chain E.B. et al. (1940) 'Penicillin as a chemotherapeutic agent', *Lancet*, 2: 226–8.

Chain E.B. (1971) 'Thirty years of penicillin therapy', *Proc. RSL*, B, 179: 293.

Chain E.B. (1991) 'Penicillin and beyond', *Nature*, 353: 492–4.

Chamak B. (2004) 'Un scientifique pendant l'occupation: le cas d'Antoine Lacassagne', *Revue d'Histoire des Sciences*, 57: 101–33.

Chandler A.D. (1977) *The Visible Hand: the managerial revolution in American business*, Cambridge, Mass.: Harvard University Press.

Chandler A.D. (1990) *Scale and Scope: the dynamics of industrial capitalism*, Cambridge, Mass.: Belknap.

Chandler A.D. (2005) *Shaping the Industrial Century: the remarkable story of the evolution of the modern chemical and pharmaceutical industries*, Cambridge, Mass.: Harvard University Press.

Chandler A.D. and Daems H. (eds.) (1980) *Managerial Hierarchies: comparative perspectives on the rise of the modern industrial enterprise*, Cambridge, Mass.: Harvard University Press.

Chandler A. D., Hagström P. and Sölvell O. (eds.) (1988) *The Dynamic Firm: the role of technology, strategy, organization, and regions*, Oxford: OUP.

Chapman A.W. (1955) *The History of a Modern University*, Sheffield: OUP.

Chauveau S. (1998) 'Entreprises et marchés du médicament en Europe occidentale des années 1880 à la fin des années 1960', *Histoire, Economie et Société*, 1 : 49–81.

Chauveau S. (1999) *L'invention pharmaceutique: la pharmacie entre l'Etat et la société*, Paris: Institut d'Edition Sanofi-Synthélabo.

Chauveau S. (2000) 'l'Etat français et l'industrie pharmaceutique: modernism, corporatisme, réquisitions', in O. Dard, J.-C. Daumas, and F. Marcot (eds.), *L'Occupation, l'état français et les entreprises*, Paris: Association pour le Développement de l'Histoire Economique, pp. 347–360.

Chen W. (1992) 'The laboratory as business: Almroth Wright's vaccine programme and the construction of penicillin', in A. Cunningham and P. Williams (eds.) *The Laboratory Revolution in Medicine*, Cambridge: CUP, pp. 245–92.

Chevassus-au-Louis N. (2004) *Savants sous l'Occupation: enquête sur la vie scientifique française entre 1940 et 1944*, Paris: Seuil.

Chick H. (1957) 'C.J. Martin, 1866–1955', *Bio. Mem. FRS*, 2: 173–208.

Chick H., Hume M. and Macfarlane M. (1971) *War on disease: a history of the Lister Institute*, London: Deutsch.

Chin-Dusting J., Mizrahi J., Jennings G. and Fitzgerald D. (2005) 'Finding improved medicines: the role of academic industrial collaborations', *Nature Reviews Drug Discovery*, 5: 891–7.

Church R. and Tansey T. (forthcoming in 2006) *Knowledge, Trust, and Profit: a history of Burroughs Wellcome & Co. and the transformation of the British Pharmaceutical Industry*, Lancaster: Carnegie Publishing.

Clark R.W. (1965) *Tizard*, London: Methuen.

Clark R. W. (1985) *The Life of Ernst Chain: penicillin and beyond*, London: Weidenfeld & Nicolson.

Clarke H.T. (1949) *The Chemistry of Penicillin*, Princeton: Princeton University Press.

Cohen A. (1993) *Persécutions et sauvetages: juifs et français sous l'occupation et sous Vichy*, Paris: Ed. du Cerf.

Cook J. G. (Nov. 1947) 'Penicillin at Trafford Park', *ICI Magazine*.

Cooter R. (1993) *Surgery and Society in Peace and War: orthopaedics and the organization of modern medicine, 1880–1948*, Basingstoke: Macmillan.

Cooter R., Harrison M. and Sturdy S. (eds.) (1998) *War, Medicine and Modernity*, Stroud: Sutton.

Cope Z. (1966) *Almroth Wright: founder of modern vaccine-therapy*, London: Nelson.

Corley T.A.B. (1994) 'The Beecham group in the world's pharmaceutical industry', *Zeitschrift für Unternehmensgeschichte*, 39: 18–30.

Corley T.A.B. (2003) 'The British pharmaceutical industry since 1851', in L. Richmond, J. Stevenson and A. Turton (eds.), *The Pharmaceutical Industry: a guide to historical records*, Aldershot: Ashgate, pp. 14–32.

Courvoisier S. et al. (1953) 'Propriétés pharmacodynamiques du chlorhydrate de chloro-3-(diméthylamino-3'propyl)-10 phénothiazine (4560 RP)', *Arch. Int. Pharmacodyn.*, 92: 305–61.

Crawford E., Shinn T. and Sörlin S. (1992) 'Introductory essay', in E. Crawford, T. Shinn and S. Sörlin (eds.) *Denationalizing Science: the contexts of international scientific practice*, Dordrecht: Kluwer Academic, pp. 1–42.

Crawford E., Shinn T. and Sörlin S. (eds.) (1992) *Denationalizing Science: the contexts of international scientific practice*, Dordrecht: Kluwer Academic.

Crouzet F. (1985) *De la Supériorité de l'Angleterre sur la France*, Paris: Perrin.

Cunningham A. and Williams P. (eds.) (1992) *The Laboratory Revolution in Medicine*, Cambridge: CUP.

Dahan A. and Pestre D. (2004) *Les Sciences pour la guerre*, Paris: Ed. de l'EHESS.

D.A.F.S.A. (1981) *L'Industrie mondiale de la pharmacie: structures et strategies*, Paris, .

Dale H.H. (1930) 'Letter to the editor', *Lancet*, 2: 1149–50.

Dale H.H. (1939) 'George Barger', *Obit. Not. FRS*, 3: 63–85.

Dale H.H. (1939–1941) 'Sir Patrick Playfair Laidlaw, 1881–1940', *Obit. Not. FRS*, 3: 427–47.

Dale H.H. (1949) 'Introduction', in M. Marquardt, *Paul Ehrlich*, London: W. Heinemann Medical Books, pp. xiii–xx.

Dale H.H. (1958) 'Arthur James Ewins, 1882–1958', *Bio. Mem. FRS*, 4: 81–91.

Dale H.H., Himmelweit F. and Marquardt M. (eds.) (1960) *The collected papers of Paul Ehrlich*, London: Pergamom Press, 3 vols.

Dard O., Daumas J.-C., and Marcot F. (eds.) (2000) *L'Occupation, l'état français et les entreprises*, Paris: Association pour le Développement de l'Histoire Économique.

Davenport-Hines R.T.P. and Jones G. (eds.) (1988) *The End of Insularity: essays in comparative business history*, London: Cass.

Davenport-Hines R. T.P. and Slinn J. (1992) *Glaxo: a history to 1962*, Cambridge: CUP.

David P. (1993) 'Path dependence and predictability in dynamic systems with local network externalities: a paradigm for historical economics', in D. Foray and C. Freeman (eds.) *Technology and the Wealth of Nations: the dynamics of constructed advantage*, London: OECD, pp. 209–31.

David P. (1994) 'Why are institutions the 'carriers of history'? Path dependence and the evolution of conventions, organizations and institutions', in *Structural Change and Economic Dynamics*, 5: 205–20.

David P., Foray D. and Steinmueller W.E. (1999) 'The research network and the new economics of science: from metaphors to organizational behaviors', in A. Gambardella and F. Malerba (eds.) *The Organization of Economic Innovation in Europe*, Cambridge: CUP, pp. 303–42.

Debru C., Gayon J. and Picard J-F. (eds.) (1994) *Les Sciences biologiques et médicales en France 1920–1950*, Paris: Editions CNRS.

de Chadarevian S. and Kamminga H. (eds.) (1998) *Molecularizing Biology and Medicine: new practices and alliances, 1910s–1970s*, Amsterdam: Harwood Academic.

de Chadarevian S. (2002) *Designs for Life: molecular biology after World War II*, Cambridge: CUP.

Delaunay A. (1962) *L'Institut Pasteur, des origines à aujourd'hui*, Paris: France Empire.

Delay J. and Deniker P. (1961) *Méthodes chimiothérapiques en psychiatrie: les nouveaux médicaments psychotropes*, Paris: Masson.

Delépine M. (1950) 'Ernest Fourneau, sa vie, son oeuvre', *Bulletin de la Société Chimique de France*, 1–75.

Delépine M. (1950) 'Notice sur la vie et les travaux de Ernest Fourneau, 1872–1949', *Bulletin de la Société Chimique de France*, 17: 953–82.

de Solla Price D. (1965) *Little Science, Big Science*, New York: Columbia University Press.

Desnuelle P. (n.d.) 'Claude Fromageot, 1899–1958', in *Mémorial Claude Fromageot, 1899–1958*, Paris: 5–27.

Dickens F. (1975) 'Edward Charles Dodds', *Bio. Mem. FRS*, 21: 227–67.

Direction des Recherches, Rhône-Poulenc Santé (1982) *Rhône-Poulenc 40 years of research in the field of health care*, Besançon: Direction Information of Rhône-Poulenc.

Dixit A. and Nalebuff B.J. (1991) *Thinking Strategically: the competitive edge in business, politics and everyday life*, New York: Norton, 1991.

Dobson A.P. (1986) *Wartime Aid to Britain*, London: Croom Helm.

'Documentation française: de Pasteur à Fleming' (Dec. 1945– Jan. 1946), *Exposition de la Pénicilline au Palais de la Découverte*.

Dollery, C. (1978) *The End of an Age of Optimism: medical science in retrospect and prospect*, London: Nuffield Provincial Hospitals Trust.

Duclert V. (1997) 'Les revues scientifiques: une histoire de la science et des savants français sous l'Occupation', *La Revue des Revues*, 24: 161–95.

Dyhouse C. (1995) *No Distinction of Sex? Women in British universities, 1870–1939*, London: UCL Press.

Earle E.M. (ed.) (1964) *Modern France: problems of the Third and Fourth Republic*, New York: Russell and Russell.

Edgerton D.E.H. (1987) 'Science and technology in British business history', *Bus. His.*, 29: 84–103.

Edgerton D.E.H. (1990) 'Science and war', in R.C. Olby, G.N. Cantor, J.R.R. Christie and M.J.S. Hodge (eds.) *Companion to the History of Modern Science*, London: Routledge, pp. 934–45.

Edgerton D.E.H. (1994) 'British industrial R&D, 1900–1970', *J. Europ. Econ. His.*, 23: 49–68.

Edgerton D.E.H. (1996) *Science, Technology and the British Industrial 'Decline', 1870–1970*, Cambridge: CUP.

Edgerton D.E.H. (2006) *Warfare State: Britain, 1920–1970*, Cambridge: CUP.

Edgerton D.E.H. and Horrocks S.M. (1994) 'British industrial research and development before 1945', *Econ. His. Rev.*, XLVII: 213–38.

'Edmond Emile Blaise (1872–1939)' (1989) in C. Charle and E. Telkès (eds.) *Les Professeurs de la Faculté des Sciences de Paris: dictionnaire biographique, 1901–1939*, Paris: Ed. du CNRS, pp. 40–2.

'Sir Edward Abraham' (12 May 1999) Obituary, *Times*, 21.

Elbaum B. and Lazonick W. (1986a) 'An institutional perspective on British decline', in Elbaum and Lazonick (eds.) *The Decline of the British Economy*, Oxford: Clarendon Press, pp. 1–17.

Elbaum B. and Lazonick W. (eds.) (1986b) *The Decline of the British Economy*, Oxford: Clarendon Press.

Elder A. E. (ed.) (1970) 'The History of Penicillin Production', *Chem. Eng. Series*, 66, New York.

Etkowitz H. and Leydersdorff L. (1998) 'The endless transition: a 'triple helix' of university-industry-government relations', *Minerva*, 1998, 36: 203–8.

Evang K. (1960) *Health Service, Society and Medicine*, London: OUP.

Fabre R. and Dillemann G. (1971) *Histoire de la pharmacie*, Paris: PUF.

Faure M. (1991) 'Cent années d'enseignement à l'Institut Pasteur', in M. Morange (ed.) *L'Institut Pasteur: contributions à son histoire*, Paris: La Découverte, pp. 62–74.

Federation of British Industries (1946), *Industry and Research: the full report of a two-day conference held at the Kingsway Hall*, London: Isaac Pitmona, 1946.

Feldberg W.S. (1969) 'Henry Halett Dale, 1875–1968', *Bio. Mem. FRS*, 16: 77–173.

Ferry G. (1998) *Dorothy Hodgkin: a life*, London: Granta Books.

Fleming A. (1939) 'Recent advances in vaccine therapy', *BMJ*, 2: 99–115.

Fleming A. (ed) (1946) *Penicillin: its practical applications*, London: Butterworth & Co.

Florey H.W. (1949) *Antibiotics: a survey of penicillin, streptomycin, and other antimicrobial substances from fungi, actinomyces, bacteria, and plants*, Oxford: OUP, vols. 1 and 2.

Florey H.W. (1956) 'The medical aspects of the development of resistance to antibiotics', *Giornale di Microbiologia*, 2: 361–71.

Florey H.W. (1960) 'Medical science in the twentieth-century', *Yale Journal of Biology and Medicine*, 33: 212–26.

Florey H.W. (1962) 'Prestige in academic scientific research', *Nature*, 193: 1017–8.

Foray D. and Freeman C. (eds.) (1993) *Technology and the Wealth of Nations: the dynamics of constructed advantage*, London: OECD.

Foreman-Peck J. (1995) *Smith and Nephew in the Health Care Industry*, Aldershot: Edward Elgar.

Foster W.D. (1961) *A Short History of Clinical Pathology*, Edinburgh: E.&S. Livingstone.

Fourneau E. and Tiffeneau M. (1905) 'Sur quelques oxydes d'éthylène aromatiques monosubstitués', *Comptes rendus de l'Académie des Sciences*, 140: 1595.

Fourneau E. and Tiffeneau M. (1914) 'Détermination de la constitution des halohydrines par action des amines tertiaires. Iodhydrines dérivées du styrolène', *Bull. Soc. Chim. Fr.*, 15: 4, 275.

Fourneau E. and Tiffeneau M. (1926) 'Sur les propriétés anésthésiques des alcoxybenzhydrylamines', 12ᵉ Congrès de Stockholm.

Fox D. M. (1986) 'The National Health Service and the Second World War: the elaboration of consensus', in H.L. Smith (ed.) *War and Social Change: British society in the Second World War*, Manchester: Manchester University Press, pp. 32–57.

Fox R. (1986) 'Contingency or mentality? Technical innovation in France in the age of science-based industry', in M. Kranzberg (ed.), *Technological Education — Technological Style*, San Francisco: San Francisco University Press, pp. 59–68.

Fox R. (1990) 'Research, education, and the industrial economy in modern France', in *The Academic Research Enterprise within the Industrialized Nations: comparative perspectives*, Washington, D.C.: National Academic Press, pp. 95–107.

Fox R. (1991) 'An Uneasy Courtship: rhetoric and reality in the relations between academic and industrial chemistry, 1770–1914', IV National Meeting 'Storia e Fondamenti della Chimica' (Venezia, 7–9 Nov. 1991).

Fox R. (ed.) (1996) *Technological Change: methods and themes in the history of technology*, Amsterdam: Harwood Academic.

Fox R. and Weisz G. (eds.) (1980) *The Organisation of Science and Technology in France 1808–1914*, Cambridge: CUP.

Fox R. and Guagnini A. (1985) 'Britain in perspective: the European context of industrial training and innovation, 1880–1914', *History and Technology*, 2: 133–50.

Fox R. and Guagnini A. (1992) 'Life in the slow lane: research and engineering in Britain, France and Italy, ca. 1900', in P. Kroes and M. Bakker (eds.) *Technological Development and Science in the Industrial Age*, Amsterdam: pp. 133–53.

Fox R. and Guagnini A. (1993a) 'Introduction', in R. Fox and A. Guagnini (eds.), *Education, Technology and Industrial Performance in Europe, 1850–1939*, Cambridge, Mass.: CUP, pp. 1–2.

Fox R. and Guagnini A. (eds.) (1993b) *Education, Technology and Industrial Performance in Europe, 1850–1939*, Cambridge: CUP.

Fox R. and Guagnini A. (1999) *Laboratories, Workshops and Sites. Concepts and practices of research in industrial Europe, 1800–1914*, Berkeley: Berkeley Papers in History of Science.

Frances J., Levacic R., Mitchell J., and Thompson G. (1991) 'Introduction', in Thompson, Frances, Levacic, and Mitchell (eds.) *Markets, Hierarchies and Networks: the coordination of social life*, London: Sage, pp. 1–19.

Frank R. (1993) 'La mémoire empoisonnée', in J.-P. Azéma and F. Bédarida (eds.) *La France des années noires*, Paris: Seuil, vol 2, pp. 483–514.

Freidson E. (1986) *Professional Powers: a study of the institutionalisation of formal knowledge*, Chicago: Chicago University Press.

Galambos L. with Eliot Sewell J. (1995) *Networks of Innovations: vaccine development at Merck, Sharpe & Dohme, and Mulford, 1895–1995*, Cambridge, Mass.: CUP.

Galdston I. (1943) *Behind the Sulfa-Drugs: a short history of chemotherapy*, New York: D. Appleton-Century Co. Inc.

Galison P. (1987) *How Experiments End*, Chicago: Chicago University Press.

Galison P. and Kevly B. (eds.) (1992) *Big Science: the growth of large-scale research*, Stanford, CA: Stanford University Press.

Gambardella A. and Malerba F. (eds.) (1999) *The Organization of Economic Innovation in Europe*, Cambridge: CUP.

Gambetta D. (1988) 'Can we trust trust?', in D. Gambetta (ed.) *Trust: making and breaking cooperative relations*, Oxford: Basil Blackwell, pp. 213–37.

Gambetta D. (ed.) (1988), *Trust: making and breaking cooperative relations*, Oxford: Basil Blackwell.

Garber E. (ed.) (1990) *Beyond History of Science: essays in honor of Robert E. Scholfield*, Cranbury, N.J.: Lehigh University Press.

Gambrelle F. (1995) *Innovating for Life: Rhône-Poulenc, 1895–1995*, Paris: Albin Michel.

Gaudillière, J.-P. (1991) 'Catalyse enzymatique et oxydations cellulaires. L'oeuvre de Gabriel Bertrand et son héritage', in M. Morange (ed.) *L'Institut Pasteur: contributions à son histoire*, Paris: La Découverte, pp. 118–36.

Gaudillière J.-P. (1994) 'Les biochimistes français entre légitimité médicale et légitimité biologique', 1930–1960', in C. Debru, J. Gayon and J-F. Picard (eds.) *Les Sciences biologiques et médicales en France 1920–1950*, Paris: Editions CNRS, pp. 265–82.

Gaudillière J.-P. and Löwy I. (eds.) (1998) *The Invisible Industrialist: manufactures and the production of scientific knowledge*, Basingstoke: Macmillan.

Gaudillière J.P. (2002) *Inventer la biomédecine: la france, l'amérique et la production des savoirs du vivant*, Paris: La Découverte.

Gaudillière J.-P. (2004) 'Hormones, régimes d'innovation et stratégies d'entreprise: les exemples de Schering et Bayer', *Entreprises et Histoire*, 36: 84–102.

Geertz C. (1993) *The Interpretation of Cultures*, London: Fontanal.

Geison G. L. (1995) *The Private Science of Louis Pasteur*, Princeton, N.J.: Princeton University Press.

Geilijns A.C. and Their S.O. (2002) 'Medical innovation and institutional interdependence: rethinking university-industry connections', *JAMA*, 287: 72–7.

Goldsmith M.L. (1946) *The Road to Penicillin: a history of chemotherapy*, London: Lindsay Drummond.

Gilmann H. and Shirley D.A. (1944) 'Some derivatives of phenothiazine', *Am. J. Chem. Soc.*, 66: 888–93.

Goldsworthy N.E. and Florey H.W. (1930) 'Some properties of mucus with specific references to its antibacterial functions', *B. J. Ex. Path.*, 11: 192–208.

Goodman J. (1998) 'Can it ever be pure science? Pharmaceuticals and the pharmaceutical industry and biomedical research in the twentieth-century', in J.-P. Gaudillière and I. Löwy (eds.) *The Invisible Industrialist: manufactures and the production of scientific knowledge*, Basingstoke: Macmillan, pp. 143–65.

Goudemand M. (1992) 'La situation hospitalière avant et immédiatement après l'introduction de Largactil', in J.-P. Olie, D. Ginestet, G. Jollès and H. Lôo (eds.) *Histoire d'une découverte en psychiatrie: 40 ans de chimiothérapie neuroleptique*, Paris: Doin, pp. 19–27.

Granovetter M. (1973) 'The strength of weak ties', *Am. J. Soc.*, 1973, 78: 1360–80.

Granovetter M. (1983) 'The strength of weak ties: a network theory revisited', *Sociological Theory*, 1: 201–33.

Greene N.M. (ed.) (1968) *Halothane*, Philadelphia: F.A. Davis Co.

Gross A.G. (1996) *The Rhetoric of Science*, Cambridge, Mass.: Harvard University Press, 2nd edn.

Guerlac H.E. (1964) 'Science and French national strength', in E.M. Earle (ed.), *Modern France: problems of the Third and Fourth Republic*, New York: Russell and Russell, pp. 81–105.

Guillaume P. (1996) *Le Rôle du médecin depuis deux siècles (1800–1945)*, Paris: Assocation pour l'Histoire de la Sécurité Sociale.

Gummett P. (1980) *Scientists in Whitehall*, Manchester: Manchester University Press.

Haber L.F. (1971) *The Chemical Industry 1900–1930: international growth and technological change*, Oxford: Clarendon Press.

Hakenbec R., Höltje J.-V. and Labischinski H. (eds.) (1983) *The Target of Penicillin: the nurein sacculus of bacterial cell walls, architecture and growth*, Berlin: W. de Gruyter.

Hall A.R. and Bembridge B.A. (1986) *Physic and Philanthropy: a history of the Wellcome Trust, 1936–1986*, Cambridge: CUP.

Halpern B.N. (1942) 'Les antihistaminiques de synthèse. Essais de chimiothérapie des états allergiques', *Archives Internationales de Pharmacodynamie et de Thérapie*, 68 : 339–408.

Hamburger J. (ed.) (1947) *Medical Research in France during the War (1939–1945)*, Paris: Flammarion.

Hancher L. (1990) *Regulating for Competition: government, law and the pharmaceutical industry in the United Kingdom and France*, Oxford: Clarendon Press.

Hannah L. (1980) 'Visible and invisible hands in Great Britain', in A.D. Chandler and H. Daems (eds.), *Managerial Hierarchies: comparative perspectives on the rise of the modern industrial enterprise*, Cambridge, Mass.: Harvard University Press, pp. 41–71.

Hancock W.K. and Gowing M.M., *British War Economy*, London: HMSO.

Hare R. (1970) *The Birth of Penicillin: and the disarming of microbes*, London: George Allen & Unwin.

Hare R. (1982) 'New light on the history of penicillin', *Med. His.*, 26: 1–24.

Harington C.R. (1956) 'Harold King, 1887–1956', *Bio. Mem. FRS*, 2: 157–71.

Hayes P. (1987) *Industry and Ideology: IG Farben in the Nazi era*, Cambridge: CUP.

Heaman E.A. (2003) *St Mary's: the history of a London teaching hospital*, Montreal and Kingston: McGill-Queen's University Press.

Hecht G. (1998) *The Radiance of France: nuclear power and national identity after World War II*, Cambridge, Mass.: MIT Press.

Hendry J. (1989) *Innovating for Failure: government policy and the early British computer industry*, Cambridge, Mass.: MIT Press.

Hewison R. (1995) *Culture and Consensus: England, art and politics since 1940*, London: Methuen.

Higby G.J. and Stroud E.C. (eds.) (1997) *The Inside Story of Medicines: a symposium*, Madison, Wis.: American Institute of the History of Pharmacy.

Hobby G.L. (1985) *Penicillin: meeting the challenge*, Yale: Yale University Press.

Hodgkin D.C. and Maslen E.N. (1961) 'The X-ray analysis of the structure of cephalosporin C', *Biochem. J.*, 79: 393–402.

Hofstede G. (1991) *Cultures and Organizations: software of the mind*, London: McGraw Hill.

Hofstede G. (1997) 'Motivation, leadership and organization: do American theories apply abroad?', in D.S. Pugh (ed.), *Organization Theory: selected readings*, London: 4th ed., pp. 223–50.

Hounshell D. A. and Smith J. K. (1988) *Science and Corporate Strategy: DuPont R&D, 1902–1980*, Cambridge: CUP.

Holton R.J. (1992) *Economy and Society*, London: Routledge.

Homburg E. (1992) 'The emergence of research laboratories in the dyestuffs industry, 1870–1900', *BJHS*, 25: 91–111.

Horrocks S.M. (1995) 'Technology and chocolate: research in the British food industry before 1940', in F. Caron, P. Erker, and W. Fisher (eds.), *Innovations in the European Economy between the wars*, Berlin: de Gruyter, pp. 131–48.

Horrocks S.M. (1999) 'Enthusiasm constrained? British industrial R & D and the transition from war to peace, 1942–1951', *Bus. His.*, 41: 42–63.

Hughes J. (2002) 'Craftsmanship and social service: W.H. Bragg and the Modern Royal Institution', in F.A.J.L. James (ed.) *'The Common Purposes of Life': science and society at the Royal Institution of Great Britain*, Aldershot: Ashgate, pp. 225–47.

Hughes T.P. (1983) *Networks of Power. electrification in Western Society, 1880–1930*, Baltimore: Johns Hopkins University Press.

Hughes T.P. (1986) 'The seamless web: technology, science, etcetera... etcetera...', *Soc. Stud. Sci.,* 16: 281–92.

Hunt J.A. (1991) 'Pioneering penicillin production in Britain', *Pharm. J.,* Dec. 21/28: 807–10.

Hunt L. (1989) 'Introduction: history, culture, and text', in L. Hunt (ed.) *The New Cultural History*, Berkeley: University of California Press, pp. 1–22.

Hunt L. (ed.) (1989) *The New Cultural History*, Berkeley: University of California Press, pp. 1–22.

Inkster I. (1983) 'Introduction: Aspects of the History of Science and Science Culture in Britain, 1780–1850 and beyond', in I. Inkster and J. Morrell (eds.) *Metropolis and Province: science in British culture, 1780–1850*, London: Hutchinson, pp. 11–55.

Inkster I. and Morrell J. (eds.) (1983) *Metropolis and Province: science in British culture, 1780–1850*, London: Hutchinson.

James F.A.J.L. (ed.) (2002) *'The Common Purposes of Life': science and society at the Royal Institution of Great Britain*, Aldershot: Ashgate.

Jamous H. (1969) *Sociologie de la décision: la réforme des études médicales et des structures hospitalières*, Paris: Ed. CNRS.

Jewkes J., Sawyers D. and Stillerman B. (eds.) (1969) *The Sources of Invention,* London: Macmillan, 2nd edn.

Jones E. (2001) *The business of Medicine*, London: Profile Books.

Jones T. (1991) 'The value of academia/industrial links in R&D', in S.R. Walker (ed.), *Creating the Right Environment for Drug Discovery*, Lancaster: Quay Publishing, pp. 77–84.

Johnson P.S. (ed) (1980) *The Structure of British Industry*, London: Granada.

Jordanova L.J. (1995) 'The social construction of medical knowledge', *Med. His.,* 8: 361–421.

Keith S.T. (1981) 'Inventions, patents, and commercial development from governmentally financed research in Great Britain: the origins of the National Research and Development Corporation', *Minerva*, 19: 92–122.

Kelly T. (1981) *For Advancement of Learning: the University of Liverpool 1881–1981*, Liverpool: Liverpool University Press.

Kennedy C. (1986) *ICI: the company that changed our lives*, London: Hutchinson.

Knorr-Cetina K. and Mulkay M. (eds.) (1983) *Science Observed: perspectives on the social study of science*, London: Sage.

Kohler R.E. (1982) *From Medical Chemistry to Biochemistry: the making of a biomedical discipline*, Cambridge: CUP.

König W. (1996) 'Science-based industry or industry-based science? Electrical engineering in Germany before World War 1', *Tech. and Cult.*, 37: 70–101.

Kragh H. (1998) 'The take-off phase of the Danish chemical industry, ca. 1910–1940', in A.S. Travis, H.G.Schröter, E. Homburg and P.J.T. Morris (eds.), *Determinants in the Evolution of the European Chemical Industry, 1900–1939*, Dordrecht: Kluwer Academic, pp. 321–39.

Kranzberg M. (ed.) (1986) *Technological Education — Technological Style*, San Francisco: San Francisco University Press.

Krige J. and Pestre D. (1997) 'Introduction', in D. Pestre and J. Krige (eds.) *Science in the Twentieth Century*, Amsterdam: Harwood Academic, pp. xxi–xxxv.

Krige J. and Pestre D. (eds.) (1997) *Science in the Twentieth Century*, Amsterdam: Harwood Academic.

Krige J. (2006) *American Hegemony and the Postwar Reconstruction of Science in Europe*, Cambridge, Mass.: MIT Press.

Kroes P. and Bakker M. (eds.) (1992) *Technological Development and Science in the Industrial Age*, Amsterdam: Kluwer Academic.

Kuhn T.S. (1970) *The Structure of Scientific Revolutions*, Chicago: Chicago University Press, 2nd edn.

Kuisel R.F. (1981) *Capitalism and the State in Modern France: renovation and economic management in the twentieth century*, New York: CUP.

Kuisel R.F. (1993) *Seducing the French: the dilemma of Americanization*, Berkeley: University of California Press.

Kunkel. J.H. (1970) *Society and Economic Growth: a behavioural perspective of social change*, London: OUP.

Lacroix- Riz A. (1997) 'Les élites françaises et la collaboration économique: la banque, l'industrie, Vichy et le Reich', *Revue d'Histoire de la Shoah*, Janvier-Avril: 8–123.

Landes D. S. (1969) *The Unbound Prometheus: technological change and industrial development in Wetsern Europe from 1750 to the present*, Cambridge: CUP.

Lane F.C. and Riemersma J.C. (eds.) (1953) *Enterprise and Secular Change: readings in economic history*, London: George Allen & Unwin.

Lapresle C. (1991) 'Le rôle de l'hôpital de l'Institut Pasteur dans l'application à la médecine des recherches fondamentales', in M. Morange (ed.) *L'Institut Pasteur: contributions à son histoire*, Paris: La Découverte, pp. 45–51.

Latour B. (1983) 'Give me a laboratory and I will raise the world', in K. Knorr-Cetina and M. Mulkay (eds.) *Science Observed: perspectives on the social study of science*, London: Sage, pp. 141–70.

Latour B. and S. Woolgar (1979) *Science in Action: how to follow scientists and engineers through society*, Beverly Hills: Sage.

Latour B. (1999) 'On recalling ANT', in J. Law and J. Hassard (eds.) *Actor Network Theory and After*, Oxford: Blackwells, pp. 15–25.

Law J. and Hassard J. (eds.) (1999) *Actor Network Theory and After*, Oxford: Blackwells.

Lawrence C. (1997) 'Clinical research', in J. Krige and D. Pestre (eds.) *Science in the Twentieth Century*, Amsterdam: Harwood Academic, pp. 439–60.

Lawrence C. and Weisz G. (eds.) (1998) *Greater than the Parts: holism in biomedicine, 1920–1950*, Oxford: OUP.

Lax E. (2004) *The Mould in Dr Florey's Coat: the remarkable true story of the penicillin miracle*, London: Little, Brown.

Lazell H.G. (1975) *From Pills to Penicillin: the Beecham story*, London: Heinemann.

Lederer E. (1989) 'La chimie des substances naturelles', *Cah. His. CNRS*, 2: 43–54.

Le Fanu J. (1999) *The Rise and Fall of Modern Medicine*, London: Abacus.

Le Roux M. (2003) 'Genèse des textes de Pierre Potier, chimiste des substances naturelles', *Genesis*, 20: 91–125.

Le Roux M. (2006) 'Hommage à Pierre Potier (1934–2006)', *Bulletin de L'Association des Anciens Amis du CNRS*, 41: 5–27.

Lesch J.E. (1993) 'Chemistry and biomedicine in an industrial setting: the invention of the sulfa-drugs', in S.H. Mauskopf (ed.) *Chemical Sciences in the Modern World*, Philadelphia: Philadelphia University Press, pp. 158–215.

Lesch J.E. (1997) 'The discovery of M & B 693 (Sulfapyridine)', in G.J. Higby and E.C. Stroud (eds.), *The Inside Story of Medicines: a symposium*, Madison, Wis.: American Institute of the History of Pharmacy, pp. 101–9.

Levy-Leboyer M. (1976) 'Innovation and business strategies in nineteenth- and twentieth-century France', in E.C. Carter, R. Foster and J.N. Moody (eds.) *Enterprise and Entrepreneurs in Nineteenth- and Twentieth-century France*, Baltimore: Johns Hopkins University Press, pp. 87–135.

Levy-Leboyer M. (1980) 'The large corporation in modern France', in A.D. Chandler and H. Daems (eds.), *Managerial Hierarchies: comparative perspectives on the rise of the modern industrial enterprise*, Cambridge, Mass.: Harvard University Press, pp. 117–60.

Liebenau J., 'Industrial R&D in pharmaceutical firms in the early twentieth century', *Bus. His.*, 26: 329–46.

Liebenau J. (1987a) *Medical Science and Medical Industry: the formation of the American pharmaceutical industry*, Baltimore: Johns Hopkins University Press.

Liebenau J. (1987b) 'The British success with penicillin', *Soc. Stud. Sci.*, 17: 69–86.

Liebenau J. (1988a) 'Ethical business: the formation of the pharmaceutical industry in Britain, Germany and the US before 1914', in R.T.P. Davenport-Hines and G. Jones (eds.), *The End of Insularity: essays in comparative business history*, London: Cass, pp. 117–29.

Liebenau J. (1988b) 'Patents and the chemical industry: tools of business srtategy', in J. Liebenau (ed.) *The Challenge of New Technology: innovation in British business since 1850*, Aldershot: Gower, pp. 135–50.

Liebenau J. (1989) 'The MRC and the pharmaceutical industry: the model of insulin', in J. Austoker and L. Bryder (eds.) *Historical Perspectives on the Role of the MRC*, Oxford: OUP, pp. 163–80.

Liebenau J. (1990a) 'The rise of the British pharmaceutical industry', *BMJ*, 301: 724–33.

Liebenau J. (1990b) 'The twentieth-century British pharmaceutical industry in international context', in J. Liebenau, G.J. Higby and E.C. Stroud (eds.) *Pill Peddlers: essays on the history of the pharmaceutical industry*, Madison, Wis.: American Institute of the History of Pharmacy, pp. 123–33.

Liebenau J., Higby G.J. and Stroud E.C. (eds.) (1990) *Pill Peddlers: essays on the history of the pharmaceutical industry*, Madison, Wis.: American Institute of the History of Pharmacy.

Liebenau J. and Robson M. (1991) 'L'Institut Pasteur et l'industrie pharmaceutique', in M. Morange (ed.) *L'Institut Pasteur: contributions à son histoire*, Paris: La Découverte, pp. 52–61.

Lindenberg D. (1990) *Les Années souterraines (1937–1947)*, Paris: La Découverte.

'The Lister Institute of Preventive Medicine', (1975) Editorial, *Lancet*, 1: 54.

Lôo H. (1992) 'Une révolution thérapeutique en psychiatrie: la chlorpromazine', J.-P. Olie, D. Ginestet, G. Jollès and H. Lôo (eds.) *Histoire d'une découverte en psychiatrie: 40 ans de chimiothérapie neuroleptique*, Paris: Doin, pp. 13–9.

Lorenz E.H. (1988) 'Neither friends nor strangers: informal networks of subcontracting in French industry', in D. Gambetta (ed.) *Trust: making and breaking cooperative relations*, Oxford: Basil Blackwell, pp. 194–210.

Löwy I. (ed.) (1992a) *Medicine and Change: historical and sociological studies of medical innovation*, Montrouge: John Libbey Eurotext.

Löwy I. (1992b) 'The strength of loose concepts: boundary objects, federative experimental strategies and discipline growth: the case of inmmunology', *His. Sci.*, 30: 371–96.

Löwy I. (1994) 'On hybridizations, networks and new disciplines: the Pasteur Institute and the development of microbiology in France', *Stud. Hist. Phil. Sci.*, 25: 655–88.

Löwy I. (2005) 'Biotherapies of chronic diseases in the interwar period: From Witte's peptone to Penicillium extract', *Studies in History and Philosophy of Biology and Biomedical Sciences*, 2005, vol. 36 .

Lundgren A. (1991) *Technological Innovation and Industrial Evolution: the emergence of industrial networks*, Stockholm: Routledge.

Lundgreen P. (1980) 'The organisation of science and technology in France: a German perspective', in R. Fox and G. Weisz (eds.) *The Organisation of Science and Technology in France 1808–1914*, Cambridge: CUP, pp. 309–32.

Lwoff A. (1979) 'Jacques Lucien Monod', in A. Lwoff and A. Ullmann (eds.) *Origins of Molecular Biology: a tribute to Jacques Monod*, New York: Academic Press, pp. 1–23.

Lwoff A. and Ullmann A. (eds.) (1979) *Origins of Molecular Biology: a tribute to Jacques Monod*, New York: Academic Press.

Macdonald G. (1980) *One Hundred Years Wellcome, 1880–1980*, London: the Wellcome Foundation Ltd.

Macfarlane G. (1979) *Howard Florey: the making of a great scientist*, Oxford: OUP.

Macfarlane G. (1985) *Alexander Fleming: the man and the myth*, Oxford: OUP.

MacLeod R. and K. (1970) 'The origins of the DSIR: reflections on ideas and men', *Pub. Admin.*, 48: 23–32.

MacLeod R. and K. (1975) 'War and economic development: government and the optical industry in Britain, 1914–8', in J.M. Winter (ed.), *War and Economic Development: essays in memory of David Joslin*, Cambridge: CUP, pp. 165–203.

MacLeod R. (1998) 'Chemistry for King and Kaiser: revisiting chemical enterprise and the European war', in A.S. Travis, H.G. Schröter, E. Homburg and P.J.T. Morris (eds.) *Determinants in the Evolution of the European Chemical Industry, 1900–1939*, Dordrecht: Kluwer Academic, pp. 25–49.

Magnello E. (2002) 'The introduction of mathematical statistics into medical research: the roles of Karl Pearson, Major Greenwood, and Austin Bradford Hill', in E. Magnello and A. Hardy (eds.) *The Road to Medical Statistics*, Amsterdam: Rodopi, pp. 95–123.

Magnello E. and Hardy A. (eds.) (2002) *The Road to Medical Statistics*, Amsterdam: Rodopi.

Major R.T. (1948) 'Cooperation of science and industry in the development of the antibiotics', *Chem. and Eng. News*, 25 Oct., 26: 3186–91.

Maienschein J. (1993) 'Why collaborate?', *J. His. Biol.*, 26: 167–83.

Margairaz M. and Rousso H. (1992) 'Vichy, la guerre et les entreprises', *Histoire, Economie et Société*, 3: 337–68.

Marks H.M. (1992) 'Cortisone, 1949: a year in the political life of a drug', *Bull. Hist. Med.*, 66: 419–39.

Markus A.I. (1990) 'From Erhlich to Waksman: chemotherapy and the seamed web of the past', in E. Garber (ed.) *Beyond History of Science: essays in honor of Robert E. Scholfield*, Cranbury, N.J.: Lehigh University Press, pp. 266–83.

Marquardt M. (1949) *Paul Ehrlich*, London: W. Heinemann Medical Books.

Marteret M.J. (1954) 'Le Centre de Recherche Nicolas Grillet de la Societé Rhône-Poulenc', *L'Industrie Nationale*, 1: 36–46.

Marwick A. (1978) *War and Social Change in the Twentieth Century: a comparative study of Britain, France, Russia and the United States*, London: Macmillan.

Massé P. (1984) *Aléas et progrès. Entre Candide et Cassandre*, Paris: Economica.

Matthews R.C.O., Feinstein C.H. and Odling-Smee J.C. (1982) *British Economic Growth, 1856–1973*, Oxford: Clarendon Press.

Matthews J. Rosser (1995) 'Major Greenwood versus Almroth Wright: contrasting visions of "scientific" medicine in Edwardian Britain', *Bulletin of the History of Medicine*, 69: 30–43.

Mauskopf S.H. (ed.) (1993) *Chemical Sciences in the Modern World*, Philadelphia: Philadelphia University Press.

Maxwell R.A. and Eckhardt S.B. (1990) *Drug Discovery: a casebook and analysis*, Clifton, N.J.: Humana Press.

McGraw D. J. (1991) 'On leaving the mine: historiographic resource exhaustion in antibiotics history', *Dynamis*, 11: 415–36.

McKeown T. (1976) *The Role of Medicine. Dream, Mirage, or Nemesis?*, London: Nuffield Provincial Hospitals Trust.

Mead M. (1937) *Cooperation and Competition among Primitive Peoples*, New York: McGraw Hill, 1st edn.

Melville H. (1964) *The Department of Scientific and Industrial Research*, London: George Allen & Unwin.

Mémorial Claude Fromageot, 1899–1958 (Paris, n.d.).

Mendelsohn A. (2003) 'Bacteriology and microbiology', in J. Heilbron (ed.) *The Oxford Companion to the History of Modern Science*, New York: Oxford University Press, pp. 75–77.

Mioche P. (1987) *Le Plan Monnet: genèse et élaboration, 1941–1947*, Paris: Ed. de la Sorbonne.

Mitchell D. (1995) 'There's no such thing as culture: towards a reconceptualization of the idea of culture in geography', *Transactions of the Institute of British Geographers*, 20: 102–16.

Moberg C.L. and Cohn Z.A. (eds.) (1990) *Launching the Antibiotic Era: personal accounts of the discovery and use of the first antibiotics*, New York: Rockefeller University Press.

Moberg C.L. (1991) 'Penicillin's forgotten man: Norman Heatley', *Science*, 16 Aug., 253: 734–5.

Monnet J. (1978) *Memoirs*, London: Collins.

Morange M. (ed.) (1991) *L'Institut Pasteur: contributions à son histoire*, Paris: La Découverte.

Morange M. (1998) *A History of Molecular Biology*, Cambridge, Mass.: CUP.

Morrell J.B. (1972) 'The chemist breeders: the research schools of Justus Liebig and Thomas Thomson', *Ambix*, 19: 2–47.

Morrell J.B. (1990) 'Professionalisation', in R.C. Olby, G.N. Cantor, J.R.R. Christie and M.J.S. Hodge (eds.) *Companion to the History of Modern Science*, London: Routledge, pp. 980–9.

Morrell J.B. (1996) *Science at Oxford, 1914–1939: transforming an arts university*, Oxford: Clarendon Press.

Moses H. and Martin J.B. (2001) 'Academic relationships with industry: a new model for biomedical research', *JAMA*, 285: 933–5.

Moulin A.-M. (1991) 'L'inconscient Pasteurien: l'immunologie de Metchnikoff à Oudin, 1917–1940', in M. Morange (ed.) *L'Institut Pasteur: contributions à son histoire*, Paris: La Découverte, pp. 144–64.

Moulin A.-M. (1992) 'Patriarchal science: the network of the overseas Pasteur Institutes', in P. Petitjean, C. Jami and A.-M. Moulin (eds.) *Science and Empires*, Dordrecht: Kluwer Academic, 1992, pp. 307–22.

Moulin A.-M. and Guénel A. (1993) 'L'Institut Pasteur et la naissance de l'industrie de la santé', in J.-C. Beaune (ed.) *La Philosophie du remède*, Paris: PUF, pp. 91–109.

Mowery D.C. (1986) 'Industrial Research, 1900–1950', in B. Elbaum and W. Lazonick (eds.) *The Decline of the British Economy*, Oxford: Clarendon Press, pp. 189–222.

Mowery D.C. (1989) 'The organisation of industrial research in Great Britain, 1900–1950', in D.C. Mowery and N. Rosenberg (eds.) *Technology and the Pursuit of Economic Growth*, Cambridge: CUP, pp. 98–119.

Mowery D.C. and Rosenberg N. (eds.) (1989) *Technology and the Pursuit of Economic Growth*, Cambridge: CUP.

Mukerji C. (1989) *A Fragile Power: scientists and the state*, Princeton, N.J.: Princeton University Press.

Mulholland K. (1991) 'Introduction', *'French Science since 1945'*, special issue, *Fr. His. Stud.*, 17: 1–5.

Nelson R. and Rosenberg N. (1989) 'Science, technological advance and technological growth', in A. D. Chandler, P. Hagström and O. Sölvell (eds.) *The Dynamic Firm: the role of technology, strategy, organization, and regions*, Oxford: OUP, pp. 45–59.

Neushul P. (1998) 'Fighting research: army participation in the clinical testing and mass production of penicillin during the Second World War', in R. Cooter, M. Harrison and S. Sturdy (eds.) *War, Medicine and Modernity*, Stroud: Sutton, pp. 203–24.

Nye M.-J. (1986) *Science in the Provinces: scientific communities and provincial leadership in France, 1860–1930*, Berkeley: University of California Press.

Nye M.-J. (1993) 'National styles? French and English chemistry in the 19th and early 20th century', in G.L. Geison and F.L. Holmes (eds.) *'Research Schools: historical reappraisals'*, special issue, *Osiris*, 8: 30–53.

Offer A. (1997) 'Between the gift and the market: the economy of regard', *Econ. His. Rev.*, 50: 431–45.

Ogilvie M. B. (1987) 'Marital Collaboration: an approach to science', in P.G. Abir-Am and D. Outram (eds.) *Uneasy Careers and Intimate Lives: women in science, 1789–1979*, New Brunswick: Rutgers University Press, pp. 104–25.

Olby R.C., Cantor G.N., Christie J.R.R. and Hodge M.J.S. (eds.) (1990) *Companion to the History of Modern Science*, London: Routledge.

Olie J.-P., Ginestet D., Jollès G. and Lôo H. (eds.) (1992) *Histoire d'une découverte en psychiatrie: 40 ans de chimiothérapie neuroleptique*, Paris: Doin.

Oliviero A. (1994) 'Daniel Bovet, 1907–1992', *Bio. Mem. F.R.S.*, 39: 59–70

Ord M. G. and Stocken L. A. (1990) *The Oxford Biochemistry Department: its history and activities, 1920–1985*, Oxford: Department of Biochemistry, University of Oxford.

Oudshorn N. (1993) 'United we stand: the pharmaceutical industry, laboratory and clinic in the development of sex hormones into scientific drugs, 1920–1940', *Science, Technology and Human Values*, 18: 5–24.

Oudshorn N. (1998) 'Shifting boundaries between industry and science: the role of WHO in contraceptive R&D', in J.-P. Gaudillière and I. Löwy (eds.) *The Invisible Industrialist: manufactures and the production of scientific knowledge*, Basingstoke: Macmillan, pp. 345–67.

Pace D. (1991) 'Atomic energy and the ideology of science in post-war France', *Fr. His. Stud.*, 17: 38–61.

Parascandola J. (1990) '"The Preposterous Provision": the American Society for Pharmacology and Experimental Therapeutics ban on industrial pharmacologists, 1908–1941', in J. Liebenau, G.J. Higby and E.C. Stroud (eds.) *Pill Peddlers: essays on the history of the pharmaceutical industry*, Madison, Wis.: American Institute of the History of Pharmacy, pp. 29–47.

Parish H.J. (1968) *Victory with Vaccines*, London: E.S. Livingstone.

Parnham M.J. and J. Bruinvels (eds.) (1987) *Discoveries in Pharmacology*, Amsterdam: Elsevier.

Paul H.W. (1985) *From Knowledge to Power: the rise of the science empire in France, 1860–1939*, Cambridge: CUP.

Pavitt K. (1993) 'What do firms learn from basic research?', in D. Foray and C. Freeman (eds.), *Technology and the Wealth of Nations: the dynamics of constructed advantage*, London: OECD, pp. 29–40.

Paxton R. O. (1972) *Vichy France: old guard and new order, 1940–1944*, New York: A.A. Knopf.

Pelis K. (1997) 'Prophet for profit in French North Africa: Charles Nicolle and the Pasteur Institute of Tunis, 1903–1936', *Bull. His. Med.*, 71: 583–622.

'Penicillin: an antiseptic of microbic origin', (1941) Editorial, *BMJ*, 2: 310.

'Penicillin in warfare' (1944) Editorial, *Brit. J. Surgery*, 32: 124.

'Penicillin and modern research' (1950) Ediorial, *Lancet*, 1: 76–7.

Perkin H. (1996) *The Third Revolution: professional elites in the Modern World*, London: Routledge.

Perlman D. (1970) 'The evolution of penicillin manufacture', in A. E. Elder (ed.) *'The history of penicillin production'*, special issue, *Chem. Eng. Series*, 66: 23–30.

Perkin H. (1996) *The Third Revolution: profeesional elites in the modern world*, London: Routledge.

Perrin M.W. (1953) 'The story of polythene', *Research*, 6: 111–8.

Pestre D. (1984) *Physique et physiciens en France, 1918–1939*, Paris: Ed. des Archives Contemporaines.

Pestre D. (1992) 'Les physiciens dans les sociétés occidentales de l'après-guerre: une mutation des pratiques techniques et des comportements sociaux et culturels', *Rev. His. Mod. Contemp.*, 39: 56–72.

Pestre D. (1997) 'The moral and political economy of French physicists in the first half of the XXth century', *La Lettre de la Maison Française d'Oxford*, 6: 106–13.

Petitjean P., Jami C. and Moulin A.-M. (eds.) (1992) *Science and Empires*, Dordrecht: Kluwer Academic.

Peyrefitte A. (1976) *Le Mal français*, Paris: Plon.

Pickstone J.V. (ed.) (1992) *Medical Innovations in Historical Perspective*, Basingstoke: Macmillan.

Pharmaceutical Division, ICI ltd (Jan. 1972) 'Fermentation Products Department'.

Picard J.-F. (1992) 'Poussée scientifique ou demande de médecins? La recherche médicale en France de l'Institut national d'hygiène à l'INSERM', *Sciences Sociales et Santé*, 10: 47–106.

Picard J.-F. (1994) 'De la médecine expérimentale (1865) à l'INSERM (1964)', in C. Debru, J. Gayon and J-F. Picard (eds.) *Les Sciences biologiques et médicales en France 1920–1950*, Paris: Ed. CNRS, pp. 329–45.

Picard J.-F. (1990) *La République des savants: la recherche française et le CNRS*, Paris: Flammarion.

Picard, J.-F. (2003) 'Aux origines de l'INSERM, l'Institut national d'hygiène et la recherche médicale', *Sciences Sociales et Santé*, 21: 5–30.

Pickstone J.V. (1985) *Medicine and Industrial Society*, Manchester: Manchester University Press.

Pickstone J.V. (ed.) (1992) *Medical Innovations in Historical Perspective*, Basingstoke: Macmillan.

Picon A. (1996) 'Towards a history of technological thought', in R. Fox (ed.) *Technological Change: methods and themes in the history of technology*, Amsterdam: Harwood Academic, pp. 37–49.

Pieters T. (2005) *Interferon: the science and selling of a miracle drug*, London: Routledge.

Piganiol P. (1959) 'Les Gouvernements et la Science', *Publicis*, 7: 15.

Piganiol P. (1962) 'Sizing up France's science', *Chemical Weekly*, 91: (n.p.).

Pilcher R.B. (1938) *The Profession of Chemistry*, London: Royal Institute of Chemistry, 4th edn.

Pinch T. (1996) 'The Social Construction of Technology: a review', in R. Fox (ed.) *Technological Change: methods and themes in the history of technology*, Amsterdam: Harwood Academic, pp. 17–35.

Poggendorff (1904–22), *Bio. Lit. Hand.*, v–vi.

Polanco X. (1990) 'La mise en place d'un réseau scientifique: les rôles du CNRS et de la DGRST dans l'institutionalisation de la biologie moléculaire en France (1960–1970)', *Cah. His. CNRS*, 7: 49–90.

Ponting C. (1990) *1940: myth and reality*, London: Cardinal.

Porter R. and Teich M. (eds.) (1996) *Drugs and Narcotics in History*, Cambridge: CUP.

Prager D.J. and Omen G.S. (1980) 'Research, innovation, and university-industry linkages', *Science*, 379: 303–42.

Prévot A.R. (1947) 'Rapid Method for the titration of penicillin', in J. Hamburger (ed.), *Medical Research in France during the War (1939–1945)*, Paris: Flammarion, pp. 231–233.

Pugh D.S. (1997) *Organization Theory: selected readings*, London: Penguin, 4th edn.

Pycior H.M., Slack N.G., and Abir-Am P. (eds.) (1996) *Creative Couples in the Sciences*, New Brunswick, N.J.: Rutgers University Press.

Quirke V. (1997) 'Penicillin and post-war reconstruction in Britain and France: science and industry in the balance', *La Lettre de la Maison Française d'Oxford*, 6: 87–98.

Quirke V. (1998) 'Howard Florey -medicine maker', *Chem. in Britain*, 34: 35–8.

Quirke V. (2002) '"A big happy family": the Royal Institution under William and Lawrence Bragg, and the History of Molecular Biology', in F.A.J.L. James (ed.) *'The Common Purposes of Life': science and society at the Royal Institution of Great Britain*, Aldershot: Ashgate, pp. 249–71.

Quirke V. (2004) 'War and change in the pharmaceutical industry: a comparative study of Britain and France in the twentieth century', *Entreprises et Histoire*, 36: 64–83.

Quirke V. (2005a) 'Making *British* cortisone: Glaxo and the development of corticosteroid drugs in Britain in the 1950s and 1960s', *Studies in History and Philosophy of Biology and Biomedical Sciences*, 36: 645–74.

Quirke V. (2005b) 'From alkaloids to gene therapy: a brief history of drug discovery in the twentieth century', in S. Anderson (ed) *A Brief History of Pharmacy*, London: the Pharmaceutical Society, pp. 177–201.

Rasmussen N. (2002) 'Steroids in arms: government, industry and the hormones of the adrenal cortex in the United States, 1930–1950', *Med. His.*, 46: 299–324.

Rasmussen N. (2004) 'The moral economy of the drug company-medical scientist collaboration in interwar America', *Soc. Stud. Sci.*, 34: 161–85.

Raventos J. (1956) 'Action of Fluothane: a new volatile anaesthetic, *Brit. J. Pharmacol.*, 11: 394.

'Raymond Paul', *Who's Who in France* (1997–8), 1334.

Rayner-Canham M. and G. (1999) 'Hoppy's ladies', *Chem. in Britain*, 35: 47–9.

Reader W.J. (1975) *Imperial Chemical Industries: a history*, London: OUP, 2 vols. 1 and 2.

Reed P. (1992) 'The British chemical industry and the indigo trade', *BJHS*, 25: 113–25.

Reekie W.D. (1980) 'Pharmaceuticals', in P.S. Johnson (ed.) *The Structure of British Industry*, London: Granada, pp. 106–30.

Reich L. S. (1985) *The Making of American Industrial Research: science and business at GE and Bell, 1876–1926*, Cambridge: CUP.

Reinhardt C. (1998) 'Basic research in industry: two case-studies at IG Farbenindustrie in the 1920's and 1930's', in A.S. Travis, H.G.Schröter, E. Homburg and P.J.T. Morris (eds.) *Determinants in the Evolution of the European Chemical Industry, 1900–1939*, Dordrecht: Kluwer Academic, pp. 67–88.

Reinhardt C. and Schröter H.G. (2004) 'Academia and industry in chemistry: the impact of state intervention, and the effect of cultural values', *Ambix*, 2: 99–106.

'Research in industry: report of the F.B.I. Committee' (1943), *Research and Industry*, 62: 424–5.

Rey R. (1994) 'René Leriche (1875–1955): une oeuvre controversée', in C. Debru, J. Gayon and Picard (eds.) *Les Sciences biologiques et médicales en France 1920–1950,* Paris: Eds. CNRS, pp. 297–309.

Richmond L., Stevenson J. and Turton A. (eds.) (2003) *The Pharmaceutical Industry: a guide to historical records*, Aldershot: Ashgate.

Roberts G.K. (1997) 'Dealing with issues at the academic-industrial interface in inter-war Britain: University College London and Imperial Chemical Industries', *Sci. Pub. Pol.*, 24: 29–35.

Roberts K.B., Florey H.W. and Joklik W.K. (1952) 'The influence of cortisone on cell division', *Quart. J. Exp. Physio.*, 37: 239–57.

Robson M. (1990) 'The French pharmaceutical industry, 1919–39', in J. Liebenau, G.J. Higby and E.C. Stroud (eds.), *Pill Peddlers: essays on the history of the pharmaceutical industry*, Madison, Wis.: American Institute of the History of Pharmacy, pp. 107–22.

Roche L., Sabatini J. and Serange-Fonterme R. (1982), *L'Economie de la santé*, Paris: PUF.

Romano T. M. (1997) 'Gentlemanly versus scientific ideals: John Burdon Sanderson, medical education and the failure of the Oxford School of physiology', *Bull. His. Med.*, 71: 224–48.

Rosenberg N. (1990) 'Why do firms do basic research (with their own money)?', *Res. Pol.*, 19: 165–74.

Ross R. (1986) 'Academic research and industry relationships', *Clinical and Investigative Medicine*, 9: 269–72.

Rousso H. (ed.) (1986) *De Monnet à Massé: enjeux politiques et objectifs économiques dans le cadre des quatre premiers Plans (1946–1965)*, Paris: Ed. CNRS.

Rudwick M. J.S. (1985) *The Great Devonian Controversy: the shaping of scientific knowledge among gentlemanly specialists*, Chicago: Chicago University Press.

Ruffat M. (1996) 175 Ans d'industrie pharmaceutique française: histoire de Synhélabo, Paris: La Découverte.

Rupke N. A. (1990) *Vivisection in Historical Perspective*, London: Routledge.

Russell C. A., Coley N. G. and Roberts G.K. (eds.) (1977) *Chemists by Profession*, Milton Keynes: Open University Press.

Sadove M. S. and Wallace V. E. (1962) *Halothane*, Oxford: Blackwell Scientific.

Sanderson M. (1972) 'Research and the firm in British industry, 1919–39', *Sci. Stud.*, 2: 107–51.

Sanderson M. (1972) *The Universities and British Industry, 1850–1970*, London: Routledge and Kegan Paul.

Saville J. (1993) *The Politics of Continuity: British foreign policy and the labour government, 1945–46*, London: Verso.

Sawers D., Jewkes J. and Stillerman B. (1969) *The Sources of Invention*, London: Macmillan.

Schild H.O. (1962) *Adventures with Histamine*, London: H.K. Lewis & Co.

Schild H.O. (1997) 'Dale and the development of pharmacology', *Br. J. Pharmacol.*, 120 (4 suppl.): 504–8.

Schueler F.W. (1960) *Chemobiodynamics*, New York: McGraw Hill.

Servier J. (1986) *Le Médicament Français: une industrie de pointe en voie de liquidation*, Paris: Institut Economique de Paris.

Sheehan J. C. (1982) *The Enchanted Ring: the untold story of penicillin*, Cambridge, Mass.: MIT Press.

Shinn T. (1980) 'The genesis of French industrial research, 1880–1940', *Soc. Sci. Info.*, 19: 607–40.

Shinn T. (2002) 'The triple helix and the new production of knowledge', *Soc. Stud. Sci.*, 32: 599–614.

Sidebottom E. (2004) 'Norman Heatley: last survivor of the team that developed penicillin', obituary, *The Independent*, 23 Jan. 2004, 22.

Sigvard J. (1975) *l'Industrie du medicament*, Paris: Calman-Lévy.

Silverstein A. M. (1989) *A History of Immunology*, San Diego: Academic Press.

'Sir Edward Abraham' (12 May. 1999) *Times*, Obituary, 21.

'Sir Ian Fraser' (13 May 1999) *Daily Telegraph*, Obituary, 33.

Sjöström H. and Nilsson R. (1972) *Thalidomide and the Power of the Drug Companies*, Harmondsworth: Penguin.

Slater L.B. (2000) 'Industry and academy: the synthesis of steroids', *His. Stud. Phys. Sci.*, 30: 443–79.

Slinn J. (1984) *May & Baker, 1834–1984*, Cambridge: Hobsons Ltd.

Slinn J. (1996) 'Research and development in the UK pharmaceutical industry from the nineteenth century to the 1960s', in R. Porter and M. Teich (eds.) *Drugs and Narcotics in History*, Cambridge: CUP, pp. 168–86.

Slinn J. (1996) 'Innovation at Glaxo and May & Baker, 1945–65', *His. and Tech.*,13: 133–47.

Slinn J. (2005) 'Drug-guzzlers or medicine junkies? Regulating the cost and consumption of prescription pharmaceuticals in the UK 1948–1967', *Business History*, 47: 352–66.

Smith H.L. (ed.) (1986) *War and Social Change: British society in the Second World War*, Manchester: Manchester University Press.

Sneader W. (1996) *Drug Prototypes and Their Exploitation*, Chichester: John Wiley & Sons.

Sokoloff B. (1946) *Penicillin: a dramatic story*, London: Allen & Unwin.

Sondheimer J. (1957) *History of the British Federation of University Women*, London.

Stankiewics R. (1986) *Academics and Entrepreneurs: developing university-industry relations*, London: Pinter.

Staub A.-M. and Bovet D. (1937) 'Action de la thymoxyéthydiéthylamina (929F) et des éthers phénoliques sur le choc anaphylactique du cobaye', *Comptes rendus des séances de la Société de Biologie*, 125 : 818–21.

Sturdy S. (1992) 'Medical chemistry and clinical medicine: academics and the scientisation of medical practice in Britain', in I. Löwy (ed.) *Medicine and Change: historical and sociological studies of medical innovation*, Montrouge: John Libbey Eurotext, pp. 371–93.

Sturdy S. (1998) 'War as experiment. Physiological innovation and administration in Britain, 1914–1918: the case of chemical warfare', in R. Cooter, M. Harrison and S. Sturdy (eds.) *War, Medicine and Modernity*, Stroud: Sutton, pp. 65–84.

Suckling C.W. (1957) 'Some chemical and physical factors in the development of Fluothane', *Brit. J. Anaesth.*, 29: 466–72.

Summers W.C. (1999) *Félix d'Hérelle and the Origins of Molecular Biology*, New Haven, CT: Yale University Press.

Swann J.P. (1988) *Academic Scientists and the Pharmaceutical Industry: cooperative research in twentieth-century America*, Baltimore: Johns Hopkins University Press.

Swann J.P. (1990) 'Universities, industry and the rise of biomedical collaboration in America', in J. Liebenau, G.J. Higby and E.C. Stroud (eds.),*Pill Peddlers: essays on the history of the pharmaceutical industry*, Madison, Wis.: American Institute of the History of Pharmacy, pp. 73–90.

Swazey J.P. (1974) *Chlorpromazine in Psychiatry: a study of therapeutic innovation*, Cambridge, Mass.: MIT Press.

Swedberg R. (1993) *Explorations in Economic Sociology*, New York: Russell Sage Foundation.

Swedberg R. (1996) *Economic Sociology*, Cheltenham: Edward Elgar.

Tansey E.M. (1989) 'The Wellcome Physiological Research Laboratories 1894–1904: the Home Office, Pharmaceutical Firms and Animal Experiments', *Med. His.*, 33: 1–41.

Tansey E.M. and Milligan R.M.C.E. (1990) 'The early history of the Wellcome Research Laboratories, 1894–1914', in J. Liebenau, G.J. Higby and E.C. Stroud (eds.), *Pill Peddlers: essays on the history of the pharmaceutical industry*, Madison, Wis.: American Institute of the History of Pharmacy, pp. 91–106.

Tansey E.M. and Catterall P.P. (eds.) (1997) 'Technology transfer in Britain: the case of monoclonal antibodies', in Tansey et al. (eds.) *Wellcome Witnesses to Twentieth-Century Medicine*, London: Wellcome Trust, vol. 1, pp. 3–34.

Tansey E.M. and Reynolds L.A. (eds.) (1997) 'The Committee on Safety of Drugs', in Tansey et al. (eds.) *Wellcome Witnesses to Twentieth-Century Medicine*, London: Wellcome Trust, vol. 1, pp. 103–35.

Tansey E.M. et al. (eds.) *Wellcome Witnesses to Twentieth-Century Medicine* (London, 1997), vols. 1 and 2.

Tansey E.M. (1998) ' "They used to call it psychiatry": aspects of the development and impact of psychopharmacology', in M. Gijswijt-Hofstra and R. Porter (eds.) *Cultures of Psychiatry and Mental Health Care in Postwar Britain and the Netherlands*, Amsterdam: Rodopi, pp. 79–101.

'Team Research' (1957) Editorial, *Brit. J. Anaesth.*, 29: 437.

Thomas C.J. (1958) 'The pharmaceutical industry', in D. Burn (ed.) *The Structure of British Industry*, vol. 2, Cambridge: CUP.

Thomas L.G. (1994) 'Implicit industrial policy: the triumph of Britain and the failure of France in global pharmaceuticals', *Industrial and Corporate Change*, 3: 451–89.

Thompson G., Frances J., Levacic R. and Mitchell J. (eds.) (1991) *Markets, Hierarchies and Networks: the coordination of social life*, London: Sage.

Thomson A.L. (1973) *Half a Century of Medical Research*, London: HMSO, vols. 1 and 2.

Tissot R. (1992) 'Découverte de la chlorpromazine et hasard', in J.-P. Olie, D. Ginestet, G. Jollès and H. Lôo (eds.) *Histoire d'une découverte en psychiatrie: 40 ans de chimiothérapie neuroleptique*, Paris: Doin, pp. 47–53.

Todd Lord Alexander and Cornforth J.W. (1976) 'Robert Robinson', *Bio. Mem. FRS*, 221: 415–527.

Tomlinson J. (1996) 'Inventing "decline": the falling behind of the British economy in the post-war years', *Econ. His. Rev.*, 49: 731–57.

Travis A.S. (1998) 'Modernizing industrial organic chemistry: Great Britain between two world wars', in A.S. Travis, H.G.Schröter, E. Homburg and P.J.T. Morris (eds.), *Determinants in the Evolution of the European Chemical Industry, 1900–1939*, Dordrecht: Kluwer Academic, pp. 171–98.

Travis A.S., Schröter H.G., Homburg E. and Morris P.J.T. (eds.) (1998) *Determinants in the Evolution of the European Chemical Industry, 1900–193*, Dordrecht: Kluwer Academic.

Tréfouël J., Tréfouël T., Nitti F. and Bovet D. (1935) 'Activité du p. aminophényl-sulpfamide sur les infections streptococciques expérimentales de la souris et du lapin', *Société de Biologie*, 23 Nov: 756–8.

Triggle D. (2005) 'Patenting the sun: enclosing the scientific commons and transforming the university – ethical concerns', *Drug Development Research*, 63: 139–49.

Tweedale G. (1990) *At the Sign of the Plough: 275 years of Allen & Hanbury's and the British pharmaceutical industry, 1715–1990*, London: Murray.

Unger L. and Harris M.C. (1974) 'Stepping stones in allergy', *Ann. Allergy*, 32: 340–60.

Vagelos R. (2004) *Medicine, Science and Merck*, Cambridge and New York: CUP.

Vallery-Radot L. Pasteur (ed.) (1951) *Les Acquisitions Médicales Récentes*, Paris: Flammarion.

Varcoe I. (1970) 'Scientists and organised research in Great Britain, 1914–16: the early history of the DSIR', *Minerva*, 9: 192–217.

Varcoe I. (1974) *Organising for Science in Britain: a case-study*, Oxford: OUP.

Viaud P. (1954) 'Les amines dérivées de la phénothiazine', *Journal de Pharmacie et Pharmacologie*, 6 : 361–89.

Vig N.J. (1968) *Science and Technology in British Politics*, Oxford: Pergamom Press.

Vovelle M. (1982) *Ideologies and Mentalities*, Paris: F. Maspero.

Wainwright M. (1990) *Miracle Cure: the story of penicillin and the golden age of antibiotics*, Oxford: Basil Blackwell.

Wall I.M. (1991) *The U.S. and the Making of Postwar France, 1945–54*, Cambridge: CUP.

Walsh V. (1994) 'Invention and innovation in the chemical industry: demand-pull or discovery-push?', *Research Policy*, 13: 211–34.

Walsh V. (1998) 'Industrial R&D and its influence on the organization and management of the production of knowledge in the public sector', in J.-P. Gaudillière and I. Löwy (eds.) *The Invisible Industrialist: manufactures and the production of scientific knowledge*, Basingstoke: Macmillan, pp. 298–344.

Walsh V. and Le Roux M. (2004) 'Contingency in innovation and the role of national systems: taxol and taxotère in the USA and France', *Res. Policy*, 33: 1307–27.

Warner J.H. (1986), *The Therapeutic Perspective: medical practice, knowledge and identity in America, 1820–1885*, Cambridge, Mass.: Harvard University Press.

Watson K.D. (1995) 'The Chemist as Expert: the consulting career of Sir William Ramsay', *Ambix*, 42: 143–59.

Wear A. (ed.) (1992) *Medicine in Society: historical essays*, Cambridge: CUP.

Weart S. R. (1979) *Scientists in Power*, Cambridge, Mass.: Harvard University Press.

Weatherall Miles (1990) *In Search of a Cure: a history of pharmaceutical discovery*, Oxford: OUP.

Webster C. (1988) *The Health Services Since the War, vol. 1: Problems of Health Care: the National Health Service Before 1957*, London: HMSO.

Weindling P. (1989) *Health, Race and German Politics between National Unification and Nazism, 1870–1945*, Cambridge: CUP.

Weindling P. (1991) 'Emile Roux et la diphtérie', in M. Morange (ed.) *L'Institut Pasteur: contributions à son histoire*, Paris: La Découverte, pp. 137–43.

Weindling P. (1992a) 'Scientific élites and laboratory organisation in *fin de siècle* Paris and Berlin: the Pasteur Institute and Robert Koch's Institute for Infectious Diseases compared', in A. Cunningham and P. Williams (eds.) *The Laboratory Revolution in Medicine*, Cambridge: CUP, pp. 170–88.

Weindling P. (1992b) 'From infectious to chronic diseases: changing patterns of sickness in the nineteenth and twentieth centuries', in A. Wear (ed.) *Medicine in Society: historical essays*, Cambridge: CUP, pp. 303–16.

Weindling P. (2000) *Epidemics and Genocide in Eastern Europe, 1890–1945*, Oxford: OPU.

Weiviorka O. (1993) 'La Résistance', in J.-P. Azéma and F. Bédarida (eds.) *La France des années noires*, Paris: Seuil, pp. 65–90.

Wiener M. J. (1981) *English Culture and the Decline of the Industrial Spirit*, Cambridge: CUP.

Williams T. I. (1984) *Howard Florey: penicillin and after*, Oxford: OUP.

Williams T.I. (1990) *Robert Robinson: chemist extraordinary*, Oxford: Clarendon Press.

Wilson D. (1976) *Penicillin in Perspective*, London: Faber.

Wilson F. and Popp A. (eds.) (2003) *Industrial Clusters and Regional Business Networks in England, 1750–1970*, London: Ashgate.

Winter J.M. (ed.) (1975) *War and Economic Development: essays in memory of David Joslin*, Cambridge: CUP.

Wollmann E. (1991) 'Succès et limites de la recherche pasteurienne: introduction', in M. Morange (ed.) *L'Institut Pasteur: contributions à son histoire*, Paris: La Découverte, pp. 105–7.

Work T.S. and Work E. (1948) *The Basis of Chemotherapy*, Edinburgh: Oliver Boyd.

Wright M. (1991) 'The comparative analysis of industrial policies: policy networks and sectoral governance structures in Britain and France', Manchester: EPRU working paper.

Wurtman R.J. and Bettiker R.L. (1995) 'The slowing of treatment discovery, 1965–1995', *Nature Medicine*, 1: 1122–5.

Zallen D.T. (1989) 'The Rockefeller Foundation and French research', *Cah. His. CNRS*, 5: 35–58.

Zallen D.T. (1992) 'Le cycle Rapkine et la Mission Rapkine, le développement de la recherche médicale en France', *Sciences Sociales et Santé*, 10: 11–23.

5. UNPUBLISHED ARTICLES AND BOOKS

R. Cooter, 'Between playing fields and killing fields: the language and labour of teamwork in medicine, c. 1900–45' (Skills Conference, Wellcome Institute for the History of Medicine, April 1996).

J. Foreman-Peck, 'The long run competitiveness of British healthcare businesses' (Business History Unit Symposium, 'Future Directions in the Business History of Pharmaceuticals', 19 Nov. 1993).

R. Fox, 'An Uneasy Courtship: Rhetoric and Reality in the Relations between Academic and Industrial Chemistry, 1770–1914', (IV National Meeting 'Storia e Fondamenti della Chimica', Venezia, 7–9 Nov. 1991).

J.-P. Gaudillière, 'Screening and copying: tuberculosis chemotherapy after 1945', paper presented at the conference on 'Perspectives on 20th-century Pharmaceuticals' (St Anne's, Oxford, 14–16 July 2005).

F. Guinot, 'Chimie d'hier, chimie de demain', unpublished paper, 14/09/06.

G. Hagemann, 'Un cinquantenaire de l'époque héroïque de la pénicilline au développement de la microbiologie industrielle, dea antibiotiques et autres produits de fermentations, dans le groupe Roussel Uclaf' (Roussel-Uclaf, 1991).

D. Pestre, 'From Revanche to Competition and Cooperation: physics research in Germany and France', *Society in the Mirror of Science: the Politics of Knowledge in Modern France* (Berkeley, 30 September–1 October, 1988).

C. Suckling, 'The discovery of the anaesthetic halothane: the story of a science-based innovation' (discourse presented on 20 March 1992 at the Royal Institution).

M. Wilcox, 'Introduction', in A. Crookham et al., 'The Confederation of British Industry and Predecessor Archives', Coventry: Modern Records Centre Resources Booklet no. 7, 1997.

6. UNPUBLISHED THESES

S. Boudia, 'Marie Curie et son laboratoire: science, industrie, instruments et métrologie de la radioactivité en France, 1896–1914' (Paris VII doctoral thesis, 1997).

D. Dosso, 'Louis Rapkine (1904–1948) et la mobilisation scientifique de la France libre' (University of Paris VII Ph.D. thesis, 1998).

P. Gould, 'Feminity and Physical Science in Britain, 1870–1914' (Cambridge University Ph.D. thesis, 1998).

S.M. Horrocks, 'Consuming science: science, technology and food in Britain, 1870–1939' (University of Manchester Ph. D. thesis, 1993).

N. Jas, '"L'agriculture est une science chimique!" Eléments pour une histoire comparée des sciences agronomiques allemandes et françaises de la seconde moitié du XIXe siècle' (Florence, European Institute doctoral thesis, 1997).

M. Le Roux, 'Evolution des stratégies de recherche d'une grande entreprisee française : Pechiney 1866–1975 – le cas de l'aluminium' (Ph.D. thesis, Paris IV-Sorbonne, 1994).

S. Massat-Bourrat, 'Des phénothiazines à la chlorpromazine: les destinées multiples d'un colorant sans couleur', thèse de doctorat, Université Louis Pasteur, Strasbourg, 2004.

A. Muhammad, 'Patenting dyes and drugs in Britain, 1860–1960: case studies on the role of patents in chemical science and industry' (Ph.D. thesis, University of Manchester, 2004).

A. O'Sullivan, 'Networks of creativity: a study of scientific achievement in British physiology, 1881–1945' (Oxford University D.Phil. thesis, 2002).

M. Pinault, 'Frédéric Joliot, la science et la société: un itinéraire de la physique nucléaire à la politique nucléaire' (1900–1958)' (Paris I doctoral thesis, 1999).

M.T. Robson, 'The pharmaceutical industry in Britain and France, 1919–1939' (London School of Economics Ph.D. thesis, 1993).

A.-M. Staub (1939) *Recherches sur quelques bases synthétiques antagonistes de l'histamine* (Ph.D. thesis, Faculté des Sciences de Paris).

E.M. Tansey, 'The early scientific career of Sir Henry Hallett Dale FRS (1875–1968)' (University College, London Ph.D. thesis, 1991).

M. Weatherall, *Scientific Medicine and the Medical Sciences in Cambridge 1851–1939* (Cambridge University Ph.D. thesis, 1994).

K.J. Williams, 'British pharmaceutical industry, synthetic drug manufacture and the clinical testing of novel drugs, 1895–1939' (Ph.D thesis, University of Manchester, 2004).

7. ARTICLES ON THE WEB

M. Le Roux, 'Between academy and industry: the story of an unusual CNRS laboratory: the ICSN, 1960–2000', 5th International Congress on the History of Chemistry, Lisbon, Sept. 2005 (http://5ichc-portugal.ulusofona.pt/paperslist.asp).

J.-F. Picard, 'The Institut National d'Hygiène and Public Health in France', 1940–1946' (http://picardp1.ivry.cnrs.fr/).

Index

rhetoric of, 169, 244, 247, 281 n. 211

Bacteria, *see also* infectious diseases, chemotherapy

Antibacterial, *see* sulphanilamide, lysozyme, penicillin

Bacterial antagonism, *see* antibiosis

Bacterial anti-sera, 38

Bacterial growth, or metabolism, 18, 133

Bactericidal, 67

Bacterial infection, 30

Bacteriolytic, 103, 132

Bacteriophage, 72 Table 2.2, *see also* d'Hérelle

Gram-negative, *see* cephalosporin

Bacteriology, 17, 30-31, 36-37, 101–102, 104, 165, 229, 263 n. 38, 287 n. 175

Bacteriologists, *see* Nitti in industry, 45, 127, 160, 238

Baker, H.B., 88

Baker, Wilson, 115 Fig. 3.6, 131–132

Banting, (Sir) Frederick, 88

Barbachau, 70

Barberot, Etablissements, 150

Barger, George, 81–82, 278 n. 132

Barnes, J.M., 104

Barnett, Corelli, 207, 254 n. 21, 263 n. 33, 269 n. 172, 311 n. 145, 312 n. 3, 313 n. 8

BASF, 44, 48

Batchelor, Ralph, 238

Bayer, 17, 65, 67, 145–146, 270 n. 184

Beattie, J., 214

Beckenham, 10, 125 Tab. 3.2, *see also* Wellcome Laboratories

Beecham, 206, 208, 231, 236–239

Research Laboratories, 86, 231, 237, 288 n. 204

Beer, John, 60, 273 n. 42

Béhal, Auguste, 56, 70

Belgium, 165

Bell laboratories, 71, 276 n. 96

Bellon, Roger, 185, 194, 238, 302 n. 115

Benoît, Germaine, 60, 66, 176

Berlin, 30, 96, 141, 273 n. 22

Bernard, Claude, 197

Bernard, Jean, 193, *see also* daunorubicin

Bernthsen, August, 188, *see also* phenothiazines

Bertrand, Gabriel, 23–24, 263 n. 34

Besredka, Alexandre, 21, 263 n. 30, 264 n. 50

Bessis, Marcel, 196, *see also* Cabanel

Best, Charles, 88

Biarritz, 53 Fig. 2.1, 54

Billon, Francis, 45, 56–57, 193

Biochemistry, 19 Tab. 1.1, 23–25, 31, 35–38, 40–41, 81–82, 101–105, 132, 176, 181, 260, n. 2, 263 n. 44, 266 n. 95, 303 n. 123

Biochemists as collaborators for industry, 8, 235, 238

Biochemists in industry, 110, 123, 238

Biology, *see also* chemistry, immunology, microbiology

Biological activity, 41, 69, 106-108, 132–133, 212, *see also* chemical structure

Biological alternative to synthetic remedies, 97

Biological approach to medicine or therapy, 28, 204

Biological experiments, *see also* penicillin

Biological faction in psychiatry, 204

Biological remedies, 15, 18, 37–38, 42, 45–46, 49, 72–73 Tab. 2.2, 2.3, 87, 93–94, 97, 119, 181, *see also* antibiotics, glandular extracts, hormones, insulin, penicillin, sera, vaccines, vitamins

Biological research, 163, 179

Biological sciences, 11, 18, 19 Tab. 1.1,

Lack of development in France, 23, 29

Biological standards, 31, 81, 140 *see also* Committee on Biological Standardisation, penicillin

Biological tests, 65-68

Biological tradition in pharmaceutical research, 94

Collaboration with chemists, 40-41, *see also* chemotherapy

Immunobiology, 152

in industry, 67

Laboratories, 71, 74

Medical, 45, *see also* biomedical

Mediterranean biology and pathology, centre on, 154

Molecular, 25, 182–184